Collins

AQA GCSE English Language and English Literature

Teacher Guide

Series Editors: Sarah Darragh and Jo Heathcote

Sarah Darragh
Phil Darragh
Mike Gould
Jo Heathcote

William Collins' dream of knowledge for all began with the publication of his first book in 1819. A self-educated mill worker, he not only enriched millions of lives, but also founded a flourishing publishing house. Today, staying true to this spirit, Collins books are packed with inspiration, innovation and practical expertise. They place you at the centre of a world of possibility and give you exactly what you need to explore it.

Collins. Freedom to teach

HarperCollins Publishers
1 London Bridge Street
London SE1 9GF

Browse the complete Collins catalogue at **www.collinseducation.com**

First edition 2015

10 9 8 7 6 5 4

© HarperCollins Publishers 2015

ISBN 978-0-00-759681-2

Collins® is a registered trademark of HarperCollins Publishers Limited

www.collins.co.uk

A catalogue record for this book is available from the British Library

Commissioned by Catherine Martin
Project managed by Ben Gardiner
Edited by Hugh Hillyard-Parker
Proofread by Lily Khambata and Alison Bewsher
Designed and typeset by Hugh Hillyard-Parker
Cover design by We are Laura
Printed and bound by CPI Group (UK) Ltd, Croydon, CR0 4YY

All rights reserved. No part of this book may be reproduced, stored in a retrieval system, or transmitted in any form or by any means, electronic, mechanical, photocopying, recording or otherwise, without the prior permission in writing of the Publisher. This book is sold subject to the conditions that it shall not, by way of trade or otherwise, be lent, re-sold, hired out or otherwise circulated without the Publisher's prior consent in any form of binding or cover other than that in which it is published and without a similar condition including this condition being imposed on the subsequent purchaser.

HarperCollins does not warrant that www.collins.co.uk or any other website mentioned in this title will be provided uninterrupted, that any website will be error free, that defects will be corrected, or that the website or the server that makes it available are free of viruses or bugs. For full terms and conditions please refer to the site terms provided on the website.

ACKNOWLEDGEMENTS

The publishers gratefully acknowledge the permissions granted to reproduce copyright material in this book. Every effort has been made to contact the holders of copyright material, but if any have been inadvertently overlooked, the Publisher will be pleased to make the necessary arrangements at the first opportunity. See CD-ROM for full list of acknowledgments.

The publishers would like to thank the following for permission to reproduce pictures in these pages:

Cover images © Lebrecht Music and Arts Photo Library/Alamy, grough.co.uk/Alamy
p.191: Paul Bradbury/Getty Images;
p.239: ThreeRivers11/Shutterstock.com;
p.348 Hemis/Alamy

CD-ROM MINIMUM SYSTEM REQUIREMENTS

MS Office 2007
Acrobat Reader 5

IMPORTANT, PLEASE READ CAREFULLY – LICENCE AGREEMENT

For the purpose of this Agreement, the Publishers are HarperCollinsPublishers Ltd; the Licensee shall mean the relevant partnership, corporate body, trust charity, school, educational establishment or any other body on whose behalf the purchaser has acquired the work. The Licensee shall be entitled to install and use the CD-ROM solely for educational purposes, on computers and intranet-based VLE systems within one educational establishment only, subject to the restrictions set out below.

RESTRICTIONS ON USE

All commercial purposes including but not limited to altering, cropping, printing and other treatment of all or any part of any artwork, images, sound, music, or text held on the CD-ROM and the rental, lending, networking, resale, remote access and inclusion on a bulletin board of the CD-ROM or any of its content. There is no right, by virtue of this purchase, for the purchaser or Licensee to copy, adapt or make copies of an adaptation in connection with the CD-ROM, except as expressly permitted by law. Notwithstanding the foregoing, in the event that the Licensee is a school or other educational establishment, the Licensee shall have the right to make one back-up copy only of the CD-ROM. All moral rights of artists and all other contributors to the CD-ROM are hereby asserted. The Licence referred to is deemed to take effect when the CD-ROM installation routine is invoked. All other titles, obligations and liabilities of the Publishers, including but not limited to consequential loss, loss of profits, or any economic loss arising from the use, the inability to use, or any defect in the CD-ROM are excluded in so far as permitted by UK law. This Agreement and licence are specific to the Licence and all rights not expressly provided herein are reserved to the Publishers and no rights of any nature may be assigned, licensed or made over to any third party. This agreement is subject to English law and the jurisdiction of the English courts.

Contents

Introduction	4
Medium-term plans (Core)	6
Medium-term plans (Advanced)	15
One-year scheme of work	24
Two-year scheme of work	25
Three-year scheme of work	28

Core: Lesson plans

Chapter 1	Key technical skills	32
Chapter 2	Key concepts	48
Chapter 3	Reading, understanding and responding to texts	64
Chapter 4	Explaining and commenting on writers' methods and effects	80
Chapter 5	Working with context	94
Chapter 6	Forming a critical response	106
Chapter 7	Comparing texts	120
Chapter 8	Writing creatively	130
Chapter 9	Point of view writing	146

Core: Worksheets

Chapter 1	Key technical skills	164
Chapter 2	Key concepts	177
Chapter 3	Reading, understanding and responding to texts	182
Chapter 4	Explaining and commenting on writers' methods and effects	193
Chapter 5	Working with context	199
Chapter 6	Forming a critical response	204
Chapter 7	Comparing texts	215
Chapter 8	Writing creatively	226
Chapter 9	Point of view writing	235

Advanced: Lesson plans

Chapter 1	Key technical skills	244
Chapter 2	Key concepts	250
Chapter 3	Reading, understanding and responding to texts	256
Chapter 4	Analysing and evaluating writers' methods and effects	264
Chapter 5	Working with context	272
Chapter 6	Forming a critical response	280
Chapter 7	Comparing texts	288
Chapter 8	Writing creatively	296
Chapter 9	Point of view writing	304

Advanced: Worksheets

Chapter 1	Key technical skills	312
Chapter 2	Key concepts	317
Chapter 3	Reading, understanding and responding to texts	320
Chapter 4	Analysing and evaluating writers' methods and effects	324
Chapter 5	Working with context	329
Chapter 6	Forming a critical response	333
Chapter 7	Comparing texts	339
Chapter 8	Writing creatively	345
Chapter 9	Point of view writing	349

Introduction

The *Collins AQA GCSE English Language and GCSE English Literature Teacher Guide* is designed to support teachers using the Collins AQA GCSE Core and Advanced Student Books. The purpose of these books is to address the key skills that students need for both GCSE English Language and GCSE English Literature.

Our series is premised on the fact that both qualifications are underpinned by the same fundamental skills. It has been structured to develop these skills in a combined approach that will help you to co-teach the two GCSE courses as one coherent course. You will notice, therefore, that the majority of the chapters focus on one main Assessment Objective (AO) for English Language and one for English Literature.

The series can be used in either the mixed-ability or ability-banded classroom. The two books enable you to offer the right level of challenge to your students: the Core Student Book is intended to support students working in the Grade 2–6 range, while the Advanced Student Book revisits the same skills and AOs at a more sophisticated level for students working between Grades 6 and 9. The Teacher Guide suggests ways of adapting and differentiating some of the tasks to suit the full range of abilities in your GCSE groups.

How the books are structured

The first two chapters focus on the key technical skills and key concepts for English study. These key skills and concepts are then built upon in the rest of the book. The first two chapters could be seen as a foundation unit for the rest of the GCSE course, as the remaining chapters draw on the skills and ideas covered here. As such, they might be used before the GCSE course begins, either in Year 9 or at the start of Year 10.

There are seven further chapters in the book, each divided into a sequence of 'topics' or 'lessons', which build towards a final *Apply your skills* task for English Language and/or English Literature at the end of the chapter.

Each chapter opener explains clearly which Assessment Objectives are the focus of that chapter, although other key Assessment Objectives are also referenced within particular sections of the chapters. For instance, Chapter 5 centres on Literature AO3 but encourages students to relate their understanding of context to their comments on writers' meanings, methods and effects (AO1 and AO2).

Each lesson provides a range of tasks and activities with regular diagnostic assessment points prior to the more substantial task at the end of each chapter. These synoptic, exam-style *Apply your skills* tasks are designed to draw together the learning from that particular chapter, and from the course so far, enabling teachers and students to track progress and identify areas for further improvement.

Standards are exemplified throughout: for example, by the annotated responses in the *Apply your skills* sections that end each chapter.

Using the Teacher Guide

Each topic in the Student Book is intended to provide work for one lesson, and is supported in the Teacher Guide by a two-page lesson plan, plus worksheet(s) and PowerPoints (PPTs). PDF and Word file formats are available on the CD-Rom for easy printing and editing.

The Teacher Guide is designed to help you with the following:

Planning

- Key references to the two GCSE specifications are listed at the start of each lesson plan, with the **Assessment objectives** and links to **Examination papers and questions** identified so that the wider application of learning is clear.

- Detailed, ready-to-use **lesson plans** offer all you need to teach. These are divided into sections that match the Student Book – *Getting you thinking*, *Explore the skills*, *Develop the skills* and *Apply the skills* – ensuring progression and pace as well as opportunities for consolidation.

- The **Big question** and **Big answer** features suggest starter and plenary activities to keep the opening question from each Student Book lesson clearly in focus.

- **Worksheets** and **PowerPoint slides** (PPTs) supplement and extend activities in the Student Book and are itemised in each lesson plan, meaning that time-consuming preparation is kept to a minimum.

- A one-year, two-year and a three-year **scheme of work** suggest how you might use the books across your GCSE course. **Medium-term plans** allow you to see at a glance which AOs, exam questions and texts are covered in each chapter, and a **matching grid** (available on the CD-Rom) summarises where each exam question is addressed in the books.

- Finally, five **CPD videos** can be shared with your department to help them adjust to the new specifications in the first few years of teaching.

Differentiation

- Each lesson plan begins with **Learning outcomes** differentiated at three levels, suggesting what expected progress should look like for students targeting Grades 4, 5 and 6 in the Core Book, and Grades 6, 7 and 8 in the Advanced Book.

- Further differentiation opportunities are provided in the **Extra support** and **Extra challenge** boxes, ensuring all students are supported and stimulated.

- **Worksheets** and **PPTs** offer additional activities to suit a range of learning styles and abilities.

- A **Key terms PowerPoint slide** for each lesson enables you to introduce any unfamiliar terminology to the class either as it occurs or at the start of the lesson.

Assessment

- Peer- and self-assessment are used to help students understand how to progress towards their target grades. The **Check your progress** boxes at the end of each lesson in the Student Book suggest what expected progress on the final *Apply the skills* task should look like for students targeting Grades 4, 5 and 6 in the Core Book and Grades 6, 7 and 8 in the Advanced Book.

- Chapters 3 to 9 in each book end with an **Apply your skills lesson** in which students are given the opportunity to apply the skills they have developed in the chapter to relevant practice English Language and/or English Literature tasks, to compare two sample responses to each task and to use the larger **Check your progress** summaries at the end of each chapter to assess their own work.

Our resources are designed to enhance performance so that candidates can work towards GCSE grades they can be proud of. We hope you enjoy using them.

Chapter 1 Medium-term plan

Core Student Book
CHAPTER 1

Topic/lesson	AOs	Exam question(s)	Key terms	Big question	Texts
1.1 Words and how we spell them	**English Language** AO6 **English Literature** AO4	**English Language** Paper 1, Question 5 Paper 2, Question 5	prefixes, suffixes	How do you improve your spelling of more complex words?	Charles Dickens, from *Nicholas Nickleby*
1.2 Vocabulary and meaning: nouns and adjectives	**English Language** AO2, AO5 **English Literature** AO2, AO4	**English Language** Paper 1, Question 2, 5 Paper 2, Question 3, 5 **English Literature** key skills across all components	adjectives, determiner, nouns, noun phrase	What jobs do words do?	Edwin Morgan, 'Space Poem 3: Off Course'
1.3 Words and meaning: verbs and agreement	**English Language** AO5, AO6 **English Literature** AO2, AO4	**English Language** Paper 1, Question 2, 5 Paper 2, Question 3, 5 **English Literature** key skills across all components	auxiliaries, dialect, Standard English	How do you know what verbs do and which ones to use where?	Sophie Duffy, from *The Generation Game*
1.4 Sentences and their functions	**English Language** AO2, AO6	**English Language** Paper 1, Question 2, 5 Paper 2, Question 3, 5	command, exclamation, statement	What are sentences for?	Melvin Burgess, from *Junk* WaterAid campaign leaflet
1.5 Add meaning and clarity with punctuation	**English Language** AO6 **English Literature** AO4	**English Language** Paper 1, Question 5 Paper 2, Question 5 **English Literature** key skills across all components		Why is punctuation important in making things clear?	Lewis Carroll, from *Alice in Wonderland* Barry Hines, adapted from *A Kestrel for a Knave*
1.6 Sentences used for effect	**English Language** AO2, AO6 **English Literature** AO2	**English Language** Paper 1, Question 2, 5 Paper 2, Question 3, 5 **English Literature** key skills across all components	statement	Does using different types of sentences make any difference?	Barack Obama, from speech made as he unveiled a statue of Rosa Parks Patricia Debney, 'How Not to be a Woodlouse' William Shakespeare, from *Othello* (Act 3, Sc. 3)
1.7 Structure: using different sentence structures	**English Language** AO2, AO6 **English Literature** AO4	**English Language** Paper 1, Question 3, 5 Paper 2, Question 5 **English Literature** key skills across all components	coordinating conjunctions, main clause, pronoun, subordinate clauses	What is the difference between a simple, compound and complex sentence?	Raymond Carver, from 'Everything Stuck to Him' Lauren Child, from *The Princess and the Pea*
1.8 Structure: paragraphing	**English Language** AO2, AO6 **English Literature** AO4	**English Language** Paper 1, Question 3, 5 Paper 2, Question 5 **English Literature** key skills across all components		Does it really matter when you start a new paragraph?	

Chapter 2 Medium-term plan

Topic/lesson	AOs	Exam question(s)	Key terms	Big question	Texts
2.1 Understand literary forms	**English Language** AO1, AO2 **English Literature** AO1, AO2	**English Language** Paper 1, Questions 2, 3, 4 Paper 2, Questions 3, 4 **English Literature** key skill across all components	forms	Why do we tell stories and how do we tell them?	Charles Dickens, from *Great Expectations*
2.2 Understand non-fiction genres	**English Language** AO1, AO2 **English Literature** AO1, AO2	**English Language** Paper 1, Questions 2, 3, 4 Paper 2, Questions 3, 4 **English Literature** Paper 2, Section C	genres	What is the difference between different types of non-fiction?	Jeevan Vasagar, 'Children's Behaviour at School Deteriorating', *Guardian* 18 April 2011; Barry Hines, from *A Kestrel for a Knave* Peter Hessler, *River Town*; Abraham Lincoln, *Autobiography*; Elizabeth Gaskell, *The Life of Charlotte Brontë*; Jonathan Hayes, 'Teenage stowaway survives flight …', *Guardian* 21 April 2014
2.3 Understand narrative perspective	**English Language** AO1, AO2 **English Literature** AO1, AO2	**English Language** Paper 1, Questions 2, 3, 4 Paper 2, Questions 3, 4 **English Literature** Paper 1, Sections A and B Paper 2, Section C	perspective, pronouns	What is narrative point of view and why is it important that you understand it?	Mark Haddon, from *The Curious Incident of the Dog in the Night-Time* Mark Haddon & Simon Stephens, from *The Curious Incident of the Dog in the Night-Time: The Play*
2.4 Understand theme	**English Language** AO1, AO2 **English Literature** AO1, AO2	**English Language** Paper 1, Questions 2, 3, 4 Paper 2, Questions 3, 4 **English Literature** key skill across all components		How can a text be 'about' more than one thing at the same time?	William Blake, 'A Poison Tree' Carol Ann Duffy, 'Cold'
2.5 Understand structure	**English Language** AO1, AO2 **English Literature** AO1, AO2	**English Language** Paper 1, Questions 2, 3, 4 Paper 2, Questions 3, 4 **English Literature** key skill across all components	chronologically, flashbacks	Why does structure matter?	Margaret Atwood, from *The Year of the Flood*
2.6 Understand literal and metaphorical reading	**English Language** AO1, AO2 **English Literature** AO1, AO2	**English Language** Paper 1, Questions 2, 3, 4 Paper 2, Questions 3, 4 **English Literature** key skill across all components	connotations, figure of speech, imagery, implicit, literal	Why do writers use metaphors when they could just say what they mean?	Charles Perrault, from *Little Red Riding Hood* William Wordsworth, 'Daffodils'
2.7 Understand the effect of writers' choices	**English Language** AO1, AO2 **English Literature** AO1, AO2	**English Language** Paper 1, Questions 2, 3, 4 Paper 2, Questions 3, 4 **English Literature** key skill across all components	connotations, purpose	What are effects and how do you write about them?	NSPCC advert Carol Ann Duffy, from 'Havisham' William Blake, 'The Chimney Sweeper'
2.8 Understand attitude and viewpoint	**English Language** AO1, AO2 **English Literature** AO1, AO2	**English Language** Paper 1, Question 1 Paper 2, Questions 1, 2 **English Literature** key skill across all components		How do you know what a writer feels about what they are writing about?	Mark Sweney, 'Britons "watch four hours of TV a day"', *Guardian*, 4 May 2010 'Forget the Fiction: Live Your Own Adventure' Archibald Forbes, from 'The Suppression of the Paris Commune', *Daily News*, 26 May 1871

Chapter 3 Medium-term plan

Topic/lesson	AOs	Exam question(s)	Key term(s)	Big question	Texts
3.1 Retrieve basic information from unseen texts	**English Language** AO1 **English Literature** AO1	**English Language** Paper 1, Question 1 Paper 2, Question 1	scanning, skimming	What is 'explicit information'?	Allan Hall, 'How did Swedish man survive in this frozen car …?', *Daily Mail*, 22 February 2012 George Packer, from 'Snow Story'
3.2 Support ideas with evidence and quotation	**English Language** AO1 **English Literature** AO1	**English Language** Paper 1, Question 4 Paper 2, Questions 2, 4	colon	Isn't quotation just copying out bits of the text?	Allan Hall, 'How did Swedish man survive in this frozen car …?', *Daily Mail*, 22 February 2012 George Packer, from 'Snow Story'
3.3 Show your understanding of inference and implication	**English Language** AO1 **English Literature** AO1	**English Language** Paper 1, Question 4 Paper 2, Questions 2, 4	explicit meanings, first-person narrator, implicit meanings, inferences	What are inferences and why do you need them?	Michelle Roberts, from 'Your Shoes'
3.4 Make and present inferences about people	**English Language** AO1, AO4 **English Literature** AO1	**English Language** Paper 1, Question 4 Paper 2, Questions 2, 4		How do we know what writers want us to see about characters?	Charles Dickens, from *Great Expectations* Charles Dickens, from *Oliver Twist*
3.5 Make and present inferences about places	**English Language** AO1, AO4 **English Literature** AO1	**English Language** Paper 1, Question 4 Paper 2, Questions 2, 4		How do we know what writers want us to see about places?	Emily Brontë, from *Wuthering Heights*
3.6 Make and present inferences about ideas and attitudes	**English Language** AO1 **English Literature** AO1	**English Language** Paper 1, Question 4 Paper 2, Question 4		You can make inferences about creative writing but how can you do it with newspaper articles?	'The Secret Teacher', from *Guardian*, 3 May 2014
3.7 Summarise and synthesise: selecting and collating information from more than one text	**English Language** AO1	**English Language** Paper 2, Questions 2, 4		How do you work with two texts at once?	Extract from Captain Scott's Diary, 1912 James Cracknell and Ben Fogle, from *Race to the Pole*
3.8 Apply your skills to English Language and English Literature tasks	**English Language** AO1 **English Literature** AO1	**English Language** Paper 1, Question 4 Paper 2, Questions 2, 4 **English Literature** Paper 2, Section A			Alastair Sloan, 'Sleeping rough for charity hides the real homelessness crisis', *Guardian*, 29 October 2013 Charles Dickens, from *Sketches by Boz* Ray Bradbury, from 'The Veldt'

Chapter 4 Medium-term plan

Topic/lesson	AOs	Exam questions	Key terms	Big question	Texts
4.1 Explain and comment on writers' use of language	**English Language** AO2	**English Language** Paper 1, Questions 2, 3 Paper 2, Question 3	adverbials, effects, viewpoint	Why does it matter which words and phrases the writer chooses?	George Orwell, from *The Road to Wigan Pier*
4.2 Explain and comment on writers' use of language techniques	**English Language** AO2	**English Language** Paper 1, Questions 2, 3 Paper 2, Question 3	colloquial, rhetorical techniques	How do writers use language techniques to influence the way you think about things?	'Let's put the brakes on teen drivers…' by Joanna Moorhead, *Guardian*
4.3 Explain the way writers use language to create character	**English Language** AO2 **English Literature** AO2	**English Language** Paper 1, Questions 2, 3 Paper 2, Question 3 **English Literature** Paper 1, Section B Paper 2, Section A	connotation, first person, omniscient narrator, semantic field, third person	Do you have to pay close attention to every single word when you're writing about a fiction text? How do you choose what to write about?	Charles Dickens, from *A Christmas Carol* Lloyd Jones, from *Mr Pip*
4.4 Explain and comment on writers' use of structural features	**English Language** AO2 **English Literature** AO2	**English Language** Paper 1, Questions 2, 3 Paper 2, Question 3 **English Literature** Paper 2, Sections A, B	cohesion, dashes, structural features, tone	What does 'structure' mean and why is it important?	Dennis Kelly, from *DNA* Bill Bryson, from *A Walk in the Woods*
4.5 Explain and comment on writers' use of openings	**English Language** AO2 **English Literature** AO2	**English Language** Paper 1, Questions 2, 3 Paper 2, Question 3 **English Literature** Paper 1, Section B Paper 2, Section A	infer, inferences, narrator	Why is the opening of a story important?	Gaye Jee, from 'The Way the Pit Works' Charlotte Brontë, from *Jane Eyre*
4.6 Explain and comment on the ways writers create meanings and effects with structure and form	**English Literature** AO2	**English Language** Paper 1, Questions 2, 3 Paper 2, Question 3 **English Literature** Paper 1, Section B Paper 2, Section A	cohesion, couplet, iambic pentameter	What is the difference between structure and form, and why do they matter?	William Shakespeare, 'Sonnet 17' Carol Ann Duffy, 'Anne Hathaway'
4.7 Apply your skills to English Language and English Literature tasks	**English Language** AO2 **English Literature** AO2	**English Language** Paper 1, Questions 2, 3 Paper 2, Question 3 **English Literature** Paper 1, Section B Paper 2, Section A			Malcolm Rose, from *Bloodline* John Clare, 'First Love' Arthur C. Clarke, from *The Forgotten Enemy* (Worksheet 4.7c) Isobel Thrilling, 'Advice to a Teenage Daughter' (Worksheet 4.7d)

Chapter 5 Medium-term plan

Topic/lesson	AOs	Exam question(s)	Key terms	Big question	Texts
5.1 Understand and define context	**English Literature** AO3	**English Literature** Paper 2, Section B	allegories	What is context and how can it help you to understand literary texts?	George Orwell, from *Animal Farm*
5.2 Relate themes and language to context	**English Literature** AO2, AO3	**English Literature** Paper 1, Section A		How can understanding ideas and attitudes from the time in which a text was written help us to understand the story and its themes?	William Shakespeare, from *Macbeth*, Act 2 Scene 3
5.3 Relate context to language	**English Literature** AO2, AO3	**English Literature** Paper 1, Section B		How do the ideas of the time affect the language of the text?	Robert Louis Stevenson, from *Dr Jekyll and Mr Hyde*
5.4 Explore setting as context	**English Literature** AO3	**English Literature** Paper 2, Section A		If you want to write a political play to change people's attitudes in the modern world, why set it in the past?	J.B. Priestley, from *An Inspector Calls*
5.5 Explore the same context from different perspectives	**English Literature** AO2, AO3	**English Literature** Paper 2, Section B	perspective	How can two writers see such different things in the same setting?	William Wordsworth, 'Upon Westminster Bridge' George Eliot, 'In a London Drawingroom'
5.6 Apply your skills to an English Literature task	**English Literature** AO1, AO2, AO3	**English Literature** Paper 2, Section B			John Clare, 'The Swallow' Ted Hughes, 'Work and Play'

Chapter 6 Medium-term plan

Topic/lesson	AOs	Exam question(s)	Key terms	Big question	Texts
6.1 Critical Evaluation: form an interpretation	**English Language** AO4 **English Literature** AO1	**English Language** Paper 1 Question 4 Paper 2, Question 4 **English Literature** All components	inferences, interpretation	How is critical evaluation different from doing basic comprehension?	Vernon Scannell, 'A Case of Murder'
6.2 Critical evaluation: gather and present evidence about language	**English Language** (AO2) AO4 **English Literature** AO1 (AO2)	**English Language** Paper 1 Question 4 Paper 2, Question 4 **English Literature** All components	connotations, semantic field	Do you need your knowledge about language in evaluative essay-type questions too?	Wilfred Owen, from 'Dulce et Decorum est'
6.3 Critical evaluation: gather and present evidence about structure	**English Language** AO2. AO4 **English Literature** AO1, AO2	**English Language** Paper 1 Question 4 Paper 2, Question 4 **English Literature** All components	compound sentence, structure,	What else can you say apart from: "it's got a beginning, a middle and an end and it's made up of long sentences'?	Jon McGregor, from *If Nobody Speaks of Remarkable Things*
6.4 Critical evaluation: gather and present evidence about mood	**English Language** AO4 **English Literature** AO1, AO2	**English Language** Paper 1 Question 4 Paper 2, Question 4 **English Literature** All components	gothic horror genre, pathetic fallacy, semantic field	Why is mood important in critical evaluation?	Bram Stoker, from *Dracula*
6.5 Critical evaluation: construct a convincing response to literary texts	**English Language** AO4 **English Literature** AO1	**English Language** Paper 1 Question 4 Paper 2, Question 4 **English Literature** All components		You have gathered a lot of clues and quotations, but how do you put it all together?	P.B. Shelley, 'Ozymandias'
6.6 Critical evaluation: construct a convincing response to non-fiction texts	**English Language** AO4	**English Language** Paper 1 Question 4 Paper 2, Question 4 **English Literature** All components	minor sentences, rhetorical questions, simple sentences, tone	You can write up your ideas about poems and stories, but you find it harder with non-fiction texts. How do you improve?	Jessica Ennis, from *Unbelievable*
6.7 Apply your skills to English Language and English Literature tasks	**English Language** AO4 **English Literature** AO1	**English Language** Paper 1 Question 4 Paper 2, Question 4 **English Literature** All components			F. Scott Fitzgerald, from *The Great Gatsby* Arthur Conan Doyle, from 'The Adventure of the Speckled Band'

Chapter 7 — Medium-term plan

Topic/lesson	AOs	Exam question(s)	Key terms	Big question	Texts
7.1 Compare views and perspectives in non-literary non-fiction from the twentieth century	**English Language** AO3	**English Language** Paper 2, Question 4		How do you compare two different viewpoints?	Anonymous, 'Why I'm taking my child out of school for a holiday', *The Guardian*, 29 January 2014 Joanna Moorhead, 'Why I'll never take my children out of school for a holiday', *The Guardian*, 29 January 2014
7.2 Compare non-fiction prose texts	**English Language** AO3	**English Language** Paper 2, Question 4		How do you know what to compare when you're comparing two different texts?	Sugata Mitra, www.edutopia.org/blog/selforganized-learning-sugata-mitra Charles Dickens, 'A Sleep to Startle Us', *Household Words*, 13 March 1852
7.3 Compare the ways viewpoints are presented in texts from the early twentieth century	**English Language** AO2, AO3	**English Language** Paper 2, Question 4	emotive language, hyperbole	What kinds of things are you looking for when you're thinking about how writers present their viewpoints to the reader?	Article from *New York Times*, 19 April 1912 Adolf von Spiegel, from 'U-Boat Attack'
7.4 Structure a comparative response to poetry	**English Literature** AO1, AO2	**English Literature** Paper 2, Sections B & C		How do you know what to compare when you're comparing poems?	Tatamkhula Afrika, 'Nothing's Changed' Sophia de Mello Breyner, 'Homeland'
7.5 Apply your skills to English Language and English Literature tasks	**English Language** AO3 **English Literature** AO1, AO2	**English Language** Paper 2, Question 4 **English Literature** Paper 2, Sections B & C			Sarah Ashton, interviewed in *The Ashton Chronicle*, 23 June 1849 Michael Bartlet, 'Britain's child soldiers', *The Guardian*, 11 March 2011 Siegfried Sassoon, 'The Hero' Wilfred Owen, 'Arms and the Boy' Transcript of chimney sweep William Cooper's evidence to a parliamentary committee in 1818 Article on modern-day child slavery Brian Patten, 'The Armada' Owen Sheers, 'Not Yet My Mother'

Chapter 8: Medium-term plan

Topic/lesson	AOs	Exam question(s)	Key terms	Big question	Texts
8.1 How to describe setting and atmosphere	**English Language** AO5, AO6	**English Language** Paper 1, Question 5	adverbial, personification, prepositional phrase	How can you describe setting and atmosphere in a memorable way?	Elizabeth Gaskell, from *The Life of Charlotte Brontë* Tobias Jones, from *The Dark Heart of Italy*
8.2 How to describe people and events	**English Language** AO5, AO6	**English Language** Paper 1, Question 5	show, not tell	How can you describe people and events in a memorable way?	Charles Dickens, from *Oliver Twist* Lorna Sage, from *Bad Blood*
8.3 How to structure a description	**English Language** AO5, AO6	**English Language** Paper 1, Question 5		How can you structure your descriptions to keep readers interested?	Ameena Meer, from 'Rain'
8.4 Build ideas for a descriptive task	**English Language** AO5, AO6	**English Language** Paper 1, Question 5		How can you quickly come up with ideas for your descriptive task?	
8.5 How to structure narratives effectively	**English Language** AO5, AO6	**English Language** Paper 1, Question 5	flashback, in medias res, protagonist	How can you structure your stories to keep readers interested?	Robert Cormier, from *The Chocolate War* Edgar Allan Poe, from *The Fall of the House of Usher* George R.R. Martin, from *A Song of Ice and Fire* Anne Brontë, from *The Tenant of Wildfell Hall*
8.6 Creating convincing characterization and voice	**English Language** AO5, AO6	**English Language** Paper 1, Question 5	dialect	How can you make your characters or narrators interesting?	Andrea Levy, from *Small Island* F. Scott Fitzgerald, from 'The Ice Palace'
8.7 Generate ideas for your narrative response	**English Language** AO5, AO6	**English Language** Paper 1, Question 5		How can you come up with good ideas for a short story or short story opening in a short space of time?	
8.8 Apply your skills to an English Language task	**English Language** AO5, AO6	**English Language** Paper 1, Question 5			

Chapter 9 Medium-term plan

Topic/lesson	AOs	Exam question(s)	Key terms	Big question	Texts
9.1 What is point of view writing?	**English Language** AO5, AO6	**English Language** Paper 2, Question 5	negative, neutral, positive	What does it mean when you have to write from a particular point of view?	
9.2 Match tone and register to task and audience	**English Language** AO5, AO6	**English Language** Paper 2, Question 5		Why does it matter what tone or register you use?	
9.3 Match features to text types and conventions	**English Language** AO5, AO6	**English Language** Paper 2, Question 5		What features will make your point of view more convincing?	Helena Pielichaty, 31 March 2014, www.helena-pielichaty.com/blog/ Frederick Douglass, 'What to the slave is the fourth of July?', 5 July 1852
9.4 Select appropriate vocabulary to make an impact	**English Language** AO5, AO6	**English Language** Paper 2, Question 5	adjectives, adverbs, noun phrases	How can your choice of words influence the reader?	Naomi Mdudu, *Metro*, 20 March 2014 Naomi Klein, from *No Logo*
9.5 Key techniques: varying sentences and verbs for effect	**English Language** AO5, AO6	**English Language** Paper 2, Question 5	compound sentences, modal verbs, simple sentences, verb	How can you use different types of sentence and verbs to influence the reader?	Pam Allyn, *Huffington Post*, 3 March 2014
9.6 Key techniques: using punctuation for effect and impact	**English Language** AO5, AO6	**English Language** Paper 2, Question 5		How can punctuation help you to get your message across?	*The Times*, 5 November 2012
9.7 Shape whole texts cohesively	**English Language** AO5, AO6	**English Language** Paper 2, Question 5		How can you organise your writing as a whole to make your point of view persuasive and clear?	Information from Lattitudes website: www.lattitude.org.uk/2013/03/gap-year-by-numbers/
9.8 Shape sentences into paragraphs effectively	**English Language** AO5, AO6	**English Language** Paper 2, Question 5	determiner	How can you arrange your sentences to make your viewpoint clear and have an impact on your readers?	Hadley Freeman, 'Why black models are rarely in fashion', *The Guardian*, 18 February 2014
9.9 Apply your skills to an English Language task	**English Language** AO5, AO6	**English Language** Paper 2, Question 5			

Chapter 1 Medium-term plan

Topic/lesson	AOs	Exam question(s)	Key terms	Big question	Texts
1.1 An introduction to phrases	**English Language** AO2, AO6 **English Literature** AO2, AO4	**English Language** Paper 1, Question 5 Paper 2, Question 5 The same skills and knowledge are also required in **English Language** Paper 1, Questions 3, 4 Paper 2, Question 4 **English Literature** Paper 1, Section A Paper 2, Section A	adverb, adverbial clause, adjectival phrase, modification, phrase, prepositions	Isn't a phrase just a cluster of words?	John Donne, 'To His Mistris going to Bed' William Wordsworth, 'Daffodils' William Blake, 'Laughing Song'
1.2 Sentence structures and punctuation	**English Language** AO2, AO6 **English Literature** AO2, AO4	**English Language** Paper 1, Question 5 Paper 2, Question 5 The same skills and knowledge are also required in **English Language** Paper 1, Questions 3, 4 Paper 2, Question 4 **English Literature** Paper 1, Section A Paper 2, Section A	complex sentence, compound sentence, compound-complex sentence, simple sentence	Some texts use very complex sentences – how do you 'unpack' them?	J.K. Rowling, from *Harry Potter and the Philosopher's Stone* Virginia Woolf, from *The Waves* Jane Austen, from *Pride and Prejudice*
1.3 Structural effects in sentences	**English Language** AO2, AO6 **English Literature** AO2	**English Language** Paper 1, Question 5 Paper 2, Question 5 The same skills and knowledge are also required in **English Language** Paper 1, Questions 3, 4 Paper 2, Question 4 **English Literature** Paper 1, Section A Paper 2, Section A	minor sentence, syndetic list	Does it make any difference what types of sentence you use?	Jon McGregor, *If Nobody Speaks of Remarkable Things* Charles Dickens, from *Sketches by Boz*

Chapter 2 — Medium-term plan

Topic/lesson	AOs	Exam question(s)	Key terms	Big question	Texts
2.1 Explore meanings and interpretations	**English Language** AO1 **English Literature** AO1	**English Language** Paper 1, Section A **English Literature** Paper 2, Section B	assertion, connotations, interpretation, plurality, synonyms	What does 'interpreting' a text mean?	T.S. Eliot, 'Virginia' William Blake, 'The Sick Rose'
2.2 Explore the conventions of genre	**English Language** AO1 **English Literature** AO1	**English Language** Paper 1, Section A **English Literature** Paper 2, Section A	conventions, genre	What are conventions and how do writers use them in different ways?	Horace Walpole, from *The Castle of Otranto* Jane Austen, from *Northanger Abbey* Daphne du Maurier, from *Rebecca*
2.3 Explore narrative voices	**English Language** AO1, AO5 **English Literature** AO1	**English Language** Paper 1, Section A **English Literature** Paper 2, Section A	address, allusions, analogies, first person, ironic, narrative perspective, protagonist	How do writers create interesting narrative voices?	Edgar Allan Poe, from 'The Tell-tale Heart'

Chapter 3 Medium-term plan

Topic/lesson	AOs	Exam question(s)	Key terms	Big question	Texts
3.1 Understand more challenging texts	**English Language** AO1, AO4 **English Literature** AO1	**English Language** Paper 2, Section A	inferential reading	What techniques can you use to make sense of difficult texts?	Adapted from Charles Darwin, *The Autobiography of Charles Darwin*
3.2 Use textual support in sophisticated ways	**English Language** AO1, AO4 **English Literature** AO1	**English Language** Paper 1, Section A **English Literature** Paper 2, Section B		How can you use the text more effectively to back up your ideas?	Lord Byron, 'She Walks in Beauty' William Shakespeare, Sonnet 130
3.3 Synthesise and summarise more challenging texts	**English Language** AO1 **English Literature** AO1	**English Language** Paper 2, Section A	synthesise	How can you draw together ideas from two related texts in a clear and fluent way?	A.A. Gill, from 'My London, and Welcome to it', *The New York Times*, 27 April 2012 Thomas Miller, from *Picturesque Sketches of London Past and Present*
3.4 Apply your skills to English Language and English Literature tasks	**English Language** AO1 **English Literature** AO1	**English Language** Paper 1, Section B			Tom Phillips, 'Rio World Cup demolitions leave favela families trapped in ghost town', *The Guardian*, 26 April 2011 Gilbert Beith, from 'The Crofter Question', 1884 D.H. Lawrence, from 'Odour of Chrysanthemums'

Chapter 4 Medium-term plan

Topic/lesson	AOs	Exam question(s)	Key terms	Big question	Texts
4.1 Analyse and evaluate writers' use of language techniques	**English Language** AO2	**English Language** Paper 1, Questions 2, 3 **English Language** Paper 2, Question 3	alliteration, connotations, extended metaphor, personification, semantic field, simile	What does 'analyse the effect' mean and how do you do it successfully?	George Orwell, from *The Road to Wigan Pier*
4.2 Analyse and evaluate writers' use of structure	**English Language** AO2	**English Language** Paper 1, Questions 2, 3 **English Language** Paper 2, Question 3	anecdote, hyperbolic question, op-ed article, rhetorical question	How do structure and organisation make a difference to the ways in which a text is read and understood?	Caitlin Moran, from *How to be a Woman*
4.3 Analyse the ways writers create meanings and effects with structure and form	**English Literature** AO2	**English Literature** Paper 2, Section B Paper 2, Section C	caesura, enjambment, volta	What is the difference between 'structure' and 'form'? Why does the 'form' of a text matter?	Edmund Spenser, Sonnet 75 Ros Barber, 'How to Leave the World that Worships *Should*'
4.4 Apply your skills to English Language and English Literature tasks	**English Language** AO2 **English Literature** AO2	**English Language** Paper 1, Questions 2, 3 Paper 2, Question 3 **English Literature** Paper 1 Paper 2			William Golding, from *Lord of the Flies* Mary Oliver, 'The Swan'

Chapter 5: Medium-term plan

Topic/lesson	AOs	Exam question(s)	Key terms	Big question	Texts
5.1 Explore how writers use different settings to develop characters	**English Literature** AO1, AO2, AO3	**English Literature** Paper 2, Section A		How can ideas about a place help you to understand a character?	Penelope Lively, from 'The Darkness Out There'
5.2 Explore how writers use different time periods to develop themes and ideas	**English Literature** AO1, AO2, AO3	**English Literature** Paper 2, Section B		How can understanding a text's historical setting help you to understand its themes and ideas?	Seamus Heaney, 'At a Potato Digging'
5.3 Explore how ideas about literary context can inform your reading of a text	**English Literature** AO1, AO2, AO3	**English Literature** Paper 1, Section B	*bildungsroman*, *protagonist*	How do writers create authentic childhood narrative voices?	Charles Dickens, from *Great Expectations* Charles Dickens, from *David Copperfield* Charlotte Brontë, from *Jane Eyre*
5.4 Apply your skills to an English Literature task	**English Literature** AO1, AO2, AO3	**English Literature** Paper 2, Section A			William Shakespeare, from *Hamlet*

Chapter 6 — Medium-term plan

Topic/lesson	AOs	Exam question(s)	Key terms	Big question	Texts
6.1 Understand critical reading	**English Language** AO4 **English Literature** AO1	**English Language** Paper 1, Question 4 Paper 2, Question 4 **English Literature** key skill across all components	interpretation	How is reading critically different from doing the usual comprehension work?	Peter Bradshaw, 'Wuthering Heights – review', from *The Guardian*, 10 November 2011 Robbie Collin, 'Wuthering Heights: review', from *The Telegraph*, 10 November 2011 William Shakespeare, from *Romeo and Juliet* Walter Greenwood, from *Love on the Dole*
6.2 Construct a convincing response to literary texts	**English Language** AO4 **English Literature** AO1	**English Language** Paper 1, Question 4 Paper 2, Question 4 **English Literature** key skill across all components		You have gathered ideas about a text – how do you put it all together?	William Blake, from 'The Tyger'
6.3 Construct a convincing response to non-fiction texts	**English Language** AO4 **English Literature** AO1	**English Language** Paper 1, Question 4 Paper 2, Question 4 **English Literature** key skill across all components		You are confident when presenting your ideas about poems and stories, but you find it harder with non-fiction texts. How do you improve?	Jean Sprackland, from *Strands*
6.4 Apply your skills to English Language and English Literature tasks	**English Language** AO4 **English Literature** AO1	**English Language** Paper 1, Question 4 Paper 2, Question 4 **English Literature** key skill across all components			Khaled Hosseini, from *The Kite Runner* Thomas Hardy, 'The Convergence of the Twain'

Chapter 7 — Medium-term plan

Topic/lesson	AOs	Exam question(s)	Key terms	Big question	Texts
7.1 Compare how writers use tone to convey viewpoints and perspectives	**English Language** AO3	**English Language** Paper 2, Question 4		What is irony and how do writers use it for humorous effect?	David Sedaris, from 'Six to Eight Black Men' Mary Kingsley, from *Travels In West Africa*
7.2 Compare the influence of poetic voices over time	**English Language** AO3 **English Literature** AO2	**English Literature** Paper 2, Section B	evaluate, personification	How can two writers see such different things in the same setting?	Emily Brontë, 'Spellbound' Norman MacCaig, 'Below the Green Corrie' George Sterling, 'Night on the Mountain'
7.3 Compare and evaluate how writers explore similar ideas in poetry	**English Literature** AO2	**English Literature** Paper 2, Section C	synthesise	What is an 'evaluative comparison' and how do you do it?	Isobel Thrilling, 'Children in Wartime' Vernon Scannell, 'Incendiary'
7.4 Apply your skills to English Language and English Literature tasks	**English Language** AO3 **English Literature** AO2	**English Language** Paper 2, Question 4 **English Literature** Paper 2, Section B Paper 2, Section C			Leader, 'Ban this barbaric sport', from *The Guardian*, 18 December 2000 William Hazlitt, from 'The Fight' D.H. Lawrence, 'Piano' Tony Harrison, 'Background Material'

Chapter 8 — Medium-term plan

Topic/lesson	AOs	Exam question(s)	Key terms	Big question	Texts
8.1 Engage the reader through original forms of narration	**English Language** AO5, AO6	**English Language** Paper 1, Section B	tone	How can you engage the reader through narrative forms or voices?	From short story, 'Wreckage' Nick Hornby, from *High Fidelity*
8.2 Use imagery and symbolism to enhance narrative and descriptive power	**English Language** AO5, AO6	**English Language** Paper 1, Section B	cinquain, figurative language, imagery, literal, personification, symbolise	How can you make your stories and descriptions distinctive and powerful?	Adelaide Crapsey, 'The Warning' Ted Hughes, from 'The Rain Horse'
8.3 Use structures to create memorable texts	**English Language** AO5, AO6	**English Language** Paper 1, Section B		How can you order and structure narratives to interest and engage the reader?	Katherine Mansfield, from 'Miss Brill'
8.4 Apply your skills to an English Language task	**English Language** AO5, AO6	**English Language** Paper 1, Section B			

Chapter 9 Medium-term plan

Topic/lesson	AOs	Exam question(s)	Key terms	Big question	Texts
9.1 Convey convincing and original voices in your writing	**English Language** AO5, AO6	**English Language** Paper 2, Section B	alludes, extended metaphor, vignettes	How can you develop an original and engaging tone of voice?	Tim Dowling, 'Hounded out', from *The Guardian*, 22 March 2014 Xan Brooks, '*The Amazing Spider-Man 2* review', from *The Guardian*, 9 April 2014 Tim Lott, 'Good friends are hard to find – and even harder to keep', from *The Guardian*, 13 August 2014
9.2 Manipulate structure to create effects in point-of-view writing	**English Language** AO5, AO6	**English Language** Paper 2, Section B	foreground, polemical	How can you structure points in an opinion piece to create impact in an original, yet clear way?	George Monbiot, 'Ban neonicotinoids now – to avert another silent spring', from *The Guardian*, 16 July 2014
9.3 Match style and tone to purpose and audience	**English Language** AO5, AO6	**English Language** Paper 2, Section B		How can you pitch your style perfectly to match the task?	Harry Leslie Smith, 'This surveillance bill puts our hard-won freedom in peril', from *The Guardian*, 11 July 2014
9.4 Apply your skills to an English Language task	**English Language** AO5, AO6	**English Language** Paper 2, Section B			

One-year scheme of work

Suitable for:
- English Language re-sit candidates in school, sixth-form college or FE
- English Language candidates in sixth-form college, FE college or mature candidates in Adult Education sitting GCSE for the first time

Required skills:	Top tips for teachers:
✓ Basic reading comprehension skills (Chapter 3) ✓ Analysis of the language and structure of texts (Chapters 1, 2, 4) ✓ Writing 'mini' practical criticism essay to unseen creative texts (Chapter 6) ✓ Writing 'mini' practical criticism essay comparing non-fiction texts (Chapter 7) ✓ Descriptive writing (Chapter 8) ✓ Narrative writing (Chapter 8) ✓ Point of view writing (Chapter 9)	• Aim to keep everything linked together thematically, in order to help students connect the core skills and see the bigger picture. • Relate everything you do to the Assessment Objectives and reinforce which examination questions students are being prepared for. • Ensure that text choices and topics/themes dealt with are relevant to the age group. • Avoid repeating anything that the students may already have done in secondary school to keep up the motivation, and maintain variety and interest.

Term 1: Sharing stories (10–12 weeks)

• Recap and develop basic reading comprehension skills (Core 3.1–3.6) • Read a selection of short stories applying those skills, and practise for English Language Paper 1, Questions 1 & 4 • Link the study of short stories to basic narrative techniques (Core 2.1, 2.3–2.7) • Work on basic spellings (Core 1.1) • Work on basic punctuation (Core 1.5) **Assessment** *Short story writing/constructing your own successful narrative (Core 1.6–1.8, 8.5–8.7)*	**Recommended additional resources** • *Telling Tales – AQA Anthology of Modern Short Stories* or your own anthology of 6–8 chosen stories/extracts from novels to suit your cohort • Etymological dictionaries

Term 2: The power of words (10–12 weeks)

• Develop a basic toolkit of terms (Core 1.2–1.4) • Learn to analyse short passages from stories/poems in terms of language and structure (Core 2.4–2.5, 4.1–4.4) • Link the craft of writers studied to develop own descriptive techniques (Core 4.5–4.6, 8.1–8.2) • Write to describe (Core 8.3–8.4) • An introduction to critical evaluation (Core 6.1–6.4) **Assessment** *Mock exam: English Language Paper 1. Feedback and target setting*	**Recommended additional resources** • *Telling Tales – AQA Anthology of Modern Short Stories* • 3–4 poems with an interesting structure • 3–4 descriptive poems • AQA English Language Paper 1 for mock exam

Term 3: Perspective and interpretation (10–12 weeks)

• An introduction to persuasive and rhetorical devices (Core 2.8, 9.1–9.4) • Present your own points of view in writing (Core 9.5–9.8) • Develop comprehension skills with two texts (Core 3.7) • Develop comparative skills (Core 7.1–7.3) • Develop critical evaluation (Core 6.5–6.6) **Assessment** *Mock exam: English Language Paper 2. Feedback and target setting* • Intensive revision using the 'Apply your skills' resources **Assessment** *Final full mock exam: English Language Papers 1 and 2. Final feedback*	**Recommended additional resources** • Exemplar opinion pieces from broadsheet newspapers • AQA English Language Papers 1 and 2 for mock exams

Two-year scheme of work

Suitable for:

- 14–16-year-old secondary school students of mid to good ability: potential Levels 3–9
- Students in FE or adult education studying a combined Language and Literature course awarding two GCSEs

Required skills:

- ✓ Basic reading comprehension skills (Chapter 3)
- ✓ Analysis of the language and structure of texts (Chapters 1, 2, 4)
- ✓ Writing 'mini' and full practical criticism essay responses to single literary texts; some set, some unseen (Chapters 4, 5, 6)
- ✓ Writing 'mini' and full practical criticism essay responses comparing texts (both literary and non-fiction); some set, some unseen (Chapter 4, 5, 6, 7)
- ✓ Descriptive writing (Chapter 8)
- ✓ Narrative writing (Chapter 8)
- ✓ Point of view writing (Chapter 9)

Top tips for teachers:

- Remember the key differences within the specification and allow the full two years for the course.
- Plan holistically, linking the core skills, rather than compartmentalising.
- Remember you have no topical coursework and controlled assessment to worry about or to encourage compartmentalising.
- Begin with the familiar ground, developing skills and confidence with the modern accessible texts before adding complexity and challenge with the 19th-century texts and the Shakespeare play.
- Use whole texts as a way of developing a number of skills across both Language and Literature, rather than focusing on just one subject award.
- Use thematic links to good effect. For example, if you are studying the 'Love and relationships' poetry cluster, link other set texts to this theme to produce a cohesive course where work overlaps and skills build. You might therefore choose:
  - 'Love and relationships' poetry + *A Taste of Honey* + *Romeo and Juliet* + *Jane Eyre,* or
  - 'Power and conflict' poetry + *DNA* + *Macbeth* + *Frankenstein*.

For further advice see the accompanying videos on the CD-Rom.

Year 1

Term 1: Sharing stories (10–12 weeks)

- Recap and develop basic reading comprehension skills (Core 3.1–3.5)
- Read a selection of short stories applying those skills, and practise for English Language Paper 1, Q1 and 4
- Link the study of short stories to basic narrative techniques (Core 2.3–2.7)
- Work on basic spellings (Core 1.1)
- Work on basic punctuation (Core 1.5)
- Short story writing / construct your own successful narrative (Core 8.5, 8.6, 8.7)

Assessment

Complete a practice English Language Paper 1, Question 5; mark with mark scheme and feedback

Recommended additional resources

- *AQA Anthology of Modern Short stories for Literature* or your own anthology of 6–8 chosen stories / extracts from novels
- Etymological dictionaries
- Thesaurus
- AQA English Language Paper 1, Section B with mark scheme

Term 2: Responding to issues (10–12 weeks)

- Develop a basic toolkit of terms for non-fiction analysis (Core 2.2)
- Develop comprehension skills with non-fiction texts (Core 3.6–3.7)
- Learn to analyse and compare non-fiction texts (Core 7.1–7.2)
- Explore issue-based articles and non-fiction connected with the topic of the modern play and develop an introduction to persuasive and rhetorical devices (Core 2.8, 9.1–9.4)
- Present your own points of view in writing (Core 9.5–9.8)
- Study the modern drama (set Literature text) in terms of plot, theme, character, language and structure (Core 5.1, 5.4)

Assessment

Practice exam-style question from English Literature Paper 2, Section A; mark with mark scheme and feedback

Recommended additional resources

- *AQA Anthology of Modern Short stories for Literature* or your own selection
- Set Literature text: modern drama
- Dictionaries
- Thesaurus
- AQA English Literature Paper 2, Section A, and mark scheme

Term 3: Creativity and analysis (10–12 weeks)

- Develop a basic toolkit of terms (Core 1.2–1.4, 2.1, 2.3–2.5)
- Learn to analyse short passages from stories / unseen poems in terms of language and structure (Core 4.1–4.4)
- Work on the poetry cluster of choice (Core 5.5, 7.4)
- Link the craft of writers studied to develop own descriptive techniques (Core 4.5–4.6, 8.1–8.2)
- Write to describe (Core 8.3–8.4)
- An introduction to critical evaluation (Core 6.1–6.4)

End-of-Year-10 assessment

English Language, Paper 1 mock exam; mark with mark scheme and feedback

English Literature, Paper 2 mock exam; mark with mark scheme and feedback

Recommended additional resources

- 3–4 poems with an interesting structure
- 3–4 poems with a rich descriptive element
- AQA Anthology: poetry clusters
- AQA English Language Papers 1 and 2 for mock exams

Year 2

Term 1: Connecting with the past (10–12 weeks)

- Build skills of critical evaluation and response (Core 6.5–6.6)
- Work with extracts of 19th-century non-fiction linked to the themes and issues of the set novel, alongside modern non-fiction texts (Core 7.3)
- Read and study the 19th-century novel (set Literature text) in terms of plot, theme, character, language and structure (Core 4.5, 5.2–5.3)

Assessment

English Language Paper 2 mock exam; mark with mark scheme and feedback

English Literature Paper 1, Section B, and feedback

Recommended additional resources

- Set Literature text: 19th-century novel and accompanying non-fiction texts in context
- Dictionaries
- Thesaurus
- AQA English Language Paper 2 and mark scheme
- AQA English Literature Paper 1, Section B, and mark scheme

Term 2: The writer's craft (10–12 weeks)

- Read and study Shakespeare play (set Literature text) in terms of plot, /theme, /character, /language and structure
- Use extracts of Shakespeare play alongside unseen poetry to practise comparative and unseen skills
- Make links via theme with the modern drama text to kick start revision
- Use images and photographs connected with the play / key lines, etc., as creative writing stimulus / to describe a character or place, for example
- Revision of poetry clusters

Assessment

English Literature Paper 1 full mock exam; mark with mark scheme and feedback

Recommended additional resources

- Set Literature text: Shakespeare play
- Selection of poetry, perhaps connected to the play by theme
- Selection of photographic images
- Dictionaries
- Thesaurus
- AQA English Literature Paper 1 and mark scheme

Term 3: Consolidation and exam preparation text (10–12 weeks)

- Consolidating skills in analysing language and structure (Core 4.7)
- Revision for 19th-century novel in harness with English Language Paper 2 (Core 7.5)
- Revision of modern drama text and Shakespeare (linked by theme)
- Revision of short stories in harness with English Language Paper 1 skills (Core 3.8, 6.7)

Assessment

English Language full mock exam with feedback

Recommended additional resources

- All set English Literature texts
- AQA English Language Papers 1 and 2 for mock exams

Three-year scheme of work

Suitable for:
- 14–16-year-old secondary school students of weaker ability, potentially Levels 1–3
- Students with SEN who may require more time to work on the course
- EAL or ESL students with a developing ability in the English Language, who may require more time to develop their own language skills before tackling the more complex aspects of the course

Required skills:
- ✓ Basic reading comprehension skills (Chapter 3)
- ✓ Analysis of the language and structure of texts (Chapters 1, 2, 4)
- ✓ Writing 'mini' and full practical criticism essay responses to single literary texts; some set, some unseen (Chapters 4, 5, 6)
- ✓ Writing 'mini' and full practical criticism essay responses comparing texts (both literary and non-fiction); some set, some unseen (Chapter 4, 5, 6, 7)
- ✓ Descriptive writing (Chapter 8)
- ✓ Narrative writing (Chapter 8)
- ✓ Point of view writing (Chapter 9)

Top tips for teachers:

- Remember the key differences within the specification, and allow the full two years for the course itself using Year 9 to develop and build the right preparatory skills. Remember this is a marathon and not a sprint!

- A crucial element of the course is reading, and some of the reading is of a complex nature. In Year 9 aim to work on developing and extending – and regularly monitoring – the reading ages of the students. Use class readers, encourage library visits, ensure students have a personal reading book, and have some set-reading time planned into lessons with a reading log kept weekly. Work on spellings – first the basics, then more complex words, in patterned groups on a weekly basis. Work on basic punctuation skills to boost the overall literacy level of the students before embarking on the GCSE level work.

- Plan holistically, linking the core skills, rather than compartmentalising. Remember you have no topical coursework and controlled assessment to worry about. Begin the GCSE work on familiar ground, developing skills and confidence with the more modern and accessible texts in Year 10, before working with the most challenging texts in Year 11. Don't be tempted to do them in a rush three times and demotivate or bore the students with three helpings of *Macbeth*. Build skills slowly and steadily.

- Use whole texts as a way of developing a number of skills across both Language and Literature, rather than focusing on just one subject award. Use thematic links to good effect. For example, if you are studying the 'Love and relationships' poetry cluster, it makes sense to link other set texts to this theme to produce a cohesive course where work overlaps and skills build. You might therefore choose:
  - The 'Love and relationships' poetry cluster with *Romeo and Juliet* as your Shakespeare set text, or
  - The 'Power and conflict' cluster with *DNA*.

- Aim to make sensible set text choices for the ability range. For example, *The Strange Case of Dr Jekyll and Mr Hyde* is short, but it is a very complex read for reluctant or less confident readers.

- Suggested set texts for lower-ability students:
  - *Romeo and Juliet* or *The Merchant of Venice* (Shakespeare play)
  - *A Christmas Carol* (19th-century novel)
  - *DNA* or *A Taste of Honey* (modern texts)

For further advice see the accompanying videos on the CD-Rom.

Year 1

Term 1: Building skills and sharing stories (10–12 weeks)

- Personal reading books: 30 minutes of guided reading per week
- Ten basic spellings / common errors / homophones per week
- Basic reading comprehension skills (Core 3.1–3.2)
- Use skills to apply to collection of short stories
- Work on basic punctuation (Core 1.4–1.5)
- Explore techniques for storytelling and writing stories / narrative structures (Core 8.5)
- Write stories of their own on a theme or based on a picture
- Class reader (20th-century / accessible) for pleasure and comprehension practice

Assessment

*Using AQA KS3 Practice 'GCSE style' Paper 1 Section B.
At this stage use the Year 8 paper. Feedback*

Recommended additional resources

- Selection of two or three short stories of your choice to suit your cohort
- Own reading books
- Etymological dictionaries
- Thesaurus
- Accessible Year 9 class reader
- AQA KS3 English Language Paper 1 with mark scheme

Term 2: Creativity and analysis (10–12 weeks)

- Personal reading books: 30 minutes of guided reading per week
- Ten basic spellings per week following patterns (Core 1.1)
- Introduce basic grammar and agreement (Core 1.3)
- Analyse short persuasive texts and identify persuasive features and rhetorical devices (Core 9.1)
- Use persuasive writing in topic-based letters
- Look at two or three famous (extracts from) speeches, including one from Shakespeare, and identify techniques
- Write a persuasive speech for a class debate

Assessment

*Using AQA KS3 Practice 'GCSE style' Paper 2 Section B.
At this stage use the Year 8 paper. Feedback*

Recommended additional resources

- Own reading books
- Collins *Non-fiction for GCSE Teacher Pack*, 'Charity' and 'Travel' sections
- Dictionaries
- Thesaurus
- AQA KS3 Paper 2, Section B, and mark scheme

Term 3: Building skills in the craft of writing (10–12 weeks)

- Personal reading books: 30 minutes of guided reading per week
- Ten subject-specific spellings / English terminology words per week
- An introduction to literature (Core 2.1)
- Learn about structure and some key literary terms (perhaps 6–8 key terms with consolidation work) from your chosen poems
- Look at poems connected to pictures and complete some analysis
- Use picture stimulus to write poems developing an interesting structure and using similes and metaphors
- Introduce some descriptive tools (Core 8.3)
- Introduce effective paragraphing (Core 1.8)
- Write a descriptive piece

End-of-Year-9 assessment

AQA KS3 'GCSE style' practice Paper 1. Use the Year 9 paper. Feedback

Recommended additional resources

- 2–3 poems with an interesting structure / use of technique connected to paintings or pictures
- Own reading books
- Dictionaries
- Thesaurus
- AQA KS3 English Language Paper 1 for Year 9

Year 2

Term 1: Connecting with the past (10–12 weeks)	
<ul><li>Use news articles on a key issue/theme connected to your chosen drama piece, e.g. gangs/bullying in connection with *DNA* or teenage love/pregnancy in relation to a *Taste of Honey* (Core 7.1, 3.6)</li><li>Build comprehension skills</li><li>Class reading of the chosen set modern text exploring plot, theme, character, language and structure (Core 4.2–4.3)</li><li>Write a monologue from the perspective of a character</li><li>Study a connected short story or extract from a novel, exploring language, character and structure, and building comprehension skills (Core 3.3–3.4)</li><li>Work on sentences for effect (Core 1.6)</li><li>Create own narratives from pictures (Core 8.6)</li><li>Work on two or three unseen poems reading and discussing for pleasure and practice</li></ul>**Assessment** *AQA English Language Paper 1, Questions 1, 2, 3, 5*	**Recommended additional resources**<ul><li>Set Literature text: modern text accompanying non-fiction in context</li><li>Dictionaries</li><li>Thesaurus</li><li>2–3 extracts, stories or modern, thematically-connected novel</li><li>AQA English Literature Paper 1 and mark scheme</li></ul>
Term 2: The writer's craft (10–12 weeks)	
<ul><li>Recap on poetry analysis skills and literary terms</li><li>Begin work on the chosen poetry cluster, studying structure, theme, language, imagery, mood and making comparative links (Core 2.4–2.6, 4.4)</li><li>Introduce how to plan and structure responses to GCSE English Literature Paper 2 Section B</li><li>Use the poetry work as an opportunity for a vocabulary boost and lead into connected creative writing/descriptive work (Core 8.1–8.2)</li><li>Work on three or four unseen poems of your choice, reading and working collaboratively on activity-based study</li></ul>**Assessment** *AQA GCSE English Literature Paper 2, Section B*	**Recommended additional resources**<ul><li>AQA poetry anthology, *Poems Past and Present*: poetry clusters</li><li>Dictionaries</li><li>Thesaurus</li><li>AQA English Literature Paper 2 and mark scheme</li></ul>
Term 3: Working with a Shakespeare text (10–12 weeks)	
<ul><li>Complete a class reading and study of a Shakespeare play; establish plot, key themes and key characters (Core 5.2)</li><li>Use short, key extracts and scenes to work on language/poetry analysis</li><li>Develop essay writing skills (Core 6.1)</li><li>Recap on Point of view writing; explore a universal issue/theme from the play via modern news articles / speeches, exploring register and more complex spellings and punctuation for effect (Core 9.2–9.8)</li></ul>**End-of-Year-10 assessment** *AQA GCSE English Language Paper 2, Section B* *AQA GCSE English Literature Paper 1, Section A*	**Recommended additional resources**<ul><li>Set English Literature Shakespeare text</li><li>AQA English Language Paper 2</li><li>AQA English Literature Paper 1</li><li>Dictionaries</li><li>Thesaurus</li></ul>

Year 3

Term 1: Connecting with the past (10–12 weeks)	
• Work on three or four unseen poems linked by period to the 19th-century novel and linked by theme • Work on issue-based comprehensions using non-fiction paired texts for English Language Paper 2 (Core 7.3) • Read and study the 19th-century novel, linked contextually and thematically to the poems and comprehension work studied • Build examination responses **Assessment** *AQA English Language Paper 2 mock exam* *AQA English Literature Paper 1, Section A, timed*	**Recommended additional resources** • Own choice of 19th-century poetry • Set Literature text: 19th-century novel • Accompanying non-fiction linked by theme • Dictionaries • Thesaurus • English Language Paper 2 • English Literature Paper 1
Term 2: Joining the dots (10–12 weeks)	
• Work on three or four unseen poems using paired and individual response work where possible • Work on poetry clusters and comparative responses (Core 7.4) • Work on more detailed responses to unseen texts for English Language Paper 1 (Core 6.2–6.5) • Complete a 'refresher' reading and revision of modern text **Assessment** *AQA English Literature Paper 2 mock exam*	**Recommended additional resources** • AQA poetry anthology, *Poems Past and Present*: poetry clusters • Own choice of poems • Set Literature text: modern play • English Literature Paper 2 • Dictionaries • Thesaurus
Term 3: Consolidation and Exam preparation (10–12 weeks)	
• A walk through of English Language Paper 1 and revision of key skills (Core 3.8, 6.8, 8.8) • A walk through of English Literature Paper 1 and revision of Shakespeare and the 19th-century novel (Core 4.7, 5.6) **Assessment** *Mock exams* • A walk through of English Language Paper 2 and revision of key skills (Core 6.6, 7.5, 9.9) • A walk through of English Literature Paper 2 and revision of key skills (Core 4.7, 7.5) **End-of-Year-10 assessment** *Mock exams*	**Recommended additional resources** • All set English Literature texts • AQA English Language Papers 1 and 2 for mock exams

1.1 Words and how we spell them

Assessment objectives

English Language

AO6 Use a range of vocabulary and sentence structures for clarity, purpose and effect, with accurate spelling and punctuation

English Literature

AO4 Use a range of vocabulary and sentence structures for clarity, purpose and effect, with accurate spelling and punctuation

GCSE examinations
- **English Language** Paper 1, Question 5
- **English Language** Paper 2, Question 5

Differentiated learning outcomes
- **All students must** be able to recognise, use and spell basic words accurately.
- **Most students should** be able to recognise, use and spell more complex words.
- **Some students could** show they are able to form and use complex words which do not always follow regular patterns.

Resources
- **Student Book**: pp. 8–11
- **Worksheets**: 1.1a–c
- **PPT**: 1.1

Getting you thinking

Big question	Refer to the **Big question**: *How do you improve your spelling of more complex words?* Explain that influxes of words from overseas invaders and from other languages are some of the reasons why the spelling of English words can be tricky at times and may sometimes seem illogical. Explain that understanding the roots of our language can help with the challenge of spelling.

Display **PPT 1.1, slide 1** and read the opening paragraph of **Getting you thinking** on page 8 of the Student Book. Work through **Q1a–e** as a class, eliciting the students' ideas and suggestions, and then use **PPT 1.1, slides 2–4** to offer feedback.

Now ask the students to complete **Q2**, for which dictionaries are required, either individually or as paired or collaborative work.

> **Give extra support** by using the first word, *pyjamas*, to show the students that, in many dictionary definitions, there is also a reference to the root language the word is from and its part of speech. You could demonstrate this using an etymological dictionary or an online version.

Feed back as a class and collate on the whiteboard how many different roots the words have stemmed from.

Explore the skills

Look at the words in the box and use the first paragraph under the **Explore the skills** heading on page 9 to explain to the students more about words of Anglo-Saxon and Old Norse origin (sometimes referred to collectively as 'Germanic').

> **Give extra challenge** by asking the students if they notice anything about this collection of words – they may well note there are lots of basic, everyday terms, e.g. *house*, *food*, *friend*, but also many terms related to nature, e.g. *grass*, *sky*, *sun*, *water*. Interestingly, there are also references to feelings here, e.g. *love* and *heart*. Before setting the poetry task you could ask the students to speculate why so many words here connect to the absolute basics of human life.

32 • Key technical skills LESSON 1.1 © HarperCollins*Publishers* 2015

Allow approximately 10 minutes for the students to complete the poetry-writing task (**Q3**) using **Worksheet 1.1a**.

Now move on to explore the information on Latinate words and introduce or reinforce the terms 'prefix' and 'suffix' using the **Key terms** box. Display **PPT 1.1**, **slides 5–10** to support the explanation of how Latinate words are built from a stem, before asking the students to complete the table in **Q4**.

Allow approximately 15 minutes for the students to complete **Q4** and **Q5**, using **Worksheet 1.1b**. If preferred, this will work well as a paired or small-group activity, allowing the students to work together to apply the rule and create the new words.

Develop the skills

Consolidate the skills from **Q4** and **Q5** by drawing conclusions as to why knowledge of the stem word is important. If necessary, display **PPT1.1**, **slides 5–10** again, to show how this can lead to logical choices when spelling more complex words.

Discuss as a class the meanings of 'finish', 'finite', 'infinite', 'definite' and 'indefinite' (**Q6**).

Now ask the students to complete **Q7**, either individually or in pairs.

> **Give extra support** by working on this collaboratively and using the whiteboard and **PPT 1.1**, **slides 5–10**.
>
> **Give extra challenge** by setting up a mini competition for pairs to build as many Latinate words as they can in 10 minutes.

Apply the skills

Using the opening paragraph under **Apply the skills** on page 11 of the Student Book, draw together the ideas about Latinate vocabulary and how the students will encounter this type of vocabulary in many of the texts they will study at GCSE.

Display **PPT 1.1**, **slide 11**, the extract from *Nicholas Nickleby*, and read aloud, pausing at each stem word. Then allow 15 minutes for the students to complete **Q8**, in pairs or small groups using **Worksheet 1.1c**. Alternatively, this could be used as an individual homework task. You could explain that this task includes words of both Latinate and Germanic origin.

Feed back as a class using **PPT 1.1, slide 12** if needed.

Big answer plenary	Use the **Check your progress** to check that the work in the poem in **Q3** has allowed all learners to achieve these outcomes. Refer back to the **Big question** and use the second rung of the ladder to link back to the work in **Q4** and **Q5**. Ask how many students now feel more confident about building complex words using this method.

1.2 Vocabulary and meaning: nouns and adjectives

Assessment objectives

English Language

AO2 Explain, comment on and analyse how writers use language and structure to achieve effects and influence readers, using relevant subject terminology to support their views

AO5 Communicate clearly, effectively and imaginatively, selecting and adapting tone, style and register for different forms, purposes and audiences; organise information and ideas, using structural and grammatical features to support coherence and cohesion of texts

English Literature

AO2 Analyse the language, form and structure used by a writer to create meanings and effects, using relevant subject terminology where appropriate

AO4 Use a range of vocabulary and sentence structures for clarity, purpose and effect, with accurate spelling and punctuation

GCSE examinations
- English Language Paper 1, Question 2, 5
- English Language Paper 2, Question 3, 5
- English Literature key skills across all components

Differentiated learning outcomes
- **All students must** know what the terms noun, adjective and noun phrase mean.
- **Most students should** be able to recognise nouns, adjectives and noun phrases and understand the idea of modification.
- **Some students could** recognise how the placing of a word in a sentence gives it its word class and that, by modifying nouns, we create different meanings.

Resources
- **Student Book**: pp. 12–15
- **Worksheet**: 1.2
- **PPT**: 1.2

Getting you thinking

| Big question | Refer to the **Big question**: *What jobs do words do?* Recap that nouns, adjectives and determiners are all some of the 'job titles' of words. |

Ask the students if they know, or have been told, what the first words they ever said were. Take some examples from the class. Then read the first two paragraphs and the **Key terms** box on page 12 of the Student Book.

Now ask the students to complete **Q1–Q3**, using **Worksheet 1.2**. Take feedback as a class and collect the noun phrases from **Q3** on the whiteboard.

Ask the students to complete **Q4** either in pairs or as a whole class exercise.

Refer them to the **Key term** 'noun phrase' on page 12 to consolidate and check understanding before moving on.

Explore the skills

Display **PPT1.2, slides 1–4** to introduce the idea of modification.

Allow 10 minutes for the students to work individually on **Q5**. They could collate their ideas for each type of house in spider diagrams.

Give extra support by using the first noun phrase, 'a newly built house', and taking collaborative ideas.

If time allows, take feedback as a class and discuss some of the different impressions the adjectives have given to different students.

34 • Key technical skills LESSON 1.2 © HarperCollins*Publishers* 2015

 Now display **PPT 1.2, slide 5**, the extract from 'Space Poem 3: Off Course' and allow 5–10 minutes for the students to work individually to select four noun phrases and jot down their thoughts (**Q6**).

> **Give extra support** by pairing up the students so they can discuss their impressions before making their notes.

Allow a further 10 minutes for the students to complete **Q7**. If time allows take feedback as a class, asking the students to share their ideas.

Develop the skills

 Display **PPT1.2, slide 6**, the complete poem. The examples of 'the golden flood' and 'the hot flood' have been highlighted. Ask the students to work in groups to complete **Q8** and then feed back to the class. If you have an interactive whiteboard, work as a whole class on this task, highlighting and discussing the findings.

 Work on **Q9a** collaboratively with the students. Aim to elicit that early on in the poem a 'crackling headphone' might suggest that the spacecraft is still in contact with Earth, but that later on in the poem 'the crackling somersault' feels more dangerous, as though there is too much heat in the cabin and a disaster of some kind is happening.

Then use **Q9b** as a way of building on this idea.

Use **Q10** to introduce the idea of some words doing more than one job. For example, 'orbit' is an adjective in the first and third phrases ('the orbit wisecrack'; 'the orbit mouth-organ') but is a noun in the second phrase ('the smuggled orbit').

Practise and consolidate the idea of words doing more than one job, by asking the students to complete **Q11** individually.

 If time allows, feed back as a class and allow the students to share some of their combinations.

Apply the skills

Set up the **Apply the skills** task (**Q12**) and allow approximately 20–25 minutes for the students to complete their poems. This could be done as homework if preferred.

Big answer plenary	Use the **Check your progress** outcomes to begin the plenary. Ask the students to write down what nouns, adjectives and noun phrases are to ensure everyone is able to achieve Outcome 1.
	Ask the students to explain to a partner what modification is and ask each pair to agree on a definition.
	Ask the students to look back at their work for **Q11**, and to label the determiners, adjectives and nouns in each of their pairs of noun phrases.

1.3 Words and meaning: verbs and agreement

Assessment objectives

English Language

AO5 Communicate clearly, effectively and imaginatively, selecting and adapting tone, style and register for different forms, purposes and audiences; organise information and ideas, using structural and grammatical features to support coherence and cohesion of texts

AO6 Use a range of vocabulary and sentence structures for clarity, purpose and effect, with accurate spelling and punctuation

English Literature

AO2 Analyse the language, form and structure used by a writer to create meanings and effects, using relevant subject terminology where appropriate

AO4 Use a range of vocabulary and sentence structures for clarity, purpose and effect, with accurate spelling and punctuation

GCSE examinations

- **English Language** Paper 1, Questions 2, 5
- **English Language** Paper 2, Questions 3, 5
- **English Literature** key skills across all components

Differentiated learning outcomes

- **All students must** have a clear idea of what a verb is and its role in a sentence.
- **Most students should** be able to understand tense as well as verbs and how to use different tenses effectively with some control of agreement.
- **Some students could** show that they understand what verbs and tenses are and are able to demonstrate subject/verb agreement accurately.

Resources

- **Student Book**: pp. 16–19
- **Worksheet**: 1.3
- **PPT**: 1.3

Getting you thinking

Big question	Refer to the **Big question**: *How do you know what verbs do and which ones to use where?* Read and comment on the opening two paragraphs on page 16 of the Student Book, asking for examples of 'movements and actions' and ensuring the students know what is meant by 'states of being'.

Display **PPT 1.3, slide 1** and ask the students to consider and respond to **Q1a** and then **Q1b**. They should notice that the phrase 'have slept' places the action in the past and 'is going to be' places the action in the future.

Explore the skills

Reiterate the information about tense at the bottom of page 16 of the Student Book, and then read aloud the passage from *The Generation Game* on page 17 (**Q2**).

Allow approximately five minutes for the students to complete **Q3** individually, using **Worksheet 1.3**.

Gather the students' ideas and impressions for **Q4** collaboratively. Then ask them to write answers to the two questions individually.

For **Q5**, review the table with the class, explaining how to create the simple past with *-ed* endings and how to create the future with *will*. Allow five minutes for the students to complete the table using **Worksheet 1.3**, if necessary.

Then display **PPT 1.3, slide 2**, which contains the answers to **Q5**.

Develop the skills

Explain how the verbs 'to have' and 'to be' are not regular verbs and create their own individual patterns. Give the students five minutes to complete **Q6** using **Worksheet 1.3b**.

> **Give extra support** by asking the students to place the verbs within a sentence to help them change tense. For example:
> - 'I am hungry.' What would this become in the simple past? 'I was hungry.'
> - 'I am hungry.' What would this become in the future tense? 'I will be hungry.'
>
> The students could peer or self-mark their tables. If necessary, display **PPT 1.3**, **slide 3**, which contains the answers to **Q6**.

Introduce the idea of 'auxiliaries' using the **Key terms** box on page 18 of the Student Book and the examples given. Then allow five minutes each for the students to complete **Q7** and **Q8**.

> **Give extra support** by selecting some action verbs to get the students started.

Pause to spend some time on the key idea of agreement, that is, matching the correct form of the verb to the subject or pronoun. Ask the students to comment on 'We was marching.' What is the correct auxiliary? Where should *was* be used? Can they identify why this common mistake might happen?

Ask the students about the difference between Standard English and dialect and consolidate these terms using the **Key terms** box on page 19 of the Student Book. This may generate some useful discussion about the differences between written and spoken mode, about the importance of Standard English in written work, and about the way some of our dialect words can cause confusion when we write.

Use this discussion to lead into the transcript on page 19. Invite two confident students to read out the parts of Jack and Bill before allowing 10–15 minutes for the students to work on **Q9a** and **Q9b** in pairs. If necessary, display **PPT 1.3**, **slide 4**, which contains the answers to **Q9a**.

Give the students some time to discuss **Q9b** with their partners and make notes, before sharing their ideas with the class. This will allow the tricky topic of subject–verb agreement to be fully discussed and brought to the attention of all the students.

Apply the skills

Use **Q10** to consolidate how to form the past tense. Answers to **Q10**: *liked; liked; liked; stocked; liked; was happiest; was; helped; mastered; was.*

> **Give extra support** by asking students to comment on how the text has a different feel when placed in the past tense. Does it lose anything? Does it gain anything?

Big answer plenary	Use the **Check your progress** outcomes. Refer back to the **Big question** and ask the students to write down their own definition of a verb and what it does, to check that everyone can achieve Outcome 1.
	Play a game of 'tense tennis' in plenary. Throw a small ball to a student and give them a verb in a sentence in the present tense. As they catch it, they must change the verb to a different tense before passing the ball along. Ensure everyone has a turn to help them decide if they have achieved Outcome 2.
	Use the answers for **Q9a** to help the students evaluate whether they have achieved Outcome 3.

1.4 Sentences and their functions

Assessment objectives

English Language

AO2 Explain, comment on and analyse how writers use language and structure to achieve effects and influence readers, using relevant subject terminology to support their views

AO6 Use a range of sentence structures for clarity, purpose and effect, with accurate punctuation

GCSE examinations

- **English Language**
  Paper 1, Questions 2, 5
- **English Language**
  Paper 2, Questions 3, 5

Differentiated learning outcomes

- **All students must** show their understanding of the fact that sentences have different functions.
- **Most students should** be able to name the different sentence functions and understand how they can add to the meaning of a text.
- **Some students could** show their understanding of the fact that different sentence functions can add to the impact of a text and help to fulfil its purpose and engage its reader.

Resources

- **Student Book**: pp. 20–3
- **Worksheets**: 1.4a–b
- **PPT**: 1.4

Other Student Book pages

- Lesson 1.1, pp. 8–11

Getting you thinking

Big question	Read the introductory paragraph on page 20 of the Student Book and link it to the **Big question**: *What are sentences for?* Ask the students to think about sentences: • Why do we use them? • Do we use them in spoken English? • Are we conscious of when we use them and when we don't? • Where did the concept of the sentence come from?

Ask the students to complete **Q1**, either as a teacher-led, class activity or as a five-minute discussion in small groups or pairs. The students are likely to think of examples such as text messages, informal conversations, casual emails and social-media posts.

Ask the students to think about the root of the word 'sentence' and what they learned about Latinate vocabulary in Lesson 1.1. Then ask them to think about the origins of the sentence and complete **Q2**. The students should pick up on the idea of the law and a 'sentence' meaning prison or punishment. Help them to see the link in meaning between this and 'judgement', linking it to the Ben Jonson quotation given on page 20.

Explore the skills

Display **PPT 1.4, slide 1** and discuss the answers to **Q3** with the class. Encourage the students to identify the differences between each sentence.

Reinforce the terms 'statement', 'command' and 'exclamation' using the **Key terms** box, before asking the students to complete the matching exercise in **Q3**. This could also be done as a class activity.

Now read aloud the extract from Melvin Burgess's novel, *Junk*, on page 21 of the Student Book (**Q4**). Allow 5–10 minutes for the students to work through the extract and identify the sentence functions in **Q5a** using **Worksheet 1.4a**.

Give extra support by collating the answers to **Q5a** on the board, before working on questions **Q5b–e** orally with the class.

Give extra challenge by allowing the students 10 more minutes to work on questions **Q5b–e** individually, making notes, and then take feedback collectively. If necessary, display **PPT 1.4, slide 2**, which contains the answers to **Q5**.

Develop the skills

Display **PPT 1.4, slide 3**, and read aloud the opening four lines of the WaterAid advertisement. Then complete **Q6** with the class. If necessary, display **PPT 1.4, slide 4**, which contains the answers to **Q6**.

Read aloud the complete WaterAid advertisement on page 22 of the Student Book.

Now ask the students to complete **Q7**, using the annotated text on page 22 of the Student Book and **Worksheet 1.4b**. The questions in the seven annotations lend themselves to some exploratory, small-group investigation work. Allow 20 minutes to explore the leaflet in detail, and ensure the students either make notes or annotate their copy of the text with their findings.

Collate the students' responses in a plenary. Aim to elicit the following points:

- The shock value of the facts, the stark reality of the figures and the simple problem of 'dirty water'. The question is directed to the reader and seems hard hitting – the reference to 'stomach' seems deliberate and links to 'sickening' on the next line – making us think of upset stomachs and how serious they are for the children needing help.

- The second lot of facts in the fourth paragraph provide a contrast, but the 100 people helped by the charity seem fewer than the 2000 mentioned before, even though the time factor is different.

- The later statements are practical – showing exactly what simple response is needed. They repeat and reinforce the idea of 'safe, clean water'.

- The final statement has impact in case we choose to ignore the required action.

Apply the skills

The **Apply the skills** task (**Q8**) is a fun task to help the students apply the knowledge of sentence types, and consolidate the investigative work from **Q6** and **Q7**. The activity should take about 30–45 minutes and may be suited to a follow-up homework task.

Big answer plenary	Refer back to the **Big question** and use the following questions to elicit responses to it: • Is a sentence a group of words that begins with a capital letter and a full stop? Yes, it is – but what else is it? • How can sentences be used? • How do they help us to communicate more effectively? • How can they help us, as writers, to achieve our purpose more clearly? Refer the students to the **Check your progress** outcomes on page 23 of the Student Book. In the final task, the students should have used all four sentence functions within their poster to achieve Outcome 1. Use peer assessment, encouraging the students to look at each other's posters to help them assess who has reached Outcome 3 – which of the posters are the most realistic and effective, matched to purpose and audience?

1.5 Add meaning and clarity with punctuation

Assessment objectives

English Language

AO6 Use a range of vocabulary and sentence structures for clarity, purpose and effect, with accurate spelling and punctuation

English Literature

AO4 Use a range of vocabulary and sentence structures for clarity, purpose and effect, with accurate spelling and punctuation

GCSE examinations

- **English Language** Paper 1, Question 5
- **English Language** Paper 2, Question 5
- **English Literature** key skills across all components

Differentiated learning outcomes

- **All students must** show they can use full stops, question marks and exclamation marks to mark the end of their sentences, sometimes remembering to use apostrophes.
- **Most students should** be able to demarcate sentences and use both forms of apostrophe in the right place, as well as use the comma correctly most of the time.
- **Some students could** demonstrate that their use of demarcation, both forms of apostrophe, commas and speech punctuation is accurate nearly all of the time.

Resources

- **Student Book**: pp. 24–7
- **Worksheet**: 1.5
- **PPT**: 1.5

Other Student Book pages

- Lesson 1.4, p. 21

Getting you thinking

Big question	Refer to the **Big question**: *Why is punctuation important in making things clear?* Introduce the idea in the introductory paragraph on page 24 of the Student Book, which may well be a historical fact that the students are unaware of. Ask them to imagine what all of their school books, reading books and textbooks would look like without punctuation.

In pairs, allow the students 2–3 minutes to try and read the extract from *Alice in Wonderland* to each other on page 24 of the Student Book, or ask for volunteers to attempt to read it aloud to the whole group. Then briefly discuss with the class how difficult they found it compared to the kinds of texts they are used to (**Q1**).

Explore the skills

For **Q2**, allow 10 minutes for the students to produce their copies of the text. You could pre-print some larger – A3-sized – sheets of lined paper for the students to use for this task.

Display **PPT 1.5, slide 1** for the students to check their answers.

Give extra support by providing pre-printed copies of the spaced text on A3 paper and have the students complete **Q3** and **Q4** in small groups.

Recap on the four sentence functions from Lesson 1.4 (Student Book page 21) and elicit from the students which punctuation mark is used for which sentence function (**Q3**).

Allow time for the students to correctly punctuate all the statements, questions and exclamations in their copies of the text (**Q4**). If they are using A3-sized paper, you could provide them with coloured felt pens or marker pens. Display **PPT 1.5, slide 2** for the students to check their answers.

Now introduce the ideas about apostrophes, reinforcing the rules and examples for each on page 25 of the Student Book. If required, model some further examples of each on the whiteboard before asking the students to complete **Q5**.

Display **PPT 1.5, slide 3** for the students to check their answers.

Ask the students to complete **Q6** in their notebooks. Then display **PPT 1.5, slide 4** and ask them to self-mark their answers.

Develop the skills

Spend some time working through the information on commas on page 26 of the Student Book, before asking the students to complete **Q7**. If time allows, share some of the students' examples of each usage on the whiteboard, selected from effective ones you may have spotted while monitoring this work.

Refer the students to the annotated sentences on page 27 of the Student Book. Elicit the answer to the five questions from the class, to ensure everyone is clear about the correct placement of punctuation in dialogue.

Allow 10 minutes for the students to complete **Q8**. The students could use different coloured pens to indicate the commas and speech punctuation.

Display **PPT 1.5, slide 5** and allow the students 2–3 minutes to check their answers.

Apply the skills

Allow approximately 15 minutes for the students to complete the main task (**Q9**), using **Worksheet 1.5**. If possible, provide different coloured pens for the students to mark the apostrophes, commas and speech marks.

Display **PPT 1.5, slide 6** and ask the students to peer mark their answers to **Q9** with a partner. The pairs should then discuss and use the **Check your progress** outcomes on page 27 to apply a level to each other's work.

Big answer plenary	Refer back to the **Big question** and the extract from *Alice in Wonderland* on page 24 of the Student Book. Ask the students to reflect on the need for clarity in punctuation and ask which they would rather read, **PPT 1.5, slide 1** or **slide 5**, showing both in sequence.

1.6 Sentences used for effect

Assessment objectives

English Language

AO2 Explain, comment on and analyse how writers use language and structure to achieve effects and influence readers, using relevant subject terminology to support their views

AO6 Use a range of vocabulary and sentence structures for clarity, purpose and effect, with accurate spelling and punctuation

English Literature

AO2 Analyse the language, form and structure used by a writer to create meanings and effects, using relevant subject terminology where appropriate

GCSE examinations

- **English Language** Paper 1, Questions 2, 5
- **English Language** Paper 2, Questions 3, 5
- **English Literature** key skills across all components

Differentiated learning outcomes

- **All students must** show they can identify the four different sentence functions and try to use a variety in their own work.
- **Most students should** be able to explain how the different functions can create different moods and feelings within a text and aim to use this in their own work.
- **Some students could** demonstrate and explain that they understand how writers use those functions to create specific impact on a reader or audience and seek to apply that in their own work.

Resources

- **Student Book**: pp. 28–31
- **Worksheets**: 1.6a–b
- **PPT**: 1.6

Other Student Book pages

- Lesson 1.4, p. 21

Getting you thinking

| Big question | Read the **Big question**: *Does using different types of sentences make any difference?* At this stage, recap the four sentence functions; then briefly discuss the question with the class to elicit some preliminary thoughts. |

Display **PPT 1.6, slide 1**, and ask the students to practise saying the sentences in different tones of voice. Ask the students to confirm which sentence functions are used – *statement* and *question* – and why that makes a difference to the purpose, the meaning and the tone we might say them in (**Q1**).

Explore the skills

Read aloud the extract from Barack Obama's speech on page 28 of the Student Book, or play the excerpt from the speech being delivered, which is available online at:

- www.youtube.com/watch?v=ekr21tnxG0k, or
- www.whitehouse.gov/photos-and-video/video/2013/02/27/president-obama-dedicates-statue-honoring-rosa-parks#transcript (@47:30).

Alternatively, go to www.youtube.com and search for 'President Barack Obama dedicates a statue honoring Rosa Parks'.

Read through **Q2–Q6**, ensuring all students have retained the necessary terminology from Lesson 1.4 (Student Book page 21).

Then work through **Q2–Q6** with the class, prompting discussion and eliciting suggestions. Encourage the students to think about how:

- the added credibility of the declarative tone, created through the numerous statements, gives a definite, factual undertone and feel
- this adds to the serious and respectful tone and the overall nature of the occasion

- the use of the present tense suggests the legacy of Rosa Parks's bravery is still felt today – Obama links it to his own opportunity to become president: '... I stand here today.'
- Obama maintains this serious, declarative tone; he is not persuading us – he presents what he is saying as definite and true.

Give extra challenge by having the students complete **Q2–Q6** in small groups. Provide copies of **Worksheet 1.6a**, which could be enlarged onto A3 paper for students to annotate collaboratively, using the questions to guide the exploration.

Audio/Video versions of the speech are also available online should the students have computer access in the lesson. Allow approximately 15 minutes before taking feedback as a class.

Display **PPT 1.6, slide 2**, and read aloud the poem: 'How Not to be a Woodlouse'. Then ask the students to complete **Q7–Q10**.

If preferred, the students could work in pairs on **Q7–Q10**, or if they have worked in groups on **Q2–Q6**, these questions would make a useful, teacher-led, whole group activity.

Encourage the students to identify the imperatives, but also to note that here the tone is gentler. The writer is not issuing 'commands'; instead the poem seems to be gently offering advice. The gentleness is the surprising element. Introduce the idea that the woodlouse is a metaphor before exploring the possibilities of the final question (**Q10**).

Develop the skills

Set the context for the extract from *Othello* using the opening paragraph on page 30 of the Student Book. Then allow 25–30 minutes for the students to complete **Q11**. You may wish to provide the students with versions of the text on **Worksheet 1.6b** for them to annotate.

This is a more challenging text so you may prefer the students to view the extract in performance. See www.youtube.com/watch?v=hWW3ryV5Jeg (@48:00). Alternatively go to www.youtube.com and search for *Othello full movie*.

Give extra support by working through the extract in short instalments, allowing each annotation to be considered individually.

Give extra challenge by asking the students to act out the extract in pairs, or read an interpretation to each other before using the annotations as the basis for a paired investigation and short presentation of feedback.

Apply the skills

Allow 30 minutes for the students to look back at their notes, and to write up responses to the main task (**Q12**). There are three texts in this lesson, so this will allow for some differentiation in terms of guided choices. Refer the students to the **Checklist for success** on page 31 before they begin. If preferred, this could be used as a homework task.

Big answer plenary	Use the **Big question** in plenary to ask the students what they have learned about the effects of the four sentence functions. Ask them how they could use this knowledge in their own writing.
	On the whiteboard collate a list of 'Hints from Professional Writers' about how to use sentences for effect.

1.7 Structure: using different sentence structures

Assessment objectives

English Language

AO6 Use a range of vocabulary and sentence structures for clarity, purpose and effect, with accurate spelling and punctuation

English Literature

AO4 Use a range of vocabulary and sentence structures for clarity, purpose and effect, with accurate spelling and punctuation

GCSE examinations

- **English Language** Paper 1, Questions 3, 5
- **English Language** Paper 2, Question 5
- **English Literature** key skills across all components

Differentiated learning outcomes

- **All students must** be able to show they understand that sentences are structured in different ways and recognise the terms 'simple', 'compound' and 'complex'.
- **Most students should** be able to understand the key differences between simple, compound and complex sentences.
- **Some students could** demonstrate that they are aware of how each sentence type may be constructed and how it can be used to create effects in their writing and the writing of others.

Resources

- **Student Book**: pp. 32–5
- **Worksheet**: 1.7
- **PPT**: 1.7

Getting you thinking

| Big question | Refer to the **Big question**: *What's the difference between a simple, compound and complex sentence?* Ask the students if they are confident in distinguishing between these three main sentence structures and their effects. |

Display **PPT 1.7**, and ask the students to identify the main idea in each sentence (**Q1**).

Work through **Q2–Q5** with the class, encouraging the students to discuss and agree on the answers as a group. For **Q3**, allow the students to identify the main clause in sentence **c**, then ask them to consider how the ideas in the sentence seem to contradict each other without the word 'until' – elicit or point out that the sense of the second part depends on the first. In **Q4**, the additional information in sentence **d** is that the book was read in class.

Answers to **Q5**: **a** simple; **b** compound; **c** complex; **d** compound-complex.

Explore the skills

Reinforce the key information about simple sentences on page 33 of the Student Book. Emphasise the effect of this kind of sentence before reading the extract from 'Everything Stuck to Him' by Raymond Carver – aloud if possible.

Allow 10 minutes for the students to complete **Q6a–e**, using **Worksheet 1.7**. This could be done as a paired investigation, and answers could then be shared with the class. Answers to **Q6a–e**:

a stared; took up; went; started; went; making a job of it; scraped away; turned off; sat; got out; went back; was; was asleep; was asleep; took off

b sentences 1, 3, 7, 8, 9, 10

c The students might note that there is the sense of an argument from 'stared' and the fact the boy seems to be walking out. By the end of the extract he changes his mind and comes back.

d They are not simple because they contain two ideas.

e The two ideas are linked with the conjunction 'and'.

Develop the skills

Follow the class feedback from **Q6** with the key information about compound sentences on page 34 of the Student Book. Spend some time focusing on the use of the incorrect 'comma splice', as this is a very common error in students' writing.

Allow 10 minutes for the students to complete **Q7a–c**, either in pairs or as a whole group. Accept all valid suggestions from the group, but ensure the students are aware of the following points:

- The simple sentences create a clipped, tense feel.
- The full stops allow for longer pauses, giving the sense of time passing and a slow, measured pace as the boy decides what to do.
- They also make the images of the girl, the baby and the boy taking off his boots more stark and cut and dried, as though not leaving them is the only choice the boy really had.

Reinforce the key information about complex sentences on page 34 of the Student Book and ask the students to work individually on **Q8a**, to allow you the opportunity to check their understanding. Then ask the students to read through their passage carefully and make notes for **Q8b**. Allow time for some students to share and read out their work on **Q8** with the class.

Apply the skills

Spend some time with students talking about books they read when they were very young. Then examine the student analysis on page 35 of the Student Book and question students as to where this perception might have come from and why. Ask them to consider the words 'simple' and 'complex': do they alter their perception of the sentences? For example, does the word 'simple' suggest that the meaning is likely to be very easy to understand? Does the word 'complex' suggest the sentence is going to be very difficult to understand?

The key point for the students to grasp is that it is the structure of the simple sentence that has a simple format, but the idea within it may *not* be so simple. Likewise, it is the structure of a complex sentence that has complexity, yet it may contain very straightforward ideas.

> **Give extra support** by exploring the passage on page 35 from the children's book, *The Princess and the Pea*, first with the students, collaboratively deciding on the sentence types used.
>
> **Give extra challenge** by looking at a number of children's picture books – say for the under 5s – as a research opportunity, noting how many employ complex structures to present ideas.

If preferred, the students could complete **Q9** as an individual homework task, once they have debated in class.

Big answer plenary	Refer back to the **Big question** and ask each student to write three sentences about themselves – a simple, a compound and a complex. Ask them to use the **Check your progress** outcomes to self-check their work on the task in **Q9** before handing it in.

1.8 Structure: paragraphing

Assessment objectives

English Language

AO6 Use a range of vocabulary and sentence structures for clarity, purpose and effect, with accurate spelling and punctuation

English Literature

AO4 Use a range of vocabulary and sentence structures for clarity, purpose and effect, with accurate spelling and punctuation

GCSE examinations

- **English Language**
  Paper 1, Questions 3, 5
- **English Language**
  Paper 2, Question 5
- **English Literature**
  key skills across all components

Differentiated learning outcomes

- **All students must** be able to understand that writing needs paragraphs to be clear and show that they can use them.
- **Most students should** be able to demonstrate the ability to logically organise paragraphs and use topic sentences.
- **Some students could** demonstrate that they are able to create effects in their writing by marking topic shifts with their paragraphs and using varied and effective lengths of paragraphs.

Resources

- **Student Book**: pp. 36–40
- **Worksheets**: 1.8a–b
- **PPT**: 1.8

Getting you thinking

Big question	Elicit a definition of a paragraph from the class (a section of a piece of writing that contains at least one sentence). Then read the **Big question**: *Does it really matter when you start a new paragraph?*, and elicit some initial thoughts.

Read the introduction to **Getting you thinking** on page 36 of the Student Book, and ask the students to imagine their journey to school, visualising it in silence with their eyes closed for 60 seconds. Then ask the students to complete **Q1**.

Discuss **Q2** with the whole group before using the concluding paragraph that follows it to link back to the **Big question**.

Explore the skills

Read the introduction to **Explore the skills** on page 36 of the Student Book.

Then display **PPT 1.8, slide 1**, and complete the true-or-false exercise as a whole group (**Q3**). Ask the students to make a note of their own responses to see whether the activities that follow prove their initial thoughts to be correct or not.

Display **PPT 1.8, slide 2**, and ask the students to complete **Q4** individually. Give the students a full minute to look at the picture before listing the details in order.

Read the paragraph just above the photograph on page 37, which introduces the idea of the description working in a logical order, with a single focus for each paragraph.

Recap briefly on the use of topic sentences before asking the students to complete **Q5** using **Worksheet 1.8a**.

Discuss **Q6** with the class. The discussion should help the students to reflect on the planning they have done so far. Encourage them to see how the 'zoom lens' effect of specific focus can add interest and originality to their work.

Use **Q7** to recap on the basics of paragraphing, by reminding the students of the rules about topic shifts between person, place, subject and speaker. Help them to appreciate how this can also lead to more depth in writing – by providing focus and by creating a logical 'journey' for the reader to follow and imagine – and thereby creating more effective writing.

Develop the skills

Display **PPT1.8, slide 2**, again – the picture of the Greek village – and use the introductory paragraph of **Develop the skills** on page 38 of the Student Book, to enable the students to 'see' the picture in a different context.

Ask the students to complete **Q8** in pairs, using **Worksheet 1.8a** to cut out and re-order the topic sentences. Then feed back as a class. A suggested order might be: d), c), a), b), e), f).

Display **PPT 1.8, slide 3**, and read the extract aloud.

Then ask the students to complete **Q9** using **Worksheet 1.8b**. The questions could be done individually, using page 39 of the Student Book, or collaboratively with the whole group using the PPT slide. Suggested responses may include:

- The opening paragraph introduces a memory and indicates time.
- This creates pause and dramatic tension. It is isolated from the remaining text, suggesting this is how the writer feels at this moment. Although he is revisiting a familiar place, the narrator feels like a stranger.
- The repetition of the one-sentence paragraph emphasises the narrator's sense of estrangement and perhaps loss. The image of the bar helps us to connect with the idea of the person the writer is looking for. It describes the bar, but also introduces another character who has a sense of mystery about her.

As before, the repetition adds a poetic quality to the writing. Juxtaposed with the idea of the tourists with their eyes shielded behind expensive sunglasses, it adds to the sense of isolation and the sense of desperate hope the writer seems to have that there could be someone familiar still in the bar, 'after all these years'.

Apply the skills

Allow 25 minutes for the students to continue the story by adding three more paragraphs, reminding them to use the four bullet points (**Q10**). You could use **Worksheet 1.8b** as a starting point for this work.

Big answer plenary	You could provide copies of the Examination mark scheme for English Language Paper 1 Question 5, to enable the students to peer assess their work. Relate the descriptors for 'Organisation' back to the **Big question** and reflect on the key words describing paragraphs in the different bands of the mark scheme.
	Use the **Check your progress** outcomes and match the statements against the mark scheme descriptors to see if candidates can recognise which outcome their skills would equate to.

2.1 Understand literary forms

Assessment objectives

English Language

AO1 Identify and interpret explicit and implicit information and ideas

AO2 Explain, comment on and analyse how writers use language and structure to achieve effects and influence readers, using relevant subject terminology to support their views

English Literature

AO1 Read, understand and respond to texts, maintaining a critical style and developing an informed personal response

AO2 Analyse the language, form and structure used by a writer to create meanings and effects, using relevant subject terminology where appropriate

GCSE examinations

- **English Language** Paper 1, Questions 2, 3, 4
- **English Language** Paper 2, Questions 3, 4
- **English Literature** key skill across all components

Differentiated learning outcomes

- **All students must** be able to recognise the main differences between literary forms.
- **Most students should** be able to explain some of the key differences of convention between literary forms.
- **Some students could** link literary form more precisely to its conventions, explaining why particular forms have particular conventions.

Resources

- **Student Book**: pp. 42–5
- **PPT**: 2.1

Getting you thinking

Big question	Read the **Big question**: *Why do we tell stories and how do we tell them?* Ask for responses from the students. The students might offer some examples of different kinds of stories, such as written/oral storytelling, TV soaps, plays or films. All of these are relevant at this stage.

For **Q1**, ask the students to look at the picture of a cave painting on page 42 of the Student Book. Draw attention to the idea that, even without written language, human beings want to communicate their 'story' to each other. A cave painting is simply a pictographic representation of a sequence of events; in other words, it's telling a story.

Display **PPT 2.1, slide 1**, an alternative picture of a cave painting, if preferred.

Allow 10 minutes for the students to read the statements about stories on page 42 of the Student Book and to complete **Q2a**, the diamond ranking exercise. The statements about stories can be displayed from **PPT 2.1, slide 2**, if preferred.

The students can complete the diamond ranking exercise in pairs or small groups if preferred, also discussing their suggestions in response to **Q2b**.

Read the statements attached to **Q3**, either from page 43 of the Student Book or from **PPT 2.1, slide 3**, and ask the students to identify the three ways of telling a story being described by the statements (**a** = fiction, **b** = poetry, **c** = drama).

Give extra challenge by asking the students to write their own description of a play, a poem and a story before reading the definitions in **Q3**. The students can then compare their ideas with the statements.

Explore the skills

Explain the idea of 'convention' and ask the students to make a note of the definition of the **Key term** 'forms' on page 43. Ask for suggestions of the kinds of conventions they might expect to see in order to identify that a poem is a poem.

Now explain that for this lesson, the focus will be on the different conventions of form between novels, short stories, poems and plays. Read the descriptions of a short story and a novel on page 43 of the Student Book and allow five minutes for the students to complete **Q4**, summarising the differences between these two forms. Explain that the term 'fiction' (or 'prose fiction') is generally used to refer to these two forms.

Q5 asks students to summarise a novel that they know well into 50 words or fewer. This could be done as either an individual or a whole-class activity. It might be useful to base this activity on a novel that the students have previously studied in school.

Now ask the students to read the paragraph describing poetry, on page 44 of the Student Book. Then ask them to read the statements in **Q6**. For this activity, the students can either select the three statements that they feel are the most relevant, or complete another diamond ranking exercise. The idea with this activity is to encourage the approach that poetry is not to be feared – it's just a different way of communicating and exploring ideas.

> **Give extra challenge** by asking the students to undertake some independent research on the rise of printing and how it influenced what, when and where humans read the printed word. The British Library has a timeline of the development of literary texts, which might be useful. This can be found at
> www.bl.uk/learning/langlit/evolvingenglish/accessvers
> (or search for *British Library English timeline*).
>
> **Give extra support** by explaining to the students that the novel as a literary form is a relatively recent development compared to poetry and drama.

Q7 and **Q8** focus on the conventions of form of a play. For the second question in **Q7**, the students might suggest these key conventions of a play:

- divided into acts and scenes
- characters moving around on the stage
- staging itself – costume, stage props and backdrops.

For **Q8**, the students might suggest these ways of turning a play into something 'live':

- using sound effects and music to add to the sensory experience
- actors' use of voice, expression and emotion to bring the characters to life
- involving the audience by bringing the action into or around the people watching.

Develop the skills

Q9 asks the students to identify the conventions that are being used in this passage. Draw attention to: narrative voice; written in prose; description of a character.

Using the passage from *Great Expectations* and the descriptions of 'story' and 'poem' that they have been working with, allow 10–15 minutes for students to complete **Q10**.

Q11 can be a discussion or a reflection activity if preferred, with the students identifying which conventions they adapted and used in order to turn the prose passage into a piece of poetry.

Apply the skills

This section of the lesson asks students to reflect on what they have learned in this section and make some notes on the four main forms they have considered (**Q12**).

Big answer plenary	Returning to the **Big question**, ask the students to write a sentence explaining in their own words why human beings tell stories.
	An additional task might be to consider the four literary forms and write an additional sentence explaining which form they think is the best way to tell a story.

2.2 Understand non-fiction genres

Assessment objectives

English Language

AO1 Identify and interpret explicit and implicit information and ideas

AO2 Explain, comment on and analyse how writers use language and structure to achieve effects and influence readers, using relevant subject terminology to support their views

English Literature

AO1 Read, understand and respond to texts, maintaining a critical style and developing an informed personal response

AO2 Analyse the language, form and structure used by a writer to create meanings and effects, using relevant subject terminology where appropriate

GCSE examinations

- **English Language**
  Paper 1, Questions 2, 3, 4
- **English Language**
  Paper 2, Questions 3, 4
- **English Literature**
  Paper 2, Section C

Differentiated learning outcomes

- **All students must** be able to identify the difference between various non-fiction genres.
- **Most students should** be able to explain some of the key differences of convention between the various non-fiction genres.
- **Some students could** explain the key differences in language and form between different non-fiction genres.

Resources

- **Student Book**: pp. 46–9
- **Worksheet**: 2.2
- **PPT**: 2.2

Getting you thinking

Big question	Read the **Big question**: *What is the difference between different types of non-fiction?* The purpose of this question is to clarify what the term 'non-fiction' means and also to ensure that the students know the difference between fiction and non-fiction. At this stage, allow the students to explore the wide variety of ways non-fiction texts can be produced and the variety of ways they can be received: for example, in newspapers, blogs, articles, advertisements and online magazines.

Q1 aims to ensure that the students understand the difference between fiction and non-fiction first of all. Once this is established, ask the students to make a quick list of as many non-fiction forms as they can think of (**Q2**).

Read the two extracts under **Q3** and ask the students to identify which is fiction and which is non-fiction. Ask them to explain briefly how they know which is which. Use **PPT 2.2, slides 1–2**, to display the extracts if preferred.

Ask the students to complete **Q4**, the table of features, using **Worksheet 2.2**. This task is designed to consolidate their ability to identify some of the differences between fiction and non-fiction texts.

Explore the skills

Ask the students to read the statement on page 48 of the Student Book, which summarises the main purposes of fiction and non-fiction texts. Explain that this is quite a sweeping statement and ask them to refine it with further ideas about the range of different purposes of these two types of text. The students might offer:

- designed to get the reader to act or behave in a certain way
- to change the reader's opinion or beliefs
- to present a strong point of view about something
- to share an experience.

Draw attention to the **Key term** 'genres' and ask the students to compare this explanation with the explanation of 'forms' from the previous lesson. They can then write a sentence explaining the difference between 'form' and 'genre'.

For **Q5**, allow 10 minutes for the students to read the definitions of the four main non-fiction text types and then match each type to its definition.

> **Give extra challenge** by first giving the students the list of the four genres in **Q5** and asking them to work in pairs or small groups to create their own list of defining features without reference to the Student Book. These can then be compared with the definitions in the Student Book for the students to see how accurately they defined each text type.
> - Did they manage to include all the features listed?
> - Did they suggest other features not mentioned in the Student Book?

Develop the skills

Using the descriptions of each non-fiction genre, ask the students to read the four extracts on pages 48–9 of the Student Book and to identify which genre applies to which text (**Q6a**). They should identify:

- Text A: travel writing
- Text B: autobiography
- Text C: biography
- Text D: broadsheet article

Use **PPT 2.2**, **slides 3–6** to provide copies of the extracts for class discussion if preferred.

As an extension to this activity, ask the students to select one sentence or phrase from each extract and explain why that particular piece of evidence helps to define it as that genre of text (**Q6b**).

Apply the skills

The table on page 49 of the Student Book is designed for the students to draw together their findings on the four extracts and select three pieces of evidence from each text that demonstrate how it follows the conventions of each particular genre (**Q7**).

Finally, ask the students to carry out the task in **Q8**, updating their glossary with a description of the conventions of the non-fiction genres.

Big answer plenary	Return to the **Big question** and ask the students to write an answer of one or two sentences. The purpose of the lesson is to enable them to respond clearly to this question, so the students should be able to answer this question fairly confidently if they have identified the key differences between the four text types.

2.3 Understand narrative perspective

Assessment objectives

English Language

AO1 Identify and interpret explicit and implicit information and ideas

AO2 Explain, comment on and analyse how writers use language and structure to achieve effects and influence readers, using relevant subject terminology to support their views

English Literature

AO1 Read, understand and respond to texts, maintaining a critical style and developing an informed personal response

AO2 Analyse the language, form and structure used by a writer to create meanings and effects, using relevant subject terminology where appropriate

GCSE examinations

- English Language
  Paper 1, Questions 2, 3, 4
- English Language
  Paper 2, Questions 3, 4
- English Literature
  Paper 1, Section A
- English Literature
  Paper 1, Section B
- English Literature
  Paper 2, Section C

Differentiated learning outcomes

- **All students must** be able to explain the difference between first-, second- and third-person narrative perspectives, and try these in their own writing.
- **Most students should** be able to explain how and why writers use different narrative perspectives, and try these out in their own writing.
- **Some students could** explain in detail how writers use different narrative perspectives to explore ideas and present characters; they could use these to create effects in their own writing.

Resources

- **Student Book**: pp. 50–3
- **PPT**: 2.3

Getting you thinking

Big question	Ask students to read the **Big question**: *What is narrative point of view and why is it important that you understand it?*. At this stage, elicit some responses to the first part of the question: 'narrative' is story; 'point of view' is the viewpoint from which the reader hears the story, and so on.
	Explain that the second part of the question is the focus for this lesson.

Read the **Key term** definition of 'perspective' on page 50 of the Student Book and ask students to link this to the discussion they have just had about 'point of view'.

Ask students to explain the difference between first, second and third person and suggest which pronouns (I/you/he/she/they) tend to go with which.

Give students five minutes to read the three texts on page 50 of the Student Book and to work through **Q1** and **Q2**, identifying which text is written in the first person (Text 1); which in the third person (Text 2); and which uses a mixture of second and third person (Text 3). Then ask them to scan the texts again and, for each one, make a list of the pronouns used (**Q3**).

Q4 draws together this short piece of learning by paying particular attention to narrative perspective. Students could write one sentence for each of the three texts, explaining what they can identify about the narrator of each one. Suggest that students might consider: whether the narrator is there, whether they seem to know the person/people being described, to whom they are speaking, and how much information they seem to have.

Explore the skills

Ask students to read the descriptions and examples of first-person, second-person and third-person perspective on page 51 of the Student Book.

> **Give extra challenge** by asking students to suggest examples from their own reading of different narrative perspectives.

Draw attention to the statement on page 51 of the Student Book: 'Sometimes the person who tells the story can't be trusted.' Give the term 'unreliable narrator' at this stage and allow students 10 minutes to complete **Q5**, either as an individual task or in pairs. The aim of this activity is to highlight the importance of taking account of narrative perspective when we read a fiction text, and also to highlight the importance of separating the narrator of the text from the writer of the text.

Develop the skills

This part of the lesson develops the idea introduced in **Explore the skills**. It uses examples from the novel *The Curious Incident of the Dog in the Night-Time*. For students not familiar with this novel, explain that Christopher is the narrator of the book but, due to his condition, he finds it very difficult to process his experiences and therefore the reader infers a good deal from what Christopher says, does and describes.

In the first extract (**Q6**), ideally students should notice that Christopher seems very distant from events; he is being arrested but is more focused on the actual words the police officer uses rather than their implications. The fact that he is calmed by the officer's words is also very surprising, and highlights his condition.

Students should now be able to respond to **Q7** independently, as it once again shows a disparity between the implications and expected reactions to events, and the way that Christopher receives them. Draw attention to the complete lack of emotional vocabulary once again.

All four of these extracts from *The Curious Incident of the Dog in the Night-Time* are also on **PPT 2.3, slides 1–3**.

Q8 is prompting students to think about the level of empathic engagement. Ask students to focus in particular on the sentence from the play transcript: 'His thrashing has exhausted him'. Why might this sentence be out of place in the novel, but more appropriate in the third-person stage direction?

Apply the skills

For this task, give students five minutes to read the further extract from the novel on page 53 of the Student Book and the summary that contextualises this extract.

Allow 15 minutes to complete the written task, which is to rewrite this moment from the story using a different narrative perspective (i.e. that of Christopher's father). Students should focus on how the father will be feeling about his son, and how these feelings might be communicated in a piece of writing. Remind students of how Christopher presents his story with no reference or acknowledgement of emotional ideas or vocabulary, and how his father might present this moment in a very different style.

Finally, ask the students to carry out the task in **Q9**, updating their glossary.

Big answer plenary	Return to the **Big question** and this time, ask students to respond to the second part of the question. They may include ideas such as: • Understanding who is telling the story helps to understand the story. • The person narrating the story isn't always to be trusted. • It is important to read between the lines to make sure you take the narrator's point of view into account.

2.4 Understand theme

Assessment objectives

English Language

AO1 Identify and interpret explicit and implicit information and ideas

AO2 Explain, comment on and analyse how writers use language and structure to achieve effects and influence readers, using relevant subject terminology to support their views

English Literature

AO1 Read, understand and respond to texts, maintaining a critical style and developing an informed personal response

AO2 Analyse the language, form and structure used by a writer to create meanings and effects, using relevant subject terminology where appropriate

GCSE examinations

- English Language Paper 1, Questions 2, 3, 4
- English Language Paper 2, Questions 3, 4
- English Literature key skill across all components

Differentiated learning outcomes

- **All students must** be able to understand that there is a difference between content and theme.
- **Most students should** be able to explain the difference between content and theme and explain how writers use content to present themes.
- **Some students could** explain in detail how writers use content to explore themes and ideas.

Resources

- **Student Book**: pp. 54–7
- **Worksheet**: 2.4
- **PPT**: 2.4

Getting you thinking

Big question	Display or read the **Big question**: *How can a text be 'about' more than one thing at the same time?* Discuss this question with the class in order to elicit some preliminary thoughts, possibly using examples of texts you know they have studied in previous English lessons. At this stage the purpose is to gauge to what extent the students can differentiate between content and wider ideas and purpose.

Read the introductory example: the short dialogue about content and theme.

The two definitions in **Q1** give an opportunity to set up a working definition of 'content' and 'theme' for this lesson. If students have been keeping a glossary of terms, these two could be added at this stage.

Explore the skills

Read the poem 'A Poison Tree' by William Blake on page 55 of the Student Book. If preferred, display **PPT 2.4, slide 1**, which is a copy of the poem.

Q2 and **Q3** are straightforward questions, which should be answered without the need to write them down; their purpose is to show very simply that often the content is a vehicle to explore the theme. If students point out that these questions are very easy, all the better because it means they are finding distinction between content and theme very easy to spot.

Q4 starts to develop the skill. Discuss the point about Adam and Eve and draw attention to the use of the apple and what it might represent. Students may offer ideas about the apple symbolising temptation, or being something other than it seems.

Q5 again could be undertaken as a class discussion, or as a paired discussion activity. Students may stick to the idea of the Garden of Eden, or may start to explore more metaphorical uses of the tree, such as:

- A tree has many branches – bad feeling grows and spreads.
- A tree grows deep roots – it is difficult to dig up.
- A tree grows from a tiny seed – a small amount of bad feeling can grow huge if you are not careful.

Develop the skills

The idea of this part of the lesson is to demonstrate the variety of ways in which a theme can be unpicked and interpreted from a text.

Ask students to look at the painting *Landscape with the Fall of Icarus* on page 56 of the Student Book. **PPT 2.4, slide 2**, is a copy of the painting for class display.

One way of approaching **Q6** is to display the painting for a few seconds then remove it from the screen and ask students to say what they noticed. The most common responses will be: the ploughman; the ship; the sea; the cliffs.

It might be useful not to tell students the title of the painting until they have looked at it. Then give them the title and, if they don't already know it, tell them the story of Icarus. They will find it easier to 'spot' Icarus once this has been explained.

Read the two 'student' interpretations of why the painter has constructed the painting in the way he has. Leaving the painting on display, allow 10 minutes for completion of **Q7**, **Q8** and **Q9** either in pairs or as a class activity.

> **Give extra challenge** by providing students with copies of the poems 'Musée des Beaux Arts' by W.H. Auden and/or 'Landscape with the Fall of Icarus' by William Carlos Williams, for use as further inspiration.

Apply the skills

Read the poem 'Cold' by Carol Ann Duffy. **PPT 2.4, slide 3**, is a copy of the poem for class display as students complete **Q10** and **Q11**.

These two tasks are also reproduced on **Worksheet 2.4**.

If students haven't already done so, ask them to complete definitions of 'content' and 'theme' in their glossary and write a summary of the difference between the two (**Q12**). As an extension task, they can use examples from the poem to illustrate these explanations.

Big answer plenary	Using the **Check your progress** outcomes at the end of this section, ask students to either self-assess or pair-mark their paragraphs about the poem 'Cold' and identify which outcomes they have achieved.

2.5 Understand structure

Assessment objectives

English Language

AO1 Identify and interpret explicit and implicit information and ideas

AO2 Explain, comment on and analyse how writers use language and structure to achieve effects and influence readers, using relevant subject terminology to support their views

English Literature

AO1 Read, understand and respond to texts, maintaining a critical style and developing an informed personal response

AO2 Analyse the language, form and structure used by a writer to create meanings and effects, using relevant subject terminology where appropriate

GCSE examinations

- English Language Paper 1, Questions 2, 3, 4
- English Language Paper 2, Questions 3, 4
- English Literature key skill across all components

Differentiated learning outcomes

- **All students must** be able to identify some structural features in a text.
- **Most students should** be able to explain the effect of some structural features on the reader.
- **Some students could** examine the ways in which specific structural features have been used to engage the reader.

Resources

- **Student Book**: pp. 58–61
- **Worksheet**: 2.5
- **PPT**: 2.5

Getting you thinking

Big question	Read the **Big question**: *Why does structure matter?* Ask the students for ideas about what the word 'structure' might refer to. Students might refer to structure in a range of genres.

Display **PPT 2.5, slide 1**, to give some ideas about the word 'structure', and how it might be relevant to looking at writing. Draw out ideas about:

- holding things together
- the foundations that whole things are built on
- how structure gives shape and definition.

If you have a whiteboard, take feedback on ideas, which can be collated and compared with the list in the **Explore the skills** activity below.

Display **PPT 2.5, slide 2**, which is a copy of the mini-saga.

Allow 5–10 minutes for the students to work in pairs on **Q1**, adding information to the mini-saga. Take feedback on some suggestions for this activity.

Explore the skills

Read the information on 'structure' on page 58 of the Student Book. Alternatively, the students could first work in pairs or groups to discuss how the term 'structure' refers to the organisation of a text, and then compare the list with their own ideas.

Display **PPT 2.5, slide 3**, which is a copy of the Freytag pyramid. Give the students a minute to read it and then explain that the pyramid describes how most narratives are structured.

Using **PPT 2.5, slide 4**, rather than the Student Book, ask the students if they recognise the story from the description.

Once the students have established that even very simple stories have a defined, recognisable structure, their task (**Q2**) is to transform another story that they know using the Freytag pyramid. The table on page 59 of the Student Book gives them a structure for doing this, and **Worksheet 2.5** provides a table to use if required. If any need additional suggestions, the following work well:

- *Shrek*
- *Aladdin*
- *Harry Potter.*

Read the next part of this section and ask the students to make a note of the **Key terms** 'chronologically' and 'flashbacks' in their glossary.

Discuss **Q3** and take verbal responses. The main idea to elicit is that writers might use this technique as a way of capturing the reader's attention and arousing their curiosity.

Develop the skills

Ask for suggestions as to what the title, and then the opening two paragraphs of *The Year of the Flood* might suggest (**Q4a** and **Q4b**). The students might pick up on the Biblical suggestion in the title (a reference to Noah's Flood), or that it seems to be referring to some kind of natural disaster.

Read the passage on pages 60–1 of the Student Book, either as a class or individually, and allow at least 10 minutes for the students to look at the annotations on the passage and complete **Q5**. This could be undertaken as a paired or group activity at this stage, as the final task will be individual.

Take feedback on ideas here, possibly collating on the whiteboard for reference when the students do the final independent task.

> **Give extra support** by focusing on the first two paragraphs only. Ask the students to look at what the reader is told and what we have to work out for ourselves. Alternatively, focus just on the different kinds of sentences and ask the students to identify one example each of a very short sentence and a question.

Apply the skills

Allow at least 20 minutes for completion of the final task (**Q6**). Remind the students that they can use the annotations on page 60 of the Student Book as well as any suggestions that have been collated on the class whiteboard for reference.

Big answer plenary	Refer back to the **Big question** and ask the students to suggest one structural feature. These could be collated as a wall display and saved for future reference. Using the **Check your progress** outcomes on page 61 of the Student Book, ask the students to reflect on their written task and identify which outcomes they have achieved.

2.6 Understand literal and metaphorical reading

Assessment objectives

English Language

AO1 Identify and interpret explicit and implicit information and ideas

AO2 Explain, comment on and analyse how writers use language and structure to achieve effects and influence readers, using relevant subject terminology to support their views

English Literature

AO1 Read, understand and respond to texts, maintaining a critical style and developing an informed personal response

AO2 Analyse the language, form and structure used by a writer to create meanings and effects, using relevant subject terminology where appropriate

GCSE examinations

- **English Language** Paper 1, Questions 2, 3, 4
- **English Language** Paper 2, Questions 3, 4
- **English Literature** key skill across all components

Differentiated learning outcomes

- **All students must** be able to identify examples of imagery and give some examples.
- **Most students should** be able to identify and explain the effect of an image on the reader.
- **Some students could** explain in detail how a writer uses imagery to create a range of meanings.

Resources

- **Student Book**: pp. 62–5
- **Worksheet**: 2.6
- **PPT**: 2.6

Other Student Book pages

- 2.4, p. 56

Getting you thinking

Big question	Read the **Big question**: *Why do writers use metaphors when they could just say what they mean?* Ask the students to make a note of it for now. Explain that they will return to this question later.

Ask the students to look at the list of suggested purposes of non-fiction texts given on page 62 of the Student Book. Then ask for suggestions of different types of text that might fit these purposes. Encourage any suggestions at this stage; even a road sign counts as a 'text' in that it communicates information, instructions and possibly a warning. Display **PPT 2.6, slide 1** as part of this activity.

Read the start of *Little Red Riding Hood* and ask for suggestions as to its possible purpose and audience (**Q1** and **Q2**). Although the students might simply say 'to entertain' at this stage, when they have read the next section, they will start to understand the allegorical function.

If they are creating their own glossaries, ask the students to add 'allegory' and 'implicit'.

Explore the skills

Read the explanation of literal and implicit meaning, with particular reference to the story of *Little Red Riding Hood*.

Display **PPT 2.6, slide 2** as a way of reinforcing the idea of 'implicit' meaning. Draw students' attention to the fact that the majority of the iceberg is out of sight, and how this metaphor works well to explain how, when we read, we are looking more deeply for the things 'under the surface'.

Ask the students to add the **Key term** 'literal' to their glossaries.

Give extra challenge by asking the students to think about what the characters in the allegorical story of *Little Red Riding Hood* might actually represent: the girl, the wolf, the grandmother, the huntsman who kills the wolf.

Ask the students to look at the three sentences:

- *The girl was very thin.*
- *The girl was very slender.*
- *The girl was very scrawny.*

Remind the students of the **Key term** 'connotations' and ask them to suggest which of these sentences has a positive, which a negative, and which a neutral connotation. The students might also want to suggest which sounds like a criticism and which sounds like a compliment.

Allow five minutes for completion of **Q3** and **Q4**, either individually or in pairs.

Take feedback on their ideas before moving on to the next part of the lesson.

Develop the skills

Read the definitions of the **Key terms** 'imagery' and 'figure of speech' on page 64 of the Student Book and add these to the glossary. The students will probably be familiar with simile, metaphor and personification already, so ask for definitions before they complete **Q5** to consolidate their understanding.

Read 'Daffodils' on page 65 of the Student Book, paying particular attention to the highlighted sections. For future reference, it might be useful to explain that Wordsworth was a Romantic poet, and that this poem is one of the most famous examples of a common Romantic theme: the uplifting power of the natural world.

Allow 10 minutes for the students to identify the similes, metaphors and examples of personification in 'Daffodils' (**Q6** and **Q7**). Then ask them to select one image and write a paragraph about its effect (**Q8**). **Worksheet 2.6** provides a full copy of the poem with highlighted examples of imagery.

Display **PPT 2.6**, **slide 3**, which shows a model paragraph describing the effect of the metaphor 'wealth'. You could display this either before the students complete their paragraph (for **Q8**) or after the students have attempted their own.

Give extra challenge by asking the students to extend the model paragraph even further, linking it to other examples of imagery in 'Daffodils'.

Read the point about learning to 'read the picture', in the middle of page 65, and refer the students back to the lesson using the painting *Landscape with the Fall of Icarus* in Chapter 2, Topic 4.

Apply the skills

Display **PPT 2.6**, **slide 4**, and ask the students to read the list of discussion prompts on page 65 of the Student Book (**Q9**).

Either use this task as stimulus for a class discussion or collate ideas and then allow 10 minutes for the students to produce a short written response to the task.

Big answer plenary	Return to the **Big question**. Allow five minutes for the students to complete the following sentence: *Writers use metaphorical language because …*

2.7 Understand the effect of writers' choices

Assessment objectives

English Language

AO1 Identify and interpret explicit and implicit information and ideas.

AO2 Explain, comment on and analyse how writers use language and structure to achieve effects and influence readers, using relevant subject terminology to support their views

English Literature

AO1 Read, understand and respond to texts, maintaining a critical style and developing an informed personal response

AO2 Analyse the language, form and structure used by a writer to create meanings and effects, using relevant subject terminology where appropriate

GCSE examinations

- **English Language** Paper 1, Questions 2, 3, 4
- **English Language** Paper 2, Questions 3, 4
- **English Literature** key skill across all components

Differentiated learning outcomes

- **All students must** be able to identify that a writer is doing deliberate things in order to create a particular effect.
- **Most students should** be able to explain what a writer is doing in order to create a particular effect.
- **Some students could** explain precisely why a particular technique has a specific effect on the reader.

Resources

- **Student Book**: pp. 66–9
- **PPT**: 2.7

Getting you thinking

Big question	Read the **Big question**: *What are effects and how do you write about them?* Explain that the purpose of this lesson is to learn how to explain exactly what the effects of a particular choice are, rather than merely identifying that the writer has done something on purpose.

PPT Display the images on **PPT 2.7, slide 1** and ask students to explain what the 'effect' of shaking a can or bottle of fizzy drink would be.

Read the explanation of 'effect' on page 66 of the Student Book, and ask students to give some examples from their learning so far. These might include the effect of using:

- simile, metaphor or personification
- particular word choices
- structural features: sentence forms and types.

PPT Display **PPT 2.7, slide 2** and ask students to make a note of the questions to ask themselves, either using this slide or the same list on page 66 of the Student Book.

PPT Display **PPT 2.7, slide 3** and allow 10 minutes for students to study the leaflet and answer the related questions (**Q1–Q3**), either using the slide or the image on page 66 of the Student Book.

PPT For **Q4**, display **PPT 2.7, slide 4**, which provides an example answer. Students could either read this example before completing their own sentence, or write their sentence first and then compare their work with the model answer.

When responding to the picture (**Q5**), stress that the picture is part of the text and is helping to communicate meaning in the same way that the words, and the position of the words, are doing.

Explore the skills

Ask students to read the information about 'effect' on page 67 of the Student Book.

Display **PPT2.7**, slide **5**, which is the checklist for reading a literary text.

Display **PPT2.7**, **slide 6** and read the line from 'Havisham'. Take some initial suggestions for what effect this image has on the reader (**Q6**), and then compare these with the two sample responses at the bottom of page 67 (**Q7**). It may be necessary to contextualise the poem for students who aren't familiar with it or with the character of Miss Havisham (from Dickens's *Great Expectations*) on whom the poem is based. The poem concerns a woman rejected and abandoned who has been consumed by bitterness as a result.

Draw particular attention to the three phrases in sample A:

- 'to create an effect'
- 'to make the line stand out'
- 'to make the reader want to read on'

Ask students whether these three phrases are particularly effective and actually demonstrate any knowledge or skill, or if sample B actually expresses their ideas much more effectively.

Now ask students to read the two paragraphs describing a holiday scene on page 68, and to select some details that have a positive connotation.

Then ask them to work in pairs to identify the purpose of the text and the effects the writer wants to achieve (**Q8**). Take feedback as a class.

Add the **Key term** 'connotations' to the glossary, explaining that this is one word that can be used to write about the effects of particular word choices; 'suggests', 'highlights' and 'implies' are also very useful words to use in explanations.

Ask students to identify some details that suggest the memory described by the two paragraphs is a happy one (**Q9**). Then give them 10 minutes to read the example of the changed second paragraph and adapt the first paragraph accordingly (**Q10**). Take some feedback on their suggestions.

Develop the skills

Read the first verse of 'The Chimney Sweeper' on page 69 of the Student Book and the accompanying annotations. Take some ideas in response to the question prompts about what effect Blake wants to create (**Q11**), and then read the sample paragraph, which shows students how to write more efficiently about writers' effects.

Allow a further 10 minutes for students to choose their own word or phrase from this verse and to write a paragraph on its effect (**Q12**). Remind students to avoid the three phrases from sample A on page 67, and instead make sure there is a clear, specific comment on what the effect might be.

Apply the skills

Ask students to read the list of terms and add definitions for each one to their glossaries (**Q13**). Encourage them to write an example to illustrate each, either using the poem or the passage of description from this lesson.

Big answer plenary	Ask students to write a definition of *effect* in one sentence. Using the **Check your progress** outcomes on page 69 of the Student Book, ask the students to reflect on the paragraph they wrote for **Q12** and to identify which outcomes they have achieved.

2.8 Understand attitude and viewpoint

Assessment objectives

English Language

AO1 Identify and interpret explicit and implicit information and ideas

AO2 Explain, comment on and analyse how writers use language and structure to achieve effects and influence readers, using relevant subject terminology to support their views

English Literature

AO1 Read, understand and respond to texts, maintaining a critical style and developing an informed personal response

AO2 Analyse the language, form and structure used by a writer to create meanings and effects, using relevant subject terminology where appropriate

GCSE examinations

- **English Language** Paper 1, Question 1
- **English Language** Paper 2, Questions 1, 2
- **English Literature** Key skill across all components

Differentiated learning outcomes

- **All students must** be able to identify the tone of a text.
- **Most students should** be able to explain the tone of a piece of writing and identify some of the ways the writer's attitude is communicated.
- **Some students could** use details and techniques from a text to provide a thoughtful consideration of how a writer is presenting a particular attitude and viewpoint.

Resources

- **Student Book**: pp. 70–3
- **Worksheet**: 2.8
- **PPT**: 2.8

Getting you thinking

Big question	Read the **Big question**: *How do you know what a writer feels about what they are writing about?* Ask the students to give some initial thoughts. Explain that they will return to this question at the end of the lesson and will be able to give a fuller response then.

For **Q1** and **Q2**, read the two sentences and discuss possible responses to the questions/prompts. The students can either make notes or give oral responses at this stage. For **Q2**, ensure they notice that it is the pause created by the full stop that suggests a negative attitude.

For **Q3**, allow the students a couple of minutes to rewrite the sentence and suggest some ways of demonstrating a positive attitude without explicitly saying so. Then ask the students to read out some of their sentences to the class.

Explore the skills

Ask the students to make a note of the two terms 'objective' and 'subjective' and to explain what they mean. Then read the explanations on page 70 of the Student Book and ask the students to compare them with their definitions. Check that all students are clear about the difference, referring back to the sentences about Portugal in **Q1** and **Q2** in order to clarify the difference, if necessary.

For **Q4**, display **PPT 2.8, slide 1**, which is a list of the text types. Ask the students to suggest which ones are likely to be objective and which are more likely to be subjective. Some may suggest ways in which certain ones could be either:

- a news report (objective)
- a letter to a friend about a recent holiday (subjective)
- a review of a rock album (could be either, but more likely to be subjective)
- a science textbook (objective)
- a recipe (objective)
- an article about child labour in Bangladesh (could be either).

Read **Text 1** and ask the students to identify if there are any ways in which the writer's point of view can be seen (**Q5**). Draw attention to the impersonal tense, the use of statistics and the reporting of facts.

Now read **Text 2** and ask the students to notice how this text much more clearly expresses a strong opinion (**Q6**).

Using **Worksheet 2.8** or by referring to the table on page 72 of the Student Book, allow 10 minutes for the students to look at both texts and identify some of the ways in which the writers are expressing, or not expressing, their opinion (**Q7**).

Develop the skills

Read the four sentences **a–d** in **Q8**, and give the students 10 minutes to identify the tone of each one by matching the correct word to each sentence (**Q9a**). Then ask the students to identify a particular detail in each sentence that helped them to decide (**Q9b**).

If preferred, the students could work in pairs to identify the tone of each sentence. Then take feedback by asking the students to select one particular feature about each sentence to explain how they identified the tone to the class.

Apply the skills

Display **PPT 2.8, slide 2**, which is a copy of the text on page 73 of the Student Book.

Refer the students to the **Checklist for success** at the bottom of page 73 and allow 20 minutes for them to read the text and complete the written task (**Q10**).

> **Give extra support** by explaining that the writer is on the side of the people he is describing and wants the reader to also see them from his point of view. Suggest that the students highlight some of the vocabulary the writer uses to show that he feels sorry for the prisoners he is describing.
>
> **Give extra challenge** by focusing on the admiration the writer expresses for the people being described.

Add the terms 'tone', 'attitude' and 'viewpoint' to the glossary (**Q11**). The students can illustrate their definitions with examples from the texts in this lesson if preferred.

Big answer plenary	Using the **Check your progress** outcomes, ask the students to identify which outcomes they feel their work demonstrates they have achieved. Then ask them to swap with a partner, who should identify one way in which the work could be improved.
	Ask the students to complete the following task, which is also on **PPT 2.8, slide 3**:
	Writers use lots of ways to communicate how they feel about what they are writing about. These can include: ...

3.1 Retrieve basic information from unseen texts

Assessment objectives

English Language

AO1 Identify and interpret explicit and implicit information and ideas; select and synthesise evidence from different texts

English Literature

AO1 Read, understand and respond to texts, maintaining a critical style and developing an informed personal response; use textual references, including quotations, to support and illustrate interpretations

GCSE examinations
- English Language Paper 1, Question 1
- English Language Paper 2, Question 1

Differentiated learning outcomes
- **All students must** be able to show they can read texts carefully and select the required information with help.
- **Most students should** be able to read texts and then select the required information without help.
- **Some students could** read texts and then select information, presenting it in a clear format.

Resources
- **Student Book**: pp. 76–9
- **Worksheet**: 3.1
- **PPT**: 3.1

Other Student Book pages
- Lesson 3.2, pp. 80–3

Note: You may wish to teach Lessons 3.1 and 3.2 together, depending on the time you have available. They are designed to work consecutively, as they use the same groups of texts and develop the very basic skills of comprehension.

Getting you thinking

Big question	Read the **Big question**: *What is 'explicit information'?* and elicit some initial responses.

Read the introductory paragraph on page 76 of the Student Book and work through **Q1** with the class. You could organise this as a simple poll, either by having a show of hands or asking the students to write their ideas on mini whiteboards. Use this activity to link back to the **Big question**, and explain, or reiterate, that explicit information is information that is on the surface, i.e. the key factual information within a text.

Now ask the students to complete **Q2** individually. If time allows, share some responses with the class.

Explore the skills

Ask the students to look at the newspaper article on page 77 of the Student Book, and read it aloud to the class.

Now ask the students to complete **Q3** using **Worksheet 3.1**. Refer the students to the suggested techniques for identifying and marking up information, on page 78 of the Student Book.

Feed back as a class and ask the students to self-mark their work. Some suggested answers to **Q3** are given below.

Things we know about the man:
- He is Swedish
- He survived for two months in his car.
- He was 44.

- He survived by eating handfuls of snow.
- He was in a poor state when found.

Things we know about his car:

- His car was covered in snow.
- His car was stranded in snowdrifts in northern Sweden.
- The dashboard and seats were covered in ice.
- The car was off the main road on forest tracks.
- The fuel had run out.

Develop the skills

Reinforce the opening statement in **Develop the skills** on page 78 of the Student Book, before reading aloud the extract from 'Snow Story' by George Packer.

Ask the students to complete **Q4**. Explain to the students that they will need to look carefully at statements **a–f** and decide whether they are true or false. The key information for the task has been highlighted. This task may be done in pairs if preferred and self-marked.

Answers to **Q4**:

a True

b False

c False

d False

e True

f True

Apply the skills

Allow no more than five minutes for the students to skim the article about Peter Skyllberg's ordeal again and complete **Q5** individually. Encourage them to highlight or annotate the copy of the extract on **Worksheet 3.1**. Before they begin the task, make sure they refer to the **Checklist for success** on page 79. Relevant points that the students should identify include the following:

- He was discovered by a man passing by on a snowmobile.
- The man scraped some snow off the windscreen and saw movement inside the car.
- An emergency services team was deployed to rescue Peter.
- He was wrapped up in a sleeping bag in the car when he was found.
- Peter was in a very poor state when he was found and could barely speak.

The students could mark each other's answers in pairs, using the article to check the accuracy of each other's statements.

Big answer plenary	Have the students use the **Check your progress** outcomes to assess their own progress so far.

3.2 Support ideas with evidence and quotation

Assessment objectives

English Language

AO1 Identify and interpret explicit and implicit information and ideas; select and synthesise evidence from different texts

English Literature

AO1 Read, understand and respond to texts, maintaining a critical style and developing an informed personal response; use textual references, including quotations, to support and illustrate interpretations

GCSE examinations

- **English Language** Paper 1, Question 4
- **English Language** Paper 2, Questions 2, 4

Differentiated learning outcomes

- **All students must** remember to put quotations in their reading responses.
- **Most students should** be able to use quotations to support the point they are making.
- **Some students could** choose quotations carefully to support their points and show that they understand texts fully.

Resources

- **Student Book**: pp. 80–3
- **PPT**: 3.2

Other Student Book pages

- Lesson 3.1, pp. 76–9

Getting you thinking

Big question	Moving on from Lesson 3.1, ask the students what quotations are, and why we use quotations in English and English Literature.
	Read the **Big question**: *Isn't quotation just copying out bits of the text?* Discuss this briefly with the class to elicit some preliminary thoughts.

For **Q1**, present the scenario of a lawyer in a courtroom to introduce the idea of using supporting evidence to back up our points, and briefly discuss the questions with the class.

Explore the skills

If you are completing this lesson separately from Lesson 3.1, re-read the article on page 77 of the Student Book.

Read the first student's response to the task, on page 80 of the Student Book. Then work through **Q2a–c** with the class and take responses collaboratively to reinforce the teaching point.

Read the second student's response, on page 81, aloud and highlight the key differences using the annotations (**Q3**).

Now ask the students to complete **Q4** either individually or in pairs.

Develop the skills

For **Q5**, refer to the model comprehension question and ask the students to identify the focus of the task. Reinforce that, in order to select appropriate support material, they must always keep the focus of the question in mind – in this instance, the impact of the snowstorm.

Read the annotated extract on page 82 of the Student Book aloud. If you are combining Lessons 3.1 and 3.2, then ask the students to re-read the extract for themselves.

PPT Focus on the chosen quotations, and display them using **PPT 3.2, slide 1**. Use annotations to reinforce the good practice demonstrated.

Keeping the quotations on **PPT 3.2, slide 1** on display, ask the students to complete **Q6** individually. If time allows, feed back as a class and share some of the variations constructed by the group.

If necessary, ask the students to complete **Q7**, which contains extension ideas regarding longer quotations. Answers to **Q7**:

1. The quotation is not embedded into the text but begins on a new line and is preceded by a colon.
2. The extract is indented away from the margin.
3. When quoting from a character in a play, the colon is also used to separate the character name from the dialogue itself.
4. The new line in the quotation must match the layout of the original text and be indented also.

Apply the skills

For the main task (**Q8**), read the introductory overview of the story and the task itself. Ask the students to identify the focus – the girl's feelings. Then refer the students to the **Checklist for success** and recap on the key skills.

Allow the students no more than 15 minutes to read the extract independently and complete the task.

Big answer plenary	Before handing in their work on the final task, ask the students to check it against the **Check your progress** outcomes and decide which outcomes they think they have achieved.
	Return to the **Big question** and ask the students to write down one clear suggestion to complete the sentence:
	Using supporting quotations is important because …
	Collate the students' suggestions on the board and share the responses in plenary.

3.3 Show your understanding of inference and implication

Assessment objectives

English Language

AO1 Identify and interpret explicit and implicit information and ideas; select and synthesise evidence from different texts

AO4 Evaluate texts critically and support this with appropriate textual references

English Literature

AO1 Read, understand and respond to texts, maintaining a critical style and developing an informed personal response; use textual references, including quotations, to support and illustrate interpretations

GCSE examinations

- **English Language** Paper 1, Question 4
- **English Language** Paper 2, Questions 2, 4

Differentiated learning outcomes

- **All students must** be able to make some simple inferences, showing what a text means to them following statements and quotations.
- **Most students should** be able to demonstrate some ability to read between the lines and present some clear inferences to follow supported statements.
- **Some students could** show they are able to form a clear and detailed understanding of a text by presenting clear inferences which link effectively to their supported statements.

Resources

- **Student Book**: pp. 84–7
- **Worksheets**: 3.3a–b
- **PPT**: 3.3

Getting you thinking

Big question	Refer students to the **Key term** *inferences* on page 84 of the Student Book. Then read the **Big question**: *What are inferences and why do you need them?* and the introduction to **Getting you thinking** on page 84. Explain that, when writing about a text in class or in an examination, the students need to show their real, in-depth understanding of the text. In order to do this, they need to understand the implicit ideas within a text as well as the explicit and literal ones.

For **Q1**, ask students to look at the transcript or use two volunteers to read it aloud to the class. Discuss the questions with the class and take suggestions. It should be clear to the students that person B certainly doesn't think person A's new top is cool; she doesn't say it explicitly or openly, but we can *infer* this from her words.

Refer students to the **Key terms** box and use the definitions to reinforce the three **Key terms**: 'explicit meanings', 'inferences' and 'implicit meanings'. You could ask students to make a note of these in their books.

Explore the skills

Use the introductory paragraph of **Explore the skills** on page 85 to introduce, or recap, how to make inferences, before reading aloud the extract from 'Your Shoes' by Michelle Roberts.

Allow approximately 10 minutes for students to complete **Q2**, using **Worksheet 3.3a**. Feed back and take suggestions from the whole group.

Give extra support by putting students in pairs or small groups.

Work through **Q3** with the class. Elicit the answers to the two questions to help overall understanding.

Develop the skills

For **Q4**, read the question and reinforce the instructions – for the students to select four quotations of their own – before reading aloud the second extract from 'Your Shoes' on page 86.

For **Q5**, students should work individually. Allow approximately 15 minutes for students to write out the four quotations they have selected, and make notes on their inferences in the same way as they did in **Q2**.

Allow a further five minutes for the students to look at these and draw some conclusions about **Q5a** and **Q5b**. Then feed back as a class and take suggestions from the whole group. The students should be able to infer from the second extract that the person who has gone missing is the speaker's child. The child is probably a teenager, which can be inferred from the references to 'as you got older' and getting 'home from school'.

Read the example student response on page 87 of the Student Book and reinforce the method using the bullet points at the end of **Q5**. Ask students to identify which part of the student response is the key information, which is the quotation and which is the inference (**Q6**).

Apply the skills

Read the main task on page 87, reinforcing the instructions in **Q7** and asking students what the focus of the task is.

Refer students to the **Checklist for success** and remind them of the ways they can highlight key information and quotations, from Lesson 3.2, page 82.

Allow approximately 25–30 minutes for students to complete the main task (**Q7**). **Worksheet 3.3b** includes the text of both extracts from Michelle Roberts's story; encourage the students to work with this text, highlighting and annotating it as they read it again.

Alternatively, this task could be set as homework.

Big answer plenary	Ask students to read over their work and look at the inferences they have made. Using the **Check your progress** outcomes, ask students to identify whether all of their inferences are clear or whether in some cases they are simply paraphrasing the key information statement or the quotation. Use this to decide between Outcomes 1 and 2.
	If all of the points made are supported and have interesting inferences (which do not employ paraphrase), students have achieved Outcome 3.

3.4 Make and present inferences about people

Assessment objectives

English Language

AO1 Identify and interpret explicit and implicit information and ideas; select and synthesise evidence from different texts

AO4 Evaluate texts critically and support this with appropriate textual references

English Literature

AO1 Read, understand and respond to texts, maintaining a critical style and developing an informed personal response; use textual references, including quotations, to support and illustrate interpretations

GCSE examinations
- **English Language** Paper 1, Question 4
- **English Language** Paper 2, Questions 2, 4

Differentiated learning outcomes

- **All students must** be able to look at character descriptions and imagine what characters look like.
- **Most students should** be able to look at character descriptions and pick out specific quotations to help them work out what the characters are like.
- **Some students could** make interesting inferences about the characters in the extracts by selecting specific details from the text as evidence.

Resources
- **Student Book**: pp. 88–91
- **Worksheet**: 3.4
- **PPT**: 3.4

Other Student Book pages
- Lesson 3.3, pp. 84–7

Getting you thinking

Big question	Read the **Big question**: *How do we know what writers want us to see about characters?* Ask the students to speculate about whether it is actually possible to know what writers want us to see about characters. Ask them to think about characters in films or TV dramas and the clues we pick up as to what that character is like. • What techniques are used in performance to create impressions of characters? For example: their costumes; facial expressions; hair; make-up; mannerisms; and way of speaking. • Do any of those aspects translate to characters in print?

Read the opening paragraphs about Charles Dickens in **Getting you thinking** on page 88 of the Student Book.

Then display **PPT 3.4, slide 1**, and read out the names of some of Dickens's characters. Allow the students one minute to each select one character to focus on (**Q1**). Allow a further five minutes for the students to jot down initial ideas using the prompts in **Q2**. This would work equally well as a paired activity.

Display **PPT 3.4, slide 2**, and allow approximately 10 minutes for individuals (or pairs) to complete a spider diagram for their chosen character (**Q3**). Feed back and present some students' ideas to the class.

Explore the skills

Read the opening paragraph in **Explore the skills** on page 89. Then ask the students to read the extract from *Great Expectations* (**Q4**).

Allow approximately 10 minutes for the students to complete **Q5**, using **Worksheet 3.4**. The students should identify key ideas about wealth and the notion of a wedding about to take place. They should be able to infer that Miss Havisham is someone packing for their future, or their honeymoon, and that they are in the process of getting ready. You may wish to encourage the students to speculate on the confusion apparent in the final sentence.

> **Give extra support** by making **Q5** a small-group activity where the students can work together to collect ideas.

Develop the skills

Move on to **Q6**, allowing a further 10 minutes for the additional inferences to be added to the students' notes. The students should pick up from this second extract the contrast of past meeting present, and that Miss Havisham, and her bridal gown, are showing the signs of no longer being young/new. They should grasp the notion of things fading and ageing, and that Miss Havisham has potentially been wearing the dress since she was young. This may lead some to conclude she has been disappointed in love and/or abandoned by her lover just prior to their marriage.

> **Give extra support** by making **Q6** a small-group activity where the students can work together to collect ideas.

Take feedback as a class, discussing all the inferences the students have made about Miss Havisham so far, and draw some conclusions about her character.

Read **Q7** and ask the students to highlight the focus of the task. Reinforce the methodology used and practised in Lesson 3.3. Allow approximately 20 minutes for the students to complete **Q7**, writing up their four separate ideas.

Apply the skills

Q8 is an opportunity for independent work testing the skills acquired so far. This could be used as a homework task or as a 30-minute individual task in class.

Allow approximately 30 minutes for the students to complete **Q8**, using the copy of the extract on **Worksheet 3.4** to allow for annotations and highlighting of key quotations. Before the students begin, reinforce the method and **Checklist for success** from Lesson 3.3.

Big answer plenary	First ask the students to evaluate their own work against the outcomes listed in the **Check your progress** on page 91 of the Student Book. Which of the outcomes do they think they have achieved?
	Then ask the students to work in pairs to read each other's responses to **Q8**. Display **PPT 3.4, slide 3**, which contains peer-evaluation criteria that will help the students evaluate which outcomes from **Check your progress** their partners have achieved.

3.5 Make and present inferences about places

Assessment objectives

English Language

AO1 Identify and interpret explicit and implicit information and ideas; select and synthesise evidence from different texts

AO4 Evaluate texts critically and support this with appropriate textual references

English Literature

AO1 Read, understand and respond to texts, maintaining a critical style and developing an informed personal response; use textual references, including quotations, to support and illustrate interpretations

GCSE examinations
- English Language Paper 1, Question 4
- English Language Paper 2, Questions 2, 4

Differentiated learning outcomes
- **All students must** be able to show a basic understanding of what the two places in the extracts are like through making simple inferences.
- **Most students should** be able to work out the differences between the two places by picking out key quotations and making some clear inferences.
- **Some students could** show they can form a clear picture of what the two places are like by making interesting and valid inferences based on the selection of specific details within the text.

Resources
- **Student Book**: pp. 92–5
- **Worksheet**: 3.5
- **PPT**: 3.5

Other Student Book pages
- Lessons 3.3 and 3.4, pp. 84–91

Getting you thinking

Ask students to complete **Q1**. This would work well as a class discussion, with you collating ideas on spider diagrams on the board. Alternatively, have students work in groups of three, with each student having to imagine and give suggestions about one of the bulleted places.

Big question	Take feedback as a class. Then spend two to three minutes focusing on the information in the final paragraph of **Getting you thinking** on page 92, linking this to the **Big question**: *How do we know what writers want us to see about places?* You could ask students if they have a vivid memory of a place they read about in a novel recently or a storybook they read as a child.

Explore the skills

Recap on the skills learned in Lesson 3.4. Then read the opening paragraph in **Explore the skills** on page 92 of the Student Book, and reinforce the suggested method for dealing with, and making inferences about, place.

Read the extract from *Wuthering Heights* aloud (Student Book, page 93). Before you read, you might wish to let students know this is from a 19th-century text; that the novel is set in Yorkshire; that Cathy and Heathcliff are from a neighbouring farm to this beautiful house; and that Mr and Mrs Linton are the owners of the house and Edgar and Isabella are their children. Allow approximately 20 minutes for students to work through the questions in the annotations (**Q2**).

Give extra support by putting students in small groups so that they can discuss and explore the questions in a collaborative way, recording all of their ideas.

Display **PPT 3.5, slide 1**, and feed back as a class, taking ideas for each question from selected students or each group.

Develop the skills

Display **PPT 3.5, slide 2**, and read aloud the second extract from *Wuthering Heights*. Spend some time ensuring all students understand the vocabulary and help out by explaining more difficult vocabulary, where required.

For **Q3a–e**, explain that students need to answer each question with a clear sentence, or sentences, in their own words, and use a quotation to support each answer. Allow approximately 20–25 minutes for students to complete **Q3**, either individually or in pairs, using **Worksheet 3.5** to aid note-taking, annotation and highlighting.

> **Give extra support** by modelling a response to **Q3a** on the whiteboard using ideas gathered from the whole group reading of the text.

Apply the skills

For **Q4**, spend five minutes unpacking the task with the students. Ask them to speculate on why these two places might be so significant in the novel and why the writer chose to make them so different. Invite students to speculate on whether the two places might be symbolic in any way – for example, on the one hand is the ancient, shabby but solid working farm, hunkering down in the landscape, which stands in contrast to the luxury and light-coloured frippery of Thrushcross Grange, where all seems light and superficial.

Reiterate and recap on the now practised method from Lessons 3.3 and 3.4, revisiting the **Checklist for success** in Lesson 3.3, page 87, if required.

Allow 20–30 minutes for students to complete **Q4**. Encourage students to use the planning grid on **Worksheet 3.5** as the basis for their answer.

Big answer plenary	Use the **Check your progress** outcomes (Student Book, page 95) in plenary as a basis for paired discussion on the outcomes of the work from Lesson 3.5. Ask students to rate themselves against each outcome to evaluate their own skills, using: • *Agree strongly* • *Agree* • *Agree somewhat* • *Disagree somewhat* • *Disagree* Ask students to write down one key thing they need to gain more confidence with in their next lesson.

3.6 Make and present inferences about ideas and attitudes

Assessment objectives

English Language

AO1 Identify and interpret explicit and implicit information and ideas; select and synthesise evidence from different texts

English Literature

AO1 Read, understand and respond to texts, maintaining a critical style and developing an informed personal response; use textual references, including quotations, to support and illustrate interpretations

GCSE examinations
- English Language
  Paper 2, Question 4

Differentiated learning outcomes
- **All students must** be able to read the text and work out the main ideas and point of view through making simple inferences and drawing on key quotations.
- **Most students should** be able to work out the main viewpoint and attitudes in a text, selecting evidence or quotations to support their ideas and making sensible, clear inferences from them.
- **Some students could** explain the viewpoint, attitudes and ideas clearly, showing understanding through clear inferences and well-chosen support.

Resources
- **Student Book**: pp. 96–9
- **Worksheets**: 3.6a–b
- **PPT**: 3.6

Getting you thinking

Big question	Read the **Big question**: *You can make inferences about creative writing but how can you do it with newspaper articles?* Briefly discuss this question with the class to see how many students feel the same way. Ask students what they feel the difficulty is in transferring the skills – aim to see whether they find articles or non-fiction texts more concrete and fact-based and thus more difficult to interpret or make inferences about. Use the discussion to lead into the introductory paragraph of **Getting you thinking** on page 96 of the Student Book.

Display **PPT 3.6, slide 1**, and read the extract aloud, slowly and carefully. Ask students to make notes for **Q1** as you read. Take ideas and feedback from the class. The students should pick up on the fact that, although the writer is describing something like a schoolroom, it is not a typical school scene (the description of the learners suggests that).

Allow an additional five minutes for students to explore and discuss **Q2** and **Q3** in pairs, using **Worksheet 3.6a** as a means of recording all of their 'detective work'.

Give extra support by asking students what the phrase 'funnelled into education' implies. Are the men in the classroom by choice?

Explore the skills

The remaining activities on the text would work well as a small-group supportive investigation using **PPT 3.6** to reveal each paragraph one at a time.

Display **PPT 3.6, slide 2**, and read the second paragraph aloud.

Allow at least five minutes for students to discuss **Q4** and **Q5** in small groups, before feeding back their ideas as a class.

Allow 10 minutes for students to read the third paragraph of the article on page 98 of the Student Book, and complete the work on quotations (**Q6**), either individually or in pairs, again using **Worksheet 3.6a**.

Now complete **Q7–Q9**, as a whole-group plenary.

Develop the skills

For **Q10**, read the extract aloud and the questions in the six annotations on page 99. Allow a further 15 minutes for students to complete the questions in small groups, using the table on **Worksheet 3.6b** to record their findings. Feed back as a class and discuss what is suggested about the man in this paragraph.

> **Give extra challenge** by asking students to work individually on these questions.

Apply the skills

Ask students to read the final paragraph from the article on page 99 of the Student Book. Ensure that all students are familiar with the word 'stereotype' and check they can identify the stereotype used in the extract. Ask students why it is interesting that this stereotype of the young boy in bottom-set maths is juxtaposed with the previous paragraph of the older man struggling and working to pass his maths exam. What possible links is the writer expecting us to make between the two? Before they attempt **Q11**, explore with students why the writer wants to change our attitude towards prisoners.

Ask students to recap on their notes and evidence from **Q1–Q10** and refer them to the **Checklist for success** on page 99. They could construct a planning grid before embarking on the task like the one completed in Lesson 3.5.

Allow approximately 30 minutes for students to complete **Q11**, using the copy of the text on **Worksheet 3.6b** to make notes or annotations. Alternatively, this would make a useful homework task.

Big answer plenary	Refer back to the **Big question** and ask students to look at their final piece of work from **Q11**, and evaluate it against the three **Check your progress** outcomes.
	Take a vote as to how many students feel they are more confident than at the beginning of the lesson, and how many have changed their mind about their initial answer to the **Big question**.

3.7 Summarise and synthesise: selecting and collating information from more than one text

Assessment objective

English Language

AO1 Identify and interpret explicit and implicit information and ideas; select and synthesise evidence from different texts

GCSE examinations
- English Language Paper 2, Questions 2, 4

Differentiated learning outcomes
- **All students must** be able to read the texts and identify the key ideas that two texts have in common through making simple inferences and some use of textual support.
- **Most students should** be able to work out the main ideas and organise the ideas in a logical way, supporting them with quotations.
- **Some students could** show they are able to collate the ideas in a crisp summary supported by quotations and accompanied with inferences to show their understanding.

Resources
- **Student Book**: pp. 100–3
- **Worksheet**: 3.7
- **PPT**: 3.7

Getting you thinking

Display **PPT 3.7, slide 1**, which sets up the scenario for **Q1**, and take suggestions from the class as to how they would decide which pair of trainers to buy.

Big question | Refer to the **Big question**: *How do you work with two texts at once?* Read the further information following **Q1** in **Getting you thinking** on page 100 of the Student Book to make the link and introduce the idea of the process.

Explore the skills

Read aloud the extracts from Captain Scott's diary and *Race to the Pole* on page 101 of the Student Book. Use the opening paragraph of **Explore the skills** on page 100 to ensure students are clear about the context of each extract.

Allow 10–15 minutes for students to complete **Q2** using the grid on **Worksheet 3.7**.

Display **PPT 3.7, slide 2**, which shows an example response regarding the place. Note that this links to the example paragraph used later on. This would work well as a paired investigation, while you move around the class and check the validity of ideas and responses.

Explain the method used for summarising ideas from two texts using the bullet points in the **Checklist for success** and the example paragraph on page 102 of the Student Book. Ask students to compare this to the method they have learned already for dealing with one text, and point out the similarities and the differences.

Now allow approximately five minutes for students to work independently to produce their second paragraph (**Q3**).

Develop the skills

Read aloud the further extracts from Captain Scott's diary and *Race to the Pole* on page 103 of the Student Book.

Students should revisit the table on **Worksheet 3.7** and add in any further categories that would be useful to them. You might encourage them to think about these points before allowing a further 10 minutes to work on collating their ideas and evidence (**Q4**):

- the conditions the explorers are in
- the feelings and emotions the explorers show.

Apply the skills

Allow approximately 20–30 minutes for students to complete **Q5** using the material and ideas they have collected in **Worksheet 3.7**.

Give extra support by allowing students to use the opening paragraph from **Q2**.

Big answer plenary	Ask students to work in pairs and evaluate each other's responses, against the three **Check your progress** outcomes.
	Return to the **Big question** and ask students to write down one key tip for working with two texts at once. Encourage them to think about:
	• looking for links in themes, ideas and feelings
	• using a means of planning and organisation to collect key ideas
	• looking for ways of linking quotations or textual details that have a commonality as evidence.
	Display all the tips on the whiteboard at the end.

3.8 Apply your skills to English Language and English Literature tasks

Assessment objectives

English Language

AO1 Identify and interpret explicit and implicit information and ideas; select and synthesise evidence from different texts

English Literature

AO1 Read, understand and respond to texts, maintaining a critical style and developing an informed personal response; use textual references, including quotations, to support and illustrate interpretations

GCSE examinations

- **English Language** Paper 1, Question 4
- **English Language** Paper 2, Questions 2, 4
- **English Literature** Paper 2, Section A

Differentiated learning outcomes

- **All students must** be able to read texts carefully, sometimes making basic inferences about people and places, remembering to include quotations and showing they can identify the key ideas that two texts have in common.
- **Most students should** be able to identify the main ideas, viewpoints and attitudes of texts, organising their ideas in a logical way and supporting them with specific quotations, also making detailed and accurate comparisons.
- **Some students could** select information clearly from texts, making insightful and subtle inferences, choosing highly appropriate quotations to support their points, and making accurate and crisply presented comparisons between texts.

Resources

- **Student Book**: pp. 104–14
- **Worksheets**: 3.8a–d (3.8c–d are available on the CD-Rom only)
- **PPT**: 3.8

Start by explaining that the final lesson of this chapter provides good practice of the skills learned throughout the chapter. The activities in this lesson can be done under examination conditions, or as individual assessments if required.

Responding to English Language tasks

Read the opening paragraph on page 104 of the Student Book and ensure students are clear about the context of each extract on pages 104–106. Allow students 15 minutes to read both extracts and make notes/annotate as they read, using **Worksheet 3.8a (Q1)**.

Give extra support by reading each extract aloud for students and allowing them five minutes thinking and annotating time in-between.

Now focus on the task itself on page 106. Invite students to comment on what they think the focus of the task is, and the key skills needed to tackle the task effectively.

Display **PPT 3.8, slide 1**, the **Checklist for success**, to consolidate their ideas. Allow 30 minutes for students to plan and then write their response to the task. Once students have finished, give them five minutes to carefully proofread and check their work. Then read aloud the example **Response 1** on page 107 of the Student Book. Point out the skills that have been shown using the annotations to the text.

Ask students to annotate their own piece in a different colour to indicate where they have used any of the four skills shown in the example.

Read aloud the **Comments on Response 1**, at the bottom of page 107. Put students in pairs and allow them five minutes to look at **Response 1** and complete **Q3**. Ask each pair to write down one piece of advice they could give to this student. Feed back and share their ideas as a class.

Read aloud example **Response 2**, on page 108. Again, point out the skills that have been shown using the annotations and ask students to mark up their own work to indicate any of those skills that are evident. Then read aloud the **Comments on Response 2**, at the bottom of page 108.

Allow a further 10 minutes for students to look at **Response 2** and complete **Q4** and **Q5**, individually. Ask each student to write down one key tip they could take from this example response. Then feed back ideas as a class.

Responding to English Literature tasks

Read the opening paragraph on page 109 of the Student Book and ensure students are clear about the context of the extract from the short story 'The Veldt' and the questions they should think about.

Allow 15–20 minutes to read the extract from 'The Veldt' and make notes/annotate using **Worksheet 3.8b**.

> **Give extra support** by reading the extract aloud for students and allowing them 10 minutes thinking and annotation time.

Now focus on the task on page 111. Invite students to comment on what they think the focus of the task is, and the key skills needed to tackle the first bullet point. Point out to students that the second bullet point – how the ideas are presented in the way the author writes – deals with the language and structure of the piece, and will be covered by work in Chapters 4 and 6.

Display **PPT 3.8, slide 3**, the **Checklist for success**, to consolidate the students' ideas. Allow 30 minutes for students to plan and then write their response to the task (**Q6**). Once students have finished, allow five minutes for them to carefully proofread and check their own piece of work.

Read aloud the example **Response 1** on pages 111–12 of the Student Book. Point out the skills that have been shown using the annotations in the text.

Ask students to annotate their own piece in a different colour to show where they have used any of the four skills shown in the example. Read aloud the **Comments on Response 1**, on page 112.

Put students in pairs and allow them five minutes to look at **Response 1** and complete **Q7** and **Q8**. Ask each pair to write down one piece of advice they could give to this student. Feed back and share their ideas as a class.

Read aloud example **Response 2**, on pages 112–13. Again, point out the skills that have been shown using the annotations and ask students to mark up their own work to indicate any of those skills that are evident. Then read aloud the **Comments on Response 2**, at the bottom of page 113.

Allow a further 10 minutes for students to look at **Response 2** and complete **Q9** and **Q10**, individually. Ask each student to write down one key tip they could take from this example response. Then feed back ideas as a class.

> **Give extra challenge** by allowing students to work collaboratively in small groups to work on the two responses. Groups could spend 20–25 minutes:
> - reading the responses in turn
> - working through the annotations
> - writing a series of tips for the class
> - using the responses to peer-evaluate each other's answers and add advice
> - matching the responses – both the examples and their own – against the Level criteria in the accredited mark scheme grids.

The two additional tasks on **Worksheet 3.8c–d**, which can be found on the accompanying CD-Rom, offer further opportunities for students to develop their skills. These could be used either as extension activities or for further consolidation and practice of the skills developed throughout Chapter 3.

4.1 Explain and comment on writers' use of language

Assessment objective

English Language

AO2 Explain, comment on and analyse how writers use language and structure to achieve effects and influence readers, using relevant subject terminology to support their views

GCSE examinations
- **English Language**
  Paper 1, Questions 2 and 3
- **English Language**
  Paper 2, Question 3

Differentiated learning outcomes
- **All students must** demonstrate awareness of the writer's viewpoint and be able to refer to one or two appropriate words and phrases from the text.
- **Most students should** clearly explain the writer's viewpoint, using some relevant examples from the text to support their ideas.
- **Some students could** offer interpretations of the writer's viewpoint and make detailed comments about a range of carefully selected words and phrases to support their interpretation.

Resources
- **Student Book**: pp. 116–19
- **Worksheet**: 4.1
- **PPT**: 4.1

Getting you thinking

Display **PPT 4.1, slide 1**. Ask the students to suggest words that they might use to describe what they see. Discuss as a class what it might feel like to live in a place like the one in the photograph.

Introduce the main questions the students should ask when reading a text for the first time: What is the writer's viewpoint? How does the writer want me to think or feel?

Big question | Start with the **Big question**: *Why does it matter which words and phrases the writer chooses?* Give the students a few minutes to discuss the question in pairs before they write a short answer.

Explain that you will be returning to this question at the end of the lesson.

Ask the students to read the first extract from *The Road to Wigan Pier* in the Student Book (page 116), or read it aloud if preferred. It might be useful to explain here that the image from **PPT 4.1** is of a pottery town at the time Orwell is describing.

Display **PPT 4.1, slide 2**, which is a checklist of strategies to use when reading a new text for the first time. Refer the students to **Q1** and **Q2**. Give the students five minutes to respond to these two questions in pairs or small groups, before sharing their ideas with the class. The responses could be collated onto a whiteboard for later reference.

Explore the skills

Read the next section of *The Road to Wigan Pier* (Student Book, page 117). Make sure the students are familiar with the terminology by drawing attention to the **Key term** explanation of 'adverbials'. It might also be useful to take an example of each of the other techniques listed in the first column of the table first before the students begin their independent work in **Q3**. The students can either copy the table or use **Worksheet 4.1** to complete the second column.

The **Key term** 'effects' is central to this part of the lesson – and to following lessons. Students can slip into making vague comments on effect without grasping exactly what it means. Using this point in the lesson to reinforce what effect means can pay dividends later on in the chapter, and elsewhere. Remind the students that it refers to the effect that the word or phrase has on the reader: the mood or tone it creates;

the thoughts and feelings it provokes in the reader; the picture the reader is encouraged to have of what is being described.

Develop the skills

Display **PPT 4.1, slide 3**, and ask the students to read the sample answer. As they read, ask for responses to **Q4**. This is an opportunity to dig deeply into the meaning of 'effect' and for the students to explore ways of writing effectively about it.

The students can now respond to **Q5** by returning to their table and selecting two examples that they identified to make notes about their effect. Stress at this point that they should focus on selecting useful material – a word/phrase that can be considered in detail and linked effectively to the writer's purpose – rather than aiming for blanket coverage. This is the most important part of becoming a good, critical writer. It doesn't matter if the students' tables are not complete; they are merely using the table to note down their ideas as part of a discerning selection process.

Allow 10 minutes for the students to complete **Q6**, working independently. Refer to the **Checklist for success** as an aide memoire that the students can use before they begin their written task. If time allows, select some responses to share with the class at this point, pointing out what is working well and where the students have dealt with the idea of effect clearly.

Apply the skills

Read out the main task and make a note of it on the board. Stress the key words in the task: 'how', 'use language' and 'viewpoint'. Elicit that 'language' means the effect of particular word choices as well as language techniques.

Look at the plan in the Student Book relating to Orwell's use of language (page 119) and identify the good practice: being clear about what the writer's viewpoint is (point 1) and how the effect is created (points 2–4).

Give the students 10 minutes to look at their notes and plan their responses (**Q7**). Emphasise again that it is about selecting the most useful, effective bits of evidence to illustrate how the writer's viewpoint is created rather than trying to cover every single word a writer uses.

> **Give extra support** by keeping the model answer on display so the students can use this to scaffold their own writing.
>
> **Give extra challenge** by asking the students to make sure they include relevant technical vocabulary from this section as part of the response.

Allow 15 minutes for the students to work independently on **Q8**, crafting their answer to the task. The students could use the first sentence of the plan in the Student Book (page 119) to help them start if necessary.

| **Big answer plenary** | Ask the students to use the **Check your progress** outcomes at the end of the section to decide which of the three outcomes they think their response has achieved. When they have done this, they should share their work with a partner and ask the partner also to match the response to the appropriate outcome. Ask the students to discuss their work in pairs and identify one strategy for improvement. Refer back to the **Big question** from the start of the lesson and ask the students to write a sentence beginning with: *The words and phrases a writer chooses are essential because…* |

4.2 Explain and comment on writers' use of language techniques

Assessment objective

English Language

AO2 Explain, comment on and analyse how writers use language and structure to achieve effects and influence readers, using relevant subject terminology to support their views

GCSE examinations

- **English Language**
  Paper 1, Questions 2 and 3
- **English Language**
  Paper 2, Question 3

Differentiated learning outcomes

- **All students must** show awareness of the writer's ideas and be able to identify two or more language techniques.
- **Most students should** demonstrate clear understanding of the writer's ideas and comment in some detail on how language techniques are used to communicate these ideas to the reader.
- **Some students could** show real engagement with the writer's ideas and be able to explain clearly how specific language techniques have been used to communicate these ideas to the reader.

Resources

- **Student Book**: pp. 120–3
- **PPT**: 4.2

Getting you thinking

Big question	Draw attention to the **Big question**: *How do writers use language techniques to influence the way you think about things?* Ask the students to explain what they think a 'language technique' might be. They may offer some examples. These could be collated on the board for reference as the lesson proceeds. At this stage it might be worth returning to the idea of 'effect' from the previous lesson and reminding the students that it is important to explain *what* the effect of a particular choice actually is, rather than simply saying 'the writer does this for effect'.

Ask for some definitions/examples of rhetorical techniques. A brief explanation of rhetoric (the art of persuasion) may be useful if the students are unfamiliar with the term. The **Key terms** box provides a definition to support this activity.

Ask the students to look at **Q1** and to identify the technique (rhetorical question).

Ask the students to discuss **Q2** and **Q3** in pairs before sharing ideas with the rest of the class. Students might mention ideas about hyperbole/exaggeration here, or the ridiculousness of the question, or the shock that might come from the mental picture created by the rhetorical question. Draw the students to the understanding that, clearly, the writer sees that the question is ridiculous, and therefore it doesn't require an answer.

Explore the skills

Allow 10 minutes for the students to work through **Q4**, either independently or in pairs. Ask them to make notes as they consider each question.

Give extra support by ensuring that the students understand the terms 'direct address' and 'first person'.

Give extra challenge by focusing attention on the third question, which is more challenging than the first two.

Develop the skills

Read the next two paragraphs of the article with the class. As you read, allow time to pause and consider each annotation.

Allow around 10 minutes for the class to read the rest of the article, and its annotations, independently. As they read, the students should be encouraged to consider which of the annotated features they think they might be able to write a short paragraph about. Encourage them to choose one or two features that can be linked really clearly to the writer's overall purpose.

> **Give extra support** by ensuring the students understand terminology used in the annotations, including 'colloquial' (explained in the **Key terms** box), 'personal' 'anecdote' and 'metaphor'.
>
> **Give extra challenge** by suggesting that the students think beyond the surface and try to identify other feelings that the writer may be expressing, such as anger, frustration or grief.

Show **PPT 4.2, slide 1**, which is a copy of the student's notes in the Student Book (page 122). Discuss the strengths and limitations of these notes, and ask the students to suggest ways in which the notes might be expanded and developed in more detail. For instance, the use of personal tone and anecdote encourages empathy from the reader, which means we are far more likely to take her viewpoint on board.

Allow five minutes for the students to complete **Q5**, selecting one language technique and writing their own paragraph about it. Show **PPT 4.2, slide 2**, which is a model paragraph that the students could read as preparation for this task.

While the students are completing **Q6**, the independent reading task, ask them to make notes as they proceed.

When the students have finished reading and identifying examples of language techniques, share some of their ideas with the class. They may point out:

- use of personal details again
- use of humour in the parenthetical aside
- use of punctuation for emphasis
- use of a very dramatic final image.

Apply the skills

Read the task in **Q7** and display it on **PPT 4.2, slide 3**. Read the **Checklist for success** with the students and ensure that they make a strong opening statement about the writer's viewpoint. It might be useful to share an opening sentence such as: 'The writer believes that the driving age should be raised.' Also point out that they should be selecting two or three techniques to write about in detail, rather than trying to cover every technique that has been identified.

Students may benefit from a time limit for completing the task; 15 minutes should be enough for the majority to write around a page. They should be encouraged to use the notes they have made, the notes in the Student Book and the ideas from class discussion to help them.

Big answer plenary	When the students have completed their writing task, ask them to look at the **Check your progress** ladder and write down which of the descriptors best applies to their work.
	Returning to the **Big question**, ask the students to think of one language technique that has been used in this article and how it has influenced the way they think about things. Select some students randomly to offer their ideas to the rest of the class.

4.3 Explain the ways writers use language to create character

Assessment objectives

English Language

AO2 Explain, comment on and analyse how writers use language and structure to achieve effects and influence readers, using relevant subject terminology to support their views

English Literature

AO2 Analyse the language, form and structure used by a writer to create meanings and effects, using relevant subject terminology where appropriate

GCSE examinations
- **English Language** Paper 1, Questions 2, 3
- **English Language** Paper 2, Question 3
- **English Literature** Paper 1, Section B
- **English Literature** Paper 2, Section A

Differentiated learning outcomes
- **All students must** be able to identify at least one method and demonstrate awareness of the effect the writer is trying to create.
- **Most students should** be able to choose clear supporting evidence to explain how one or more methods help to communicate the writer's ideas.
- **Some students could** select particular methods and analyse them in detail, linking them precisely to the overall effect being created.

Resources
- **Student Book**: pp. 124–7
- **Worksheet**: 4.3
- **PPT**: 4.1; 4.3

Other Student Book pages
- Lesson 2.3, pp. 50–3

Getting you thinking

Big question — Refer to the **Big question**: *Do you have to pay close attention to every single word when you're writing about a fiction text? How do you choose what to write about?* Ask the students to suggest some reasons why it would be a very bad idea to attempt to write about every word.

Ask for suggestions as to what might influence which words students choose to write about. The students might suggest 'level of complexity of vocabulary', and it would be useful to flag up this idea and explain that the harder vocabulary is not always the most interesting or effective to write about.

Refer the students back to **PPT 4.1, slide 2**: the reading checklist.

Ask the students to read the short extract from *A Christmas Carol* in the Student Book (page 124) and simply choose one word that stands out for them. Stress that there is no right or wrong answer. Collate the students' selections to return to later.

Draw attention to the **Key term** 'omniscient narrator' and clarify the meaning: the sense that the narrator is 'all knowing'. If required, refer to the difference between third- and first-person narration here, asking the students why a writer might decide to use one or the other and what the key differences are. Students might refer to the idea of distance created by third person, or how first person allows us to view events and ideas from the narrator's perspective (which may or may not be accurate).

Now ask the students to look at the description of a 'discerning, analytical reader'. Then give them five minutes to complete **Q1** and **Q2**. Share some responses before moving to the next part of the lesson.

Explore the skills

Ask the students to complete **Q3**, either using **Worksheet 4.3** or copying and completing the table in the Student Book (page 125). Refer to the **Key term** 'connotation' and make sure the students understand what this means.

Display **PPT 4.3**, **slide 1**, which unpicks one detail from the extract and illustrates the meaning of 'connotation'. When the students have read this example, ask them to complete **Q4**, choosing a different detail from the extract.

Now refer the students to the **Key term** box and ask them to read the definition of 'semantic field'. Ask them to read the next extract describing Scrooge, either individually or as a class, and ask the students for responses to **Q5** and **Q6**. This task could be completed as independent writing if preferred.

The students should be made aware of the idea of 'cold' and how this can have emotive connotations as well as literal ones. Asking the students to write a sentence at this stage using both the **Key terms** could be a useful consolidation exercise: 'Dickens, the omniscient narrator, uses a semantic field of cold, which has connotations of …'. Stress the importance of explaining the effect of the semantic field, and not simply identifying that it exists.

Develop the skills

Refer back to the idea of narrative perspective to remind the students of the difference between first-person and third-person narrative. You may find it useful to refer back to Lesson 2.3 on pages 50–3 of the Student Book.

Ask the students to read the extract from *Mr Pip* by Lloyd Jones, either independently or as a class. Ask them to complete **Q7a**, thinking about the differences between the effect of narrative perspective in this extract compared to the extract from *A Christmas Carol*. What difference does it make having a first-person narrator? Draw the students into considering whether it means the reader can find out more, or less, about the various characters.

As preparation for **Q7b**, ask the students to think about what the reader sees that might be different from what the narrator, Matilda, sees. Is the reader being drawn to admire Dolores? Draw attention to the words and phrases that suggest Dolores's strength and her love for Matilda, for example 'My mum smiled back at me'.

Apply the skills

This task draws together the learning from the lesson. Remind the students about the 'magnifying glass' idea and how they approached the first part of the lesson, selecting one particular word to comment on. Remind them of the **Big question** and how selecting a good detail to write about is dependent on how much they can say about the effectiveness of that detail.

If preferred, students could work in small groups or pairs on this part of the lesson.

> **Give extra challenge** by drawing attention to the phraseology in the final paragraph. Notice how many words and phrases suggest that Matilda is merely observing her mother ('tended to look' / 'looked' / 'appeared to be'), rather than trying to understand or empathise with her. Encourage students to think how this might suggest that the narrator's perspective is biased or flawed.

Big answer plenary	Return to the **Big question** by asking for examples of details students selected. Draw attention to the range of details used in the class. Were some particular details used more than others?
	Ask students to pair up with someone who used the same detail and read each other's ideas. If there is time, students could then rewrite their response, using both their own and their partner's ideas.
	Ask students to use the **Check your progress** outcomes at the end of the section to assess their own work and their partner's.

4.4 Explain and comment on writers' use of structural features

Assessment objectives

English Language

AO2 Explain, comment on and analyse how writers use language and structure to achieve effects and influence readers, using relevant subject terminology to support their views

English Literature

AO2 Analyse the language, form and structure used by a writer to create meanings and effects, using relevant subject terminology where appropriate

GCSE examinations

- **English Language** Paper 1, Questions 2, 3
- **English Language** Paper 2, Question 3
- **English Literature** Paper 2, Sections A and B

Differentiated learning outcomes

- **All students must** be able to identify one or more structural technique and attempt to explain its effect on the reader.
- **Most students should** identify the writer's purpose and viewpoint and clearly explain how a range of structural techniques help to demonstrate this purpose / viewpoint.
- **Some students could** select one or two particular structural features and present a detailed commentary on how they work to reinforce the writer's purpose and viewpoint.

Resources

- **Student Book**: pp. 128–31
- **Worksheet**: 4.4
- **PPT**: 4.4

Getting you thinking

Big question Read the **Big question**: *What does 'structure' mean and why is it important?* Ask for students' suggestions as to what 'structure' means in this context. The students could either offer ideas verbally for collation on the board, or write their ideas as a list or in sentences. At this stage their suggestions may refer to aspects such as sentence length, paragraphs, beginnings and endings. You can return to the second part of the question – 'why is it important?' – at the end of the lesson.

Refer to the opening paragraph, which identifies some structural features, and make sure the students have read the **Key term** 'cohesion'. Identify the learning point: the actual words themselves are only one part of the way a writer creates meaning.

Display **PPT 4.4, slide 1**, and ask the students to complete **Q1** – the spider diagram – using the ideas in the Student Book (pages 128–9) as well as those that have come out of the initial class discussion.

Explore the skills

Reiterate the main point from this section of the lesson, which is how structure can be used to shape understanding.

Have the students complete **Q2** by reading the extract from *DNA* in pairs, in a variety of different ways. Allow at least five minutes for the students to practise this, before asking for feedback on where the pace might be different, where the overlaps might be, and what might change in terms of mood by altering the pace at different moments.

Discuss **Q3** and ask the students to suggest responses to this question. They should identify that it is Mark who has the information and Jan who is in the dark.

Allow the students 10-15 minutes to complete **Q4a**, **Q4b**, **Q5** and **Q6**. This could be done independently or as discussion in pairs or groups.

When the students feed back their ideas from this part of the lesson, it might be useful to draw their attention to the ways in which Kelly is creating a sense of tension. Also, highlight how the use of unresolved, unfinished questions creates a sense of mystery and invites the audience to want to know more about what has happened and what this conversation is about. You might also want to draw attention to the ways in which the unanswered questions suggest a shared knowledge between Jan and Mark.

Develop the skills

Display **PPT 4.4**, **slide 2**, and read the extract from *A Walk in the Woods*. Read the **Key term** description of 'structural features' and see if there are any ideas here that the students could add to their spider diagram.

Give the students 10 minutes to complete **Q7**, either using **Worksheet 4.4** or copying and completing the table in the Student Book (page 130).

Have the students complete **Q8**. Ask them to look at how the final phrase 'chronic depression' is led up to. They may notice how the rest of the paragraph builds towards this as an inevitable consequence of the rest of the ailments being listed.

Q9a asks the students to comment on the overall tone of the passage, and **Q9b** focuses attention on how the structural features add to the tone. Once the students have established the gentle tone of humour and irony, they can then suggest which particular structural features create this. For example:

* The long list of unpronounceable diseases suggests the fear he has for this place.
* The short sentence 'There is no known cure.' in the centre of the paragraph reinforces the sense of danger.
* The list of symptoms further reiterates how focused he is on the dangers.

> **Give extra support** by focusing on how the humour is created by the contrast between what should be feelings of excitement about this trip and Bryson's actual obsessing about its potential dangers.
>
> **Give extra challenge** by drawing attention to the use of dashes and how the pauses they create add even more humour to the passage, as the various lists lead up to the final, almost inevitable, 'chronic depression'. What effect does this have on the reader's impression of Bryson? Does he sound like an intrepid explorer?

Read the sample student response and annotations (Student Book, page 131). Draw attention to the ways this response deals with the writer's purpose by identifying one structural technique (use of sentence structure), followed by explanations of two effects created by this feature. Then at the end the student links back to the writer's purpose. Explain that this is important as it shows focus on the effect (from Lesson 4.2) of the structural technique, rather than simply identifying it.

Apply the skills

Display **PPT 4.4**, **slide 3**, which is the main task for this lesson. Give the students 15 minutes to complete **Q10**, using their notes and the student response from the previous question as a model for how to structure their answer.

Big answer plenary	Return to the **Big question** from the start of the lesson. The second part of the question asked the students to think about why structure is important. Ask the students to write a sentence explaining what they have learned from this lesson about the importance of structure in aiding meaning. They could use the scaffold: *'Structure refers to … and it is important because …'*. Ask the students to use the **Check your progress** outcomes to assess their written work and decide which of the three outcomes they think they have achieved.

4.5 Explain and comment on writers' use of openings

Assessment objectives

English Language

AO2 Explain, comment on and analyse how writers use language and structure to achieve effects and influence readers, using relevant subject terminology to support their views

English Literature

AO2 Analyse the language, form and structure used by a writer to create meanings and effects, using relevant subject terminology where appropriate

GCSE examinations

- **English Language** Paper 1, Questions 2, 3
- **English Language** Paper 2, Question 3
- **English Literature** Paper 1, Section B
- **English Literature** Paper 2, Section A

Differentiated learning outcomes

- **All students must** be able to identify one or more elements from the opening to a narrative and make straightforward comments on effect.
- **Most students should** infer some meaning from details in the opening to a text and use relevant examples to support their interpretations.
- **Some students could** interpret more subtle inferences a writer is making in the introduction to a text and use precise references to support their interpretations.

Resources

- **Student Book**: pp. 132–5
- **Worksheet**: 4.5
- **PPT**: 4.5

Getting you thinking

Big question

Read the **Big question**: *Why is the opening of a story important?* Ask for some verbal responses to this question, or allow a couple of minutes for students to write a sentence beginning with *'The opening of a story is really important because…'* before asking students to share with the class. Either collate ideas for reference later or ask students to make a note of the two or three ideas that they like the best.

Allow a few minutes for students to discuss **Q1** in pairs before feeding ideas back to the class.

Ask students to look at the seaside picture in the Student Book (page 133) and to write down three words to describe the mood being suggested by this picture.

Now read the opening of 'The Way the Pit Works', either from the Student Book (page 132) or on **PPT 4.5, slide 1**. Next, read the annotations on the sentence shown in the Student Book and draw attention to the fact that this student has found three separate things to infer from the one sentence.

Give students five minutes to complete **Q2b** independently.

Ask students to read the second paragraph of the story starting 'By eight o'clock…' (page 133) and to complete **Q3**. They can either read from the Student Book or look at **PPT 4.5, slide 2**. **Slide 3** has a copy of the table, which you could show students before they read the second paragraph to give them an idea of what they will be looking for.

Q4a, 4b and **4c** could either be completed independently or through class discussion. It would be useful to draw out how the writer is creating quite an ominous mood and how there are hints in these opening paragraphs that the story is not going to end happily.

Explore the skills

Draw attention to the **Key term** 'infer' and take a moment to clarify the difference between this term and 'imply' – the easiest way for students to remember is that the writer 'implies' and the reader 'infers'.

Read the opening few lines from *Jane Eyre* and discuss **Q5** as a class. You may want to collate the answers on the board.

Then ask students to complete **Q6**; they can copy the table in the Student Book (page 134) or you can hand out copies of **Worksheet 4.5**. They can then use their ideas to answer **Q7**.

Develop the skills

Read the next section from *Jane Eyre*, either from the Student Book (page 135) or from **PPT 4.5, slide 4**. When responding to **Q8**, you might want to draw attention to the vocabulary used – 'mama', 'reclined', 'darlings' – and how this suggests that Mrs Reed is a cloying, rather overprotective mother.

Q9 requires students to think carefully about the narrative perspective. For example, they could notice how Jane manages to imply criticism with the reference to the cousins 'for the time neither quarrelling nor crying', and also how Jane focuses on her separateness or distance from the others.

> **Give extra support** by focusing on the last few words. Do these emphasise the fact that Jane is neither 'contented' nor 'happy'? Why might this be? Ask students to use this detail to write a sentence inferring that Jane is unhappy or discontented and suggest a possible reason why.
>
> **Give extra challenge** by drawing attention to the ironic stance of the narrator and the oblique criticism of her aunt and cousins. How is the writer implying criticism of these characters?

Apply the skills

Ask students to complete **Q10**, using the table in **Worksheet 4.5** to add any further information about Mrs Reed and Jane. Students might notice how Jane challenges her aunt rather than merely accepting the censure, or how Mrs Reed does not approve of being challenged by a child. Some may also notice that Jane prefers solitude, and possibly link this to the idea that she will need to become independent and not reliant upon anyone.

The main task (**Q11**) offers students the opportunity to put their notes and ideas into a short piece of writing, using the guidance in the **Checklist for success**. If preferred, this could be a longer task, possibly a homework activity.

Q12 offers the opportunity for students to extend their work by writing a further paragraph about how Charlotte Brontë engages the reader in this opening. You may prefer to reserve this activity for more confident students.

Big answer plenary	Return to the **Big question** and ask students to share ideas about what they have learned about the opening of a story.
	As a plenary task, invite students to write a sentence or two to a budding writer, giving advice on how to create an effective opening and explaining why this is a crucial element in a story.
	Ask the students to consider their written responses to **Q11** (and **Q12**, if completed) and decide which rung of the **Check your progress** ladder they feel most accurately describes their attainment.

4.6 Explain and comment on the ways writers create meanings and effects with structure and form

Assessment objectives

English Language

AO2 Explain, comment on and analyse how writers use language and structure to achieve effects and influence readers, using relevant subject terminology to support their views

English Literature

AO2 Analyse the language, form and structure used by a writer to create meanings and effects, using relevant subject terminology where appropriate

GCSE examinations

- **English Language**
  Paper 1, Questions 2, 3
- **English Language**
  Paper 2, Question 3
- **English Literature**
  Paper 1, Section B
- **English Literature**
  Paper 2, Section A

Differentiated learning outcomes

- **All students must** be able to identify at least one structural feature and comment on the effect it creates, using the correct terminology.
- **Most students should** select some features of structure and form and be able to clearly explain the effects created by the writer, using the correct terminology.
- **Some students could** analyse two or more particular features of structure and form in detail, linking them precisely to the overall effect being created and using technical vocabulary as a precise shorthand to explain effects.

Resources

- **Student Book**: pp. 136–9
- **PPT**: 4.6

Getting you thinking

Big question

Refer to the **Big question**: *What is the difference between structure and form, and why do they matter?* This question is designed to get students thinking about the differences between the two terms 'structure' and 'form'. It might be useful to spend a moment recapping on Lesson 4.4 in terms of the different ways in which structure can be manipulated in order to influence meaning. Ask students to look again at their spider diagrams from that lesson.

Read the explanation of 'form' in the Student Book (page 136) and ask students to complete **Q1**. One way of completing this task is to ask students to physically draw an example of each form first of all, then annotate it to describe the particular features that indicate which form it is.

Now read **Q2**; students could either do this question independently before feeding back, or the question could be used as a stimulus for a short class discussion.

Explore the skills

Ask students to read the Shakespeare sonnet, either from the Student Book (page 137) or from **PPT 4.6, slide 1**. Because part of the aim is to be aware of the rhythm, it might be useful to ask students to work in pairs on this task, reading the poem aloud and noticing the rhythm as well as any other features of form, such as the sonnet's fourteen lines or the rhyme scheme.

Q3a and **Q3b** are short comprehension exercises. Students should work individually at first and then discuss their ideas with a partner.

Students can then work on **Q4**, either in their pairs or individually. Once they have answered all parts of the question, they can write a definition of a Shakespearean sonnet. Bear in mind that the support for this is in the Student Book so you may want to ensure they have the relevant page closed so they don't merely copy the information there.

It might be useful to explain that there are other forms of sonnet: the Petrarchan sonnet is organised into two stanzas of eight and six lines respectively, rather than the Shakespearean sonnet with its structure of four–four–four–two lines.

The **Key terms** box explains 'iambic pentameter'. Students could select a further line from the sonnet and mark it up in a similar way, showing where the stresses are.

Develop the skills

Read the poem 'Anne Hathaway', either from the Student Book (page 138) or from **PPT 4.6, slide 2**. In order to contextualise the ideas in the poem, ensure that students read the explanation of 'second-best bed' and understand that Shakespeare could be said to be offering a very romantic message to his wife in this detail from his will.

Students should then complete **Q5** and **Q6**, either individually or in pairs. For **Q5** the main point is that she is describing the wonderful relationship she shared with Shakespeare. The key learning point from **Q6** is that there is clearly a warm, loving relationship being described here, and the choice of form is significant in that message to the reader.

Students might suggest that:

- the choice of form links the speaker closely with her husband's preferred method, showing a close bond between them
- sonnets are traditionally associated with love, again suggesting the bond of love between them.

Q7 gives students the opportunity to draw their ideas together. The key point is that the form of this poem is very significant. Ask students to keep referring back to the definition of a sonnet as they approach this question. Remind students of the importance of being able to explain the impact of, or rationale behind, the poet's conscious choices of form and structure, rather than merely identifying what the features are.

> **Give extra support** by showing students the strength of the rhyme in the final couplet and asking for a suggestion as to whether this means the love is strong or weak.
>
> **Give extra challenge** by asking students to see what else they notice: is the rhyme scheme stronger in certain places than others? Might this suggest that hers is a 'version' of a sonnet rather than the genuine article?

Apply the skills

Students can now use their notes and ideas to complete the main task (**Q8**). This would make an ideal extended homework task of around 300 words. The **Checklist for success** highlights the importance of linking comments about form and structure to the actual content and ideas of the poem.

Big answer plenary	Return to the **Big question** and ask students to see if they can now answer the question in one sentence. They will probably understand by now that there is a lot of crossover between the two terms, in that structure plays a part in, or helps to determine, form. Form generally refers to aspects such as genre, type, style and shape, whereas structure refers to particular cohesive features. Finally, students should use the **Check your progress** ladders at the end of the section to assess their work and set themselves a target for improvement.

4.7 Apply your skills to English Language and English Literature tasks

Assessment objectives

English Language

AO2 Explain, comment on and analyse how writers use language and structure to achieve effects and influence readers, using relevant subject terminology to support their views

English Literature

AO2 Analyse the language, form and structure used by a writer to create meanings and effects, using relevant subject terminology where appropriate

GCSE examinations

- **English Language** Paper 1, Questions 2, 3
- **English Language** Paper 2, Question 3
- **English Literature** Paper 1, Section B
- **English Literature** Paper 2, Section A

Differentiated learning outcomes

- **All students must** be able to identify the writer's ideas and viewpoint and select two or more features of language and structure for straightforward comment.
- **Most students should** be able to explain the writer's ideas and viewpoint clearly, selecting relevant material to comment on and explaining how this helps to present the ideas/viewpoint.
- **Some students could** infer meaning from a range of subtle clues, reading between the lines and using quite precise selection(s) of detail to support their interpretation of ideas and viewpoint.

Resources

- **Student Book**: pp. 140–52
- **Worksheets**: 4.7a–d (4.7c–d are available on the CD-Rom only)
- **PPT**: 4.7

Introduction

This section is designed to enable the students to draw together their learning from the chapter as a whole and undertake some examination-style independent assessments. This section may take about three lessons if the tasks themselves are completed in class.

Display **PPT 4.7, slide 1**, and ask the students to write a sentence in their own words explaining what skills they have to demonstrate for AO2.

Explain that AO2 refers to anything that the writer has done deliberately in order to make meaning; anything that shows understanding that the writer is 'the maker of the text' and as such, is making conscious decisions about particular words, particular techniques, particular structural features and the order in which they are used.

Responding to an English Language task about language

Have the students complete **Q1**. Display **PPT 4.7, slide 2**, and ask them to read the passage from *Bloodline*, using either the Student Book (pages 140–2) or **Worksheet 4.7a**. At this stage they are gaining an overview of the extract. Encourage them to highlight, annotate and underline anything they notice. Remind the students about what they have learned in previous lessons, in particular that making good selections of specific details that can be commented on in detail is very important when working with previously unseen material in examination conditions.

Alternatively, the students could work in pairs or small groups, annotating the extract together.

Display **PPT 4.7, slide 3**, and ask the students to select three details from the extract that they feel they could comment on in detail.

At this stage, ask the students to complete **Q2**, taking no more than 10 minutes.

The students could then complete **Q3** and **Q4** by reading the two sample responses in the Student Book (pages 143-5), and discuss the relative merits of the two responses. The mark schemes for GCSE English Language could be copied and given to the students. For each response ask them to work up the descriptors like a ladder, answering yes or no as to whether they see the skills in place. For **Response 1** they are likely to see Level 2 descriptors in place; for **Response 2** they are likely to see Level 3 descriptors evident. Focusing on the descriptors will help the students as they tackle **Q5**.

As a variation on **Q4**, the students could take one section from **Response 1** and rewrite it, using the comments on **Response 2** in order to improve it.

Responding to an English Language task about structure

Display **PPT 4.7, slide 8**, which is a copy of the second task (Student Book, page 145). This time, the students can work independently to respond to this question on whole-text structure. Ask the students to think about how they would approach the task (**Q6**) and draw attention to the **Checklist for success** from the Student Book (also on **PPT 4.7, slide 4**). Explain that this can be used to scaffold and organise their response.

When the students have finished this task, read the two sample responses in the Student Book (pages 146-8). **Q7-Q10** take the students through this process and can be used to identify:

- one element of their own work that they are particularly pleased with
- one element of their own work that needs to be improved.

Responding to an English Literature task

Display **PPT 4.7, slide 9**, and point out that even though this is referring to a very different genre of text, the skills required for reading are exactly the same.

For **Q1**, either read the poem (Student Book, page 148) with the class or allow around five minutes for independent reading. If using **Worksheet 4.7b**, the students can mirror the activity from earlier in the lesson, annotating or highlighting any features they notice. This is a useful message as it reinforces the transferability of reading skills, and reminds students that the overall approach is the same regardless of form, genre or examination question.

The next task in this section (**Q2**) is for the students to write an independent response to the poem 'First Love'. Display **PPT 4.7, slide 10**, which is a copy of the task from the Student Book (page 148).

If you prefer, ask the students to work through **Q3-Q5** first, reading **Response 1** and **Response 2** in the Student Book (pages 149-51) before they undertake their own response to this task. They could select one element of good practice and aim to incorporate it into their response. The GCSE English Literature mark scheme for Paper 2 Section B could be given to the students to place the responses into the appropriate Level (Level 3 for **Response 1**, Level 4 for **Response 2**).

The two additional tasks on **Worksheet 4.7c-d**, which can be found on the accompanying CD-Rom, offer further opportunities for the students to develop their skills. These could either be used as extension activities or for further consolidation and practice of the skills developed throughout Chapter 4.

5.1 Understand and define context

Assessment objective

English Literature

AO3 Show understanding of the relationships between texts and the contexts in which they were written

GCSE examinations
- English Literature Paper 2, Section A

Differentiated learning outcomes
- **All students must** be able to explain contextual ideas and give one or two examples from the story.
- **Most students should** be able to explain how contextual ideas influenced the story.
- **Some students could** link the story closely to contextual ideas.

Resources
- **Student Book**: pp. 154–7
- **Worksheet**: 5.1
- **PPT**: 5.1

Getting you thinking

Big question | Read the **Big question**: *What is context and how can it help you to understand literary texts?* Ask the students to suggest what extra things you might need to know about a writer, or about the historical/cultural/social period a text has been written or set in, in order to understand it more clearly.

Display **PPT 5.1, slide 1**, and ask the students to complete **Q1** by selecting the statement that they agree with most strongly.

Feed back as a class, and encourage the students to explain why they disagree with the ones they did not select.

Now ask the students to look at the list of four famous stories on page 154 of the Student Book, and complete **Q2**. The students could do this in pairs or small groups if preferred. Feed back ideas as a class. Ensure all the students understand what is meant by the **Key term** 'allegories'.

> **Give extra challenge** by asking the students to think of another allegorical story they know. What is the hidden meaning in the story?

Explore the skills

Display **PPT 5.1, slide 2**, which is a picture of Napoleon from *Animal Farm*, and ask the students to complete **Q3** in pairs, using the summary of *Animal Farm* on page 155 of the Student Book.

Feed back ideas as a class. The students might notice that:

- The story starts positively as the animals take over the farm and create a more equal world.
- This does not last long because of the pigs and their lust for power.
- When the pigs take power, they use it to control the other animals for their own purposes.
- The pigs end up behaving exactly like Mr Jones the farmer.
- The overall moral could be that power corrupts.

Develop the skills

PPT

Display **PPT 5.1, slide 3**, which is a picture of Stalin. Ask the students to read the summary of events in twentieth-century Russia/USSR on page 155 of the Student Book and to compare it with the summary of *Animal Farm*, making notes on any similarities they find (**Q4**).

Feed back as class. The students' suggested connections might include:

- Both places – Russia and Animal Farm – are ruled by a wealthy elite, and the ordinary people are very poor.
- Revolutions are inspired by political ideas (Karl Marx/Old Major).
- Both are renamed after the revolution (USSR/Animal Farm).
- Things begin well in both places after the revolution.
- Power is seized by one person (Stalin/Napoleon).
- Napoleon and Stalin both get rid of their respective rivals (Trotsky/Snowball).
- Both set up secret police forces (KGB/dogs).
- Things become worse for ordinary people than before the revolution.

Apply the skills

Draw attention to the main learning in this section: that the contextual ideas inform your reading of the text and that it is vital to use the text as the main focus when writing about context. To illustrate this, read Orwell's quotation from the preface of *Animal Farm* on page 156 of the Student Book.

Now read aloud the extract from *Animal Farm* on page 156 of the Student Book.

Allow 15–20 minutes for the students to complete the main task independently, using evidence to support their points (**Q5**).

Before the students begin, refer them to the **Checklist for success** on page 157.

PPT

Give extra support by displaying **PPT 5.1, slide 4**, which contains some sentence stems to support the written task.

Give extra challenge by providing the students with a copy of **Worksheet 5.1**, which contains further reading about Orwell and how *Animal Farm* has been received since its publication.

Big answer plenary	Ask the students to answer the following question: *Why did Orwell choose to write this as a story that could be understood by anybody with a basic education rather than just telling people how bad Stalin was?* This question asks the students to think more deeply about ideas about empathy and engagement through narrative. Refer back to the **Big question** and ask the students to write a sentence explaining how knowledge of political/social/historical context aids understanding of *Animal Farm*. What other situations could *Animal Farm* be an allegory of?

5.2 Relate themes and language to context

Assessment objectives

English Literature

AO2 Analyse the language, form and structure used by a writer to create meanings and effects, using relevant subject terminology where appropriate

AO3 Show understanding of the relationships between texts and the contexts in which they were written

GCSE examinations
- English Literature Paper 1, Section A

Differentiated learning outcomes
- **All students must** be able to explain at least one idea about context from one of the two extracts, using some relevant evidence.
- **Most students should** be able to explain ideas and language choices clearly, making clear links to context.
- **Some students could** use context to help them examine ideas and language choice in detail.

Resources
- **Student Book**: pp. 158–61
- **PPT**: 5.2

Getting you thinking

| Big question | Read the **Big question**: *How can understanding ideas and attitudes from the time in which a text was written help us to understand the story and its themes?* Then briefly discuss the question with the class and elicit some initial responses. |

Ask the students to complete **Q1** by ranking the occupations in order of importance. Do not give them any criteria at this stage. If preferred, the students could undertake this activity as a group discussion.

Feed back as a class, and ask the students to explain how they ranked the occupations. Criteria might include:

- how much each job pays
- how much status each job has
- how much use each job is to society
- how hard you have to work at each job
- how much talent you have to have
- how clever you need to be.

Explore the skills

In order for the students to understand Shakespeare better, it is important that they learn that the social structure was much more rigid in Shakespeare's time. They must also understand that if the social structure was disturbed, it was believed that this could lead to other disturbances in nature.

Display **PPT 5.2, slide 1**, and explain to the students that during Shakespeare's time, by and large, people kept their social status from birth for the rest of their lives. Ask the students to look at the descriptions of the top and bottom ranks in society, and to suggest advantages and disadvantages of this system (**Q2**). Responses could include:

- Advantage – society is more stable.
- Advantage – you do not see yourself as a failure if your social status is low; it is not your fault.
- Disadvantage – you are not rewarded for your talents and abilities, so what is the point of trying to improve?
- Disadvantage – lots of talent is wasted.
- Disadvantage – people do not earn status so society is very unfair.

Now read the summary of the story of *Macbeth* and the paragraph that follows it on page 159 in the Student Book. The point to reinforce here is that people in Shakespeare's time believed that upsetting the natural order led to disturbances in nature or in the wider world.

Now read the extract from Act 2 Scene 3 of *Macbeth* on page 159, and ask the students to identify the natural disturbances Lennox is describing (**Q3**). They may pick out:

- chimneys blown down
- lamentings in the air
- strange screams of death
- obscure bird clamoured
- earth shaking.

For **Q4**, ask the students to identify the specific words and phrases that add to the idea of the events being extreme and unnatural. Draw attention to particular words and phrases that suggest danger, noise and confusion.

Now ask the students to link the language being used to the ideas in the passage (**Q5**). Key phrases include:

- 'strange screams of death'
- 'prophesying, with accents terrible'
- 'the obscure bird' (owl).

Develop the skills

Allow 10 minutes for the students to complete **Q6** and **Q7** in pairs.

If preferred, the students could read the extract aloud in their pairs a few times, stressing any words/phrases that sound particularly linked with danger, death, noise or confusion. The students may identify the following points:

- It is the worst night the old man has encountered in all his years on earth.
- It is dark in the daytime.
- A falcon was killed by an owl.
- The king's horses went mad and ate each other.

Apply the skills

Read through the task with the students (**Q8**). Then display **PPT 5.2, slide 2**, which is a copy of the sample response on page 161 of the Student Book. Draw attention to the annotations that highlight the strengths of the response and ask the students to read these carefully before answering **Q9**, either individually or in pairs.

Allow at least 15 minutes for the students to write their own independent response to **Q10**. Before they begin, remind the students of the ideas from the lesson (the natural order being disturbed) and how to structure a response (referring to the model answer on page 161).

> **Give extra support** by selecting three key quotations from the extract on page 159 only.
>
> **Give extra challenge** by encouraging the students to link language and ideas from both extracts in their answer.

Big answer plenary	Ask the students to work in pairs, reading each other's response to **Q10** and identifying three things from their partner's work that they think are as good as, or better than, what is written in the model paragraph on page 161 of the Student Book.

5.3 Relate context to language

Assessment objectives

English Literature

AO2 Analyse the language, form and structure used by a writer to create meanings and effects, using relevant subject terminology where appropriate

AO3 Show understanding of the relationships between texts and the contexts in which they were written

GCSE examinations
- English Literature
  Paper 1, Section A

Differentiated learning outcomes

- **All students must** be able to pick out some interesting choices of language and explain what they might mean; they must be able to refer to some ideas about context to help.
- **Most students should** be able to explain clearly the effects of some language choices and sometimes link them to context.
- **Some students could** examine language choices in some detail and use ideas about context to help them develop their ideas.

Resources
- **Student Book**: pp. 162–5
- **Worksheet**: 5.3
- **PPT**: 5.3

Getting you thinking

Big question — Read the **Big question**: *How do the ideas of the time affect the language of the text?* Elicit some initial thoughts from the class.

In groups of three or four, ask the students to read the 'news report' at the top of page 162 of the Student Book. One student could take the role of a newsreader, while the other members of the group are watching/listening to the 'broadcast'. Ask them to discuss how this news might be received.

Now ask the students to complete **Q1**, either as a short written exercise or as a class discussion.

Read the information about Darwin on page 162 of the Student Book aloud to the class. Ask the students to complete **Q2**, either as a class discussion or as a short written activity. It might be useful to reinforce the idea that more people in the Western world held Christian beliefs at the time that Darwin was publishing his ideas.

Explore the skills

Now identify the key learning for this section: that when writing about context, it is important to link your ideas to the text and to the writer's language.

Read the extract from *Dr Jekyll and Mr Hyde* on page 163 and ask the students to complete **Q3** and **Q4**. The students may do this as a bulleted list or in complete sentences. The students may pick out the following points:

- Everyone notices that there is something not right about Mr Hyde, but they can't explain what exactly it is ('pale and dwarfish', 'an impression of deformity', 'a displeasing smile', 'murderous mixture', 'husky, whispering and somewhat broken voice').
- Hyde is linked to an earlier form of man ('troglodytic').
- Hyde is linked to the devil ('Satan's signature upon [his] face').

Develop the skills

For **Q5**, read the opening paragraphs of **Develop the skills** on page 164 and ensure the students understand the context of the quotations in the table. Then ask them to complete the table, using **Worksheet 5.3**, by commenting on the effects of the language. The students may notice:

- the use of verbs that are powerful and reflect an obsession with the physical nature of Hyde to the exclusion of rationality and thought: 'stamping', 'brandishing', 'clubbed'
- that Hyde is linked to violent natural events: 'great flame', 'storm of blows'
- the use of metaphorical language: 'ape-like fury', 'storm of blows'.

Apply the skills

Display **PPT 5.3, slide 1**, the model student answer, and discuss the positive and negative aspects of the response, using the annotations either in the PPT slide or on pages 164–5 of the Student Book. Ask the students to identify two things they feel the model answer has done particularly well, and set themselves these two targets to aim for in their own writing (**Q6**).

Now ask the students to complete the main writing task (**Q7**). Before they begin, refer them to the **Checklist for success** on page 165 of the Student Book and remind them that the annotations in the model answer are designed to help them with this task. This could either be completed as an independent writing activity or as a homework task.

If **Q7** is undertaken as a class activity, display **PPT 5.3, slide 2**, the **Checklist for success**, in order to scaffold the writing task.

> **Give extra support** by suggesting the students use the opening stem in **Checklist for success** on page 165 of the Student Book.
>
> **Give extra challenge** by asking the students to link Stevenson's portrayal of Hyde closely to nineteenth-century scientific and religious ideas.

Big answer plenary	Ask the students to use the **Check your progress** outcomes to self-assess their work. You may wish to use WWW (*What Went Well*) / EBI (*Even Better If*) as a structure within which the students can set themselves a target for the next lesson.

5.4 Explore setting as context

Assessment objective

English Literature

AO3 Show understanding of the relationships between texts and the contexts in which they were written

GCSE examinations
- English Literature Paper 2, Section A

Differentiated learning outcomes
- **All students must** be able to incorporate some references to contextual ideas into their response.
- **Most students should** explain contextual ideas clearly and link them to the text and to the writer's ideas.
- **Some students could** use context about historical settings in order to develop ideas about the text in detail.

Resources
- **Student Book**: pp. 166–9
- **Worksheet**: 5.4
- **PPT**: 5.4

Getting you thinking

Big question	Draw students' attention to the **Big question**: *If you want to write a political play to change people's attitudes in the modern world, why set it in the past?* Ask for some initial responses. It is important to clarify that 'setting' here refers to time as opposed to place. It might be useful to refer to other works that the students have studied that were set in a different time to when they were written.

Read the list of events on page 166 of the Student Book. Ask the students to work in small groups to place the events on a timeline similar to that on page 166 (**Q1**). This activity could be scaffolded with ICT access if available, or the students could use their smartphones to search for the information they might need.

Give extra support by telling students that each of the longer lines marks the start of a new decade, and they should be labelled as 1910, 1920, 1930, 1940 and 1950.

Display **PPT 5.4, slide 1**, which provides the date of each event. Ask the students to self-mark/correct their work.

Discuss with the class what Priestley's world might be like and what kinds of things might be preoccupying him and his audience: issues of social welfare, concerns that capitalism leads to war, and disasters like the 'unsinkable' *Titanic*, etc.

Explore the skills

Read the two introductory paragraphs of **Explore the skills** on page 166.

Then display **PPT 5.4, slide 2**, the picture of a pantomime, to illustrate the concept of dramatic irony. Explain that this can be seen as a key factor in Priestley's decision to set *An Inspector Calls* in 1912 because his audience would have known that *The Titanic* had sunk and that World War I started shortly afterwards. The characters in the play, however, do not know this; therefore the dramatic irony is used to draw attention to whether the characters and their respective ideologies are right or wrong.

Read aloud Arthur Birling's speech from page 167 of the Student Book and give the students 10–15 minutes to complete **Q2**, using **Worksheet 5.4**.

Now ask the students to complete **Q3**, using their tables in **Q2**, which should provide all the evidence they need to complete the task. A typical response might focus on the fact that Arthur is wrong about almost everything he says in this speech, and that

Priestley's audience would recognise this. This would therefore discredit Birling's capitalist views.

> **Give extra support** by reading through the first line of the table on page 167 of the Student Book, which models how to answer **Q3**, and discuss the ideas that arise from it.
>
> **Give extra challenge** by encouraging the students to use the term 'dramatic irony' in their response.

Develop the skills

Display **PPT 5.4, slide 3**, which contains Inspector Goole's final speech from page 168 of the Student Book.

Ask the students to come up to the board and highlight words and phrases that give the Inspector's political views. They could also start to suggest how these views are different from Arthur Birling's.

Now ask the students to complete **Q4** and **Q5**, using the information from this discussion. Answers might include:

- The Inspector holds opposite views to Arthur Birling.
- Priestley is using dramatic irony to show that the socialist views he holds were proved to be correct by history.

Apply the skills

Read the main task with class.

Display **PPT 5.4, slide 4**, the sample student answer, and discuss the positive and negative aspects of the response, using the annotations either in the PPT slide or on pages 168–9 of the Student Book.

Use the annotations to guide the students towards appropriate writing targets for the main task. Ask the students to identify two things they feel the sample answer has done particularly well, and set themselves these two targets to aim for in their own writing (**Q6**). Then ask them to identify two places where the ideas in the sample answer could be more developed (**Q7**). Refer them also to the **Checklist for success** on page 169, which reminds students of the key assessment objectives for this type of writing activity.

Allow about 30 minutes for the students to complete the final written task (**Q8**). Alternatively, it could be set as a homework task, in which case a writing plan could be produced in class.

Big answer plenary	Return to the **Big question** and to the definition of dramatic irony on page 166 of the Student Book. Ask the students to finish the following sentence: *Priestley set* An Inspector Calls *in 1912 because ...*

5.5 Explore the same context from different perspectives

Assessment objectives	GCSE examinations
English Literature AO2 Analyse the language, form and structure used by a writer to create meanings and effects, using relevant subject terminology where appropriate AO3 Show understanding of the relationships between texts and the contexts in which they were written	• English Literature Paper 2, Question B

Differentiated learning outcomes	Resources
• **All students must** be able to make at least one clear point about the writer's viewpoint and select an appropriate piece of evidence to support their point. • **Most students should** make several clear points about the writers' viewpoints, selecting relevant evidence and commenting effectively on the effects of particular language choices. • **Some students could** link ideas about the poets' viewpoints closely to the poems, commenting in detail on how the poets convey these ideas through language, form and structure.	• **Student Book**: pp. 170–3 • **Worksheet**: 5.5 • **PPT**: 5.5

Getting you thinking

Big question — Display **PPT 5.5, slide 1**, which is a copy of the **Big question**: *How can two writers see such different things in the same setting?* Allow two to three minutes for the students to note down some initial responses to this question. Alternatively, note these together on the slide to refer back to later in the lesson.

Allow 10 minutes for the students to discuss the relative merits of where they live, either in pairs or small groups (**Q1a**). For **Q1b**, they could take on two personae: that of a young person describing the place, and that of an older person.

Then ask the students to make notes about their discussions and list three advantages/good points and three disadvantages/bad points (**Q2**).

Feed back as a class and ask some students to share their answers. Draw attention to the explanation of perspective as context in this lesson – the idea that a person's attitudes, age, experiences and history might affect their feelings towards a particular place.

Explore the skills

Display **PPT 5.5, slide 2**, which is a copy of William Wordsworth's poem 'Upon Westminster Bridge'.

Use the annotations on page 171 of the Student Book to elicit ideas for discussion and facilitate the students' responses to **Q3–Q5**. The annotations cover the majority of the ideas they might include. Draw attention to the fact that Wordsworth is looking at a distance, from a remove, rather than in close detail, and that the description is taking place on a very pleasant morning.

Draw attention to the **Key term** 'perspective' on page 172 of the Student Book and ask the students to write a sentence explaining what Wordsworth's perspective of London is. Explain that Wordsworth is a Romantic poet. For him, therefore, poetry was a way of expressing powerful feelings and emotions that some people might consider to be rather exaggerated.

Now ask the students to complete **Q3–Q5**.

Develop the skills

Read the introduction to George Eliot's 'In a London Drawingroom' on page 172 of the Student Book, and draw attention to the fact that this is a poem describing the same location, but from a very different perspective. The speaker's view of London is more claustrophobic, as it is framed by a window and the speaker is inside, which means they can only see a small portion of the view rather than a wide vista.

Read aloud the poem and ask the students to complete **Q6–Q8** independently. These tasks will provide some useful practice for tackling Unseen Poetry. Before the students begin, refer them to the annotations, which will help them to answer the questions.

> **Give extra challenge** by encouraging the students to consider why the two writers selected these two very different perspectives from which to write about London. How does the view of London change given these two different perspectives?

Responses might include:

- Eliot's poem gives a more negative point of view than that expressed by Wordsworth.
- Eliot focuses on realistic details and daily life.

When the students have completed **Q6–Q8**, explain that Eliot was not a Romantic, and she felt that it was important to depict everyday life in a realistic way in order to effect social change, among other reasons.

Apply the skills

Read aloud the main task and the sample response on page 173 of the Student Book.

Read through **Q9** and draw attention to the sample student sentence. Ask the students to select one detail from the sample response and rewrite it, making sure they comment effectively on a language detail from the poem.

Now ask the students to complete **Q9**, using **Worksheet 5.5** to highlight or annotate the response. They should have developed some knowledge of how to incorporate ideas about context in a response. They should also have developed some understanding of how to comment on writers' use of language.

Allow at least 20 minutes for the students to complete their own, independent response to **Q10**, using their notes from the lesson to support them. Before they begin, refer them to the **Checklist for success** at the top of page 173 of the Student Book.

The students could also refer to the **Check your progress** outcomes at the end of the section in order to set themselves a target before they begin the written task.

Big answer plenary	Return to the students' initial responses to the **Big question** from the beginning of the lesson. Having completed the activities in this section, what could they now add to this list? For example, they could add: *It can be useful to know something about the writer's views in order to understand their perspective and methods more thoroughly.* Reinforce that perspective and viewpoint can depend upon a number of factors: the location itself, the time of day, and the weather – all of these influence the mood of the text.

5.6 Apply your skills to an English Literature task

Assessment objectives

English Literature

AO1 Read, understand and respond to texts

AO2 Analyse the language, form and structure used by a writer to create meanings and effects, using relevant subject terminology where appropriate

AO3 Show understanding of the relationships between texts and the contexts in which they were written

GCSE examinations
- English Literature Paper 2, Section B

Differentiated learning outcomes

- **All students must** be able to show awareness of some Romantic ideas and write some clear comments about how context is linked to what the writer is trying to say.
- **Most students should** be able to link aspects of Romanticism to a writer's ideas and techniques and clearly explain the ways context affects the way the writer uses language, or structure, or form, to create meanings.
- **Some students could** use ideas about Romanticism as an overview to aid a detailed examination of themes and techniques, with detailed explanation of the influence of the context on the writer.

Resources
- **Student Book**: pp. 174–82
- **Worksheets**: 5.6a–b (5.6b is available on the CD-Rom only)
- **PPT**: 5.6

Introduction

The purpose of this lesson is to draw together ways in which contextual ideas can be used to develop an English Literature response to texts. The preliminary parts of the lesson might take at least two sessions in themselves, with the extended written task to be completed in examination conditions in around 45 minutes.

To get the most from this lesson, the students need to be aware of some of the important ideas that influenced the Romantic movement. Begin by reading aloud the paragraph outlining the history of Romanticism on page 174 of the Student Book and reinforce that some of these ideas are still very influential.

The table of Romantic ideas on page 175 of the Student Book outlines important Romantic ideas in more detail. Remind the students that they should use this as a reference guide throughout the lesson, to enable them to relate contextual information to examples from the poems they are going to respond to.

> **Give extra support** by asking the students to write a summary of Romantic ideas in 50 words or fewer. At this stage, this could be completed as a bulleted list of points. This will help reinforce their understanding of ideas in the table and give them a ready reference list of the main ideas of Romanticism.

Now read the information about John Clare on pages 175–6.

Display **PPT 5.6, slide 1**, which is a copy of John Clare's poem 'The Swallow', and ask the students to complete **Q1**. Remind them to refer back to the table of Romantic ideas as they complete this task.

Feed back ideas on **Q1** as a class, before asking the students to write a paragraph of their own in response to the poem (**Q2**). Encourage the students to use the sentence stems on page 176. Use of the stems will enable the students to view the poem as an example of a literary movement's work and so help them to explore literary context.

Read aloud the information about Ted Hughes on page 176. Then ask the students to read the poem, 'Work and Play', on page 177, in pairs, making notes of their initial ideas about what this poem is about. Encourage the students to think about:

- what happens in the poem
- the speaker's point of view
- interesting uses of language and structure
- anything that might make the poem 'Romantic' in terms of ideas, point of view, language and structure.

Feed back and discuss the students' ideas as a class, before asking the students to complete **Q3**, using **Worksheet 5.6a**. Draw the students' attention to the two completed examples, which could act as models to support their completion of the table.

Now ask the students to complete **Q4**, by producing a similar table about Hughes' portrayal of the people in 'Work and Play'. Again, one row of this table, on page 178 of the Student Book, has been completed and can act as a model. The students may pick examples like:
- 'searching to slake its fever'
- 'collapsed on the beach'
- 'Nude as tomatoes'
- 'sand in their creases'
- 'laid out like wounded'
- 'Roasted and basting'.

Then ask the students to complete **Q5**, which encourages them to make explicit links between Hughes' poem and Romantic ideas. The students might notice the following:
- People are portrayed as slaves to the everyday world.
- The day at the beach just becomes another unpleasant task when it should be something that should be enjoyed.
- The poet notices the freedom and beauty of the swallows, whereas the 'holiday people' do not.
- The traffic jam to and from the beach could represent the modern world stifling individual freedom and creativity.

Ask the students to complete **Q6** in pairs or small groups, or, if preferred, as a class discussion.

Responding to an English Literature Task

Display **PPT 5.6, slide 2**, which is a copy of the main task and the **Checklist for success**. Ask the students to note down one or two targets that they will particularly focus on for this task (**Q1**).

Before the students plan their own answers, read the two sample responses from pages 179–181 of the Student Book. Use the annotations and **Comments** features to elicit from the students successful ways of responding to this main task (**Q2–Q4**).

Now allow approximately 45 minutes for the students to complete their own response to the main task. Encourage the students to aim for around 500 words, or two sides of A4. This could be accomplished in one lesson if the previous lesson or homework task has been used to create an individual plan.

The additional task on **Worksheet 5.6b**, which can be found on the CD-Rom, offers a further opportunity for the students to develop their skills. This could be used either as an extension activity or for further consolidation and practice of the skills developed throughout Chapter 5.

6.1 Critical evaluation: form an interpretation

Assessment objectives

English Language

AO4 Evaluate texts critically and support this with appropriate textual references

English Literature

AO1 Read, understand and respond to texts, maintaining a critical style and developing an informed personal response; use textual references, including quotations, to support and illustrate interpretations

GCSE examinations

- **English Language** Paper 1 Question 4
- **English Language** Paper 2, Question 4
- **English Literature** key skill across all components

Differentiated learning outcomes

- **All students must** show they can read the text and pick up on some of the clues left by the writer in their exploration.
- **Most students should** be able to read a text and explore it with growing confidence in their own questioning to build up a picture of its meaning.
- **Some students could** show they can read and question texts, and then present all of the clues they have gathered in an organised way to show their own interpretation.

Resources

- **Student Book**: pp. 184–7
- **PPT**: 6.1

Other Student Book pages

- Chapter 3, pp. 75–114
- Chapter 4, pp. 115–152

Getting you thinking

Big question	Refer to the **Big question**: *How is critical evaluation different from doing basic comprehension work?* Elicit some initial responses from the class.

Display **PPT 6.1, slide 1** and read the introduction to **Getting you thinking** on page 184 of the Student Book.

Focus on the **Key term** 'interpretation' and what it means using the dictionary definition on **PPT 6.1, slide 2**. Invite the students to comment on what this might mean in terms of their study of English Language and Literature. What method or skill have they already learned that enables them to draw clues or read between the lines of a text and 'unravel' it?

Refer back to Chapter 3 if required and explain that the students' skills in making inferences are vital in addressing the Assessment Objectives for this lesson. Use the definition of 'inferences' in the **Key terms** box on page 184 as a reminder. Then display **PPT 6.1, slide 3**, and recap on the SQI method: *statement + quotation + inference*.

Invite the students to recap on the method they use to comment on language and structure. Refer back to Chapter 4 if required. Then display **PPT 6.1, slide 4**, to recap the method: *word/phrase/language or structural feature + example/quotation/reference to it + comment on the effect of it.*

Now read the first extract of 'A Case of Murder' by Vernon Scannell on page 185 of the Student Book. Allow 10 minutes for the students to explore the text and complete **Q1–Q3**, in pairs or small groups.

Take feedback as a class. The students should have realised that:

- 'they' refers to the parents
- 'only' suggests he was very young – too young and vulnerable to be left
- 'basement flat' sounds dark, oppressive – connotations of cellars, not child friendly
- repetition of 'alone' raises our concerns for the boy, his welfare and how he might be feeling.

Explore the skills

Read aloud the second extract of 'A Case of Murder'. Ask the students to read and take note of the annotations as you read (**Q4**).

Allow a further 5–10 minutes for the students to discuss **Q5** and **Q6** in pairs or small groups, or use this as a whole-class discussion if preferred.

The students may now consider a different side to the boy through his brooding hatred of the cat, described in a way which makes it seem evil and somewhat dangerous – certainly not the stereotype of a warm, friendly, family pet.

Read aloud the third extract from the poem on page 186 and allow 15–20 minutes for the students to complete **Q7** in pairs or small groups.

> **Give extra support** by asking the students to work in small groups, but with half of the class working on **Q7a** and half on **Q7b**.
>
> **Give extra challenge** by asking the students to work in pairs, with one student in each pair working on **Q7a** and the other on **Q7b**.

Take feedback and share the students' ideas with the class.

Now work through **Q8** and **Q9**, eliciting answers from the class.

Develop the skills

Display **PPT 6.1**, **slide 5**, the final extract from 'A Case of Murder', and read it aloud to the class.

Use the information in the opening paragraphs of **Develop the skills** on page 186 of the Student Book to reinforce the difference between reading on the surface and reading between the lines – the difference between explicit and implicit meaning.

Now ask the students to read the two student interpretations on page 187. Elicit opinions of each interpretation and ask them to find evidence from the text to support each interpretation (**Q10**). Then invite any other ideas and interpretations from the class (**Q11**). Draw together the learning from the lesson so far, defining 'critical evaluation' for the students.

Apply the skills

Read through the main task (**Q12**) with the students and refer them to the **Checklist for success** on page 187 of the Student Book. This task would now work well as a follow-up homework task. If the students prefer to use their own interpretation, ask them to write this as a header before beginning their piece of work. Likewise, ask them to cite Student A or Student B's interpretation as a header to help maintain focus with the task.

Big answer plenary	Ask the students to work in pairs, to read the work they have produced and discuss with reference to the **Checklist for success**. Which of the skills have they demonstrated? Where could they improve?
	Ask the students to look at the **Check your progress** outcomes on page 187 of the Student Book and decide which outcome best describes how they currently feel about their skills so far.

6.2 Critical evaluation: gather and present evidence about language

Assessment objectives

English Language
AO4 Evaluate texts critically and support this with appropriate textual references
(Also supports work for AO2)

English Literature
AO1 Read, understand and respond to texts, maintaining a critical style and developing an informed personal response; use textual references, including quotations, to support and illustrate interpretations
(Also supports work for AO2)

GCSE examinations
- English Language Paper 1 Question 4
- English Language Paper 2, Question 4
- English Literature key skill across all components

Differentiated learning outcomes
- **All students must** show they can recognise some features of language in texts and mention them in their written response.
- **Most students should** be able to select some features of language and use examples of them in their written response.
- **Some students could** show they can select and exemplify features of language and use the effect of them to add to their interpretation of the text.

Resources
- **Student Book**: pp. 188–91
- **Worksheet**: 6.2
- **PPT**: 6.2

Getting you thinking

Big question	Refer to the **Big question:** *Do you need your knowledge about language in evaluative essay-type questions too?* Reinforce that knowledge about language is necessary in evaluative essay-type questions.
	Read the first three paragraphs in **Getting you thinking** on page 188 of the Student Book, and introduce the idea of being 'selective' in the choices of language features to include in an essay of this type.

For **Q1**, read aloud the task about Wilfred Owen on page 188 of the Student Book.

Display **PPT 6.2, slide 1**, which shows the three words selected from the poem.

Refer the students to the definition of 'semantic field' in the **Key terms** box, if required, and ask them to complete **Q1a–c**, individually and without looking at the poem itself. Then take feedback and ideas from the whole group.

Explore the skills

Read aloud the extract from 'Dulce et Decorum est' on page 189 of the Student Book.

Explore the three words again in the context of the poem, asking whether the students agree with the notes made by the student in **Q2** on page 189. Ask the students whether they have anything to add, or whether they disagree with any of the ideas presented and why (**Q2**).

Now allow 10–15 minutes for the students to complete **Q3–Q5** individually, using the table in **Worksheet 6.2**.

The students should pick up on the similes highlighted in yellow – that the references to age contradict what we know about WW1 soldiers being mostly young men. The dreadful state of the soldiers ('beggars'/'hags') conflicts with the idea of a proud army, well-equipped, and the notion of the smart soldier in pristine kit.

The words and phrases in pink again all refer to physical infirmities and disabilities – many of which we connect with age, not youth or a fighting force. There is something chilling in that 'all' of the soldiers seem to have these infirmities, suggesting just how vulnerable and weak they were as a force.

Develop the skills

For **Q6**, read the main task on page 190 of the Student Book and elicit answers to the four questions from the class.

Move on to the sample student response in **Q7**. Read the task, noting the important sentence: *Remember this is not a complete evaluation – just **one** aspect of it.*

Read aloud the sample paragraph on page 191, and allow 5–10 minutes for the students to complete **Q7** in pairs, using the checklist on **Worksheet 6.2**. Remind the students that this response just deals with the three words identified at the beginning of the lesson:

- 'hags'
- 'cursed'
- 'haunting'.

Apply the skills

Read the main task again and ask the students to identify the focus of the task.

Before they begin, recap on the checklist from **Q7** as a guide for their own work in this task, and also refer the students to the **Checklist for success** on page 191. Suggest to the students that they practice their method by using the words and language features they noted in the table in **Q5** as the basis for their response.

Allow 20–25 minutes for the students to complete the main task individually (**Q8**).

Big answer plenary	Ask the students to read through their own work against the **Check your progress** outcomes by: • circling in pencil their language features • underlining their quotations or examples • asking themselves whether each has an inference that adds to the interpretation, and labelling each inference. Refer back to the **Big question** and encourage the students to answer positively about how the analysis of language can add to the interpretation of a text and help to demonstrate their skills.

6.3 Critical evaluation: gather and present evidence about structure

Assessment objectives

English Language
AO4 Evaluate texts critically and support this with appropriate textual references
(Also supports work for AO2)

English Literature
AO1 Read, understand and respond to texts, maintaining a critical style and developing an informed personal response; use textual references, including quotations, to support and illustrate interpretations
(Also supports work for AO2)

GCSE examinations
- English Language Paper 1 Question 4
- English Language Paper 2, Question 4
- English Literature key skill across all components

Differentiated learning outcomes
- **All students must** show they can identify some of the ways the writer structures or organises the text and mention them in their written response.
- **Most students should** be able to identify and give examples of some of the effective structural features the writer uses.
- **Some students could** show they can select and exemplify features of structure and comment on how the effect of using them adds to the meaning of the text.

Resources
- **Student Book**: pp. 192–5
- **Worksheets**: 6.3a–b
- **PPT**: 6.3

Other Student Book pages
- Lesson 6.2, pp. 188–91

Getting you thinking

Big question	Ask the students to look at the title of this unit and recall what the structure of a text includes. Refer to the **Big question**: *What else can you say apart from: 'it's got a beginning, a middle and an end and it's made up of long sentences?* Elicit some ideas as to the kinds of techniques that make up those beginnings, middles and ends. Use the definition of *structure* in the **Key term** box to help facilitate this. Ensure that the students are aware that writers make the same conscious choices about structure as they do about language.

PPT Display **PPT 6.3, slide 1**, and read the first extract from Jon McGregor's *If Nobody Speaks of Remarkable Things* (**Q1**).

For **Q2–Q4**, use the questions and the bullet points on structure as the basis for class discussion to help all the students understand and recap on the concept of structure and how it works. They should note the following key points:

- This is a wedding anniversary.
- It's written in the present tense, giving a sense of the here and now.
- The second paragraph places emphasis on the two cards – his wife is still alive – and opens a door to the past.
- The pace is slow and measured – like his actions – through their complexity and number of subordinate clauses.
- We get the sense that he's waiting for her – tender/gentle.
- The compound sentence joins the present to the past – their wedding day. This is likely to take us back in time – perhaps to their wedding day.

Explore the skills

Read the next extract from the novel on page 193 of the Student Book.

Allow 15–20 minutes for the students to explore the second extract in pairs or small groups, using **Worksheet 6.3a** to take notes and make annotations (**Q5**). You may want to provide a copy on an A3-sized sheet of paper if they are working in groups.

Take feedback and ask the groups or pairs to share their ideas with the class. Encourage them to consider the effects of the features they have been looking at.

Develop the skills

Read the introductory text in **Develop the skills** on page 194 of the Student Book. Link the student feedback from the exploration in **Q5** to the bullet points. Use spot-questioning to check that all the students know what each of the structural features is.

Allow 15 minutes for the students to complete **Q6** individually, using **Worksheet 6.3b**.

Give extra support by setting this in the original small groups or pairs.

Take feedback as a class. The students should note the following:

- It is set in the past and uses the past tense, but her dialogue uses the future tense (he clearly did come home safely to be there as an old man with the anniversary card in extract one).
- The paragraphs focus on each of them as an individual – maybe representing how they are about to be separated by his leaving to go to war.
- Again we see long, complex sentences creating a slow pace, gentle and tender, nostalgic and dream-like – his memories floating back to him through time.
- He tells her a story of their future – of how their life together is going to be.
- Her speech is indirect – as he remembers it – not being directly spoken now.

Now ask the students to complete **Q7a–c** individually, using the feedback from **Q6** to help them consolidate their ideas. Before they begin, explain how it is the structural features of both extracts that allow the readers to make those conclusions and aid their understanding of the text itself.

Apply the skills

For **Q8**, read the main task and ask the students to identify the focus of the task. Recap on the work done in presenting a clear paragraph of analysis in Lesson 6.2 and the checklist the students applied, and remind them that this time the focus is on structure, rather than language.

Allow 20–25 minutes for the students to complete the main task (**Q8**). Before they begin, refer them to the **Checklist for success** on page 195 of the Student Book. Remind them that they only need to write about *three* features in this instance and they should choose the ones they feel most confident with from their explorations.

Display **PPT 6.3, slide 2**, the example opening, and leave this in place during the task.

Give extra support by allowing the students to use the example opening as their starting point.

Big answer plenary	Ask the students to self-evaluate their work using the checklist of statements on **Worksheet 6.2** to help them see which outcome of **Check your progress** they have reached.
	Refer back to the **Big question**. Ask all the students to write down one structural feature they have worked on in the lesson that is not 'beginning', 'middle' or 'end'. Collate these onto the whiteboard, so the students can see the variety and their growing confidence.

6.4 Critical evaluation: gather and present evidence about mood

Assessment objectives

English Language

AO4 Evaluate texts critically and support this with appropriate textual references

English Literature

AO1 Read, understand and respond to texts, maintaining a critical style and developing an informed personal response; use textual references, including quotations, to support and illustrate interpretations

(Also supports work for AO2)

GCSE examinations
- English Language Paper 1 Question 4
- English Language Paper 2, Question 4
- English Literature key skill across all components

Differentiated learning outcomes

- **All students must** show they understand that different texts can have different moods or atmospheres and can identify some of the clues to the mood or atmosphere in the text.
- **Most students should** be able to identify some of the different techniques the writer uses to create mood in their written response.
- **Some students could** show they can identify and comment on the different techniques the writer uses to create mood as part of their interpretation of the text.

Resources
- **Student Book**: pp. 196–9
- **Worksheets**: 6.4a–b
- **PPT**: 6.4

Getting you thinking

Big question	Read the opening sentence in **Getting you thinking** on page 196 of the Student Book. Use this to lead into the **Checklist for success** that follows it. Focus on the words 'tone' and 'mood', and ask the students in what context they might use them – for example, in well-known phrases like 'tone of voice' or 'I don't like your tone', and 'He's in a bit of a mood'.
PPT	Collate all the phrases on the board to illustrate the difference between 'tone' and 'mood'. Then display **PPT 6.4, slide 1**, and use it to conclude, and reinforce the difference. Link the second bullet point about mood back to the **Big question**: *Why is mood important in critical evaluation?*

Discuss **Q1** briefly with the class and elicit some ideas.

Explore the skills

Read aloud the extract from Bram Stoker's *Dracula* on pages 196–7 of the Student Book. Do not reveal the title or the author yet.

Allow 15–20 minutes for the students to complete **Q2a–e** in pairs or small groups.

> **Give extra support** by making this a teacher-led class discussion.
>
> **Give extra challenge** by asking the students to work individually for the first 15 minutes, and then ask them to share their findings with a partner and debate their responses.

Feed back as a class. The students' ideas might include the following:

- The setting is midnight – sense of the witching hour – the stereotype from horror stories and films, and linked to ideas connected to the supernatural.

- The use of howling dogs is a stereotype from horror films and links to the sound of howling wolves; also links to the genre of horror and the gothic – dogs become unsettled and sense fear more readily than humans do.
- The weather changes, the wind picks up and carries the howling, adding to its echoes and haunting quality.

Ask the students to work in pairs and discuss the ideas given in the student's response on page 197 of the Student Book, adding in more ideas of their own, using **Worksheet 6.4a (Q3)**. Move around the room, checking responses, then share the good ideas with the group during class feedback.

Develop the skills

Reveal that the novel is *Dracula* by Bram Stoker.

Display **PPT 6.4, slide 2**, and ask the students what their associations with Count Dracula are – use the images on the PPT slide to stimulate ideas.

Introduce the term 'gothic horror' and display **PPT 6.4, slide 3**, which lists some of its conventions. Link these conventions to the checklist in **Q4**.

Now read aloud the second extract on page 199 of the Student Book.

Allow 15–20 minutes for the students to complete **Q4** using **Worksheet 6.4b**. This activity would work well as a small-group quotation quest.

Feed back responses as a class, and then revisit the checklist of conventions on **PPT 6.4, slide 3**, to lead into **Apply the skills**.

Apply the skills

Set up the creative writing task, explaining that the students are going to write the next paragraph of the story (**Q5**).

Display **PPT 6.4, slide 3**, the conventions of the genre, and leave this showing while the students plan their work.

> **Give extra support** by compiling a collaborative plan of ideas on the whiteboard.
>
> **Give extra challenge** by giving the students 10 minutes of silent planning and thinking time with blank paper and a marker to gather/list/mind map their ideas.

If working in class, allow 45 minutes for the students to complete **Q5** and **Q6**, to mirror the writing time in the examination. This would also make a useful extended homework task for creative writing practice.

Big answer plenary	Refer back to the **Big question**. Ask the students to define, in a couple of sentences, what they now understand by the term 'mood' and to give one effect it can add to a piece of creative writing.

6.5 Critical evaluation: construct a convincing response to literary texts

Assessment objectives

English Language

AO4 Evaluate texts critically and support this with appropriate textual references

English Literature

AO1 Read, understand and respond to texts, maintaining a critical style and developing an informed personal response; use textual references, including quotations, to support and illustrate interpretations

GCSE examinations

- English Language Paper 1 Question 4
- English Language Paper 2, Question 3
- English Literature key skill across all components

Differentiated learning outcomes

- **All students must** be able to read a literary text and plan some points about ideas, language, structure and mood in their written work.
- **Most students should** be able to read a literary text and use supporting evidence to back up their ideas when they write their response.
- **Some students could** plan, write and support a response to a literary text that shows they have made their own convincing interpretation of the text.

Resources

- **Student Book**: pp. 200–3
- **Worksheets**: 6.5a–b
- **PPT**: 6.5

Note: this lesson provides a model for constructing effective and convincing essay-style responses. Depending on your available lesson times and how you use the **Apply your skills** section, there may be enough material here to cover two to three lessons.

Getting you thinking

| Big question | Refer the students to the **Big question**: *You have gathered a lot of clues and quotations, but how do you put it all together?* Explain that this lesson will provide them with a model for constructing effective essay-style responses to critical evaluation tasks about literary texts. |

Display **PPT 6.5, slide 1**, the task from **Q1** on page 200 of the Student Book.

Use the bullet points as a basis for a teacher-led, class discussion (**Q1**). First, try to engage the students with what is meant by 'abuse of power', and take some examples, leading them towards thinking about: authority; governments, monarchs and leaders of the past. Ask the students to think about the phrase 'how the poet seems to view' and reiterate the need for inferential reading for implicit meanings.

Then read the remaining paragraphs and bullet-pointed checklist on page 200 and recap on critical evaluation. Reinforce the key message – careful selection – and link this back to the **Big question**.

Explore the skills

Read aloud the poem 'Ozymandias' by P.B. Shelley on page 201 of the Student Book, then allow a further five minutes for the students to read the poem and the annotations individually. Referring to the annotations in the four different categories, elicit responses to the following questions:

- Do the students agree with the language ideas? Can they see supporting evidence?
- Can they work out who is speaking when, and the three 'voices' within the poem?
- Focus on the word 'civilisation': can the students name any of the world's great ancient civilisations? How does this inform the poem and link to the final notes?
- Ask whether any of the students know at what time in history Shelley was writing.

Now allow 30 minutes for the students to complete **Q2** as a small-group investigation, using **Worksheet 6.5a** so that all the students have an individual set of notes. If it can be arranged, some research time on computers would help the students to check information on sonnets and when Shelley was writing.

> **Give extra support** by splitting the class into a *language* group, a *structure* group, a *mood* group and an *ideas* group. Allow time for collaborative feedback with this approach.

Develop the skills

Display the task on **PPT 6.5**, **slide 1** again.

Read through **Q3** and **Q4** with the class and emphasise the key points. Then allow 5–10 minutes for the students to complete this planning phase individually.

Display **PPT 6.5**, **slide 2**, Student A's response.

Discuss Student A's approach with the class (**Q5**). The students should note that the response is about Shelley himself, not his views and there is only a very general comment about Romantic poets. This introduction wastes time as it does not address the task or follow the recommended method.

Now display **PPT 6.5**, **slide 3**, Student B's response.

Discuss Student B's response with the class (**Q6**). The students should note that the opening statement is clear, definite, and linked to the question – it is related directly to the poem, and gives a clear overview statement using a key word from the question: 'power'. The student then begins their analysis of the language of the poem straight away. Some subject terminology is included. There are short, crisp supporting quotations – some of which are embedded. The student has also already made some inferences.

Ask the students to compare the two passages and list how many different skills from the Assessment Objectives are displayed in each.

Then use the **Checklist for success** on page 203 of the Student Book to summarise the key learning points from this activity.

Allow 10–15 minutes for the students to write a paragraph evaluating the language used in the poem (**Q7**), working independently, and using **Worksheet 6.5b**.

Now allow 10 minutes for the students to look at the example concluding paragraph on page 203 of the Student Book, and discuss **Q8a–d** in pairs or small groups. Then take feedback as a class and use the students' ideas as a basis for compiling a 'Good practice in writing conclusions' list on the whiteboard, which they should add to their notebooks.

Apply the skills

For the main task (**Q9**), the students should produce a longer, essay-style response. This will be a longer, more developed response than the students might be expected to write under timed conditions in an exam. However, it is a chance to develop and consolidate the key skills required for Analytical Literature essays and Evaluative Language short essay tasks. Allow at least 45 minutes, or an extended homework period, to ensure the students are able to work to the best of their ability on this task.

Big answer plenary	Ask the students to self-evaluate their work, using the **Check your progress** ladder on page 203 of the Student Book to help them see which outcome they have achieved.

6.6 Critical evaluation: construct a convincing response to non-fiction texts

Assessment objective

English Language

AO4 Evaluate texts critically and support this with appropriate textual references

GCSE examinations

- English Language
  Paper 2, Question 4

Differentiated learning outcomes

- **All students must** be able to read a non-fiction text and plan and write some things to say about its ideas, language, structure and tone.
- **Most students should** be able to read a non-fiction text, plan and write their response and use supporting evidence to back up their ideas.
- **Some students could** plan, write and support a response to a non-fiction text that shows their own convincing interpretation.

Resources

- **Student Book**: pp. 204–7
- **Worksheets**: 6.6a–b
- **PPT**: 6.6

Other Student Book pages

- Lesson 6.5, pp. 200–3

Note: This lesson provides a model for constructing effective and convincing essay-style responses. Depending on your available lesson times and how you use the **Apply your skills** section, there may be enough material here to cover two lessons.

Getting you thinking

Big question	Refer to the **Big question**: *You can write up your ideas about poems and stories, but you find it harder with non-fiction texts. How do you improve?* Explain that this lesson will provide the students with a model for constructing effective essay-style responses to critical evaluation tasks about non-fiction texts, using the same method as with literary texts.

Display **PPT 6.6, slide 1**, the bullet points showing the key methodology for evaluating texts.

Allow 15 minutes for the students to put together revision notes of key elements for writing about texts critically (**Q1**). Encourage them to present the information in the way that will be easiest for them to remember. They could use coloured pens, and include definitions or a glossary of key terms using previous chapters of the Student Book to help. Ensure the students are clear on key terms such as 'language' and 'structure'.

Give extra support by using the videos explaining terms from Collins Connect.

Give extra challenge by encouraging the students to write a set of notes for use by another student in the group.

Explore the skills

Recap on the skills and method applied in Lesson 6.5 before reading out the task linked to the Jessica Ennis extract. As usual, ensure all students are clear on the focus of the task itself: the experience of competing in the Olympics and *how* it is presented.

Read aloud the extract from *Unbelievable* by Jessica Ennis, on page 205 of the Student Book. If possible, you could also show the first two minutes of a video clip of Jennifer Ennis winning an Olympic gold medal during the London 2012 Olympics, to illustrate who Jennifer Ennis is and the atmosphere she describes in the text. The video clip can be found at: www.youtube.com/watch?v=5ogwLIPAjKk (or go to Youtube.com and search for *Jessica Ennis Seals Heptathlon Gold – London 2012 Olympics*).

Allow five minutes for the students to read the extract on page 205 again, for themselves, this time considering the questions that the passage is annotated with (**Q2**). Draw attention to the colour coding and reinforce what each colour represents.

Allow 20 minutes for the students to work in pairs or small groups, and to annotate the passage with their ideas and notes in response to the questions, using **Worksheet 6.6a**. Then take feedback, sharing the ideas from each pair/group with the class.

> **Give extra support** here by nominating a 'language group' to deal with the yellow questions, a 'structure group' to deal with the green questions, and so on.

This activity would work equally well if you displayed the text in **PPT 6.6**, **slides 2 and 3**, and used the questions as a basis for a class discussion, with you annotating the extract on the whiteboard. Some of the ideas the students should pick up on are:

- the use of 'I', 'my', 'me' and the focus on Jessica's inner thoughts in the first paragraph
- the metaphor of the 'assault' linked to the volume of noise and the brightness
- how overwhelmed she is and how the first-person focus makes her seem like one tiny individual in the midst of it all, under immense pressure to perform
- how many times 'This is ...' begins the sentences and how the present tense creates impact; the tense mirrors the clipped thoughts of the athlete and we sense her fear and tension
- the way she questions herself and shows self-doubt
- the use of 'first time ... last chance', which highlights the focus on time and the amount of training done, the culmination not just of hard work but pain and dedication
- the way she reinforces her background and her ordinariness
- the metaphor of 'melting pot of hopes and dreams', as though this is where her whole life so far has been leading.

Develop the skills

Allow 15 minutes for the students to use their notes and annotations from **Q2** to compile their individual plans, using **Worksheet 6.6b** (**Q3**).

Recap on the advice in Lesson 6.5 about strong opening paragraphs and reinforce the advice in **Q4**. Then ask the students to write their opening paragraph (**Q4**).

Apply the skills

Now ask the students to complete the rest of their response to the task (**Q5**). As in Lesson 6.5, this is an opportunity to present a complete answer, practising all of the required skills. This will therefore be a longer, more developed response than students might be expected to write under timed conditions in an exam. Allow at least 45 minutes of quiet classroom time, or an extended homework period to ensure the students are able to work to the best of their ability.

Encourage the students to use the openers to the two paragraphs on page 207 of the Student Book. This will help them get started; it will also help them to cover a wide range of skills and show a wide range of knowledge in their response, as well as help them to follow the structure of their plan and learn a clear method for success.

| Big answer plenary | Display **PPT 6.6**, **slides 4–7**. Allow students two to three minutes per slide and ask them to self-evaluate their work, using the checklists to help them see which outcomes they have achieved. |

6.7 Apply your skills to English Language and English Literature tasks

Assessment objectives

English Language
AO4 Evaluate texts critically and support this with appropriate textual references

English Literature
AO1 Read, understand and respond to texts, maintaining a critical style and developing an informed personal response; use textual references, including quotations, to support and illustrate interpretations

GCSE examinations
- **English Language** Paper 1 Question 4
- **English Language** Paper 2, Question 4
- **English Literature** key skill across all components

Differentiated learning outcomes
- **All students must** be able to read a text, and plan and write some things to say about its ideas, language, structure and tone.
- **Most students should** be able to read a text, plan and write their response, and use supporting evidence to back up their ideas.
- **Some students could** plan, write and support a response to a text that shows their own convincing interpretation.

Resources
- **Student Book**: pp. 208–18
- **Worksheets**: 6.7a–d (6.7c–d are available on the CD-Rom only)
- **PPT**: 6.7

Introduction

The purpose of the lesson is to provide practice of the skills learned in this chapter. These practice tasks can be done under examination conditions, as individual assessments, if required.

Responding to an English Language task

Display **PPT 6.7, slide 1**, and allow 15 minutes for students to read the extract from *The Great Gatsby* by F. Scott Fitzgerald (Student Book, pages 208–9) and highlight/annotate it using **Worksheet 6.7a** (**Q1**).

> **Give extra support** by reading the extract aloud for students and allowing them five minutes' thinking and annotating time before they begin **Q1**.

Now display **PPT 6.7, slide 2**, which is a copy of the main task. Discuss the focus of the task, and the key skills needed to tackle it. Refer students to the **Checklist for success** on page 209 of the Student Book, to consolidate their ideas.

Then allow 45–50 minutes for students to plan and write their response to the task.

Allow five minutes for students to carefully check and proofread their own work.

Now read aloud **Response 1** on page 210 of the Student Book. Point out the skills that have been shown using the annotations.

Ask students to annotate their own work in different coloured ink to show where they have used any of the four skills shown in the example.

Read aloud the **Comments on Response 1** on page 211.

Allow five minutes for students to discuss in pairs how **Response 1** could be improved (**Q3**). Ask each pair to write down one piece of advice they could give to this student. Feed back and share ideas with the class.

Read aloud **Response 2** on pages 211–12. Again, point out the skills that have been shown in the annotations and ask students to annotate any of those skills that are evident in their own work.

Read aloud the **Comments on Response 2** on page 212, and ask students to complete **Q4** individually. Ask each student to write down one key tip they could take from this example response.

Feed back and share ideas with the class.

Responding to an English Literature task

Display **PPT 6.7**, **slide 3**, and allow 15–20 minutes for students to read the extract from 'The Adventure of the Speckled Band' by Arthur Conan Doyle (Student Book, pages 213–14) and highlight or annotate it using **Worksheet 6.7b** (**Q1**).

> **Give extra support** by reading the extract aloud for students and allowing them five minutes' thinking and annotation time before beginning **Q1**.

Read the task on page 215 of the Student Book and elicit the focus of the task and the key skills needed to tackle it. Refer students to the **Checklist for success** on page 215 of the Student Book, to consolidate their ideas.

Then allow 45 minutes for students to plan and write their response to the task.

Allow five minutes for students to carefully check and proofread their own work.

Now read aloud **Response 1** on pages 215–16 of the Student Book. Point out the skills that have been shown using the annotations (**Q2**).

Ask students to annotate their own work in different coloured ink to show where they have used any of the skills shown in the example.

Read aloud the **Comments on Response 1** on page 216.

Allow five minutes for students to discuss in pairs how **Response 1** could be improved (**Q3**). Ask each pair to write down one piece of advice they could give to this student. Feed back and share ideas with the class.

Read aloud **Response 2** on pages 216–17. Again, point out the skills that have been shown in the annotations and ask students to annotate any of those skills that are evident in their own work.

Read aloud the **Comments on Response 2** on page 217, and ask students to complete **Q4** individually. Ask each student to write down one key tip they could take from this example response.

Feed back and share ideas with the class.

> **Give extra challenge** by allowing students to work collaboratively on the two responses in small groups. Allow 20–25 minutes for students to:
> - read the samples in turn
> - work through the annotations
> - write a series of tips for the class
> - use the responses to peer-evaluate each other's responses and to add advice
> - match the responses – both the examples and their own – against the Level criteria in the accredited mark scheme grids.

The two additional tasks on **Worksheets 6.7c–d**, which can be found on the accompanying CD-Rom, offer further opportunities for students to develop their skills. These could be used either as extension activities or for further consolidation and practice of the skills developed throughout Chapter 6.

7.1 Compare views and perspectives in non-literary non-fiction from the twentieth century

Assessment objective

English Language

AO3 Compare writers' ideas and perspectives, as well as how these are conveyed, across two or more texts

GCSE examinations
- English Language Paper 2, Question 4

Differentiated learning outcomes
- **All students must** be able to identify the different viewpoints and explain what the similarities or differences are between them.
- **Most students should** be able to make clear comparisons of viewpoint based on inferences from the text.
- **Some students could** present a detailed comparison of the different viewpoints expressed in two texts, inferring meaning from a range of evidence.

Resources
- **Student Book**: pp. 220–3
- **Worksheets**: 7.1a–c
- **PPT**: 7.1

Getting you thinking

Big question

Introduce the **Big question**: *How do you compare two different viewpoints?* by displaying the following statements about school uniform, either using **Worksheet 7.1a** or **PPT 7.1, slide 1**:

a If you have to wear uniform then there is no competition about clothes, so it makes it fairer for everyone.

b Uniform takes away your individuality.

c It's much cheaper to have uniform because you don't need a different outfit for every day.

d Uniform helps you to feel you belong to the school.

e Uniform costs a fortune and the quality is rubbish.

f Uniform is a nightmare for teachers because they have to spend all their time telling the students off for not wearing it properly.

Ask the students to sort the viewpoints into those that approve of school uniform and those that disapprove of it (**Q1**). Then ask them to choose one viewpoint that might be held by a student, one that might be held by a teacher, and one that might be held by a parent, and ask them to explain what might influence each of these viewpoints (**Q2**).

Explore the skills

Ask the students to read the article on pages 220–1 of the Student Book or using **Worksheet 7.1b**, and to either highlight or annotate whenever they identify one of the reasons the writer gives for their viewpoint.

Allow 10 minutes for the students to complete **Q3**. They should aim to find a short piece of evidence for each reason they identify. These could include:

- The family need a break.
- It will be cheaper to go during term-time rather than in the school holidays.
- Her son is only four, so will not be disadvantaged by missing one week of school.
- The idea that there would be 'half-empty classrooms' is spurious.
- The benefits of foreign travel mean that a holiday can be an education in itself.

- A family holiday benefits the family.
- New 'stimulating' environments are more important than Ofsted targets.

Display **PPT 7.1**, **slide 2**, and explain the SQI (statement–quotation–inference) way of formulating a response. Explain that this moves away from the ubiquitous 'PEE' (point–evidence–explanation) method into something that enables the students to develop their thinking in a more advanced way. You may wish to illustrate this by asking the students to think about the word 'inference' and how it enables reading at a deeper level. **PPT 7.1**, **slide 3** could be used to scaffold this – the iceberg shows that only a small amount of valuable reading is 'literal' and the rest is inferential.

Read the sample response on page 221 of the Student Book, which illustrates SQI. Then ask the students to pick one of the ideas they selected from the article to construct an SQI paragraph of their own (**Q4**).

Ask the students to read the second article, either on page 222 of the Student Book, or using **Worksheet 7.1c**. Allow between 5–10 minutes for the students to answer the five questions given as annotations down the side of the article.

Now ask the students to complete **Q5**, which draws together their understanding of the writer's viewpoint in the second article.

Develop the skills

Introduce the use of the words 'both', 'however' and 'whereas' for comparing viewpoints, and display **PPT 7.1**, **slide 4**, which is a model of this construction.

For **Q6**, the students now need to look at the two articles together and think about the similarities and differences between them.

> **Give extra support** by suggesting statements like: 'both are parents, so they will have strong views'; 'both care about their children's education'. Point out that it is important to avoid the obvious statement – 'both are about school holidays' – as this isn't going to enable them to develop a good point.
>
> **Give extra challenge** by drawing attention to the tone: is it ironic/angry/frustrated/light-hearted in either text?

Apply the skills

Allow 15 minutes for the students to complete the main task in **Q7**. The notes they have taken in the lesson will be a useful scaffold for this writing task. Remind the students that they are looking for similarities and differences, supported with relevant quotations, and to infer meaning from the evidence they select about the writers' viewpoints. It may be useful to point out that 'compare' doesn't mean just similarities; it also means differences.

Big answer plenary	Ask the students to write a short answer to the **Big question**. It may help to imagine they are explaining this to a student who has been absent or who will be undertaking this learning later.
	The students should aim to use the following words in their answers to the **Big question**:
	similarities differences both however whereas viewpoint

7.2 Compare non-fiction prose texts

Assessment objective

English Language

AO3 Compare writers' ideas and perspectives, as well as how these are conveyed, across two or more texts

GCSE examinations
- English Language
  Paper 2, Question 4

Differentiated learning outcomes

- **All students must** be able to identify the viewpoints in both texts and be able to explain what the main similarities and differences are.
- **Most students should** be able to make clear comparisons of viewpoint based on inferences from the text.
- **Some students could** present a detailed comparison of the viewpoints being expressed in both texts, inferring meaning from a range of evidence.

Resources
- **Student Book**: pp. 224–7
- **Worksheet**: 7.2
- **PPT**: 7.2

Getting you thinking

Big question | Read the **Big question**: *How do you know what to compare when you're comparing two different texts?* and display **PPT 7.2, slide 1**, which shows two well-used comparative idioms (**Q1**).

Draw attention to the alliteration of 'chalk' and 'cheese', which implies an initial connection to mask complete difference. Then ask the students to think of as many connections as they can between 'sugar' and 'sand'. Refer to the prompts in **Q2** if they need help.

Draw the learning point together with a sentence:

Sugar and sand both ... However, the main difference between them is ...

Explore the skills

Display **PPT 7.2, slide 2**, which shows some children using a 'hole in the wall' computer.

Now ask the students to read the article on page 225 of the Student Book. As they read, they should think about what the writer does to test the slum children's ability to learn (**Q3**).

When the students have finished reading, ask them to complete **Q4a** and **Q4b**. The question prompts for **Q4b** are also available on **PPT 7.2, slide 3**.

Ask the students to copy and complete the table on page 225 of the Student Book or use **Worksheet 7.2** (**Q5**). This will develop their ability to find appropriate evidence and infer ideas from this evidence. This is building on the skills introduced in Lesson 7.1. Ideas might include:

- The children were interested in the computer: 'they came running'; 'glued themselves'; 'they couldn't get enough'. The inference here is that they were engaged in learning, or that they were enthusiastic about the prospect of learning, or that they didn't see learning as something to be frightened of, or as something beyond their capability.

- The children learned how to use it very quickly: 'A few hours later ... surfing the Web'; 'learned all the mouse operations ...'. The inference here is that the children are intelligent, or that their keenness to learn meant they mastered the skills easily, or that their poverty did not prove a barrier to their ability to learn.

Q6 gives the students the opportunity to draw their ideas together into a short piece of writing explaining the writer's viewpoint. It might be useful to give an opening statement such as: *This writer thinks that children in very deprived areas…*

Develop the skills

The students will now compare the first text with one written by Charles Dickens.

Display **PPT 7.2**, **slide 4**, which provides some strategies to use when reading a new text for the first time, particularly if it is one from the nineteenth century, in which the written style is more dense in construction. You could also display **PPT 7.2**, **slide 5**, which gives a visual image of the kind of society Dickens is writing about.

Now ask the students to read the article on page 226 of the Student Book. **Worksheet 7.2** also includes a copy of the article for the students to highlight or annotate if required. For **Q7**, the students should aim to find supporting evidence for each of the three statements.

Draw attention to what Dickens appears to be saying about these children, and how we have to read carefully in order to unpick his actual viewpoint. It might be easy for the students to slip into thinking that he thinks these children are beyond help, or not worthy of help.

Q8 is aiming to draw attention to the connections between these two articles by asking the students to undertake a similar task to that in **Q4b**. Display **PPT 7.2**, **slide 3** again as a scaffold if required.

Q9 and **Q10** draw together the viewpoints in the two articles: **Q9** asks the students to identify similarities, while **Q10** draws out the differences between the articles.

> **Give extra support** by suggesting starter prompts such as: 'Both articles are about education in deprived areas'.
>
> **Give extra challenge** by encouraging the students to make further inferences by including terms such as 'seems', 'appears' and 'on the surface'. The purpose of this is to delve deeper into how both writers – but especially Dickens – have clear sympathy for work being undertaken and how both see hope for the future in the work being done.

Apply the skills

Display **PPT 7.2**, **slide 6**, which provides a copy of the main task (**Q11**) and some prompts. Encourage students to use the prompts to help them select the points they want to make and the evidence they want to include to support their points. Remind the students to use SQI and to use the construction '*both … however … whereas*' to structure their responses.

Big answer plenary	Refer back to the **Big question** and ask the students to suggest possible answers. Alternatively, give the students the following three sentences and ask them to pick one which they think is the most useful: *You have to find out what the main connection is first of all.* *It is vital to understand the main points both writers are making in order to find the connections between the two texts.* *When you have made the main connection, it is easier to look for the differences in viewpoint.*

7.3 Compare the ways viewpoints are presented in texts from the early twentieth century

Assessment objectives

English Language

AO2 Explain, comment on and analyse how writers use language and structure to achieve effects and influence readers, using relevant subject terminology to support their views

AO3 Compare writers' ideas and perspectives, as well as how these are conveyed, across two or more texts

GCSE examinations
- English Language Paper 2, Question 4

Differentiated learning outcomes
- **All students must** be able to identify the different viewpoints in two texts and explain what the similarities or differences are between them.
- **Most students should** be able to make clear comparisons of the ways writers use language and structure to express their viewpoints.
- **Some students could** present a detailed comparison between the ways the writers use language and structure to express their viewpoints.

Resources
- **Student Book**: pp. 228–33
- **Worksheets**: 7.3 a–b
- **PPT**: 7.3

Getting you thinking

Big question	Start the lesson by referring to the **Big question**: *What kinds of things are you looking for when you're thinking about how writers present their viewpoints to the reader?* Ask the students to suggest ways in which writers might imply a viewpoint to the reader. These might include: • what information they choose to share/withhold • the vocabulary they select • the ways they structure and organise their writing • the language features they use.

Display **PPT 7.3, slide 1**, and ask the students to consider whether the language used by the person shown would be emotive or not (**Q1a**). Look at the **Key term** 'emotive language' on page 228 of the Student Book to support this activity.

Then display **PPT 7.3, slide 2**, and allow the students to look at the two sentences in order to scaffold the understanding of 'emotive'. Ask the students to suggest ways in which the second sentence clarifies the viewpoint of the writer (**Q1b**). The students can then look at the way this sentence has been annotated at the bottom of page 228 of the Student Book.

Now ask the students to select, modify and annotate a further sentence of their own (**Q2**). They can choose to imply enthusiasm or condemnation for the information in the sentence they have chosen. Alternatively, the students can work in pairs, using the same sentence and taking it in turns to make it first positive, and then negative.

Explore the skills

Ask the students to read the account written by Harry Senior, either individually or as a class (Student Book, page 229). It may be useful to ask the students what they know about the *Titanic* disaster prior to reading this extract, eliciting their knowledge of how the class system operated on the boat and how a much greater proportion of 'third class' passengers perished compared to those in 'first class'.

Before reading the account, it may also be useful to ask the students what they might expect in terms of emotive language from an account written by a survivor of the *Titanic*. Would they expect the content itself to be emotive? Would they expect it to contain emotive language and express a strong viewpoint?

You may find it useful to display images relating to the *Titanic* disaster, such as stills from the 1999 movie *Titanic*, showing the ship sinking (search the internet using search terms '*Titanic* sinking movie') or the front page of the *New York Times* from 16 April 1912 (search the internet using the search terms '*New York Times* front page *Titanic*'). It will provide a useful talking point, as it highlights the fact that 'notable' names were deemed to be the newsworthy victims/survivors.

After they have read the article, ask the students to complete **Q3** and **Q4**, either individually or as a class. **Worksheet 7.3a** provides a copy of the account that the students can use to highlight or annotate sentences.

Develop the skills

Display **PPT 7.3**, **slide 3**, which shows an image of a U-Boat, and ask the students to read the account on pages 230–1 of the Student Book. Ask the students to mentally compare this account with the preceding one as they read, and then complete **Q5**.

Ask the students to complete **Q6**, either by copying and completing the table on page 232 of the Student Book, or using **Worksheet 7.3b**.

As they work through **Q5** and **Q6**, the students will have implicitly begun to compare the two accounts. Now ask them to complete **Q7**, which starts to make the comparison more explicit. They may notice the use of punctuation, the clear expression of a strong opinion, and the use of an exclamatory phrase in the second sentence.

> **Give extra support** by reminding the students of the ways they have been using 'both ... however ... whereas' to structure a comparison. Draw attention to the fact that both are personal accounts that recount very dramatic experiences; however, it is the ways these accounts have been written which is the key difference.
>
> **Give extra challenge** by drawing attention to the difference between the two writers. Although both are professionals, one is a commander, and therefore has much higher status and more responsibility. The students could also suggest some reasons why Harry Senior's account appears to be so dispassionate, such as shock, lack of confidence, the facts speaking for themselves without embellishment.

Apply the skills

Ask the students to read the sample student response on page 233 of the Student Book and identify how the comparison has been structured (**Q8a**). Remind the students of the '*both ... however ... whereas*' structure from Lesson 7.1 if necessary. Ask for suggestions for direct evidence to use when they rewrite this paragraph, and remind them of the benefit of short, embedded evidence rather than lengthy quotations (**Q8b**).

Display **PPT 7.3**, **slide 4**, which is a copy of the task plan, and ask the students to attempt the main task (**Q9**). Remind the students that they are looking at how the viewpoints are presented to the reader, and how the reader works out what those viewpoints are from the ways the texts have been written. The key language features include: vocabulary choice; use of personal opinion; sentence structure and phrasing.

Big answer plenary	Return to the **Big question** and ask the students to make a list of the ways in which these two writers present their viewpoints to the reader. Which account do they find more effective and why? Ask for some opinions, supported with a piece of direct evidence.

7.4 Structure a comparative response to poetry

Assessment objectives

English Literature

AO1 Read, understand and respond to texts, maintaining a critical style and developing an informed personal response; use textual references, including quotations, to support and illustrate interpretations

AO2 Analyse the language, form and structure used by a writer to create meanings and effects, using relevant subject terminology where appropriate

GCSE examinations
- English Literature
  Paper 2, Section B
  Paper 2, Section C

Differentiated learning outcomes
- **All students must** be able to find some connections between two poems and make some links between how the ideas have been presented.
- **Most students should** be able to compare the ways a similar idea or topic is presented in two poems.
- **Some students could** find some connections between two poems and make some links between the ways a similar idea or topic is presented.

Resources
- **Student Book**: pp. 234–7
- **Worksheets**: 7.4a–b
- **PPT**: 7.4

Getting you thinking

Big question	Read the **Big question**: *How do you know what to compare when you're comparing poems?* and ask the students to look at the series of images under **Q1** on page 234 of the Student Book. Give the students five minutes to look at the images and to come up with a list of different connections that can be made.

Display **PPT 7.4, slide 1**, if required, either as the students complete **Q1** or after they have completed it. This list of connections is by no means definitive but can provide a scaffold if necessary.

Now ask the students to complete **Q2**, in which they must find the two items that they feel have the most connection between them in order to construct a 'both ... however ... whereas' paragraph.

Share some of these responses in order to see who has found the most connections.

Display **PPT 7.4, slide 2**, which is an example answer, for the students to compare against their own paragraphs from **Q2**. This sample answer is rather basic; ask for suggestions as to how it could be improved. Could more detail be added?

This activity is designed to scaffold the key learning point, which is that the easiest way to form a comparison is by finding a strong connection of meaning between two texts. It may be worth pointing out here that if this is not achieved, any comparison will quickly run out of steam.

Explore the skills

Display **PPT 7.4, slide 3**, an image of a shanty town, and ask the students to read the poem 'Nothing's Changed', either from page 235 of the Student Book or from **Worksheet 7.4a**. You may wish to contextualise the reading of 'Nothing's Changed' with an explanation of Apartheid prior to reading the poem.

Ask the students to identify details being used to help paint a picture of the place described in the poem (**Q3**). These might include:

- negative descriptions of the shanty town
- positive descriptions of the new restaurant
- negative descriptions of the 'working man's café'.

Now have the students complete **Q4**, in which they must explain what they learn about the place from the way it is described in the poem. Draw attention to:

- what it looks like (adjectives used to describe it – in particular, the use of sensory images)
- how the speaker feels about the place (vocabulary used to describe his thoughts and feelings as he describes it).

Read the annotations of stanza one on page 236 of the Student Book. Then ask the students to look at the list of features described under **Q5** and identify one annotation for each of the four features before completing **Q6**.

Now ask the students to find words in the poem associated with angry, bitter, resentful feelings, either by creating a list or annotating or highlighting on **Worksheet 7.4a** (**Q7**). **PPT 7.4, slide 4** provides a list of some of the words the students may identify.

Develop the skills

Individually or in pairs, ask the students to read 'Homeland', either on pages 236–7 of the Student Book or on **Worksheet 7.4b**. As the students read, they can either make a list of, or highlight or annotate, the details that create a connection between this poem and 'Nothing's Changed' (**Q8**).

> **Give extra support** by focusing on words used to describe the place or the people.
>
> **Give extra challenge** by focusing on the ways in which contrast is used in both poems – in particular, black/white, natural/unnatural.

For **Q9**, the students need to find words associated with warmth, nostalgia, or longing in the poem 'Homeland'. Use **PPT 7.4, slide 5** to support this activity if required.

Now ask the students to complete **Q10**, which develops the learning by asking them to put the two poems side by side to make some strong connections between them. It may be useful to place **Worksheets 7.4a** and **7.4b** next to each other in order to make it easier to physically look for the connections.

Apply the skills

The students can either complete this final task (**Q11**) as an individual piece of written work or as a home learning opportunity.

Big answer plenary	Return to the **Big question** and remind the students that connections are the building blocks of any good comparison.
	The main learning point of this lesson is that the strongest hooks are created by ideas, feelings and attitudes. Building comparisons on ideas creates the strongest foundations.
	Ask the students to share their written work and to use the **Check your progress** outcomes at the end of this section to assess each other's written responses and set a target for the next lesson.

7.5 Apply your skills to English Language and English Literature tasks

Assessment objectives

English Language

AO3 Compare writers' ideas and perspectives, as well as how these are conveyed, across two or more texts

English Literature

AO1 Read, understand and respond to texts, maintaining a critical style and developing an informed personal response; use textual references, including quotations, to support and illustrate interpretations

AO2 Analyse the language, form and structure used by a writer to create meanings and effects, using relevant subject terminology where appropriate

GCSE examinations
- English Language
  Paper 2, Question 4
- English Literature
  Paper 2, Section B
  Paper 2, Section C

Differentiated learning outcomes
- **All students must** be able to identify some similarities and differences between two texts, using relevant references to support their points.
- **Most students should** clearly explain the main connections between ideas and viewpoints in two texts as well as the differences between them, using effective details to support their points.
- **Some students could** begin to analyse the subtle differences between the ways ideas and viewpoints in two texts have been presented to the reader, comparing the ways language has been used to imply a viewpoint.

Resources
- **Student Book**: pp. 238–48
- **Worksheets**: 7.5 a–e (7.5d–e are available on the CD-Rom only)
- **PPT**: 7.5

Introduction

Begin with a recap of the learning from this chapter by asking the students to write a couple of sentences explaining the most useful ways of approaching and constructing a comparative task. They should aim to include:

- looking for the key 'hooks' or connections between the texts
- using *'both ... however ... whereas'* to structure their response.

Responding to an English Language task

Display **PPT 7.5, slide 1**, and ask the students to read **Source 1** and complete **Q1**, either using pages 238–9 of the Student Book or **Worksheet 7.5a**. At this stage they are gaining an overview of the passage. Encourage them to highlight, annotate or underline anything they notice. Remind the students of the learning from previous lessons in this chapter – in particular that good selections of particular details, which can be commented on in detail, are very important when working with previously unseen material in examination conditions.

Alternatively, the students could work in pairs or small groups, annotating the extract together.

Now display **PPT 7.5, slide 2**, and ask the students to read **Source 2** and complete **Q2**, using either pages 239–40 of the Student Book or **Worksheet 7.5b**.

Allow 10–15 minutes for the students to read both texts and make brief notes on the similarities and differences between them – it may be useful for the students to put the two sources side by side as they read. These may include the following points:

- Both are about children.
- Both are about children suffering hardship and difficulties.
- Source 1 is more personal than Source 2.

- Source 1 is less emotively written than Source 2.
- Both potentially evoke strong feelings from the reader.

Display **PPT 7.5, slide 3**, which is a copy of the task and the **Checklist for success**. If the task is being used for examination practice, allow the students at least 15 minutes to work independently.

Once the students have completed the task, ask them to read **Response 1** and **Response 2**, on pages 231 and 242–3 of the Student Book, and to complete **Q3–Q5**. These activities can be used to identify:

- one aspect of their work that they are particularly pleased with
- one aspect of their work that needs further improvement.

Give extra support by reading Response 1 before students begin the independent task. Elicit or identify what has been done well and what needs further scaffolding.

Responding to an English Literature task

Now display **PPT 7.5, slide 4** and ask the students to read 'The Hero' and complete **Q1**, either using page 244 of the Student Book or **Worksheet 7.5c**. Draw attention to the fact that, although the poem is on a different examination paper and in a different genre, the reading skills are exactly the same.

Still displaying **PPT 7.5, slide 4**, now ask the students to read 'Arms and the Boy' and complete **Q2**, either using page 245 of the Student Book or **Worksheet 7.5c**.

Allow 5–10 minutes for the students to read both poems quickly and summarise the similarities and differences between them. These might include:

- Both poems are about war.
- Both are about attitudes towards the waste of young life.
- Both present young soldiers as innocent and vulnerable.

Now ask the students to place the two poems side by side and highlight or underline:

- one particular line, phrase or couplet from each poem that they feel presents one of these strong connections
- three words from each poem that particularly stand out for them.

The final task is a comparative response to 'Hero' and 'Arms and the Boy'.

Display **PPT 7.5, slide 5**, which is a copy of the task and the **Checklist for success**.

If preferred, ask students to read **Response 1** and **Response 2** before undertaking their own response to this task. They could select one element of good practice and aim to incorporate it into their own response.

Once the students have completed the task, ask them to read **Response 1** and **Response 2**, on pages 246 and 247 of the Student Book, and to complete **Q3–Q5**.

Big answer plenary	The **Check your progress** outcomes on page 248 of the Student Book give an opportunity for the students to reflect on their learning and progress. They can be applied either to both tasks in this topic or just to the final one.

The two additional tasks on **Worksheet 7.5d–e**, which can be found on the accompanying CD-Rom, offer further opportunities for the students to develop their skills. These could either be used as extension activities or for further consolidation and practice of the skills developed throughout Chapter 7.

8.1 How to describe setting and atmosphere

Assessment objectives

English Language

AO5 Communicate clearly, effectively and imaginatively, selecting and adapting tone, style and register for different forms, purposes and audiences; organise information and ideas, using structural and grammatical features to support coherence and cohesion of texts

AO6 Use a range of vocabulary and sentence structures for clarity, purpose and effect, with accurate spelling and punctuation

GCSE examinations
- English Language Paper 1, Question 5

Differentiated learning outcomes

- **All students must** be able to describe settings precisely and choose some vocabulary for effect.
- **Most students should** describe settings using appropriate vocabulary and language features, including imagery in places.
- **Some students could** describe settings using a wide range of vocabulary, and thoughtfully selected language features, such as imagery.

Resources
- **Student Book**: pp. 250–3
- **Worksheet**: 8.1
- **PPT**: 8.1

Other Student Book pages
- Lesson 6.4, pp. 196–9

Getting you thinking

Explain that the lesson is going to focus on 'setting' and 'atmosphere' and briefly ask the class to suggest synonyms for both. Collate all the suggestions on the board, such as 'place', 'location' or 'environment', and 'mood', 'feel' or 'tone'.

Big question	Read the **Big question**: *How can you describe settings and atmosphere in a memorable way?* Ask the students to work in pairs for two to three minutes to discuss what makes a description of a place or setting 'memorable'. Take brief feedback, eliciting ideas such as 'vivid and colourful', 'unusual or original', 'has meaning for writer'.

Allow five minutes for the students to write a paragraph describing the photo on page 250 of the Student Book (**Q1**). Move around the class to pick out any student's work that has referenced the foreground and background in its description, and also mentioned something about the 'feel' these create. Contrast that with the work of another student who has perhaps interpreted the atmosphere in a different way.

Explore the skills

Ask the students to read the extract from *The Life of Charlotte Brontë* by Elizabeth Gaskell on page 251 of the Student Book; this is a description of Howarth Parsonage, the house that is in the photo. Then ask them to discuss **Q2–Q4**, in pairs. Take feedback on **Q2** and **Q3**:

- The factual elements are: the 'grey stone'; the 'two stories'; 'flags' on the roof (tiles); the 'four rooms' on each storey and the position of the windows. These can convey atmosphere too – in this case, a sense of order, as Gaskell herself indicates.

- The overall atmosphere is of 'order' and 'cleanliness', as Gaskell herself says, as indicated by words such as 'dainty', 'spotless' and 'purity'. You might want to elicit other nuances: an idea of religious cleanliness, perhaps, in the house's 'essence'.

Take brief feedback on the differences the students noticed between their paragraphs and Gaskell's (**Q4**). Encourage them to be precise about *how* they describe atmosphere – 'reflective', 'gloomy', 'joyful', etc.

Now ask the students to complete **Q5a–b**, individually. Take feedback as a class:

- 'gloomy', 'echoey', 'looming', 'long' or 'thin', 'smothered'
- Effects are: 'echoey' refers to repeating sounds that die away, suggesting 'empty' or 'vacant', so almost lifeless; 'looming' means taking on an ominous or threatening form, which creates a frightening effect; 'long' and 'thin' tell us the shape of the shadows, implying that they reach out like fingers, almost as if alive; 'smothered' means 'choked' or 'suffocated' and gives a claustrophobic effect.

> **Give extra support** by providing the synonyms or close meanings to the selected words in **Q5**, before asking what effect is created.
>
> **Give extra challenge** by asking why echoes in particular could create a lifeless effect. Elicit that echoes come from a 'real' sound or voice, but the repetition sounds as if other voices are answering you, but they're not 'real'.

For **Q6**, encourage the students to focus on at least two words in their sentences (either verbs or adjectives) and to think very carefully about how they convey a particular atmosphere.

Develop the skills

For **Q7**, allow two to three minutes for the students to think of appropriate words for the gaps. You could write the text on the board and then ask the students to come up to the front and write their chosen words into the gaps, explaining the effect created.

For **Q8**, elicit that the phrase Gaskell uses is 'glitter like looking-glass', which gives the effect of something precious and personal.

Now ask the students to read the extract from *The Dark Heart of Italy* by Tobias Jones and complete the table using **Worksheet 8.1** (**Q9**). Take feedback as a class:

- The key metaphors are: 'puncture the mountains', which makes the roads sound like active, living, powerful beings; 'villages huddle', which is suggestive of a communal group protecting themselves.
- Simile: 'like random piles of matchboxes' suggests they are small and fragile, and gives the sense of accidental evolution rather than careful planning.

Allow five minutes for students to complete **Q10** individually. Ask them to write their sentences on slips of paper. If time permits, pin these to the wall and ask the students to vote for the top three based on how appropriate and striking the phrases are.

Ask the students to discuss **Q11** in pairs, then take feedback and share ideas as a class.

Apply the skills

Display **PPT 8.1, slide 1**, and briefly explain the task in **Q12**, emphasising the success criteria in the **Checklist for success** on page 253 of the Student Book.

Display **PPT 8.1, slide 2**, which shows how the students might begin by generating ideas for their description. Then display **PPT 8.1, slide 3**, and explain that for planning it is best to simply describe what can be seen and then begin to add colour, imagery, etc. Leave **PPT 8.1, slide 3** for the students to refer to, and ask them to create their own spider diagrams as preparation for the main writing task.

> **Give extra support** by brainstorming writing suggestions as a class.

Allow 20 minutes for the students to complete the main writing task (**Q12**).

Big answer plenary	Ask the students to write down three things they have learned about how to make their description of setting memorable. Take feedback and share these as a class. Key aspects are likely to be: using concrete descriptions (actual things, objects), drawing on the senses, and using original imagery to make us see things afresh.

8.2 How to describe people and events

Assessment objectives

English Language

AO5 Communicate clearly, effectively and imaginatively, selecting and adapting tone, style and register for different forms, purposes and audiences; organise information and ideas, using structural and grammatical features to support coherence and cohesion of texts

AO6 Use a range of vocabulary and sentence structures for clarity, purpose and effect, with accurate spelling and punctuation

GCSE examinations
- English Language Paper 1, Question 5

Differentiated learning outcomes

- **All students must** be able to write about people and experiences with some reference to how people look, speak and behave.
- **Most students should** use well-chosen vocabulary to portray an experience and the people involved.
- **Some students could** write about people and experiences in convincing ways by carefully selecting from a wide range of vocabulary and using similes or metaphors where appropriate.

Resources
- **Student Book**: pp. 254–7
- **Worksheet**: 8.2
- **PPT**: 8.2

Other Student Book pages
- Lesson 3.4, pp. 91–4
- Lesson 4.3, pp. 124–7

Getting you thinking

Explain to the class that creating memorable characters in their writing will make it stand out and create an impression on the reader. Emphasise the idea that a key aspect of this is 'showing' rather than 'telling' the reader information.

Big question	Refer to the **Big question**: *How can you describe people and events in a memorable way?* Ask the students to write down the name of a character from a film, book or television programme that they think of as 'memorable', and list four or five things about them that make them stick in their mind. Take feedback and share some of these character choices with the class.

Display **PPT 8.2, slides 1–7**, and ask the students to identify which of the descriptions 'shows' something about a character, and which 'tells' us. Once the students have responded, point out that when you 'show' information, it has a double effect – you both see that person and find out information.

Ask the students to complete **Q1** independently, and take brief feedback on what they noted and why.

Explore the skills

Read aloud the description of Sikes in the extract from *Oliver Twist*, and briefly go over the annotations on page 255 of the Student Book, so that the students are clear about what is being shown.

Ask the students to work in pairs on **Q2** and Q3, and then take feedback as a class. Stress that Dickens does not tell us, 'Sikes was a violent, rough man', but allows us to infer that from what is shown in Dickens's description of him. The detail about the dog allows us to infer that Sikes mistreats it, as the dog seems to cower from him ('skulks').

For **Q4**, commend any attempt by students to suggest the character of Sikes by describing how Sikes acts – for example: 'Sikes grasped the grubby stick with its sharp end in his rough, leathery hands, and occasionally raised it in the air as if to bring it down suddenly on someone.'

Develop the skills

Ask the students to read the extract from *Bad Blood* by Lorna Sage on pages 255–6 of the Student Book, and make notes independently. Then, put the students into small groups of three or four to answer **Q5–Q8**. One person should act as note-taker for the group. The group should ensure they take turns to speak, and work co-operatively, disagreeing or clarifying in a positive way. Take feedback on one question from each group, asking the other groups if they agree/disagree. Possible responses could be:

Q5: We learn that she has her own individual sounds and phrases; that she has asthma; that she had a 'ghoulish' appearance with a pale face.

Q6: Sound: e.g. 'wheezing fits', 'cackles'; sight: 'powdery', 'pale skin'; touch: 'soft...powdery'; taste/smell: referred to in the way she savours other people's 'tastes'.

Q7: The fairy tale could be Hansel and Gretel with the witch's house made of cake/sweets that acts as a trap so the witch can catch and eat the children.

Q8: The writer uses the simile 'as though she'd been dusted all over with icing sugar like a sponge cake'. It is an appropriate simile, as this is the sort of thing an older person without any teeth might eat! The 'dusting' also suggests the grandmother's advanced age.

For **Q9**, the students should work independently to write their paragraph.

Now ask the students to read the second extract from *Bad Blood* on page 256 and to complete **Q10–Q12** independently Ask the students to share their responses with a partner before taking brief feedback as a class.

Q10: The public baths – not very pleasant; the mere: more natural, but not perfect; 'goose droppings', 'soupy', 'warm' – also very communal 'other...kids'.

Q11: Gym mistress: cruel (pushed them in) and disapproving ('horrified'); the other kids are standoffish ('didn't much speak to us'); Gail is robust both physically ('good at gym') and mentally ('determined'). The impression Lorna Sage wants us to have is that she and Gail were independent and didn't always fit in.

Q12: The phrase 'horrible baths' links back to their description in the second sentence.

Apply the skills

Read through **Q13**. Ask the students to spend 10 minutes choosing their experience and then making notes, using **Worksheet 8.2**. The students could then share some of their ideas with the class; allow a further five minutes for them to refine or add to their notes. Remind them that the skill is to 'show' what happened, rather than simply telling the reader, so lots of descriptive detail will be needed.

> **Give extra support** by putting the students into guided-writing groups according to ability and working with a less confident group to prompt them with ideas. You could jointly compose a group description before they have a go at their own, or they could use the start of the group description and develop/finish it themselves.
>
> **Give extra challenge** by asking more confident students to develop the description into a longer piece that expands on particular aspects such as the location.

Once the students have completed their descriptions, ask them to peer-assess them, using the **Check your progress** outcomes at the end of the unit. Using a pencil, they could highlight particularly clear or vivid descriptions in each other's work that create an effective and memorable picture in the mind.

Big answer plenary	Ask the students to write down one key target they will try to meet in their next piece of descriptive writing about people or experiences. You might also suggest they read further extracts from *Oliver Twist*, readily available online, to identify further evocative descriptions of people, such as the Artful Dodger, Fagin or Nancy.

8.3 How to structure a description

Assessment objectives

English Language

AO5 Communicate clearly, effectively and imaginatively, selecting and adapting tone, style and register for different forms, purposes and audiences; organise information and ideas, using structural and grammatical features to support coherence and cohesion of texts

AO6 Use a range of vocabulary and sentence structures for clarity, purpose and effect, with accurate spelling and punctuation

GCSE examinations
- English Language Paper 1, Question 5

Differentiated learning outcomes
- **All students must** be able to write a description that is split into different paragraphs, each with a new focus.
- **Most students should** use topic sentences and paragraphs that deal with separate parts of their description, and vary their structure.
- **Some students could** use a wide variety of sentence and paragraph styles to sequence the ideas in their description, and create engaging texts.

Resources
- **Student Book**: pp. 258–61
- **Worksheet**: 8.3
- **PPT**: 8.3

Other Student Book pages
- Lesson 6.3, pp. 192–5

Getting you thinking

Explain that when thinking about description, we tend to consider the obvious things such as similes or vivid vocabulary, as shown in Lessons 8.1 and 8.2, but how we organise that description is also important as we are directing where our readers should look.

Big question | Read the **Big question**: *How can you structure your descriptions to keep readers interested?* Ask the students to spend two minutes making notes in spider-diagram form around the word 'structure'. Then create a class spider-diagram on the whiteboard and collate ideas from the class. You could draw out the idea that it is about the 'shape' of a text – the particular places where things go.

Allow five minutes for the students to complete **Q1** and **Q2** independently.

Explore the skills

Now read aloud to the class the extract from 'Rain' by Ameena Meer on pages 258–9, and for **Q3**, ask the students to note down what the writer's focus is in each paragraph. If any are unsure, read it aloud again and get them to consider what is being described primarily in each case. Take feedback as a class:

- Paragraph 1: the coming storm (important to be specific, not just 'the weather')
- Paragraph 2: the sweat on the main character's neck
- Paragraph 3: her experiences in the crowded tube/subway train; the air/heat/smells
- Paragraph 4: the people on the subway.

For **Q4**, ask students to plan their paragraphs independently. Stress that the descriptions should have a purpose – to emphasise how uncomfortable she feels, or the suspense of the storm, or some other aspect of the city and how she feels about it.

Give extra support by providing some suggestions for paragraphs 6 and 7 in **Q4**, which the weaker students could expand on: for example, shop windows she passes, a beggar, traffic lights, a taxi, litter, and so on.

Give extra challenge by asking the students to plan for four more paragraphs – i.e. 6, 7, 8 and 9 – all building the picture of the woman in the city, and considering whether one particular order would work better than another.

For **Q5**, ask students to re-read the extract on pages 258–9 and then spend two to three minutes discussing the questions with a partner. The 'zoom-in' detail is the 'wiry hair', having proceeded from the 'sweat' to the 'thick black hair' to the single detail. The effect is to emphasise the physical impact of the stormy heat on her and how aware she is of it.

To reinforce understanding of the 'zoom-in' skill, display **PPT 8.3**, **slides 1–4**, which give a further description of a city scene. To check the students' understanding, you could ask the students to sketch (in very basic form) what is described in each slide, as if through the lens of a camera. Then ask the students to write their own 'zoom-in' detail (**Q6**), using the stages in **PPT 8.3** as a model. Share good examples with the class as a whole.

Ask the students to complete **Q7** independently; then take brief feedback as a class.

Develop the skills

You may wish to display the sample paragraph from page 260 of the Student Book on the board and go through the sequence of the sentences, checking the students' understanding of the term 'topic sentence'.

For **Q8** and **Q9**, the sequence and focus should now be clear. Now ask the students to write their paragraph about the storm following the established model. However, draw their attention to the slight nuance here – that the final sentence is being used as a 'summing up' sentence, to round off the description or signal a change.

Ask the students to work in pairs and prepare a rehearsed reading of the text at the top of page 261. They should decide between themselves how they will 'perform' the reading, deciding who reads what line, sentence or paragraph, using highlighter pens and **Worksheet 8.3**. They should consider how they will emphasise the repetitions or patterning, e.g. one person reading the similar lines or one stressing particular words.

Once the students have completed their rehearsed reading, they should work in the same pairs to answer **Q10–Q12**, which should now be clearer following their speaking/listening task. Then ask the students to share their answers with another pair, before taking feedback as a class. Possible responses could include:

Q10: Short opening paragraph focuses on writer 'in situ', peacefully sitting. The two very short paragraphs draw attention to the mountain and its 'smile'.

Q11: The repeated 'I am...' at the start suggests certainty and calm; the repetition of 'smiles' and 'smiling' shows the contrast and bookends the mid-part and end of the description.

Q12: The time connectives tell us the order ('At first ... In a few minutes ... soon ... Now'). But there are also references back to things – for example, the use of the definite article 'the' tells us the 'patch of blue sky' has been mentioned earlier.

Apply the skills

For the main task, allow at least five to six minutes for the students to plan the structure of their piece before they begin (**Q13**). Then, allow a further 15 minutes for the students to draft their description (**Q14**). Draw attention to the **Checklist for success** on page 261. They could complete the piece as a homework task.

Big answer plenary	Allow two to three minutes for the students to explain to each other the importance of considering structure when writing a description. Then, using the **Check your progress** outcomes, ask them to make their own evaluation of what they have achieved in the lesson. Were there any specific aspects they struggled with? If so, how could they tackle them?

8.4 Build ideas for a descriptive task

Assessment objectives

English Language

AO5 Communicate clearly, effectively and imaginatively, selecting and adapting tone, style and register for different forms, purposes and audiences; organise information and ideas, using structural and grammatical features to support coherence and cohesion of texts

AO6 Use a range of vocabulary and sentence structures for clarity, purpose and effect, with accurate spelling and punctuation

GCSE examinations

- English Language
  Paper 1, Question 5

Differentiated learning outcomes

- **All students must** be able to come up with some ideas using a spider diagram before they start writing.
- **Most students should** use different methods to generate ideas, and be able to add details to them.
- **Some students could** select from a range of ways to plan ideas, and sequence them quickly into paragraphs.

Resources

- **Student Book**: pp. 262–3
- **Worksheet**: 8.4
- **PPT**: 8.4

Other Student Book pages

- Lesson 4.1, pp. 116–19

Getting you thinking

Tell the students that it is important to remember that ideas don't often just 'pop' into their heads, or if they do, they might not necessarily be the best ones. Having a set of methods for getting ideas is therefore vital.

Big question

Refer to the **Big question**: *How can you quickly come up with ideas for your descriptive task?* Ask the students how they think professional writers get ideas when they are writing about a particular place or experience. Allow two to three minutes for the students to discuss in pairs, and then share ideas with another pair before feeding back to the class.

One thing to focus on is that most writers are very good observers: they look at aspects of life and notice particular things – colours, senses, movements.

Read aloud the task on page 262 of the Student Book. For **Q1** and **Q2**, ask the students to work on their own to generate further ideas for the website, for example:

- things you can see in the picture: gripping hands; ledges; crevices; climbing shoes
- things you can't see in the picture: blue sky; climbing partner; sea-birds; clouds; top of cliff; green rope
- climber's feelings: excitement; fear; aching limbs; taut muscles.

Then ask the students to spend two minutes thinking about which method in **Q2** they found works best for them. Is there any advantage to making a list? (It might help them to think about the sequence of description.)

Now ask the students to complete **Q3**. This activity is important: generating ideas is as much about culling material as creating it. For example, mentioning the t-shirt you're wearing might not be as interesting as the way the rope is fixed to the rock.

Explore the skills

For **Q4**, display the sentences on the board using **PPT 8.4**, **slide 1**, and give the students five minutes to come up with suitable adjectives for each one.

Ask the students to share their adjectives in pairs and between them decide which ones have added the most vivid detail. Have they covered more than two senses?

Take feedback as a class: share some suggestions for each phrase from selected students and comment on how each might alter the atmosphere or tone of the sentence.

Develop the skills

For **Q5**, ask the students to work independently to develop the further paragraphs. Suggestions could include:

- the climber's feelings as he works his way up the rock
- a sudden problem, such as the rope slipping, or climber losing his grip or feeling a spasm of pain running through his arms, or the climber inexplicably being overwhelmed by a sense of fear
- how the problem resolves – managing to cling on to the rock, or feel the pain subside, or calming his fears in some way
- a final paragraph bringing it all together – balancing the thrills and dangers of rock climbing.

> **Give extra support** by suggesting that the students use the 'zoom in' idea for their remaining paragraphs. Ask them what would be a suitable detail to zoom in on (e.g. the climber's hand and fingers as he struggles to find a secure grip).
>
> **Give extra challenge** by asking the students to rearrange their sequence and think about the effect.

Apply the skills

Reinforce the sequence and choices for generating ideas by displaying **PPT 8.4, slides 2–8**. Go through the stages with the class.

Then, ask the students to complete the main writing task (**Q6**) independently, using **Worksheet 8.4**.

> **Big answer plenary**
>
> Ask the students to tell each other what method they would use if they were given a photo to respond to in an assessment. Can they think of any other ways? On this basis, they should be able to make a judgement as to which of the **Check your progress** outcomes they have achieved.
>
> For those who are struggling to come up with more than one planning method, you may need to supply some simple templates as a reminder, for them to stick into a folder or notebook.

8.5 How to structure narratives effectively

Assessment objectives

English Language

AO5 Communicate clearly, effectively and imaginatively [...] Organise information and ideas, using structural and grammatical features to support coherence and cohesion of texts

AO6 Use a range of vocabulary and sentence structures for clarity, purpose and effect, with accurate spelling and punctuation

GCSE examinations
- English Language Paper 1, Question 5

Differentiated learning outcomes
- **All students must** be able to plan a story with an introduction, complication, climax and conclusion.
- **Most students should** plan a story and choose different ways of opening it to get the reader interested.
- **Some students could** adapt and alter their plan so that it engages the reader's interest straight away and maintains it throughout by means of clever use of paragraph styles and focuses.

Resources
- **Student Book**: pp. 264–7
- **Worksheets**: 8.5a–b
- **PPT**: 8.5

Other Student Book pages
- Lesson 2.5, pp. 58–61

Getting you thinking

Begin by explaining that writers often spend as much time on story structure as they do on writing the story itself.

Big question	Read the **Big question**: *How can you structure your stories to keep readers interested?* Ask the students to note down three things they think a good story structure should have; then feedback some ideas to the class. They might say features such as 'an exciting opening'; 'a series of challenges for the main character'; 'something surprising happening'; 'a good ending'. In each case, try to elicit from individuals what they mean by each of these things.

Read aloud the four opening extracts on page 264 of the Student Book, using appropriate tone and stress.

Put the students in groups of three or four. Allow five minutes for them to re-read each opening and then share their feelings about each one with the rest of their group (**Q1** and **Q2**). Take brief feedback as a class, asking groups to suggest what made them want to read on, perhaps eliciting the idea of wanting to know more about a situation.

Explore the skills

Read the opening paragraph of **Explore the skills** on page 265 of the Student Book. Ask the students to complete **Q3** independently, using **Worksheet 8.5a**. Some of the story openings combine several aspects, but the students should conclude that:

- Cormier: deals with a key event/action ('murder')
- Poe: mainly setting/atmosphere
- Martin: combines all of the features, except direct contact with reader
- Brontë: direct contact with reader ('You must ...').

Give extra challenge by asking individuals to consider whether there are any disadvantages to having texts that refer directly to the reader. (Answer: it has to be sustained throughout; it can come across as forced and unnatural, even comic.)

Now allow 15 minutes for the students to complete **Q4–Q6** independently. Take feedback as a class and share some students' 'location and mood' sentences.

Give extra support by providing ideas about protagonists: for example, prompt them to think about aspects such as jobs/roles, ages, people they come across every day, whether they are authority figures or weak figures.

Develop the skills

Read the opening extracts on page 264 again, before asking the students to note down answers to **Q7**. Take feedback and elicit that the shorter sentences obviously hold back more information, but the first one in particular raises questions (Who murdered whom? Why? Where? When?).

Complete **Q8** as a class discussion. Elicit that the use of personal pronouns rather than names, and the use of the phrase 'the house' rather than who owns it, all create expectation and the desire to know more.

Now ask the students to complete **Q9** in pairs. Remind them that keeping back key information as long as possible is one way of doing it, though it does have to be revealed eventually. Take feedback as a class and share their suggestions.

Give extra support by displaying **PPT 8.5, slides 1–3**, which shows how the text might be altered, before the students attempt to write their own versions.

Read the story structure on page 266 of the Student Book. For **Q10**, ask the students to discuss the possibilities in pairs, and then take feedback as a class. Elicit the idea that the story could start at any point, even the moment that he wakes up on the school coach. Ask the class:

- Are there any advantages to playing around with the time sequence in this way? (Yes, you make the reader 'work' to follow the mystery.)
- What might be the dangers? (You lose your thread and the plot becomes unclear.)

Read the four opening paragraphs to the story on page 267 and ask the students to complete **Q11–Q14** independently. Ask them to make notes for each question, before comparing answers with a partner. Take feedback as a class, eliciting the following:

Q11: The opening begins with the rising action, just before the really scary part.

Q12: He doesn't mention the visit directly – just lets us work it out through the mention of the 'teacher'.

Q13: The single word paragraph highlights his situation and his view of himself at this point.

Q14: Before the students do this, it is worth pointing out that filling in background detail can be a useful technique after you have grabbed attention with action.

Give extra support by telling the students that if they are going to refer back to earlier events (**Q14**), then they need to think carefully about tenses; point this out in the example given: *His school **had** arrived at the museum at 2pm. Dai **hadn't wanted** to go...he hated history, so...* These are completed actions in the past, now overtaken by current or recent events. Why is 'hated' not 'had hated'? Because Dai continues to hate history – that's an unchanged element of the story (so far).

Apply the skills

For **Q15**, read the task aloud and ask students to work independently to write the first two or three paragraphs of the story, using **Worksheet 8.5b**.

Big answer plenary	Ask the students to look back over their plan for **Q15**, 'The Visit', and the first two or three paragraphs they have written. Ask them to evaluate what they have done, using the **Check your progress** outcomes. Remind them that if they have stuck to the conventional approach that is fine, as long as they have done so consciously.

8.6 Creating convincing characterisation and voice

Assessment objectives

English Language

AO5 Communicate clearly, effectively and imaginatively, selecting and adapting tone, style and register for different forms, purposes and audiences; organise information and ideas, using structural and grammatical features to support coherence and cohesion of texts

AO6 Use a range of vocabulary and sentence structures for clarity, purpose and effect, with accurate spelling and punctuation

GCSE examinations
- English Language Paper 1, Question 5

Differentiated learning outcomes
- **All students must** be able to use direct speech to tell the reader something about their character.
- **Most students should** use dialogue and description to tell the reader what is happening and convey character.
- **Some students could** use dialogue convincingly to convey character and also adapt sentence style to suggest voice and viewpoint.

Resources
- **Student Book**: pp. 268–71
- **Worksheet**: 8.6
- **PPT**: 8.6

Other Student Book pages
- Lesson 1.5, pp. 24–7
- Lesson 2.3, pp. 50–3

Getting you thinking

Big question	Refer to the **Big question**: *How can you make your characters or narrators interesting?* Explain that 'characterisation' is the process writers use to build a picture of someone in the reader's head. Write the word on the board and ask the students to suggest different ways this might be done. You could begin by writing 'manner of speaking' at the top of the list and provide the example of how a 'thin, reedy voice' would give a different idea of someone than a 'strong, booming voice'.

Ask the students to read the extract from *Small Island* to themselves (Student Book, page 268) and imagine they can hear Gilbert and Hortense speaking (**Q1**).

Now, either read the extract aloud to the class, or get them to read it in groups of three, with one person narrating, one reading Hortense's words, and one Gilbert's. Encourage them to make the characters' voices distinctive: the breathless, surprised tone of Gilbert contrasted with Hortense's precise and ironic/sarcastic tones.

For **Q2** and **Q3**, give the students five minutes to work in pairs, reading the passage for a third time and answering the questions. Students should note that Hortense has obviously arrived from some way away (reference to 'letter') and has a trunk. Gilbert has failed to turn up, so she has found her own way to his house. Gilbert comes across as rather uncontrollable and disorganised (like a 'large dog'); Hortense is someone who knows her own mind, and has a sharp tongue.

Explore the skills

Begin by stressing that the 'manner of speaking' in the extract from *Small Island* on page 268, is key to our understanding of the two characters: not simply *what* is said, but *how* it is said, and the accompanying actions. Use the annotated example on page 269 as an opportunity to check not just the students' understanding of how characterisation works, but also the fundamentals of setting out direct speech.

Display **PPT 8.6, slides 1–5**. This contains a number of examples of similar passages. Ask the students to correct the speech punctuation errors for slides 2 and 3, and for slides 4 and 5 to suggest how characterisation can be built by adding an 'action'.

Once the students feel comfortable building characterisation around dialogue, allow 15 minutes for them to complete **Q4** independently.

> **Give extra support** by providing possible reasons why Gilbert didn't meet her: he missed the bus, or got the wrong day, or he was there but Hortense didn't see him. Whatever reasons the students decide on, they should try to maintain the same frosty reaction from Hortense and the defensive tone of Gilbert.
>
> **Give extra challenge** by asking some students to write a second paragraph that builds the characters further, based on what they have already read. Encourage the students to read the original novel and find out what Gilbert's actual excuse was.

For **Q5**, once the students have written their paragraphs, ask them to check speech layout against the extract on page 268, or any other extract from the book. Then ask them to swap their paragraphs with a partner for checking.

Develop the skills

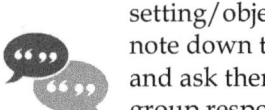

Ask the students to read the extract from 'The Ice Palace' on pages 269–270 on their own. Emphasise that here they are looking at how a character's observations or the setting/objects around them can also be used to emphasise character. Ask them to note down their answers to **Q6–Q9**. Then put the students in groups of three or four and ask them to take it in turns to share answers to the questions and then agree on group responses. Take feedback as a class. Suggested answers are:

Q6: Objects and furniture in her own house are 'old' and 'battered', maybe used for decades, but still 'luxurious'. In contrast, many of the things in the room she is in seem lacking in character and are there perhaps more for show ('some' books looked as though they had been read).

Q7: These views might suggest that she is very different from her fiancé, and perhaps they are not well matched.

Q8: Sally is observing these expensive things in a cool, almost detached way.

Q9: She likes the idea of old, familiar, comfortable things, rather than the business-like style of this room. She is perhaps a bit of a dreamer.

Now ask the students to read **Student A** and **Student B**'s responses on page 271. For **Q10** and **Q11**, ask the students to work in pairs and note down their answers:

Q10: In **Extract A**, the short, blunt sentences match the character's disappointment. In **Extract B**, the character's excitement is implied; the long sentence suggests a headlong rush of expectation and observation in a stream of vivid images.

Q11: In **Extract A**, the bitter tone of the rhetorical question reveals the character's feelings in a direct way; the adjectives 'dark' and 'gloomy' follow the list of what might have been expected; the writer chooses to focus on stark nouns ('rubbish', 'gutters') to highlight the disappointing reality. In **Extract B**, the positive vocabulary choices ('sparkling', 'glittered', 'majestically') and the metaphors ('necklaces of light', 'beating heart of the city') imply dynamism and life.

Apply the skills

For **Q12**, read the final task on page 271 and ask the students to write the two opening paragraphs of the story, using **Worksheet 8.6**. Before they begin, refer them to the **Checklist for success**.

Big answer plenary	Once the students have planned and written their paragraphs, ask them to share their drafts with a partner. Then distribute sticky notes on which they should write positive comments based on the **Check your progress** outcomes on page 271 of the Student Book, e.g. 'The direct speech here tells us that…'. Once the students have done this, ask them to pass the drafts back to their partners. If time permits, ask the students to redraft their work, aiming at a higher outcome.

8.7 Generate ideas for your narrative response

Assessment objectives

English Language

AO5 Communicate clearly, effectively and imaginatively, selecting and adapting tone, style and register for different forms, purposes and audiences; organise information and ideas, using structural and grammatical features to support coherence and cohesion of texts

AO6 Use a range of vocabulary and sentence structures for clarity, purpose and effect, with accurate spelling and punctuation

GCSE examinations
- English Language Paper 1, Question 5

Differentiated learning outcomes
- **All students must** be able to generate ideas and write a basic plan from them.
- **Most students should** generate some good ideas and create a structured plan from them.
- **Some students could** generate a range of interesting, well-developed ideas and turn these into a plan with the key ingredients of a story.

Resources
- **Student Book**: pp. 272–3
- **Worksheet**: 8.7
- **PPT**: 8.7

Other Student Book pages
- Lesson 2.1, pp. 42–5

Getting you thinking

Start by reminding the students that ideas rarely appear by 'magic' into their heads when writing or speaking; instead, thinking of and developing ideas requires the use of methods and techniques, as much as the act of writing the draft does.

Big question	Read the **Big question**: *How can you come up with good ideas for a short story or short story opening in a short space of time?* Ask the students: what is a 'good idea' when it comes to stories? Allow two to three minutes for them to note down what they think 'good' means in this sense, and then take feedback as a class. You could elicit words such as 'original', 'surprising', 'fresh', 'vivid', 'full of potential' (the idea has space to build a story around) and so on.

Ask the students to complete **Q1** and then share answers with a partner – particularly to part **b**. Elicit that, to get ideas, you need a structure or frame to 'hang' your ideas on.

Explore the skills

Read the opening paragraphs about structure in **Explore the skills** on page 272 of the Student Book, and refer the students to the sample structure of *Where? Who? What? When? Why?*. Point out how this has immediately allowed the student in question to bring life to the idea – to 'flesh it out'.

Display **PPT 8.7, slides 1–4.** Put the students in groups of three or four and allow a maximum of three minutes for each group to come up with the *Where? Who? What? When? Why?* for the title on each slide. Make it a challenge or game by asking the students to complete the elements before the time is up for each slide. There is a reason for this – they will have very little time to plan in an exam, so speed is of the essence.

Take feedback as a class. Ask some groups to share their ideas, and discuss how difficult it was to do the task. Would the students have found it easier to do it on their own? If the answer is 'yes', then that should stand as encouragement for the exam.

Keep the students in their groups, and ask them to complete **Q2** independently, and then share their ideas with the group (**Q3**). Take feedback as a class and discuss which ideas work best. Match them against the words used for 'good (idea)' at the start – i.e. 'fresh', 'original', 'full of potential', etc.

Develop the skills

This part of the lesson is designed to show the students how to make ideas 'original', as many will still struggle to do this.

Allow at least 5–10 minutes for the students to complete **Q4** and **Q5** independently.

Once they have had a chance to work through both questions, take some feedback, perhaps asking one or two students to outline their choice of character from the list and what story might be suggested.

> **Give extra support** by reminding the students of the opening parts of a story's structure: *introduction–development–problem*. This will help them think about how choosing a character (e.g. a person meeting someone they love) can be developed into action. Prompt them by asking: *What problem might there be?*
>
> **Give extra challenge** by telling selected students to choose 'main character meeting ghost of him or herself' as this may prove more complex. Apply the same structure: what problem is suggested?

Apply the skills

Ask the students to complete **Q6**, using **Worksheet 8.7**.

The worksheet will help the students plan and build a story idea. There is an option for them to write the first paragraph at the end of the worksheet, which might be useful if they wish to test or evaluate how much the planning has helped.

Big answer plenary	Once the plan (and paragraph) have been completed, ask the students to look at the **Check your progress** outcomes on page 273 of the Student Book, and make their own evaluation of which outcomes they have achieved. If they have achieved Outcomes 1 and 2, ask them to make a note of what they could do differently if they had another chance to plan. For example, were the ideas 'interesting'? If not, what could make them more interesting? (Is it a case of a more unusual central character or setting?) Take brief feedback so that the class can hear a range of responses in terms of attainment and future targets.

8.8 Apply your skills to an English Language task

> **Assessment objectives**
>
> **English Language**
>
> AO5 Communicate clearly, effectively and imaginatively, selecting and adapting tone, style and register for different forms, purposes and audiences; organise information and ideas, using structural and grammatical features to support coherence and cohesion of texts
>
> AO6 Use a range of vocabulary and sentence structures for clarity, purpose and effect, with accurate spelling and punctuation

> **GCSE examinations**
> - English Language Paper 1, Question 5

Differentiated learning outcomes
- **All students must** be able to describe settings and people precisely in separate paragraphs with some vocabulary chosen for effect.
- **Most students should** be able to describe settings using appropriate imagery and vocabulary, and vary their structure for effect.
- **Some students could** use carefully selected vocabulary, a range of language features and a wide variety of sentence/paragraph styles and structures.

Resources
- **Student Book**: pp. 274–8
- **Worksheets**: 8.8a–b (8.8b is available on the CD-Rom only)
- **PPT**: 8.8

Other Student Book pages
- Lessons 8.1–8.3, pp. 250–61

Introduction

Explain that AO5 and AO6 refer to the ways in which the students craft and compose their own descriptive and narrative writing in order to make an impact on the reader. They deal with the conscious manipulation of words, sentences and the overall text for effect and, in the case of descriptive/imaginative writing, to create vivid and powerful settings, narratives and characters.

Responding to English Language tasks

Ask the students to look at the image on page 274 of the Student Book, and read aloud the task in **Q1**. Allow five minutes for the students to work independently on the first bullet point, noting down ideas related to the image. Draw their attention to the skills they have developed so far in this chapter for generating ideas from a photo. Remind them that they should not only consider what they can see, but what might be 'off-stage' or implied by the image, for example, what might be inside one of the cars.

Take brief feedback and share ideas with the class.

Now discuss the second bullet point as a class. Ask the students to think about the key skills they would need to tackle the task and how they would plan their description. Elicit from them ideas about:

- generating words and phrases and then expanding them with further words or phrases (e.g. adjectives)
- grouping ideas into paragraphs, which can then become the focus for the description.

You could, at this stage, ask them to write a quick plan and the first paragraph of the response on their own, to get them engaged with the task as a 'real' assessment.

Now read **Response 1** on page 275 together as a class, referring to the accompanying commentary and annotations. The mark schemes for GCSE English Language could be copied and given to the students for reference. For each response, ask them to work up the descriptors like a ladder, answering 'yes' or 'no' if they see the skills in place (**Q2**). For **Response 1** they are likely to see Level 2 descriptors in place.

Now read the **Comments on Response 1** aloud and discuss with the class how **Response 1** could be improved (**Q3**).

Following the discussion of **Response 1**, you could ask the students to improve it, using the **Comments on Response 1** and **Check your progress** Outcome 2 on page 278. Display **PPT 8.8**, **slides 1–4**, to model how the first few sentences might be improved.

Now read aloud **Response 2** and the annotations, and the **Comments on Response 2** on pages 276–7. Ask the students to look at both **Response 1** and **Response 2**, and note down the key differences that they observe between the two (**Q4**). In particular, elicit from them the following features of **Response 2**:

- the developed imagery
- the way the student has 'zoomed in' on specific details
- the variety in the sentence openings
- the use of a short paragraph for effect.

The students could now complete their own, full response to a similar task, using **Worksheet 8.8a**. The photo on this worksheet shows a busy city street; the task asks the students to write a description based on it. You will need to decide whether you want the students to do a full, practice response without any assistance, or whether you wish to provide some initial guidance – for example, discussing the picture as a class first.

Completing this full response may take more than the time immediately available, in which case you could ask the students to complete the task for homework.

Once they have completed the task, they should look again at the two sample responses against their own and make a judgement as to which they think they are closer to in level.

Then, ask them to select and note down:

- one aspect or feature they are particularly pleased with in their own work
- one aspect or feature they could improve.

Alternatively, they could exchange their work with a partner and, working up from the bottom of the English Language mark scheme, decide which of the levels they feel the response fits best. They could then rewrite their response in the light of the comments proposed.

The additional task on **Worksheet 8.8b**, which can be found on the accompanying CD-Rom, offers a further opportunity for the students to develop their skills. This could either be used as an extension activity or for further consolidation and practice of the skills developed throughout Chapter 8.

9.1 What is point of view writing?

Assessment objective

English Language

AO5 Communicate clearly, effectively and imaginatively, selecting and adapting tone, style and register for different forms, purposes and audiences; organise information and ideas, using structural and grammatical features to support coherence and cohesion of texts

GCSE examinations
- English Language Paper 2, Question 5

Differentiated learning outcomes
- **All students must** be able to recognise the basic point of view of a writer.
- **Most students should** recognise the techniques a writer uses to express their point of view and apply some of them to their own work.
- **Some students could** recognise the techniques a writer uses to express their point of view and use them appropriately in their own work.

Resources
- **Student Book**: pp. 280–3
- **Worksheet**: 9.1
- **PPT**: 9.1

Other Student Book pages
- Lesson 2.8, pp. 70–4

Getting you thinking

Big question

Ask the students to discuss with a partner for two to three minutes what they believe is the biggest influence on their own point of view. Is it friends? Family? People in authority? What they see on television or online, or read in papers or magazines? Take brief feedback and share ideas with the class.

Then refer to the **Big question**: *What does it mean when you have to write from a particular point of view?* Elicit some initial responses to the question.

Introduce the topic by saying that being able to master point of view writing is an important skill not just for exams but also for life itself.

Put the students in groups of three. Ask each to take one of the points of view – A, B or C on page 280 of the Student Book – and read it aloud to their group. The three students in each group then work together to complete **Q1** and **Q2**.

For **Q1**, answers are: A is an event; B is an issue/idea; C is a person/role.

For **Q2**, encourage members of each trio to listen to each other's views patiently and, if needed, to prompt them or ask questions about why they have that belief.

Explore the skills

Keep the students in their groups and ask them to read the extracts on pages 281–2 of the Student Book and complete **Q3–Q5**.

Once the students have discussed **Q3–Q5**, display **PPT 9.1**, **slides 1–4**, and take feedback as a class asking each group to share their answers. For **Q5**, highlight the particular language that the students refer to in their answers, and ask them how this demonstrates a particular view. Answers are:

Q3: They are all about coffee bars.

Q4: Councillor: against coffee-bars run by chains, believing they are taking over the high street and damaging local businesses.

Magazine feature writer: no set view for or against, but comments on the growth of coffee shops and bars.

Student: loves coffee bars, with their enticing aromas and flavours.

Q5: See **PPT 9.1**, **slide 2** for examples of language features and evidence in the first text.

Develop the skills

Briefly concept check and elicit from the class which of the extracts is positive, which is negative and which is neutral (**Q6**).

Then, ask the students to complete **Q7**, using **Worksheet 9.1**.

> **Give extra support** by providing a list of positive adjectives and asking the students to find their opposites – for example, 'beautiful', 'tasty', 'rich', 'smooth', 'sweet', 'deep'.
>
> **Give extra challenge** by asking some students to complete the further task at the bottom of **Worksheet 9.1**. This shows that a text can contain several viewpoints even when the main viewpoint remains consistent.

Apply the skills

For **Q8**, read aloud the first paragraph of the article on page 283 of the Student Book, and ask students what, if any, viewpoint is expressed. Elicit that there isn't a specific view about whether coffee bars are a good thing, but there is an 'angle' on the issue which is the writer's surprise at the number of coffee bars, which we can infer from language such as 'I'm not kidding' and 'on a coffee planet'.

Then ask students to work independently and note down answers to the second bullet point. Take feedback as a class: they may pick out the repeated, almost rhetorical questions, but also pick up on the fact that there is little of the 'loaded' language here – it is more to do with cautionary language ('Now, I like... *but...*'), as well as reasons and evidence (no bookshops, cinemas, etc.).

For **Q9**, read the main task and draw students' attention to the techniques they should use. This includes use of adjectives and verbs, but you can also mention rhetorical questions, exaggerated surprise/shock and use of imagery. Ask the students to work independently to write a paragraph expressing their viewpoint.

Big answer plenary	Ask the students to write down their own definition of 'point of view writing', and to give three top language tips they would give to anyone wishing to write a powerful point of view article. If you wish, this could be turned into a simple A4 poster, to which they could add any further techniques they come across in their study.

9.2 Match tone and register to task and audience

Assessment objectives

English Language

AO5 Communicate clearly, effectively and imaginatively, selecting and adapting tone, style and register for different forms, purposes and audiences; organise information and ideas, using structural and grammatical features to support coherence and cohesion of texts

AO6 Use a range of vocabulary and sentence structures for clarity, purpose and effect, with accurate spelling and punctuation

GCSE examinations
- English Language Paper 2, Question 5

Differentiated learning outcomes
- **All students must** be able to understand the difference between formal and informal language.
- **Most students should** be able to write in a formal way for particular audiences, and in an informal way for other audiences.
- **Some students could** adapt their tone and register according to the task and audience.

Resources
- **Student Book**: pp. 284–5
- **Worksheet**: 9.2
- **PPT**: 9.2

Other Student Book pages
- Lesson 4.2, pp. 120–3

Getting you thinking

Read the introductory information in **Getting you thinking** on page 284 of the Student Book. Then explain to the students that understanding tone of voice in someone's writing (or speaking for that matter) can help them judge that person's point of view or attitude. It also means that they will be able to replicate it, if need be, in different contexts.

Big question	Ask the students how many different tones of voice they use during an average day. They could make a quick list, dividing up the day into seven segments: getting up/breakfast; going to school; morning lessons; lunch; afternoon lessons; going home; dinner/evening. Then read the **Big question**: *Why does it matter what tone or register you use?* Elicit some initial responses to the question.

Read aloud the extract from a reporter on page 284: you may wish to 'play up' the shocked, formal nature of the language. Then ask the students to complete **Q1–Q3** in pairs. Take feedback as a class:

Q1: The tone is 'shocked'.

Q2: The register isn't right for the audience (young people).

Q3: You could change some of the long-winded phrases to something snappier – 'I am afraid to say...' to 'I'm stunned...' – and replace some of the more complex or archaic vocabulary with something more of the moment ('attire' to 'clothes' or 'get-up').

Ask the students to work in groups of three to four to role-play a group of individuals stuck in a lift in a hospital. One is a heart surgeon; the second is a teenager visiting his grandmother; the third is a musician in a rock band who is depressed about their lack of success; the fourth is an overworked nurse on their way home. Each student should think about how their character would speak and what they would say. Ask the students to do their role-play, either sitting down or 'acted out', and then to perform it in front of the class.

Take feedback on each performance – can the class work out which character is which from what they say? How do they know?

Explore the skills

Read the annotated example on page 284 aloud. Draw attention to why it works and how it differs from the previous example.

Now ask the students to read the second formal account in the table on page 285 in pairs. They should work together to identify the language and punctuation they could change (**Q4**) and complete the writing task (**Q5**). A possible version might be:

> As for the toilets, here's the deal: you've got to queue for ages. Once you get there, you'll be shocked by how awful they are. Let's put it this way – better to bring your own toilet stuff!

At this point, revise and review the meaning of 'register' as this will be the focus of the next tasks. Display **PPT. 9.2**, **slides 1–6**, and work through the definitions and examples with the class.

Develop the skills

Read the two tasks in **Q6** and **Q7** aloud. With the students working in the same pairs, ask them to discuss and complete **Q6** and **Q7**. Take brief feedback and share ideas with the class:

Q6: The register for the first is likely to be formal, and for the second more informal.

Q7: The key points they would use to persuade the headteacher or a friend, while not strictly related to register, are related to appropriateness (which is a part of register). For example, they are unlikely to use the same arguments with both. More likely is that they might exaggerate the educational importance of the rock festival (their future career in the music industry) to the Head, and exaggerate the fun aspect to their friend (the unbelievable bands playing, all your friends will be going, etc).

Apply the skills

For **Q8**, read the main task and point out to the students that their texts should not sound overly formal or informal; they should avoid making them sound like spoofs of letters or emails, instead they should read like letters or emails the students would actually send.

Refer the students to the **Checklist for success** on page 285, and remind them that in exams they will be expected to use a formal register for the most part, albeit one that matches the audience.

> **Give extra support** by providing copies of **Worksheet 9.2**, and asking the students to write the two texts into a table so they can compare and contrast the two versions.
>
> **Give extra challenge** by asking the students to write the full text in both cases. In this situation, remind them to pay attention to the formalities of opening and closing letters and emails (e.g. 'Dear Mr/Ms XXX', 'Yours sincerely' in the formal letter).

Big answer plenary

Ask students to reflect on the work they have done in the lesson. Ask them to discuss the following questions in pairs:

- What's the difference between formal and informal language?
- When did I use formal language in the lesson? When did I use informal language?
- When and how did I adapt my language for different audiences?

9.3 Match features to text types and conventions

Assessment objectives

English Language

AO5 Communicate clearly, effectively and imaginatively, selecting and adapting tone, style and register for different forms, purposes and audiences; organise information and ideas, using structural and grammatical features to support coherence and cohesion of texts

AO6 Use a range of vocabulary and sentence structures for clarity, purpose and effect, with accurate spelling and punctuation

GCSE examinations
- **English Language** Paper 2, Question 5

Differentiated learning outcomes
- **All students must** be able to understand that certain texts have different conventions and features.
- **Most students should** use some different features according to the conventions of the type of text.
- **Some students could** adapt the content of their writing according to the conventions and features of the particular text type.

Resources
- **Student Book**: pp. 286–9
- **Worksheet**: 9.3
- **PPT**: 9.3

Other Student Book pages
- Lessons 2.1–2.2, pp. 42–9

Getting you thinking

Explain that conventions are the 'accepted ways of doing things'; this usually means that if you don't follow the conventions, your writing can appear unusual or not what the reader is expecting. In some circumstances, this can be deliberate and be used to make the reader sit up and take notice, but often it just means your work doesn't fit the purpose for which it is intended and seems 'out of place'.

Big question	Read out the **Big question**: *What features will make your point of view more convincing?* Ask the students to consider features and conventions in a different context. Ask them to think about an advert for washing powder and ask what conventions they might expect to see (e.g. comparison of two T-shirts); and then what sort of language (or features) might be used, such as comparatives or superlatives ('brighter', 'cleaner') and/or a short, imperative or summary phrase (e.g. 'For whatever life throws at you').

Read the opening paragraphs of **Getting you thinking** on page 286 of the Student Book and ask the students to complete **Q1** in pairs. Then take brief feedback as a class. Elicit the following correct responses:

a 'Dear Sir/Madam'/ 'On the one hand...'/ 'Yours faithfully'
b 'Well, what can I say...'/ 'Now, let's check out...'/ 'Marie x'
c 'I'd like to talk to you...'/ 'Another key reason...'/ 'Thank you for listening...'

Explore the skills

Read aloud the extract from Helena Pielichaty's blog on page 287, and then ask the students to work independently to identify and note down the features listed (**Q2**):

- use of the first-person narrative voice ('I think...')
- some informality – but not to the extent that the text is only understandable to close friends: 'OK'; 'that thing'; 'It's nuts really...'.
- sharing thoughts: 'I think the session went down OK.'; 'It's nuts really...' (informality suggests close contact with reader, too)
- exaggerated observations – 'even if they're bored rigid'.

Read aloud the text about the conventions of speech on page 287 of the Student Book and ask the students to read the extract from 'What to the slave is the fourth of July?' by Frederick Douglass to themselves. Then ask the students to complete **Q3** in pairs.

Now read aloud the text about the conventions of letters on page 288 and ask the students to read the letter that follows it to themselves. Then ask the students to complete **Q4** in pairs.

Take feedback and share answers to **Q3** and **Q4** with the class.

Answers to **Q3**:

- references to the audience (and the speaker himself): 'Whether we…'; 'I will…'
- examples of emotive imagery or vocabulary: 'crushed and bleeding slave'; 'fettered'; 'trampled upon'
- repetition or patterns used for rhetorical effect and impact: 'false to the past, false to the present, […] false to the future'; 'in the name of…' x 3
- a clear statement of the purpose of the speech – what needs to change: 'I will dare […] to denounce […] the great sin and shame of America!' (slavery).

Answers to **Q4**:

- introduction of issues: (first paragraph) 'I will be declining the offer'
- formal features: e.g. 'declining' as opposed to 'turning down'; 'extremely demeaning' as opposed to 'really nasty'; 'salary you propose' as opposed to 'the wages I'd get'
- logical and explanatory language: 'However […] as I felt'; 'Firstly', 'Added to that'
- the 'call to action': 'I will […] be willing to reconsider my decision if these issues are addressed'.

Develop the skills

Read the task at the top of page 289 and the extract from the student's blog. Then discuss **Q5** as a class.

Ask the students to identify the features that don't work, using **Worksheet 9.3** (**Q6**).

> **Give extra support** by spending time with targeted individuals or groups and working together through the worksheet to identify what is wrong.
>
> **Give extra challenge** by asking some students to rewrite the blog, keeping the same opinion and basic information.

Apply the skills

Now ask the students to write another blog on the same topic, but expressing their own view (**Q7**).

Before they begin the final task, display **PPT 9.3**, **slides 1–3**, and remind the students of the difference between conventions and features.

Big answer plenary	Ask the students to refer to the **Check your progress** outcomes and decide which outcome they have achieved. Do they think they have a grip on the idea of texts having particular conventions and features to match?

9.4 Select appropriate vocabulary to make an impact

Assessment objectives

English Language

AO5 Communicate clearly, effectively and imaginatively, selecting and adapting tone, style and register for different forms, purposes and audiences; organise information and ideas, using structural and grammatical features to support coherence and cohesion of texts

AO6 Use a range of vocabulary and sentence structures for clarity, purpose and effect, with accurate spelling and punctuation

GCSE examinations
- English Language Paper 2, Question 5

Differentiated learning outcomes
- **All students must** be able to make their viewpoint clear in their writing by using simple adjectives or verbs.
- **Most students should** select vocabulary carefully with awareness of how positive or negative their word choices are.
- **Some students could** make a range of detailed vocabulary choices that both tell the reader directly, or show more subtly, what their feelings are on a particular issue.

Resources
- **Student Book**: pp. 290–3
- **Worksheet**: 9.4
- **PPT**: 9.4

Other Student Book pages
- Lesson 1.2, pp. 12–15

Getting you thinking

Big question	Refer to the **Big question**: *How can your choice of words influence the reader?* Ask the students to note down briefly any words or phrases that come to mind in relation to 'influence'. Write them on the board.
	They might come up with: 'persuade', 'impact', 'change', 'make someone do something', 'shift', 'think again', etc. Suggest that although specific reasons can be given as to *why* people should do something, in fact it is often *the way* those reasons are stated that is the most influential.

The extract from the *Metro* article by Naomi Mdudu on page 290 of the Student Book is quite a complex one, so read it aloud to the students before asking them to discuss **Q1** and **Q2** in pairs.

The difficulty is that three time periods are referred to: the pre-recession culture (the early 2000s); the recession period that began in 2007/8; the present day. Allow 10 minutes for the students to discuss the questions and respond. Then take feedback as a class. Possible responses include:

Q1: in the recession: logos 'out of favour'; brands less obvious – 'tone it down'; 'understatement' more in fashion

from 2000 onwards: thoughtless, over the top – 'a bit crass', 'excessive', 'brash'

Q2: Mdudu's view about the new approaches: she appears to approve of the use of humour, light-hearted approach – 'different way'; 'fun and witty'.

Elicit the idea that being able to draw on synonyms to explain your ideas is important (for example, 'light-hearted' for 'fun').

Explore the skills

Read aloud the opening paragraph of **Explore the skills** and the two student responses on page 291. Ask the students to complete **Q3** independently, using **Worksheet 9.4**. For the first part of **Q3**, the students should underline or highlight the adverbs and adjectives. Then, they should use the table to record these selections.

Suggested solutions:

- adverbs to strengthen: 'totally'; 'incredibly'
- adjectives: 'appalled'; 'functional'; 'smart'; 'comfortable'; 'unnecessary'; 'bold'; 'instant'; 'electric'; 'powerful'; 'like-minded'
- noun phrases: 'unnecessary complication'; 'bold statement'; 'instant, electric connection'; 'like-minded people'.

For **Q4**, spend five minutes discussing the meaning of each word and its connotations (negative, neutral or positive) as a class. Then ask the students to draw a line in their notebooks and place the words with the most positive meaning on the right. There is no definitive answer to this, but one would expect words such as 'visionary', 'leader', and 'trail-blazer' to be seen as positive, whereas 'weirdo', 'loner' and 'reject' are more likely to be negative.

Then ask the students to complete **Q5** independently, noting down the correct word for each sentence. Possible answers (in order):

- 'outcast' ('reject' or 'weirdo' also possible)
- 'trail-blazer'
- 'loner'.

Develop the skills

Note: **Q6–Q8** could be treated as a guided reading/writing activity with class groups of four to six divided up according to ability.

Ask the students to read the extract from *No Logo* by Naomi Klein on page 292 and complete **Q6** and **Q7** independently.

Then ask the students to share their answers with their group and peer-evaluate their understanding. Once they have agreed answers, take feedback as a class. Possible responses:

Q6: verb: 'squeezed'; verb phrase: 'crammed in next to each other'; verb: 'extracted (from)'

Q7: workers are treated cheaply and inhumanely; place feels lifeless; machines are dominant, while women are subservient.

Now ask the students to complete **Q8**. This could be completed as a shared writing activity in pairs in their guided groups.

> **Give extra support** by providing some scaffolding prompts for the paragraph, such as: 'A ...... woman stands at a ...... machine. She looks ...... and ......'.
>
> **Give extra challenge** by asking the students to develop their paragraph to take in further details of the factory environment or other workers.

Apply the skills

Display **PPT 9.4, slides 1–4**, to remind the students how they can use language to influence the reader. Then allow 20 minutes for the students to complete the main task (**Q9**).

Big answer plenary	Once the students have completed the final task, ask them to discuss their work with a partner and point out where and how they have used vocabulary to influence the reader. Once they have done so, they can evaluate their own progress against the **Check your progress** outcomes on page 293.

9.5 Key techniques: varying sentences and verbs for effect

Assessment objectives

English Language

AO5 Communicate clearly, effectively and imaginatively, selecting and adapting tone, style and register for different forms, purposes and audiences; organise information and ideas, using structural and grammatical features to support coherence and cohesion of texts

AO6 Use a range of vocabulary and sentence structures for clarity, purpose and effect, with accurate spelling and punctuation.

GCSE examinations
- English Language Paper 2, Question 5

Differentiated learning outcomes
- **All students must** be able to write simple and long sentences that present their viewpoint.
- **Most students should** vary their sentence structures to present their viewpoints.
- **Some students could** switch between short and long sentences, including minor ones, and use various verb forms, including modals, to express their views.

Resources
- **Student Book**: pp. 294–7
- **Worksheet**: 9.5
- **PPT**: 9.5

Other Student Book pages
- Lesson 1.4, pp. 20–3
- Lesson 4.4, pp. 128–31

Getting you thinking

Big question Read out the **Big question**: *How can you use different types of sentence and verbs to influence the reader?* Allow three minutes for the students to discuss what 'different types of sentence' there are with a partner, and to list any they can think of in the form of examples. Briefly take feedback as a class and ask how often they consciously think about using such a range.

Read to the class the extract from 'Read aloud. Change the world.' by Pam Allyn on page 294 of the Student Book and then ask the students to discuss **Q1–Q3** in pairs. Take feedback as a class, establishing the link between what the writer says (her message) and how she says it (in terms of her language choices). Draw attention to the final short, summative sentence of the first paragraph – 'My mother's words changed my world.' – and also the invented, onomatopoeic 'thunked' which brings the reading alive.

You may wish to use **PPT 9.5, slides 1 and 2**, to demonstrate visually how the first paragraph of 'Read aloud. Change the world.' works. It also contains some additional skills related to other aspects, which add to the impact of the writing.

Explore the skills

Read carefully over the explanatory list of the skills used by Pam Allyn, on page 295 of the Student Book. You could look at the extract on page 294 again to concept-check some of the points. For example, ask the class to find another example of a short summative sentence ('The "read aloud" made me a reader.') or of other repetitive sentence structures (if not verbs), e.g. 'power *of* story, *of* language and *of* my mother'.

Now ask the students to complete **Q4–Q6** independently.

Once the students have completed **Q4–Q6**, put them in groups of three or four, and ask them to share responses and peer-assess what they have done.

> **Give extra support** by working with selected guided groups and rather than asking them to write the sentences straight off, get them to work in pairs, or with you, to jointly construct sentences.
>
> **Give extra challenge** by asking more confident students/groups to include at least one made-up verb in their sentences (probably the one for **Q4**) – it should be onomatopoeic if possible.

Develop the skills

Read the introductory information about compound sentences in **Develop the skills** on page 296. Then ask the students to complete **Q7–Q9**, independently. Take brief feedback as a class. Answers:

Q7: 'Yes, learning an instrument is a challenge, <u>but</u> there are countless books and videos to help you.'

'You may never be very proficient, <u>yet</u> it won't be wasted time.'

'The tunes you learn will always be there, <u>so</u> in the future, you can dig them out for generations to come.'

Q8: line of certainty: 'will occupy' (certain); 'could' (possible); 'might' (possible but less certain than 'could')

Q9: missing words: version 1 (certain): 'will', 'will'; version 2 (cautious): 'might', 'could'.

Apply the skills

Read the main task in **Q10**, and ask the students to decide which topic they will write about. (They can choose a different one if they wish, provided it allows them to apply the skills they have learned.) Then ask them to draft their opening paragraph using **Worksheet 9.5**. Before they begin, refer them to the **Checklist for success** on page 297.

Big answer plenary	Once the students have drafted their paragraph, ask them to use the checklist and features at the end of **Worksheet 9.5** to evaluate their work. If they have marked any of the features as 'not sure', ask them to pass their work to a partner or to you, to check for them.
	After they have completed the evaluation, ask them to look at the **Check your progress** outcomes on page 297 and assess which ones they have achieved.

9.6 Key technique: using punctuation for effect and impact

Assessment objectives

English Language

AO5 Communicate clearly, effectively and imaginatively, selecting and adapting tone, style and register for different forms, purposes and audiences; organise information and ideas, using structural and grammatical features to support coherence and cohesion of texts

AO6 Use a range of vocabulary and sentence structures for clarity, purpose and effect, with accurate spelling and punctuation

GCSE examinations
- English Language Paper 2, Question 5

Differentiated learning outcomes
- **All students must** be able to use some punctuation to give clarity to their work.
- **Most students should** be able to use a variety of punctuation to add clarity and begin to create effect within their work.
- **Some students could** use a range of punctuation including colons, semicolons, dashes and brackets to give impact and effect to their work.

Resources
- **Student Book**: pp. 298–9
- **PPT**: 9.6

Other Student Book pages
- Lesson 1.5, pp. 24–7

Getting you thinking

Big question

Display **PPT 9.6, slides 1–5**. These contain the following analogies:

- Punctuation is a set of traffic signs along the road as you travel along.
- Punctuation is a form of body language – it is everything that you show in your gestures when you talk to someone else.
- Punctuation is like a remote control with volume, fast forward, rewind, pause, more information, etc.

Ask the students to discuss these analogies in pairs: which of these do you think is the best comparison for punctuation in writing (and why)?

Then refer to the **Big question**: *How can punctuation help you to get your message across?* Elicit some initial responses from the students.

Now ask the students to read the short text on cycling on page 298 of the Student Book, first to themselves, and then aloud to a partner, using the punctuation to help them. Afterwards, ask each pair to discuss **Q1** and **Q2**, before reporting back to the class as a whole. Answers:

Q1: (in order) question mark; question mark; exclamation mark; brackets; full stop; apostrophe; dash; exclamation mark.

Q2: The tone could range from very cross and angry to surprised and astonished. The hint at humour – 'extreme sport', 'sharks' – probably makes it more surprised than outright mad.

Explore the skills

Read through the table on page 298 with the class, perhaps stopping to concept-check by asking individual students questions on the different usages. Then ask the students to complete **Q3** and **Q4** independently. Possible solutions are:

Q3: a Lorry drivers are the worst: they can't hear you, their mirrors are too high and they can't see you at left-hand junctions.

b Yet roads can never be completely free of danger; you take a risk whenever you get into a car or ride a bike.

c The only real solution is to educate drivers of all road vehicles; the alternative is more accidents and more anger.

Q4: In answer to the complaints of cyclists, can I say that, as an experienced driver of thirty years (with no accidents to my name), I object to being viewed as a maniac. The only maniacs – in my humble opinion! – are the cyclists themselves.

Develop the skills

For **Q5**, read the extract from *The Times* on page 299 aloud, and then ask the students to read and complete the table independently. A suggested solution is:

semicolon	Second sentence to tell us the ages of the youngest and oldest victims	Shows the contrast in age and the wide range of ages of victims, emphasising the widespread effect.
dashes	Mentions Mary as being one of the victims who survived	Reminds us this is a personal thing, not just a statistic.

Now ask the students to write out the paragraph in **Q6**, adding the semicolon and dashes as instructed. Then ask them to check their answers in pairs.

Possible response to **Q6**: 'Lorry drivers have a different perspective. City cyclists are reckless; country cyclists lack awareness. They change direction suddenly – often without signalling – so drivers have little chance of avoiding them.'

Give extra support by offering different possibilities (e.g. with the punctuation marks in incorrect places), and asking students to select which one would work.

Give extra challenge by asking the students to come up with two further paragraphs on a related topic such as dangerous sports using at least two of the following: colons, semicolons, dashes, brackets.

Apply the skills

For **Q7**, read the task and ask the students to write their paragraphs independently. Then ask them to swap their work with a partner to evaluate how well they have applied what they have learned.

Big answer plenary

Ask the students to briefly share what they think they have learned about using punctuation with the same partner they worked with in **Q7**. Then, put the students in groups of four and ask them to share again, before reporting back on the key aspects to the whole class. Try to elicit from the students the idea that punctuation is not just about 'correctness' (needing it for end of sentences), but that it can also adjust meaning. If possible elicit some specific examples from the students (possibly from their paragraphs in **Q7**).

9.7 Shape whole texts cohesively

Assessment objectives

English Language

AO5 Communicate clearly, effectively and imaginatively, selecting and adapting tone, style and register for different forms, purposes and audiences; organise information and ideas, using structural and grammatical features to support coherence and cohesion of texts

AO6 Use a range of vocabulary and sentence structures for clarity, purpose and effect, with accurate spelling and punctuation

GCSE examinations
- English Language Paper 2, Question 5

Differentiated learning outcomes

- **All students must** be able to plan an essay that has two halves – the first dealing with the pros, the second dealing with the cons.
- **Most students should** plan an essay, and write the first three paragraphs so that the arguments for and against are clear to the reader.
- **Some students could** plan an essay, considering all three possible approaches, and then vary paragraph style and content to create an impact on the reader.

Resources
- **Student Book**: pp. 300–3
- **Worksheets**: 9.7a–b
- **PPT**: 9.7

Other Student Book pages
- Lesson 4.4, pp. 128–31

Getting you thinking

Begin the lesson by asking if anyone knows what 'cohesion' is. If not, explain that it means the bonding, or linkage, between ideas or points. In the best viewpoint essays or articles this 'bonding' supports the argument and makes it stronger or more persuasive.

Big question	Allow two to three minutes for students to think about the **Big question**: *How can you organise your writing as a whole to make your point of view persuasive and clear?* (There is no need for them to write anything down.) Most people read texts such as essays, articles and reports 'in order' – that's to say they start at the beginning and read through to the end. Then discuss as a class why the 'organisation' of what you put in your text is so important.

Read the task on page 300 of the Student Book aloud and ask the students to look at **Approach 1**, the plan a student has made in preparation for this task. Elicit the obvious way this plan is cohesive (all the points relate to the topic/title). This immediately gives the students one obvious way of improving cohesion – stick to the task!

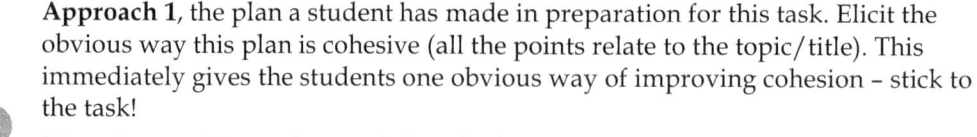

Now discuss **Q1** as a class and elicit further ideas.

Explore the skills

Ask the students to complete **Q2** and **Q3** in pairs, looking at **Approaches 2 and 3** on page 301. Briefly take feedback from two or three pairs in the class. Answers might be:

Q2: The writer alternates the 'for' and 'against' paragraphs.

Q3: a The writer is 'for' gap-years as indicated by points such as 'it will be money well spent' and 'everyone needs a break from work'.

b The arguments are contained within the same paragraph; in this case the paragraph starts with the 'against' point of view.

c The organisation of Approach 2 had just one side of the argument in each paragraph.

Display **PPT 9.7, slides 1–5**, to sum up the different ways of organising a viewpoint text. Of course, until the students try these out for themselves, this may seem a little abstract, but it should enable them to have at least three approaches they can remember at short notice. Point out the caveat about the fourth approach ('One direction').

Now return to the point/counterpoint approach. For this, they will need to consider the discourse markers mentioned in **Q4** on page 302. Read the discourse markers with the class, and then ask the students to complete **Q4**, independently.

Take feedback as a class and accept any of the solutions that grammatically fit the sentences. (The students may need to create an additional sentence at the end of each given example.) Here is one solution for part **a**:

'**While** travelling abroad for a long time could make you feel lonely, and there are many dangers you could face, **some argue that** these challenges are what make the trip worthwhile.'

Develop the skills

Ask the students to read the extract from the first essay on page 302 and write brief answers to **Q5–Q7** independently. Then ask them to compare their answers with a partner, before taking feedback as a class. Possible solutions:

Q5: The writer thinks gap years are too expensive.

Q6: The second paragraph is just one sentence.

Q7: It sums up his/her feelings in a succinct, clear way.

Now ask the students to read the extract from the second essay on page 303 and note down answers to **Q8** and **Q9** independently. Ask the students to share answers again with a partner. Then take feedback as a class. Possible solutions:

Q8: The first paragraph includes a range of statistics, such as the average cost of taking a gap year.

Q9: The second paragraph is more emotive and creates a visual example to paint a picture; it has no statistical information.

Finally, elicit the idea that the best viewpoint writing is able to order ideas in different ways, but also organise different sorts of information.

Apply the skills

Read **Q10** and the final task, and ask the students to write the first three paragraphs of their speech, using **Worksheet 9.7a** or **9.7b** according to the students' abilities.

> **Give extra support** by providing **Worksheet 9.7a**. This encourages the students to use the 'see-saw' approach, but you could simplify it further by asking them to write the essay in two distinctive halves.
>
> **Give extra challenge** by directing the students towards the additional task at the end of **Worksheet 9.7b**.

Big answer plenary	Ask the students to explain to each other in pairs what the difference between the three main models of argument writing are: 'two halves'; 'see-saw' and 'point/counterpoint'. Then ask them to say which they feel confident using and why. Take some individual feedback from the students and try to draw out any further support or guidance you may need to provide.

9.8 Shape sentences into paragraphs effectively

Assessment objectives

English Language

AO5 Communicate clearly, effectively and imaginatively, selecting and adapting tone, style and register for different forms, purposes and audiences; organise information and ideas, using structural and grammatical features to support coherence and cohesion of texts

AO6 Use a range of vocabulary and sentence structures for clarity, purpose and effect, with accurate spelling and punctuation

GCSE examinations

- English Language Paper 2, Question 5

Differentiated learning outcomes

- **All students must** be able to write paragraphs that begin with simple topic sentences explaining their views.
- **Most students should** write paragraphs that focus on one main idea and explain points clearly and fluently.
- **Some students could** write paragraphs that use a range of sentence sequences and linking words and phrases to get their point of view across to the reader.

Resources

- **Student Book**: pp. 304–7
- **Worksheet**: 9.8
- **PPT**: 9.8

Other Student Book pages

- Lesson 1.8, pp. 36–40

Getting you thinking

Start by explaining that, as with the overall structure of a text (for example, which point or paragraph comes first, which last and so on), the organisation *within* paragraphs is equally important.

Big question | Read the **Big question**: *How can you arrange your sentences to make your viewpoint clear and have an impact on your readers?* Ask the students the simple question: 'If you have a paragraph of three sentences, how many different ways can you arrange it?' They might answer 'three', but of course it is more – six, which shows that even with relatively simple paragraphs, a lot of choices can be made. Then, ask them: 'Is this *always* the case?' The answer is 'no', because sometimes words or phrases reference ideas or meanings that could only come before or after another idea. At this point, there is no need to explain or show this in action.

Read aloud the extract from the article by Hadley Freeman on page 304 of the Student Book, and ask the students to discuss **Q1–Q3** in pairs. Then briefly take feedback as a class. Answers are:

Q1 She objects to how few black models appear on magazine covers or in fashion shows.

Q2 This is made clear in the second sentence: 'blatant racism'.

Q3 It provides statistical evidence about the lack of black models in past shows and gives the (slightly) better figures from February 2014, when the article was written.

Explore the skills

Make sure all the students are looking at the first paragraph of Hadley Freeman's article on page 304, and ask them to point to each sentence as you read the bulleted explanation on page 305. The overall structure is: broader view/setting the scene; key viewpoint; detailed evidence. Point out that this is just one very effective way of conveying an argument convincingly. Ask the students to look at the extract from the article again and think about **Q4** independently then take feedback as a class.

Answers to **Q4** are:

- Sentence 2 couldn't open the paragraph because it begins with a discourse marker, 'But', which indicates a previous point.
- Sentence 3 couldn't really come at the start as it is rather blunt and feels 'out of the blue' – why would you suddenly say this? There's no 'context'.

For **Q5**, ask the students to work in pairs to discuss a possible order. Make sure you encourage them to think about *why* a particular sequence works. Take feedback as a class. For any students who may not understand, explain that the only order that really works is that shown and explained on **PPT 9.8**.

Ask the students to complete **Q6** in pairs. Take feedback as a class. Answers are:

a   It is a single, simple sentence rather than a long, complex sentence.
b   The use of 'Then' means it must come after previous points.

Now ask the students to complete **Q7**, in pairs; then take feedback as a class. Answers:

a   The first two sentences introduce the general area – 'fashion shows' – and tell us about past history, supporting the thesis of the argument.
b   The last four sentences introduce new statistics about the current situation and end by explaining how things have changed.

Develop the skills

Ask the students to read the second extract from the article by Hadley Freeman on page 306, and complete **Q8** and **Q9** independently.

Give extra support by working with less confident students to draw attention to the table in **Q9**.

Give extra challenge by asking the students to choose alternatives from the table to replace the given discourse markers in the extract.

Take feedback as a class. Answers are:

Q8:   a   'these' refers back to the previously provided factual information
      b   'But' introduces a note of caution. 'For a start' introduces a key point explaining the 'but'. 'Moreover', stresses the argument with a related point.

Q9:   Accept any word or phrase that fits the spaces. For example (in order): 'Such'/'This'; 'Furthermore'/'Moreover'/'In addition'; 'Yet'/'However'; 'For example'; 'We'.

Apply the skills

Read through the task in **Q10** with the class. To prepare for the task, put the students into groups of four or five to discuss the topic. First, though, ask them to elect a chair who will monitor proceedings and keep the discussion on track. The students should all contribute positively to the discussion, while also listening carefully to the points others make. Ask the students to note down ideas as they go along, using **Worksheet 9.8**. This should give them an accurate record of the points made. Point out that this method could be used when planning in an exam situation.

For **Q10**, you may wish to take feedback from groups and compile a table of points for and against on the whiteboard for students to use when writing their blog openings. Refer them to the **Checklist for success** on page 307, perhaps going back over any points they aren't clear about, before asking them to write their paragraphs.

Big answer plenary	Once the students have completed their blog openings, ask them to return to their discussion groups and read them to their co-group members. Ask the group to refer to the **Check your progress** outcomes on page 307 and decide which outcome they have achieved. Once they have finished the peer review, ask them to decide which piece used the widest variety of sentence structures.

9.9 Apply your skills to an English Language task

Assessment objectives

English Language

AO5 Communicate clearly, effectively and imaginatively, selecting and adapting tone, style and register for different forms, purposes and audiences; organise information and ideas, using structural and grammatical features to support coherence and cohesion of texts

AO6 Use a range of vocabulary and sentence structures for clarity, purpose and effect, with accurate spelling and punctuation

GCSE examinations
- English Language Paper 2, Question 5

Differentiated learning outcomes

- **All students must** be able to express their viewpoint clearly using a simple two-part essay structure, with topic sentences and simple adjectives and verbs.
- **Most students should** be able to write paragraphs with a clear focus, using negative and positive vocabulary, as well as appropriate formal or informal language.
- **Some students could** adapt their tone and register, use punctuation for effect, and select from a range of styles, structures and language techniques to express their views.

Resources
- **Student Book**: pp. 308–12
- **Worksheets**: 9.9a–b (9.9b is available on the CD-Rom only)
- **PPT**: 9.9

Introduction

Explain that the relevance of AO5 and AO6 to this assessment is that they refer to the ways in which the students should structure and craft their own point of view writing in order to express their viewpoint clearly and persuasively. They refer to the thoughtful organisation and deployment of language, matched to particular audiences and conventions to create influential and well-argued texts.

Responding to an English Language task

For **Q1**, read the task on page 308 of the Student Book. Then allow two to three minutes for the students to think about the first bullet point and decide what their view on the subject is. Then put them in groups of two or three to share/discuss their views.

Now ask the students to consider the second bullet and, in their groups, list key techniques or ways they could go about arguing their point of view. Draw their attention to the words 'effectively' and 'convincingly', and ask them what they understand those terms to mean.

- 'Effectively' means that whatever your viewpoint is, you are able to argue it in a way that makes it difficult for readers not to agree, to some extent at least!
- 'Convincingly' here, means that it must read as if you really share those views, whether or not that is the actual case.

Now, look at the **Checklist for success** on page 308 of the Student Book, and ask the students if they can elaborate on each of the points – can they explain what each of these actually mean? Display **PPT 9.9, slides 1–5** to help explain. You could print off copies of the slides for the students' reference.

For **Q2**, read aloud **Response 1** and the annotations and comments on pages 308–10. Ask the students a series of questions to ensure they have followed and understood the annotations. For example:

1. *What is the viewpoint expressed?* – They should note that the viewpoint isn't as clear as it should be, as it conflates not having much money and being 'cool'.
2. *In what ways is this informal?* – 'dead careful'; 'mates'; 'celebs' – Ask: *Is this tone appropriate for the paper?*
3. *What is the 'one area' it deals with?* – You can 'shop around'; this is good because the viewpoint is easy to 'get'.
4. *How, exactly, does this link?* – It links to the previous paragraph, which talked about going to the back of high street stores, whereas this one deals with charity shops.
5. *In what way does this clearly support the task title?* – Tell students to go back and check task if needed.
6. *How does this go 'off topic'?* – It talks about non-clothes items.
7. *The topic sentence is fine, but is the follow-up related to it?* – The last sentence moves off the 'rich' topic.
8. *Why is this 'rhetorical'?* – The question isn't asking for an answer (the answer is self-explanatory).
9. *How is the final short sentence clear in its viewpoint?* – It is short and to the point.

At this point the mark schemes for GCSE English Language could be copied and given to the students. For **Response 1** ask them to work up the descriptors like a ladder, answering 'yes' or 'no' as to whether they see the skills in place. For **Response 1** they are likely to see Level 2 descriptors in place (**Q3**).

For **Q4**, read aloud **Response 2** and the annotations and comments that follow it on pages 310–11. Ask the students to look at both **Response 1** and **Response 2**, and note down the key differences that they observe between them (**Q4**). Has **Response 2** met the success criteria as explained in **PPT 9.9** and the descriptors at Level 3 in the GCSE English Language mark scheme?

As before, ask them to work up the descriptors like a ladder, answering 'yes' or 'no' as to whether they see the skills in place (**Q5**).

The students could then complete their own full response to a similar task, using **Worksheet 9.9a**. This provides a task and also provides a planning template to help them get started.

You will need to decide whether you want them to do a full, practice response without any assistance, or whether you wish to provide some initial guidance – for example, discussing the title and generating ideas around the viewpoint.

Completing this full response may take more than the time immediately available, in which case you could ask the students to complete the task for homework.

Once they have completed the task, they should look again at the two sample responses against their own and make a judgement as to which they think they are closer to in level.

Then, ask them to select and note down:
- one aspect or feature they are particularly pleased with in their own work
- one aspect or feature they could improve.

Alternatively, the students could exchange their work with a partner and work up from the bottom of the English Language mark scheme to decide which of the levels they feel the response fits best. They could then rewrite their response in the light of the comments proposed.

The additional task on **Worksheet 9.9b**, which can be found on the accompanying CD-Rom, offers a further opportunity for the students to develop their skills. This could either be used as an extension activity or for further consolidation and practice of the skills developed throughout Chapter 9.

Worksheet 1.1a — Words we use every day

Student Book Q3 Using **only** the words in the box, write a short poem or description of a natural scene. You may use words more than once if you need to.

house	love	you	she	he	I	this	that	can	eat
sleep	live	water	leaf	moon	food	as	and	so	
on	in	down	to	when	where	day	night	shall	
sun	day	winter	spring	friend	evil	cold	then	we	
us	under	up	to	heart	grass	water	have	do	
be	sky	weak	die	get	give	take			

Worksheet 1.1b: Forming words using suffixes

Student Book Q4 The table below lists some common suffixes which often cause confusion when spelling words. Read the golden rule in the table then add the correct endings to the root word.

Confusing suffixes	Golden rule	Stem words	New words
–cious and –tious	If your stem ends in –**ce**, then lose the –**ce** and add –**cious**. If the stem ends in any other letters, just add –**tious**.	gra**ce** spa**ce** cau**ti**on am**bi**tion	
–ation and –able	If your stem ends in –**ce** or –**ge**, keep the –**e** before adding –**able**. Words which end in –**ation**, can usually also use –**able**.	ador**ation** no**ti**ce ma**na**ge consider**ation**	

Student Book Q5 Now look at these words ending in the prefix –*ible*.

horrible   forcible   visible   terrible

a) Work out the stem word in each case and write some golden rules to help you remember these suffixes.

Horrible: stem word = ...

Forcible: stem word = ...

Visible: stem word = ...

Terrible: stem word = ...

Golden rule for –**ible**:

....

....

....

b) Think of some more –**ible** words to try out your rule.

Examples:

....

....

....

....

Worksheet 1.1c: Dickens's use of complex words

Student Book Q8 Read the extract below, from Charles Dickens's *Nicholas Nickleby*, and work out the missing words by adding prefixes and suffixes to the word stems in brackets. Then check your answers with a dictionary.

Pale and haggard faces, lank and bony figures, children with the countenances of old men, (*form*) .... with irons upon their limbs, boys of (*stunt*) .... growth, and others whose long, meagre legs would hardly bear their (*stoop*) .... bodies, all (*crowd*) .... on the view together; there were the bleared eye, the hare-lip, the (*crook*) .... foot, and every (*ugly*) .... or (*distort*) .... that told of (*nature*) .... aversion conceived by parents for their offspring, or of young lives which, from the (*early*) .... dawn of (*infant*) ...., had been one horrible (*endure*) .... of (*cruel*) .... and neglect.

166 • Key technical skills

Worksheet 1.2: Nouns, adjectives and noun phrases

Student Book Q1 Decide whether the words in the box are nouns or adjectives. Write them in the correct column in the table below.

> black house web silvery chilly door torrential
> wispy cat moon haunted breeze rain creaking

Adjectives	Nouns

Student Book Q2 Use a pencil line to join up each noun in the table in **Q1** with an appropriate adjective.

Student Book Q3 Now create noun phrases from your pairs in **Q2**, by adding *a* or *the*. Write these in the box below.

a) ....

b) ....

c) ....

d) ....

e) ....

f) ....

g) ....

Worksheet 1.3: Using different tenses

Student Book Q2 Read this extract from *The Generation Game* by Sophie Duffy.

> School is more bearable now that I have Lucas for a friend. He might only be small and thin but he has a voice that even Miss Pitchfork must envy. A voice like a crow having a bad day. A voice he uses sparingly, for greater effect.
>
> Lucas and I soon settle into a shared routine that gets us through the six hour long haul. We play together at break in our corner. We pick each other for teams in gym. I save a place for him on the carpet. He saves a place for me in the hall at lunchtime where I give him my greens in exchange for potatoes. (He is a boy of mystery).
>
> Sophie Duffy, from *The Generation Game*

Student Book Q3 Make a list of the present tense verbs in the passage.

Student Book Q4 Thinking about the topic of the passage, why do you think the writer chose to use the present tense? Why did she use such simple verbs to convey the actions of the school day? Jot your ideas below and then aim to answer both questions in clear sentences.

Student Book Q5 Complete the table by placing the verbs in the past and the future tenses.

Present tense: *to play*	Simple past tense	Future tense
I play		
You		You will play.
S/he plays.	S/he played.	
We		
They		

Student Book Q6 Complete the table with the verb **be** and then with the verb **have**.

Present tense: *to be*	Simple past tense	Future tense
I am.		I will be.
You are.	You were.	
S/he is.		
We are.		
They are.		

Worksheet 1.4a: Identifying sentence functions

Student Book **Q5a** Read the extract from the novel *Junk* by Melvin Burgess. The character Gemma has been in a disagreement with her parents.

What function does each sentence have? Write the correct function in the space provided.

	Function of sentence
[1] I didn't go back that day.	....
[2] In fact, I stayed away all weekend as a protest.	....
[3] Response: banned from going out of the house at weekends.	....
[4] My next plot was to stay out until ten each night during the week.	....
[5] They couldn't keep me off school in the name of discipline, surely?	....
[6] They got round that by my dad picking me up from school.	....
[7] My God!	....
[8] Everyone knew what was going on.	....
[9] He actually came into the class to get me!	....
[10] I thought I was going to die of humiliation.	....

Melvin Burgess, *Junk*

Worksheet 1.4b: The effects of different sentences

Student Book Q7 Read the text of the WaterAid advert below. Think about the questions in the annotations on the right to help you explore its use of different sentences. Make notes in the space provided.

One child is dying with every minute that passes. That's 2,000 children every single day. Not because of war or disaster. But simply because of dirty water and poor sanitation.	These sentences are stark statements presented to us as facts. Why do you think the writer chose this type of sentence to be the first thing you read when you look inside the leaflet?
Hard to stomach, isn't it? What's even more sickening is that all these deaths could be so easily prevented.	Why choose a question here? Who is it addressed to? What answer is the writer expecting?
WaterAid works across the globe with some of the world's poorest people. Every hour we build a new water point. And every hour we help over 100 people to get safe, clean water.	By using more statements here, how is the charity able to communicate more about its work?
But it's still not enough. Which is why we need your help.	These sentences are still statements but they have a different tone. Can you work out what they are trying to do here? Are these statements like the more formal ones we had earlier?
Your donations will be used to buy things like cement and bricks for wells. To help communities build pumps. And to make sure children get safe, clean water and sanitation – for life.	How does changing the topic of the statements here help the charity remind you of its key message?
Have we convinced you?	Why was it important for the writer to use another question at this point?
Complete the form below and send it back to us please. Before another child dies.	The leaflet finishes with a command followed by a statement. Why put them in this order?

170 • Key technical skills

© HarperCollins*Publishers* 2015

Worksheet 1.5: Apostrophes, commas and speech marks

Student Book Q9 There are 20 punctuation marks missing from this passage from the novel *A Kestrel for a Knave* by Barry Hines. The sentence punctuation is in place, but the following have been left out:
- apostrophes
- commas
- speech marks.

Identify where all the missing punctuation marks go, using the rules you have just learned to help you.

Im sick of you boys youll be the death of me. Not a day goes by without me having to deal with a line of boys. I cant remember a day not a day in all the years Ive been in school and how longs that? … ten years and the schools no better now than it was on the day that it opened. I cant understand it. I cant understand it at all.

The boys couldnt understand it either and they dropped their eyes as he searched for an answer in their faces. Failing to find one there he stared past them out of the window.

The lawn stretching down to the front railings was studded with worm casts and badly in need of its Spring growth. The border separating the lawn from the drive was turned earth and in the centre of the lawn stood a silver birch tree in a little round bed.

Adapted from Barry Hines, *A Kestrel for a Knave*

Worksheet 1.6a: Barack Obama's speech about Rosa Parks

Look at the following extract. It is from a speech by Barack Obama as he unveiled a statue of Rosa Parks, an important figure in the American Civil Rights Movement.

> Rosa Parks tells us there's always something we can do. She tells us that we all have responsibilities, to ourselves and to one another. She reminds us that this is how change happens – not mainly through the exploits of the famous and the powerful, but through the countless acts of often anonymous courage and kindness and fellow feeling and responsibility that continually, stubbornly, expand our conception of justice – our conception of what is possible.
>
> Rosa Parks's singular act of disobedience launched a movement. The tired feet of those who walked the dusty roads of Montgomery helped a nation see that to which it had once been blind. It is because of these men and women that I stand here today. It is because of them that our children grow up in a land more free and more fair; a land truer to its founding creed.
>
> www.whitehouse.gov/the-press-office/2013/02/27/
> remarks-president-dedicationstatue-honoring-rosa-parks-us-capitol

Worksheet 1.6b: Use of sentence forms in Shakespeare's *Othello*

Consider the questions in the annotations and make a note of your responses.

Iago: My noble lord!

Othello: What dost thou say, Iago?

Iago: Did Michael Cassio, when you woo'd my lady,
Know of your love?

Othello: He did, from first to last: why dost thou ask?

Iago: But for a satisfaction of my thought –
No further harm.

> Iago has been asking devious questions but now switches to the declarative. What response does he know he is going to get here?

Othello: Why of thy thought, Iago?

> Usually the person asking the questions in a situation is the one in authority but what do you notice about the questions Othello is asking so far? Do they put him in charge here or Iago? Why?

Iago: I did not think he had been acquainted with her.

Othello: O, yes; and went between us very oft.

Iago: Indeed!

> What kind of tone does Iago's exclamation suggest here? How might that add to Othello's concern?

Othello: Indeed! Ay, indeed. Discern'st thou aught in that?
Is he not honest?

> What does the repetition of the exclamation and the series of questions now tell you about Othello's thoughts and feelings?

Iago: Honest, my lord?

Othello: Honest? Ay, honest.

Iago: My lord, for aught I know.

> How does the use of the declarative here add to Iago's success in disturbing Othello?

Othello: What dost thou think?

Iago: Think, my lord?

Othello: Think, my lord! By heaven, he echoes me,
As if there were some monster in his thought
Too hideous to be shown.

> How does Othello's declarative here suggest Iago has been successful?

William Shakespeare, from *Othello* (Act 3, Scene 3)

Worksheet 1.7: The effect of simple sentences

Student Book **Q6** Read the extract from the short story, 'Everything Stuck to Him', by Raymond Carver and answer **Q6a–e**.

> They stared at each other.[1]   Then the boy took up his hunting gear and went outside.[2]   He started the car.[3]   He went around to the car windows and, making a job of it, scraped away the ice.[4]
>
> He turned off the motor and sat awhile.[5]   And then he got out and went back inside.[6]
>
> The living-room light was on.[7]   The girl was asleep on the bed.[8] The baby was asleep beside her.[9]
>
> The boy took off his boots.[10]
>
> Raymond Carver, 'Everything Stuck to Him'

a) ....

b) ....

c) ....

d) ....

e) ....

Worksheet 1.8a — Topic sentences and paragraphs

Student Book Q5 Complete the grid by compiling some more possible topic sentences.

Detail from the picture	Topic sentence
Para 1: the large red house with blue shutters	Mandula's house dominated the bay of the small Greek fishing village.
Para 2: The sweep of soft sand	Like a continuing blanket of comfort, the sweep of soft sand always dried swiftly in the sun at low tide.
Para 3: the blueness of the sea and the sky	
Para 4: the figure in blue	
Para 5: The boats on the shore	Dotted along the shore, the tiny boats with their bright paint were a reminder of the struggling livelihood of the locals.

Student Book Q8 Look at the topic sentences below. Reorder the sentences so that their paragraphs will be more coherent for the readers of the article.

a) The tourism industry has benefited from a wide range of visitors – those who have taken longer trips and those who have spent more money on luxury holidays.

b) The local Minister for Tourism concluded: 'Tourism remains an important driving force in our recovery from recession.'

c) In the past year more money came into the country than went out, which is good news at last for locals.

d) Record spending by tourists has helped the Greek economy out of a big recession.

e) A spokesperson for a major bank warned there is a long way to go.

f) This news is little help though to the 28% of Greeks who are still unemployed.

Worksheet 1.8b: Creating coherent paragraphs

Student Book **Q9** Read the following extract which was inspired by the photograph you studied earlier. Make notes in the space provided on your responses to the questions in the annotations.

It was just as I'd remembered. The village shimmered in the bright, luminous light of the morning.

Returning now, through the sun-baked streets, I looked for familiar faces that weren't there. The old women, sitting outside shops, occupied in their lace making, their black dresses stark against the white-painted walls, paid me no heed. The fishermen on the quay-side, bronzed and weather-beaten – their skin burnished through years of struggle on these waters, continued mending their nets.

Eyes that did not recognise me.

Past the harbour and across the soft, sweep of sand, the bar still dominated the view. Red walls amongst the white dots of houses, blue shutters open like a smile to the morning. It was impossible to believe she would still be here, after all these years: that she'd brought out those cold beers and dark-treacle coffees the locals sipped. A handful of tourists were seated outside, taking in the depth of the blue from shoreline to the edge of the heavens, shading their eyes with Ray Bans.

Eyes that did not recognise me.

Annotations:

- Why is the first paragraph so short and what does its change indicate a change in?

- The writer has used a paragraph that is only one sentence long. How does that make you feel as a reader? Does it tell you anything about the narrator? Does it add to the ideas connected with time?

- How does repeating the one-sentence paragraph add interest for the reader and communicate even more fully the feelings of the narrator?

Worksheet 2.2: Fiction or non-fiction?

Student Book **Q4** How did you tell the difference between the fiction and the non-fiction extract?

Complete the table of features below.

Feature	Text 1	Text 2
factual statements		
use of descriptive language		
past / present tense		
use of statistics / data		
complex punctuation		
a narrative sequence		
quotations		
objective / subjective		

Worksheet 2.4: Understanding a poem's theme

Student Book Q10 Read the poem.

> **Cold**
>
> It felt so cold, the snowball which wept in my hands,
> and when I rolled it along in the snow, it grew
> till I could sit on it, looking back at the house,
> where it was cold when I woke in my room, the windows
> blind with ice, my breath undressing itself on the air.
> Cold, too, embracing the torso of snow which I lifted up
> in my arms to build a snowman, my toes, burning, cold
> in my winter boots; my mother's voice calling me in
> from the cold. And her hands were cold from peeling
> then dipping potatoes into a bowl, stopping to cup
> her daughter's face, a kiss for both cold cheeks, my cold nose.
> But nothing so cold as the February night I opened the door
> in the Chapel of Rest where my mother lay, neither young, nor old,
> where my lips, returning the kiss to her brow, knew the meaning of cold.
>
> Carol Ann Duffy

What is the 'plot' or 'content' of this poem? What is the sequence of events?

Student Book Q11 Using the words below to help you, write a paragraph explaining what you think the poem is really about, or what you think the *theme* of the poem is.

> Childhood   Protection   Powerlessness   Parenthood
> Vulnerability   Fear   Death   Love   Grief

Worksheet 2.5: Identifying a story's structure

Student Book **Q2** Complete this table to identify the structure of your chosen story.

Part of story	Structure
	Introduction
	Inciting incident
	Rising action
	Climax
	Transformation and resolution

Worksheet 2.6: Imagery in a Wordsworth poem

Student Book Q6 & 7 Read the poem. As you read, look at the highlighted sections. How many examples of the following can you find?

- simile
- metaphor
- personification

Daffodils

I wandered **lonely as a cloud**
That floats on high o'er vales and hills,
When all at once I saw a **crowd**,
A **host**, of golden daffodils;
Beside the lake, beneath the trees,
Fluttering and **dancing** in the breeze.

Continuous as the stars that shine
And twinkle on the Milky Way,
They stretched in never-ending line
Along the margin of a bay:
Ten thousand saw I at a glance,
Tossing their heads in sprightly dance.

The waves beside them **danced,** but they
Out-did the sparkling waves in **glee**:
A poet could not but be gay,
In such a jocund company:
I gazed—and gazed—but little thought
What wealth the show to me had brought:

For oft, when on my couch I lie
In vacant or in pensive mood,
They flash upon that inward eye
Which is the bliss of solitude;
And then my heart with pleasure fills,
And **dances** with the daffodils.

William Wordsworth

Worksheet 2.8 — Identifying text features

Student Book **Q7** Which of the following features can you find in Text 1 and which in Text 2?

Feature	Text 1 examples	Text 2 examples
Facts		
Opinions		
Statistics		
Personal pronouns (I / you / we)		
Descriptive language		
Questions		

Worksheet 3.1 — Select key information

Student Book **Q3** Read this extract from a newspaper article and complete the table below.

How did Swedish man survive in this frozen car at –30C for TWO MONTHS?

A SWEDISH MAN has been pulled barely alive from his snow-covered car having survived on nothing but snow for two months in sub-zero temperatures. Peter Skyllberg, 44, had eaten nothing but handfuls of snow since December 19 when his car became bogged down in snowdrifts in northern Sweden.

Pictures of the vehicle's interior show the dashboard and seats covered in ice after temperatures plunged to –30C.

Experts think he went into a kind of human hibernation which slowed down his metabolism and pulled him through the ordeal in what they have described as the 'case of a lifetime'.

Mr Skyllberg had driven off the main road on to forest tracks where his car became stuck fast.

On Friday a passing man on a snowmobile stopped to scrape snow from the windscreen of the vehicle and saw movement inside.

[…]

Mr Skyllberg survived by taking handfuls of snow from the roof of the car.

[…]

'Absolutely incredible that he is alive, in part considering that he hasn't had any food, but also bearing in mind that it was really cold for a while there after Christmas,' said a member of the emergency services team deployed to rescue him.

[…]

'He was at the end of his tether,' said a police spokesman. 'It was doubtful he could have survived one or two more days.'

He was wrapped up in a sleeping bag in the car but he had no other warmth; the fuel had run out long ago as he kept the heater running to try to survive as the thermometer plunged on some nights to -30C.

[…]

Policeman Nyberg added: 'He was in a very poor state when we found him.

He could not speak, just a few broken sentences and the words snow … eat. And he managed to say he hadn't eaten anything since December.'

Allan Hall, *Daily Mail*, 22 February 2012

Things we know about the man who was trapped	Things we know about his car
He is Swedish.	

Worksheet 3.3a — What is implied in a text?

Student Book Q2 Look at these quotations from the text and make notes as to what is suggested to you by each one. What is implied here that isn't being said explicitly? The first one has been done for you.

a

- didn't know them as well as she thought
- suggests a secret of some kind or a shock or surprise – sounds disappointed, though
- 'I thought I knew you as well as I know this house.'
- first-person narrator and addressing the story to someone
- the person she's talking to is familiar to her – maybe lives with her?

b

'You're not here any longer so how can I speak to you?'

c

'a bed that hasn't been slept in for weeks.'

d

'Someone half-mad with grief that is, might pick up a shoe from the rug and hold it like a baby.'

Worksheet 3.3b: Show your understanding of inference and implication

Student Book **Q7** Use both extracts from the story by Michelle Roberts, your ideas and quotations and the inferences you have made so far to complete the following task.

I thought I knew you as well as I know this house. No secret places, no hidey-holes, nothing in you I couldn't see. Now I realise how you kept yourself from me, how I didn't really know you at all.

You're not here any longer so how can I speak to you? You can't speak to someone who isn't there. Only mad people talk to an empty chest of drawers, a bed that hasn't been slept in for weeks. Someone half-mad, with grief that is, might pick up a shoe from the rug and hold it like a baby. Someone like me might do that. As if the shoe might still be warm or give a clue to where you've gone.

[...]

What did you have for lunch today? I hope you ate something. Did you beg for the money to buy a burger or a sandwich? I'd like to think you had a proper lunch. Something hot. Soup, perhaps, in a Styrofoam cup. You used to love tinned tomato soup. Cream of. I always urged you to eat proper meals, meat and two veg or something salady, when you got home from school. You liked snacks better as you got older, it was the fashion amongst your friends I think, all day long you ate crisps and buns and I don't know what, at teatime when you came in you'd say you weren't hungry then late at night I'd catch you raiding the kitchen cupboards. Fistfuls of currants and sultanas you'd jam into your mouth, one custard cream after another, you'd wolf all my supply of chocolate bars.

Michelle Roberts, from 'Your Shoes'

What do you understand about the woman in the story and how she is feeling?

Write 250–300 words using the following method to show that you really understand the text.

Checklist for success

- Make clear statements in your own words addressing the question directly.
- Support those statements with your selected quotations.
- Demonstrate your understanding using the inferences you have made.

Worksheet 3.4 — Dickens's characters

Student Book **Q5** Using the categories listed below, make some detailed notes about what we can infer about the character Miss Havisham in this extract from *Great Expectations*.

She was dressed in rich materials – satins, and lace, and silks – all of white. Her shoes were white. And she had a long white veil dependent from her hair, and she had bridal flowers in her hair, but her hair was white. Some bright jewels sparkled on her neck and on her hands, and some other jewels lay sparkling on the table. Dresses, less splendid than the dress she wore, and half-packed trunks, were scattered about. She had not quite finished dressing, for she had but one shoe on – the other was on the table near her hand – her veil was but half arranged, her watch and chain were not put on, and some lace for her bosom lay with those trinkets, and with her handkerchief, and gloves, and some flowers, and a Prayerbook, all confusedly heaped about the looking-glass.

Charles Dickens, *Great Expectations*

Categories	What we can infer
Appearance	She's dressed in white with a veil and seems to be about to get married? She seems wealthy – mention of jewels, etc.
Mannerisms	
The situation they are in	
The place they are in and how they seem to be responding to it	
The mood or atmosphere surrounding them	

Student Book **Q8** What do you understand about the character of the Artful Dodger from this extract?

He was a snub-nosed, flat-browed, common-faced boy enough; and as dirty a juvenile as one would wish to see; but he had about him all the airs and manners of a man. He was short of his age, with rather bowlegs: and little, sharp, ugly eyes. His hat was stuck on the top of his head so lightly, that it threatened to fall off every moment; and would have done so very often, if the wearer had not had a knack of every now and then giving his head a sudden twitch: which brought it back to its old place again. He wore a man's coat, which reached nearly to his heels. He had turned the cuffs back, half-way up his arm, to get his hands out of the sleeves: apparently with the ultimate view of thrusting them into the pockets of his corduroy trousers; for there he kept them. He was, altogether, as roistering and swaggering a young gentleman as ever stood four feet six, or something less, in his bluchers.

'Hullo, my covey, what's the row?' said this strange young gentleman to Oliver.

'I am very hungry and tired,' replied Oliver, the tears standing in his eyes as he spoke. 'I have walked a long way. I have been walking these seven days.'

'Walking for sivin days!' said the young gentleman. 'Oh I see. Beak's order, eh? But,' he added, noticing Oliver's look of surprise, 'I suppose you don't know what a beak is, my flash com-pan-i-on?'

'Going to London?' said the strange boy.

'Yes.'

'Got any lodgings?'

'No.'

'Money?'

'No.'

The strange boy whistled; and put his arms into his pockets as far as the big coat sleeves would let them go.

Charles Dickens, from *Oliver Twist*

Worksheet 3.5 Impressions of Wuthering Heights

Student Book Q3 Answer the questions about *Wuthering Heights*, supporting your ideas with quotations from the extract below and making inferences in each response. Use the grid below to note down your ideas.

Wuthering Heights is the name of Mr Heathcliff's dwelling. 'Wuthering' being a significant provincial adjective, descriptive of the atmospheric tumult to which its station is exposed in stormy weather. Pure, bracing ventilation they must have up there at all times, indeed: one may guess the power of the north wind […] Happily, the architect had foresight to build it strong: the narrow windows are deeply set in the wall, and the corners defended with large jutting stones […] One step brought us into the family sitting-room, without any introductory lobby or passage: they call it here 'the house' pre-eminently. […] One end, indeed, reflected splendidly both light and heat, from ranks of immense pewter dishes, interspersed with silver jugs and tankards, towering row after row, in a vast oak dresser, to the very roof. The latter had never been underdrawn, its entire anatomy lay bare to an inquiring eye, except where a frame of wood laden with oatcakes, and clusters of legs of beef, mutton, and ham, concealed it. Above the chimney were sundry villainous old guns, and a couple of horse-pistols, and, by way of ornament, three gaudily painted canisters disposed along its ledge. The floor was of smooth, white stone: the chairs, high-backed, primitive structures, painted green: one or two heavy black ones lurking in the shade. In an arch, under the dresser, reposed a huge, liver-coloured bitch pointer surrounded by a swarm of squealing puppies and other dogs haunted other recesses.

Emily Brontë, from *Wuthering Heights*

Impressions of Thrushcross Grange	Supporting quotations	Different impressions of Wuthering Heights	Supporting quotations
1		1	
2		2	
3		3	
4		4	

Worksheet 3.6a: Inferences about ideas and attitudes (1)

Student Book **Q1–3** What inferences can you make from the opening paragraph of the piece of journalism on page 96 of the Student Book?

Suggestions for place:	Clues:
Ideas about people:	Clues:
Writer's attitude: positive or negative?	Evidence:

Student Book **Q6** Consider what is implied by each word or phrase highlighted in the paragraph on page 98 of the Student Book. Jot down what you can infer from each one.

Quotation	Inference
'biggest rewards'	
'makes you rethink your first impressions'	
'proves you wrong'	
'adult learner award'	
'success'	
'saw him change'	
'most dedicated learners'	
'satisfying'	
'trust'	
'they can actually do this.'	

© HarperCollins*Publishers* 2015   Reading, understanding and responding to texts

Worksheet 3.6b: Inferences about ideas and attitudes (2)

Student Book **Q10** In the extract below, the writer uses a specific anecdote. Read the extract on page 98 of the Student Book and note down your answers to the questions in the annotations.

1 How do you feel about the age of the man who is in a classroom learning basic maths?	
2 What does this tell you about the education he has had previously?	
3 What does this tell you about his capacity for learning and his character? Why might this surprise some readers?	
4 What might this tell you about his past experiences?	
5 What does this tell you about how he learned maths? What does it also tell you about his real mathematical ability?	
6 What does this achievement mean to the prisoner and the teacher?	

Student Book **Q11** Read the final extract on your own and complete the following task.

> You know that difficult, unruly lad in bottom set maths? You know that boy who's been suspended countless times? You know that one they talk about in the staffroom, who throws chairs and spits and swears and tests everyone paid to care for him to the point of tears? Recent figures show he stands a high chance of entering the criminal justice system, and even more so if he gets expelled (with pupils thrown out aged 12 four times more likely to go to jail). If he does, if he's lucky, and brave, and determined, we'll pick him up, dust him down and carry on where he left off. And maybe second, third or 20th time around, he'll succeed.

How does the writer use a stereotype here to challenge us to see things his way and change our attitude?

Worksheet 3.7 — Compare texts

	In Text A I learn …	Evidence from the text	In Text B I learn …	Evidence from the text				
The place								
The weather								
The temperature								

© HarperCollins*Publishers* 2015

Worksheet 3.8a (1) Respond to English Language tasks (1)

Student Book **Q1** Read the two texts and then carry out the task that follows.

Text A

Sleeping rough for charity hides the real homelessness crisis

The public needs to understand the true face of what life without a home means, and sleeping rough is only part of it

Organising a sponsored sleep-out is a preferred strategy for many homelessness charities up and down the country.

Jollies under the stars, making a mattress from cardboard and bedding down – these Bear Grylls excursions just perpetuate the myth that homelessness is about rough sleeping, and is therefore a much smaller problem than it really is.

The truth is that rough sleeping is the tip of the iceberg. It doesn't begin to cover the extraordinary scope of homelessness. Each year homelessness affects around 400,000 people.

Imagine if 'experiencing homelessness' was sold to you as it really is. Most homeless people do not sleep in the street. You would most likely be sofa surfing, squatting, staying in hostels or being passed around B&Bs by the local council.

During this period you would also now be three times more likely to go to hospital, 13 times more likely to be a victim of violence and 47 times more likely to be victims of theft. One in five would have been robbed. Your life-span would be reduced from a healthy 81 years to just 47.

Since 2007, running a hostel for homeless people has been completely unregulated. Some landlords are fair and generous, but many force tenants to wallow in unhygienic conditions. 'Worse than prison,' is how one charity key worker I know described conditions in some London hostels.

Long spells in these hostels are commonplace. One in 10 will stay for more than two years, most will stay for 12 months. If you don't like the conditions, or feel threatened, a refusal to take the option excludes you from any housing support in the future. Yet 8,000 people each year still take this course of action.

Every one of the 70,000 people in this hostel system is stuck in a grim and dangerous situation. The number of full-time support workers in hostels is dropping dramatically. Cuts have put countless in-house mental health and substance misuse projects at risk. As the state recedes, the proportion of truly dangerous hostels increases.

Tens of thousands more homeless live in filthy squats, far out of reach of help. Charities can only enter to offer aid when accompanied by the police, such is the danger. Interventions are rare. Frustrated landlords turn to private security, who care little for the law and prefer to beat squatters out with garden hoses and cricket bats. Hundreds of thousands more float from sofa to sofa, the legion of 'hidden homeless.'

This problem is widespread. Rough sleeping is not. Society needs to understand how bad a situation we are really in.

Alastair Sloan, *The Guardian*, 29 October 2013

Worksheet 3.8a (2): Respond to English Language tasks (2)

Text B

It is nearly eleven o'clock, and the cold thin rain which has been drizzling so long, is beginning to pour down in good earnest; the baked-potato man has departed – the kidney-pie man has just walked away with his warehouse on his arm – the cheesemonger has drawn in his blind, and the boys have dispersed.

The constant clicking of pattens on the slippy and uneven pavement, and the rustling of umbrellas, as the wind blows against the shop-windows, bear testimony to the inclemency of the night; and the policeman, with his oilskin cape buttoned closely round him, seems as he holds his hat on his head, and turns round to avoid the gust of wind and rain which drives against him at the street-corner, to be very far from congratulating himself on the prospect before him.

The little chandler's shop with the cracked bell behind the door, whose melancholy tinkling has been regulated by the demand for quarters of sugar and half-ounces of coffee, is shutting up.

The crowds which have been passing to and fro during the whole day, are rapidly dwindling away; and the noise of shouting and quarrelling which issues from the public-houses, is almost the only sound that breaks the melancholy stillness of the night.

There was another, but it has ceased. That wretched woman with the infant in her arms, round whose meagre form the remnant of her own scanty shawl is carefully wrapped, has been attempting to sing some popular ballad, in the hope of wringing a few pence from the compassionate passer-by. A brutal laugh at her weak voice is all she has gained. The tears fall thick and fast down her own pale face; the child is cold and hungry, and its low half-stifled wailing adds to the misery of its wretched mother, as she moans aloud, and sinks despairingly down, on a cold damp door-step.

Charles Dickens, from *Sketches by Boz*

Using details from both sources, write a summary of the issues that the homeless poor seem to face today compared to the past.

Checklist for success

Before you begin, remember to:
- ask yourself which key ideas the extracts have in common
- organise that information into logical categories
- select evidence that you can use in support.

A successful response should include:
- clear statements in your own words addressing the question directly
- support for those statements with selected quotations
- inferences to show your understanding.

Worksheet 3.8b: Respond to an English Literature task

'George, I wish you'd look at the nursery.'
'What's wrong with it?'
'I don't know.'
'Well, then.'
'I just want you to look at it, is all, or call a psychologist in to look at it.'
'What would a psychologist want with a nursery?'
'You know very well what he'd want.' His wife paused in the middle of the kitchen and watched the stove busy humming to itself, making supper for four.
'It's just that the nursery is different now than it was.'
'All right, let's have a look.'
They walked down the hall of their soundproofed Happylife Home, which had cost them thirty thousand dollars installed, this house which clothed and fed and rocked them to sleep and played and sang and was good to them.
Their approach sensitized a switch somewhere and the nursery light flicked on when they came within ten feet of it. Similarly, behind them, in the halls, lights went on and off as they left them behind, with a soft automaticity.
'Well,' said George Hadley.
They stood on the thatched floor of the nursery. It was forty feet across by forty feet long and thirty feet high; it had cost half again as much as the rest of the house. 'But nothing's too good for our children,'
George had said.
The nursery was silent. It was empty as a jungle glade at hot, high noon. The walls were blank and two dimensional. Now, as George and Lydia Hadley stood in the center of the room, the walls began to purr and recede into crystalline distance, it seemed, and presently an African veldt appeared, in three dimensions, on all sides, in color reproduced to the final pebble and bit of straw. The ceiling above them became a deep sky with a hot yellow sun.
George Hadley felt the perspiration start on his brow.
'Let's get out of this sun,' he said. 'This is a little too real. But I don't see anything wrong.'
'Wait a moment, you'll see,' said his wife.
Now the hidden odorophonics were beginning to blow a wind of odor at the two people in the middle of the baked veldtland. The hot straw smell of lion grass, the cool green smell of the hidden water hole, the great rusty smell of animals, the smell of dust like a red paprika in the hot air. And now the sounds: the thump of distant antelope feet on grassy sod, the papery rustling of vultures. A shadow passed through the sky. The shadow flickered on George Hadley's upturned, sweating face.

'Filthy creatures,' he heard his wife say.
'The vultures.'
'You see, there are the lions, far over, that way. Now they're on their way to the water hole. They've just been eating,' said Lydia. 'I don't know what.'
'Some animal.' George Hadley put his hand up to shield off the burning light from his squinted eyes. 'A zebra or a baby giraffe, maybe.'
'Are you sure?' His wife sounded peculiarly tense.
'No, it's a little late to be sure,' he said, amused. 'Nothing over there I can see but cleaned bone, and the vultures dropping for what's left.'
'Did you hear that scream?' she asked.
'No.'
'About a minute ago?'
'Sorry, no.'
The lions were coming. And again George Hadley was filled with admiration for the mechanical genius who had conceived this room. A miracle of efficiency selling for an absurdly low price. Every home should have one. Oh, occasionally they frightened you with their clinical accuracy, they startled you, gave you a twinge, but most of the time what fun for everyone, not only your own son and daughter, but for yourself when you felt like a quick jaunt to a foreign land, a quick change of scenery. Well, here it was!
And here were the lions now, fifteen feet away, so real, so feverishly and startlingly real that you could feel the prickling fur on your hand, and your mouth was stuffed with the dusty upholstery smell of their heated pelts, and the yellow of them was in your eyes like the yellow of an exquisite French tapestry, the yellows of lions and summer grass, and the sound of the matted lion lungs exhaling on the silent noontide, and the smell of meat from the panting, dripping mouths.
The lions stood looking at George and Lydia Hadley with terrible green-yellow eyes.
'Watch out!' screamed Lydia.
The lions came running at them.
Lydia bolted and ran. Instinctively, George sprang after her. Outside, in the hall, with the door slammed he was laughing and she was crying, and they both stood appalled at the other's reaction.
'George!'
'Lydia! Oh, my dear poor sweet Lydia!'
'They almost got us!'
'Walls, Lydia, remember; crystal walls, that's all they are. Oh, they look real, I must admit – Africa in your parlor – but it's all dimensional, superreactionary, supersensitive color film and mental tape film behind glass screens. It's all odorophonics and sonics, Lydia. Here's my handkerchief.

Ray Bradbury, from 'The Veldt'

Worksheet 4.1: Orwell's use of language

Student Book **Q3 & 5** Use the table below to find examples of Orwell's use of language (in the second column) and to make notes about their effects (in the third column).

Language choice	Example(s)	Effect: how it makes me feel and why
Adverbials	underfoot overhead ringed completely round	Create a feeling of claustrophobia because they suggest people are completely surrounded by the effects of industrialisation
References to colour		
Powerful adjectives		
Repetition		
Imagery or comparisons		

Worksheet 4.3: How Dickens creates the character of Scrooge

Student Book **Q3** Read the extract from Charles Dickens's *A Christmas Carol*. Use the table below to list a range of different techniques that Dickens uses to create impressions of Scrooge.

Technique	Example	Connotation
Adjectives	grasping	Suggests harshness and desperation, as if money is something that Scrooge feels very passionately about
Imagery	a tight-fisted hand at the grindstone	
Narrator	Oh!	

194 • Explaining and commenting on writers' methods and effects

Worksheet 4.4: Bryson's use of structural features in *A Walk in the Woods*

Student Book Q7 Use the table to find examples of Bryson's use of language in the extract from *A Walk in the Woods*. Use the third column to comment on the effects of some of these language techniques on the reader.

Structural feature	Example	Effect on reader
The list of possible diseases	Ehrlichia chafeenis, schistosomiasis, brucellosis, and shigella	So many technical terms – means he has read up on the diseases. Might suggest he is fixated with what he might catch and suggests he is afraid. However, it could also suggest he is determined to find out everything he can so he is prepared.
The use of short simple sentences that contain one idea		
The list of symptoms of Lyme disease		
The use of dashes		

© HarperCollins*Publishers* 2015 — Explaining and commenting on writers' methods and effects

Worksheet 4.5: The opening of *Jane Eyre*

Student Book **Q6** The table below gives some examples of inferences. See what you can add.

Detail	Quotation	Inference
Negative start	'no possibility of taking a walk'	First sentence negative, suggests life is hard or miserable?
Verbs	'wandering'	Suggests …
Narrator	'we'	

Worksheet 4.7a: Apply your skills: prose extract

Student Book **Tasks** (a) How does the writer's use of language create a picture of the boy's excitement?

(b) This extract is from the opening to a novel. How has the writer used structure within the extract to interest the reader?

The wide avenue with its big white-washed houses set well back in their own lush gardens was an insult. The plush white Lexus was an insult. Shadow knelt by the car's fuel tank, the perspiration glistening on his brow and arms. Like rain on dark glass, a drop of sweat ran down his left cheek, over his short muscular neck and into the cotton of his worn T-shirt. For a fifteen-year-old boy, Shadow was built big and solid. At his side were the tools of his trade: a rag, a can of gasoline. In his pocket was the means to a magical end: a box of matches.

[…]

Shadow drank the smell from the gas tank. Sheer bliss. The smell alone could transport him to paradise. Quickly, he stuffed the rag into the wound in the side of the car, letting a few inches hang out like a wick. To make sure there was enough food for the fire, Shadow splashed gasoline over the cloth and down the side of the car. Slowly, working his way backwards, away from the Lexus, he laid a trail of gasoline. In the warmth of the night, the fuel evaporated and filled the air with its sweet hungry smell. Twenty metres from the car, behind the shiny liquid fuse leading to the Lexus, Shadow stopped.

He was eager to see the greedy flames and yet he wanted to linger, to savour the moment that was about to make him important once more. He called it Shadowtime. His fingers gripped that little box, slowly extracted a match. Such a tiny thing, like an exclamation mark. One simple strike, a quick twist of the wrist, and the cleansing began with a graceful yellow plume like a candle in a church. Shadow's spine tingled, his heartbeat raced. He was about to see the most beautiful show on Earth. He dropped the lighted match and the eager fuel reached up and embraced Shadow's gift of life.

The seductive flame danced silently, slickly down the road towards the white car. The itchy yellow fingers clawed up the side of the Lexus, blistering the paint, and loitered for a few seconds on the wick before worming their way into the interior.

[…]

Fluttering yellow birds flew out into the darkness and sucked the oxygen from the night air. Some of the flames flashed beneath the Lexus and baked the car as if it were on a gas cooker. After a delicious delay, the windows blew out and the vehicle leapt a metre off the road in an exquisite explosion, engulfed by a fiery yellow sheath as if it were being carried to heaven by a host of shining angels. The flame shot upwards into the night, pushing aside the darkness, illuminating the sky. The shock wave rushed past Shadow, pushing him backwards and roaring in his ears. A split-second later, Shadow felt an extra ripple of unnatural heat wafting over him, sensing it most on his bare skin. He did not even blink. This is what he lived for. Forget school. This was what life was all about.

Only when he detected movement in the street was it time to retreat. At first, Shadow jogged backwards so that he could keep an eye on the still burning wreck, so he could keep the image on his retina for as long as possible. In the coming days he would replay it many times – until he ached for a different image. But the next one would also be that magnificent combination of yellow and black. Street-lamps at night, gold on skin, flame scavenging among charred ruins. For now, he could see it whenever he looked. The flickering flower was reflected in every window of every house and every parked car. It was like a dream that the whole world was on fire. Paradise.

Malcolm Rose, from *Bloodline*

Worksheet 4.7b: Apply your skills: unseen poetry

Student Book **Task** How does the writer present ideas about love in 'First Love'?

First Love

I ne'er was struck before that hour
   With love so sudden and so sweet,
Her face it bloomed like a sweet flower
   And stole my heart away complete.
My face turned pale as deadly pale,
   My legs refused to walk away,
And when she looked, what could I ail?
   My life and all seemed turned to clay.

And then my blood rushed to my face
   And took my eyesight quite away,
The trees and bushes round the place
   Seemed midnight at noonday.
I could not see a single thing,
   Words from my eyes did start—
They spoke as chords do from the string,
   And blood burnt round my heart.

Are flowers the winter's choice?
   Is love's bed always snow?
She seemed to hear my silent voice,
   Not love's appeals to know.
I never saw so sweet a face
   As that I stood before.
My heart has left its dwelling-place
   And can return no more.

John Clare

Worksheet 5.1 — The context of *Animal Farm*

How could you use the following two pieces of information to help develop your response to the **Apply the skills** task?

Item A

Orwell said in a preface to *Animal Farm* in 1947:

> '... it was of the utmost importance to me that people in western Europe should see the Soviet regime for what it really was. Since 1930 I had seen little evidence that the USSR was progressing towards anything that one could truly call Socialism. On the contrary, I was struck by clear signs of its transformation into a hierarchical society, in which the rulers have no more reason to give up their power than any other ruling class. Moreover, the workers and intelligentsia in a country like England cannot understand that the USSR of today is altogether different from what it was in 1917. It is partly that they do not want to understand (i.e. they want to believe that, somewhere, a really Socialist country does actually exist), and partly that, being accustomed to comparative freedom and moderation in public life, totalitarianism is completely incomprehensible to them.
>
> ... I thought of exposing the Soviet myth in a story that could be easily understood by almost anyone and which could be easily translated into other languages.'

Item B

Burma was a totalitarian country from 1962 until 2011. According to Orwell-scholar Christopher Hitchens, there is a common saying in Burma:

> 'Orwell flattered us by writing three novels about Burma: *Burmese days*, *Animal Farm* and *1984*.'

- *Burmese Days*: an Orwell novel set in colonial Burma based on his experience as a policeman
- *1984*: an Orwell novel set in a totalitarian future where Britain is part of a dictatorship led by the cruel and ruthless Big Brother

Worksheet 5.3: Stevenson's use of language

Student Book **Q5** Look closely at Stevenson's use of language in each quotation and make some notes in the table about how you might link them to ideas about context.

Quotation	Notes
And then all of a sudden he broke out in a great flame of anger	
stamping with his foot	
brandishing the cane	
clubbed him to the earth	The word 'clubbed' instantly makes us think about cavemen and perhaps how when Jekyll changes into Hyde he is evolving backwards into a more primitive, irrational and violent form.
with ape-like fury	
he was trampling his victim under foot	
hailing down a storm of blows	The words 'hailing' and 'storm' are both powerful natural images of violence. Perhaps they show that Hyde's violence is inevitable and unstoppable, like the weather.
bones were audibly shattered	

Worksheet 5.4 — Dramatic irony in *An Inspector Calls*

Student Book **Q2–3** Complete the table below to explore how the writer, J.B. Priestley, uses dramatic irony. How has Priestley used the historical setting of 1912 to discredit the views of Arthur Birling?

Facts we know	Things Arthur says	Dramatic irony
Aeroplanes were used in WW1 and WW2 to destroy cities and kill civilians	'In a year or two we'll have aeroplanes that will be able to go anywhere.'	Arthur sees aeroplanes as a sign of progress. The audience might see this differently, as over 40 000 British civilians were killed in the Blitz during WW2. So, maybe Priestley is saying that capitalism just creates more efficient ways of killing innocent people.
The Titanic sank on its maiden voyage.		
WW1 broke out two years later in 1914.		
In 1940, Britain was involved in WW2.		
The 1920s and 1930s were marked by strikes and conflict between trade unionists and capitalists, especially the General Strike in 1926.		
The Russian army entered Berlin in 1945 leading to the final defeat of Germany in WW2.		

© HarperCollins*Publishers* 2015   Working with context

Worksheet 5.5 — Explore the same context from different perspectives

Student Book **Q9**

> Imagine you are marking this student's work. They have some good ideas and they can back up their ideas with evidence. The problem is that the student does not comment in detail about the effects of the writers' language choices. For example, the student could have written:
>
> When Wordsworth uses the word 'majesty', it makes the city sound royal like a king or queen and emphasises how grand and beautiful the city is.
>
> Show how the student could have gone into more detail about some of Eliot's language choices.

Wordsworth describes London as a beautiful place and you can tell that he really likes it. He is standing on a bridge in the early morning watching the river flow by and the sunrise over the peaceful city. You can tell he likes it because he uses words like 'majesty', 'bright', 'glittering', 'calm' and 'sweet'. Eliot thinks London is a horrible place because there is nothing beautiful in her description of it. She looks through a window but finds her view blocked by 'the houses opposite' which she thinks are 'like solid fog'. She sees people hurrying everywhere, not noticing the people around them and looking 'upon the ground'.

Everybody she sees and hears is 'closed' and shut up in their own little world and so she sees London as a miserable place whereas Wordsworth really likes it. Wordsworth describes nice buildings like 'towers, domes, theatres and temples' to show how beautiful the city is. On the other hand, Eliot describes the buildings in a depressing way saying things like 'monotony of surface and of form without a break' which makes the view from the window sound very boring.

Worksheet 5.6a — Analysis of a Ted Hughes poem

Student Book **Q3** Complete the following table to help you explore how Hughes portrays the freedom and beauty of the swallows.

Quotation	Exploration
A blue-dark knot of glittering voltage	Hughes uses 'blue-dark' to precisely capture the colour of the swallows. The word 'knot' perhaps suggests a mystery that needs to be solved or unravelled – one that is not straightforward and takes time and careful thought. 'Glittering' links the swallows to the sun and 'voltage' suggests the power, speed and excitement of electricity.
A whiplash swimmer, a fish of the air	
the barbed harpoon	
She flings from the furnace, a rainbow of purples	
Dips her glow in the pond and is perfect	
the seamstress of summer	This could link to the 'Work' mentioned in the title. Hughes could be ironically contrasting the 'work' of the swallows which mainly seems to be enjoying flying freely with the 'play' of the people as they endure a hot day at the crowded beach.
She scissors the blue into shapes and she sews it, She draws a long thread and she knots it at the corners	
cartwheeling through crimson	
Touches the honey-slow river	
Returns to the hand stretched from under the eaves	
A boomerang of rejoicing shadow	

Worksheet 6.2: Gathering evidence about language features

Student Book **Q5** Collect your ideas together in the table below.

Selected quotations	Language feature	My detective work • Connotations of the words: what they suggest to the reader • My inferences
'like old beggars' 'coughing like hags'		
'bent double' 'knock-kneed' 'lame' 'blind' 'deaf'		

Student Book **Q7** Use the checklist below to identify which skills the student has shown.

✓ or ✗

☐ the paragraph focuses on language analysis right the way through

☐ uses language terminology with examples

☐ blends in supporting quotations from the poem so they still make sense within the sentences

☐ considers what the poet is doing and what he wants us to see

☐ makes inferences about the key ideas building their own interpretation of the poem

☐ presents work clearly in Standard English.

Worksheet 6.3a — Gathering evidence about structural features

Student Book Q5 A student has made the following notes on the key structural features of the extract. Add your own ideas to these notes, exploring the impact of the features on meaning and thinking about what they help the writer to communicate to you.

It wasn't a spectacular wedding. It happened in a hurry, and they only spent one night together before he went away again, went away properly.

[…]

But it was a wedding, and they looked each other in the eyes and said the words, they made their vows and they have kept them all these years.

[…]

And they took the wedding certificate back to their new house, propped it up on the chest of drawers at the foot of the bed, and spent the whole evening looking at it.

[…]

She said, tell me the story of us, tell me it the way you'll tell our children, when they ask.

[…]

And he'd always say it the same way, starting with once upon a time there was a handsome soldier boy with a smart uniform …

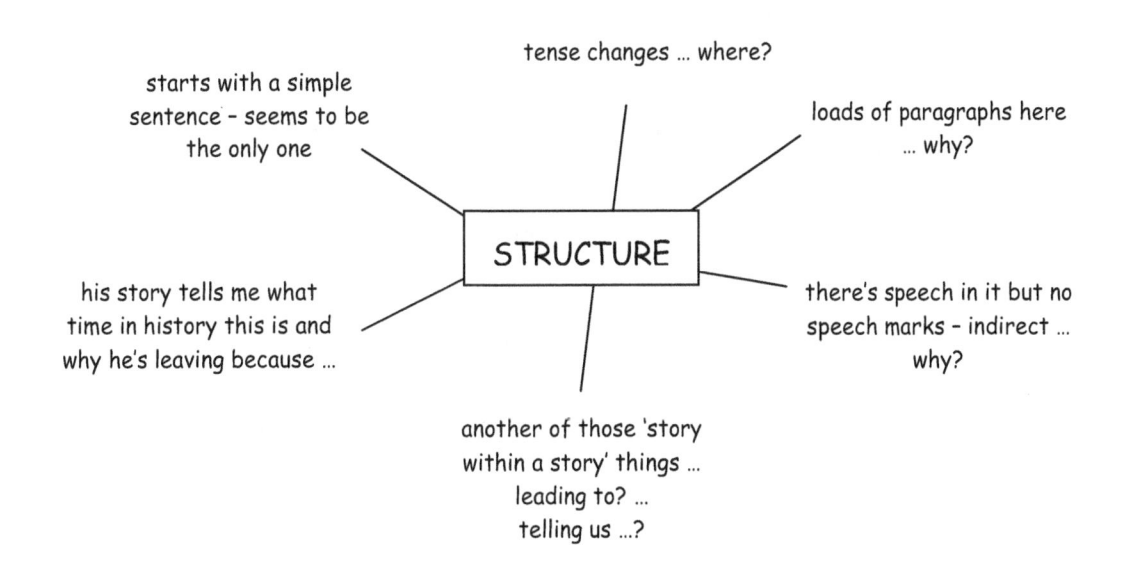

STRUCTURE (mind map):

- starts with a simple sentence – seems to be the only one
- tense changes … where?
- loads of paragraphs here … why?
- his story tells me what time in history this is and why he's leaving because …
- there's speech in it but no speech marks – indirect … why?
- another of those 'story within a story' things … leading to? … telling us …?

Worksheet 6.3b — Analysing structural features

Student Book **Q6** We know now that the following structural features are important in this text:

- past and present
- paragraph structure
- sentence structure
- story within a story
- indirect speech.

Identify and annotate for yourself the structural features that make an impact on the meaning of the story.

And that first time he'd told the story, that night, lying

side by side on the bed, fully clothed, neither of them

said anything when he finished, they just lay there

looking at the official type, the formal words.

And she'd whispered it's a good story isn't it? And the

last thing she'd said to him, just before she went to

sleep that night, quietly, almost as though she thought

he was asleep, she said you will come back won't you,

you will keep safe, please, you will come home?

Worksheet 6.4a: Evaluating comments about mood

Student Book **Q3** Do you agree with the ideas and interpretation in the student's essay about the mood of the extract? Add your own ideas in a bullet-pointed list.

---

[1] The extract creates a spooky atmosphere by using the semantic field of horror with references to 'midnight', 'fear' and 'howling' and 'agonized wailing'.

[2] There is a ghostly feel and this is increased because of the reference to midnight – the stereotypical time when bad things happen.

[3] The use of pathetic fallacy adds to the atmosphere as we know the wind 'sighed softly' like a ghost.

[4] The narrator is clearly frightened as he describes having a 'sick feeling of suspense'. He doesn't know what is going to happen and neither do we, which adds to that feeling of suspense.

Your ideas:

- ....
- ....
- ....
- ....
- ....
- ....
- ....

Worksheet 6.4b: How Bram Stoker creates the mood in *Dracula*

Student Book **Q4** Find and note down quotations that show:

- the semantic field of entrapment ....
  ....

- the use of pathetic fallacy ....
  ....

- the emotions of the narrator ....
  ....

- a mysterious character ....
  ....

- any other stereotypical conventions of the gothic horror genre – list below:
  ....
  ....
  ....
  ....
  ....
  ....

Now note down any quotations that add to the mood the text is creating.

1 ....
  ....

2 ....
  ....

3 ....
  ....

Worksheet 6.5a — Ideas about 'Ozymandias'

Student Book Q2 Read the poem 'Ozymandias'. Then use the student's initial thoughts and questions to compile your own more detailed notes on the poem. You could do this in a series of spider diagrams or a mind map.

Student's ideas	My ideas
Language: • 'antique land' makes me think of old civilisations – the past – powerful empires • person in statue not happy! Sounds fierce. Like a dictator – 'cold command' alliteration/harsh	
Structure: • a narrator • big quotation from the traveller • we get to see the inscription from the statue so must be important. • This poem has got 14 lines and some rhyming – is this a sonnet? Need to check.	
Mood: • Doesn't sound great – there is no civilisation here anymore/everything dead and gone/decayed/in ruins	
The poet's message: • What is the poet saying about past civilisations – they are all dead and gone. A warning? • When was Shelley writing? Need to check. • Is this message still/more important today? • Why end with the sand – that image quite frightening somehow.	

© HarperCollins*Publishers* 2015

Forming a critical response

Worksheet 6.5b: Evaluating the language of 'Ozymandias'

Student Book **Q7** Using your notes on language from **Q2**, write a paragraph evaluating the language used in the poem 'Ozymandias' by P.B. Shelley.

Shelley's poem Ozymandias explores how a leader of a past civilisation imposed power. The noun phrase 'an antique land' makes us think of past civilisations such as the Romans, the Ancient Greeks or the Aztecs – all powerful empires with powerful leaders.

The description of the statue of Ozymandias with his 'frown' and 'sneer of cold command' implies this leader was harsh – it is even reflected in his statue. The alliteration of 'cold command' suggests to us that …

Worksheet 6.6a — Jessica Ennis's autobiography

Student Book **Q2** The text below is from the autobiography of athlete Jessica Ennis. In it she describes the moments before her first big event in the London 2012 Olympics.

This is the day that I have dreamt about for years. This has been what all that dying on the side of a track has been about. This is the end of the raging pain. This is my one opportunity. My one shot. Walking into this arena is an assault on the senses – the purple and green and red, the crescendo of noise and the haze at the end of the straight where the Olympic flame is burning bright. This is it. This is my chance. I cannot help thinking that if it goes wrong I will never get this opportunity again. I might make another Olympics, but it won't be at home and I won't be touted as the face of the Games again. This combination of circumstances will never arise again. It is my first time and my last chance. Finally I realize just how big and scary the Olympic Games are. I follow the other girls to the start and we get into our blocks. It's like that Eminem song goes: one opportunity to seize everything you want. Will I capture the moment or let it slip?

It has taken me sixteen years to get here. Now I have seven events and two days to make it all worthwhile. There have been countless times when I have wondered if it would happen. I have been down, broken and almost out, but I have dragged myself back from the brink. Part of me wonders how this has happened. I am just an ordinary girl from a run-of-the-mill street in Sheffield and yet I have been plucked out of that normality and into this melting pot of hopes and dreams and fierce competition. It is what I have wanted when I have been training every day, but it is frightening.

I feel adrenaline, excitement and fear. I have lost my crowns in the last year and there are bigger, stronger girls ready to push me around. Tatyana Chernova is the world champion. Nataliya Dobrynska is the Olympic champion. I have no titles, just one shot. We crouch and the roar drops to total silence. It is that special moment of bated breath and possibility. And then suddenly, in those, seconds before the gun, I feel a strange calmness wash over me and I am ready. It is now or never.

Worksheet 6.6b: Selecting and gathering evidence

Student Book Q3 Select and gather the evidence you would like to use in your response to the task in the grid below.

> Evaluate how Jessica Ennis has presented the experience of competing in the Olympic Games.

Key messages	
Points about tone	
Structure points	
Language points	

Worksheet 6.7a: Responding to an English Language task

There was music from my neighbor's house through the summer nights. In his blue gardens men and girls came and went like moths among the whisperings and the champagne and the stars. At high tide in the afternoon I watched his guests diving from the tower of his raft, or taking the sun on the hot sand of his beach while his two motor-boats slit the waters of the Sound, drawing aquaplanes over cataracts of foam. On week-ends his Rolls-Royce became an omnibus, bearing parties to and from the city between nine in the morning and long past midnight, while his station wagon scampered like a brisk yellow bug to meet all trains. And on Mondays eight servants, including an extra gardener, toiled all day with mops and scrubbing-brushes and hammers and garden-shears, repairing the ravages of the night before.

Every Friday five crates of oranges and lemons arrived from a fruiterer in New York — every Monday these same oranges and lemons left his back door in a pyramid of pulpless halves. There was a machine in the kitchen which could extract the juice of two hundred oranges in half an hour if a little button was pressed two hundred times by a butler's thumb.

At least once a fortnight a corps of caterers came down with several hundred feet of canvas and enough colored lights to make a Christmas tree of Gatsby's enormous garden. On buffet tables, garnished with glistening hors-d'oeuvre, spiced baked hams crowded against salads of harlequin designs and pastry pigs and turkeys bewitched to a dark gold. In the main hall a bar with a real brass rail was set up, and stocked with gins and liquors and with cordials so long forgotten that most of his female guests were too young to know one from another.

By seven o'clock the orchestra has arrived, no thin five-piece affair, but a whole pitful of oboes and trombones and saxophones and viols and cornets and piccolos, and low and high drums. The last swimmers have come in from the beach now and are dressing up-stairs; the cars from New York are parked five deep in the drive, and already the halls and salons and verandas are gaudy with primary colors, and hair shorn in strange new ways, and shawls beyond the dreams of Castile. The bar is in full swing, and floating rounds of cocktails permeate the garden outside, until the air is alive with chatter and laughter, and casual innuendo and introductions forgotten on the spot, and enthusiastic meetings between women who never knew each other's names.

The lights grow brighter as the earth lurches away from the sun, and now the orchestra is playing yellow cocktail music, and the opera of voices pitches a key higher. Laughter is easier minute by minute, spilled with prodigality, tipped out at a cheerful word. The groups change more swiftly, swell with new arrivals, dissolve and form in the same breath; already there are wanderers, confident girls who weave here and there among the stouter and more stable, become for a sharp, joyous moment the centre of a group, and then, excited with triumph, glide on through the sea-change of faces and voices and color under the constantly changing light.

F. Scott Fitzgerald, from *The Great Gatsby*

Worksheet 6.7b: Responding to an English Literature task

A lady dressed in black and heavily veiled, who had been sitting in the window, rose as we entered.

'Good-morning, madam,' said Holmes cheerily. 'My name is Sherlock Holmes. This is my intimate friend and associate, Dr. Watson, before whom you can speak as freely as before myself. Ha, I am glad to see that Mrs. Hudson has had the good sense to light the fire. Pray draw up to it, and I shall order you a cup of hot coffee, for I observe that you are shivering.'

'It is not cold which makes me shiver,' said the woman in a low voice, changing her seat as requested.

'What, then?'

'It is fear, Mr. Holmes. It is terror.' She raised her veil as she spoke, and we could see that she was indeed in a pitiable state of agitation, her face all drawn and grey, with restless frightened eyes, like those of some hunted animal. Her features and figure were those of a woman of thirty, but her hair was shot with premature grey, and her expression was weary and haggard. Sherlock Holmes ran her over with one of his quick, all-comprehensive glances.

'You must not fear,' said he soothingly, bending forward and patting her forearm. 'We shall soon set matters right, I have no doubt. You have come in by train this morning, I see.'

'You know me, then?'

'No, but I observe the second half of a return ticket in the palm of your left glove. You must have started early, and yet you had a good drive in a dog-cart, along heavy roads, before you reached the station.'

The lady gave a violent start and stared in bewilderment at my companion.

'There is no mystery, my dear madam,' said he, smiling. 'The left arm of your jacket is spattered with mud in no less than seven places. The marks are perfectly fresh. There is no vehicle save a dog-cart which throws up mud in that way, and then only when you sit on the left-hand side of the driver.'

'Whatever your reasons may be, you are perfectly correct,' said she. 'I started from home before six, reached Leatherhead at twenty past, and came in by the first train to Waterloo. Sir, I can stand this strain no longer; I shall go mad if it continues. I have no one to turn to – none, save only one, who cares for me, and he, poor fellow, can be of little aid. I have heard of you, Mr. Holmes; I have heard of you from Mrs. Farintosh, whom you helped in the hour of her sore need. It was from her that I had your address. Oh, sir, do you not think that you could help me, too, and at least throw a little light through the dense darkness which surrounds me?'

Arthur Conan Doyle, from 'The Adventure of the Speckled Band'

Worksheet 7.1a — Viewpoints on school uniform

Student Book **Q1** Look at these statements about school uniform. Sort the viewpoints into those that approve of school uniform and those that disapprove of it.

 a If you have to wear uniform then there is no competition about clothes, so it makes it fairer for everyone.

 b Uniform takes away your individuality.

 c It's much cheaper to have uniform because you don't need a different outfit for every day.

 d Uniform helps you to feel you belong to the school.

 e Uniform costs a fortune and the quality is rubbish.

 f Uniform is a nightmare for teachers because they have to spend all their time telling the students off for not wearing it properly.

Viewpoints that approve of school uniform: ....

Viewpoints that disapprove of school uniform: ....

Student Book **Q2** Choose one viewpoint that might be held by a student, one that might be held by a teacher, and one that might be held by a parent. What might influence each of these viewpoints?

One viewpoint that a **student** might hold is: ....

Factors that might influence this viewpoint are: ....

....

....

One viewpoint that a **teacher** might hold is: ....

Factors that might influence this viewpoint are: ....

....

....

One viewpoint that a **parent** might hold is: ....

Factors that might influence this viewpoint are: ....

....

....

Worksheet 7.1b: Identify a writer's viewpoint (1)

Why I'm taking my child out of school for a holiday

This half-term, my family and I are leaving the country for a much-needed break. To save around £800, I will be taking my child out of school before the term officially ends. I have not sought permission from the head teacher. Nor will I.

[...]

Firstly, I genuinely don't feel my child (aged 4) will be disadvantaged by one or two days out of school. Second, and controversially, I don't feel the school will be disadvantaged either. I know how the argument goes – if everyone behaved like me we'd be in a sorry state with half-empty classrooms. But, really, would we? Aren't those who shout the loudest about the need for attendance the ones who are rich enough for term-time holidays never to be an issue?

I do feel guilty, but only for families who don't have the same financial resources as we do, so can't have a holiday at all, term time or not. I can't imagine any teacher devaluing the chance to learn a few words of a foreign language in situ, to see geology in action by playing on black sand, or start to understand basic engineering principles by looking at how planes fly. For us, the physical, intellectual and social advantages of travel would not be financially possible if we waited until the school holidays. Of course, I agree that attendance (most of the time) is vital but so is family harmony, unfrazzled parents, time to read or explore the world without the pressures of day-to-day life. Until travel companies offer more reasonable prices during school holidays, families like mine will continue to take their children out of school. Perhaps we should go easy on parents who value spending time with their children in a new and stimulating environment over Ofsted attendance targets.

Anonymous, *The Guardian*, 29 January 2014

Worksheet 7.1c — Identify a writer's viewpoint (2)

Student Book **Q5** Read the following article and answer the five questions relating to the parts of the text indicated by the numbers.

Why I'll never take my children out of school for a holiday

As chief holiday-planner in our household of six, I could be a lot richer – and/or my children could have seen a lot more of the world – if I'd fished them out of school, or even just shaved a few days off the beginning or end of term here and there. [1] Instead, over the last 16 years while we've had school-age kids, we've kept our holidays religiously within the vacation dates: and as my youngest child is still only 11, we've got another seven years of the same ahead. [2]

It's irksome, because there are huge financial savings to be made. Also, who wants to be on the beach in August, when it's packed and baking hot, when June and September [which is when my husband and I always holidayed in those dim and distant days before our eldest was born] are so less crowded, and the temperature more agreeable?

So why not just flout the system? Well, it all comes down to respect. Like all parents, I have occasional issues with aspects of my children's education: but on the whole, I aim to support the primary and comprehensive schools where they are, and have been, pupils. And part of the way I show my respect and support is by following the rules: and rule number one is, make sure your child is in school when he or she should be there. [3]

So many parents seem not to realise that the reason their kids don't work hard, or play truant, or get into trouble with their teachers, is connected to the fact that they have an *à la carte* attitude to rules themselves. [4] If you want your child to stick two fingers up at their teachers, to think education doesn't matter, or to skimp on revising for an exam, then go ahead and take them out of school so you can jet off on an exciting holiday for a fortnight. What you are role-modelling by your behaviour is your belief that rules are for other people, not for you; and your kids will pick up on that very, very quickly.

And here's another thing. My eldest, post-uni, is currently saving up to go to Asia on a gap year. Because travel is for life; but school is only for childhood, and as holiday-loving parents we need to remember that. [5]

Joanna Moorhead, *The Guardian*, 29 January 2014

[1] What could the writer have done?

[2] What did the writer decide to do?

[3] What is the writer's main reason for keeping their child in school?

[4] How does this statement develop their argument?

[5] What is the overall viewpoint?

Worksheet 7.2 Draw inferences

Student Book **Q5** Complete the table. What inferences can you draw from the statements and quotations?

Statement	Quotation	Inference
The project deliberately chose a very deprived area.	'… desperately poor people struggling to survive'	It would be an assumption that the deprivation also leads to intellectual deprivation.
The children were interested in the computer.		
The children learned how to use it very quickly.		

Read the following article, and annotate or highlight it as instructed.

> The close, low chamber at the back, in which the boys were crowded, was so foul and stifling as to be, at first, almost insupportable. But its moral aspect was so far worse than its physical, that this was soon forgotten. Huddled together on a bench about the room, and shown out by some flaring candles stuck against the walls, were a crowd of boys, varying from mere infants to young men; sellers of fruit, herbs, lucifer-matches, flints; sleepers under the dry arches of bridges; young thieves and beggars--with nothing natural to youth about them: with nothing frank, ingenuous, or pleasant in their faces; low-browed, vicious, cunning, wicked; abandoned of all help but this; speeding downward to destruction; and UNUTTERABLY IGNORANT.
>
> […]
>
> This was the Class I saw at the Ragged School. They could not be trusted with books; they could only be instructed orally; they were difficult of reduction to anything like attention, obedience, or decent behaviour; their benighted ignorance in reference to the Deity, or to any social duty (how could they guess at any social duty, being so discarded by all social teachers but the gaoler and the hangman!) was terrible to see. Yet, even here, and among these, something had been done already. The Ragged School was of recent date and very poor; but he **had inculcated some association with the name of the Almighty**,* which was not an oath, and had taught them to look forward in a hymn (they sang it) to another life, which would correct the miseries and woes of this.
>
> Charles Dickens, 'A Sleep to Startle Us',
> *Household Words*, 13 March 1852

* introduced the children to ideas about being a good Christian person

Worksheet 7.3a — A *Titanic* survivor's account

Student Book **Q3–4** Read the following account, written by a survivor of the *Titanic* disaster, and annotate or highlight it as instructed.

HARRY SENIOR, a fireman on the Titanic, said last night:

I was in my bunk when I felt a bump. One man said. 'Hello, she has been struck.' I went on deck and saw a great pile of ice on the well deck below the forecastle, but we all thought the ship would last some time, and we went back to our bunks. Then one of the firemen came running down and yelled, 'All muster for the lifeboats!' I ran on deck, and the Captain said:

'All firemen keep down on the well deck. If a man comes up I'll shoot him.'

Then I saw the first boat lowered. Thirteen people were on board, eleven men and two women. Three were millionaires and one was Ismay.

Then I ran up on the hurricane deck and helped to throw one of the collapsible boats on to the lower deck. I saw an Italian woman holding two babies. I took one of them and made the woman jump overboard with the baby, while I did the same with the other.

When I came to the surface the baby in my arms was dead. I saw the woman strike out in good style, but a boiler burst on the Titanic and started a big wave. When the woman saw that wave she gave up. Then, as the child was dead, I let it sink, too.

I swam around for about half an hour, and was swimming on my back when the Titanic went down. I tried to get aboard a boat, but some chap hit me over the head with an oar. There were too many in her. I got around to the other side of the boat and climbed in. There were thirty-five of us on board, including the second officer, and no women. I saw any amount of drowning and dead around us. We picked one man off an overturned boat and he died just as he was pulled over the side.

New York Times, Friday 19 April 1912

Worksheet 7.3b: Writer's techniques

Student Book **Q6** Find one example of each of the following techniques used by the writer to paint an emotive picture.

Technique	Example
description to paint a picture of the events	
first-person account	
direct speech	
a range of complex punctuation	
description of the writer's feelings and attitudes	
hyperbole	
emotive language to describe the emotions and behaviour of the people	

Worksheet 7.4a: Reading a poem: 'Nothing's Changed'

Student Book **Q3** Read the following poem. The speaker is walking through a former shanty town in South Africa, remembering his childhood under Apartheid.

Nothing's Changed

Small round hard stones click
under my heels,
seeding grasses thrust
bearded seeds
into trouser cuffs, cans,
trodden on, crunch
in tall, purple-flowering,
amiable weeds.

District Six.
No board says it is:
but my feet know,
and my hands,
and the skin about my bones,
and the soft labouring of my lungs,
and the hot, white, inwards turning
anger of my eyes.

Brash with glass,
name flaring like a flag,
it squats
in the grass and weeds,
incipient Port Jackson trees:
new, up-market, haute cuisine,
guard at the gatepost,
whites only inn.

No sign says it is:
but we know where we belong.

I press my nose
to the clear panes, know,
before I see them, there will be
crushed ice white glass,
linen falls,
the single rose.

Down the road,
working man's cafe sells
bunny chows.
Take it with you, eat
it at a plastic table's top,
wipe your fingers on your jeans,
spit a little on the floor:
it's in the bone.

I back from the
glass,
boy again,
leaving small mean O
of small mean mouth.
Hands burn
for a stone, a bomb,
to shiver down the glass.
Nothing's changed.

Tatamkhula Afrika

Worksheet 7.4b: Reading a poem: 'Homeland'

Student Book **Q8** Read the following poem. The speaker in this poem has also left her childhood home.

Homeland

For a country of stone and harsh wind
For a country of bright perfect light
For the black of its earth and the white of its walls

For the silent and patient faces
Which poverty slowly etched
Close to the bone with the detail
Of a long irrefutable report

And for the faces like sun and wind

And for the clarity of those words
Always said with passion
For their colour and their weight
For their clean concrete silence
From which the named things spring
For the nakedness of awed words

Stone river wind house
Lament day song breath
Expanse root water –
My homeland and my centre

The moon hurts me the sea weeps me
And exile stamps the heart of time

Sophia de Mello Breyner

Worksheet 7.5a Respond to an English Language task (1)

Student Book **Q1** Read **Source 1**, which is a biographical account by a young girl written in the nineteenth century.

Source 1

> My father was a glass blower. When I was eight years old my father died and our family had to go to the Bristol Workhouse. My brother was sent from Bristol workhouse in the same way as many other children were – cart-loads at a time. My mother did not know where he was for two years. He was taken off in the dead of night without her knowledge, and the parish officers would never tell her where he was.
>
> It was the mother of Joseph Russell who first found out where the children were, and told my mother. We set off together, my mother and I, we walked the whole way from Bristol to Cressbrook Mill in Derbyshire. We were many days on the road.
>
> Mrs. Newton fondled over my mother when we arrived. My mother had brought her a present of little glass ornaments. She got these ornaments from some of the workmen, thinking they would be a very nice present to carry to the mistress at Cressbrook, for her kindness to my brother.
>
> My brother told me that Mrs. Newton's fondling was all a blind; but I was so young and foolish, and so glad to see him again; that I did not heed what he said, and could not be persuaded to leave him. They would not let me stay unless I would take the shilling binding money. I took the shilling and I was very proud of it.
>
> They took me into the counting house and showed me a piece of paper with a red sealed horse on which they told me to touch, and then to make a cross, which I did. This meant I had to stay at Cressbrook Mill till I was twenty one.
>
> Sarah Ashton, interviewed in *The Ashton Chronicle*, 23 June 1849

Worksheet 7.5b — Respond to an English Language task (2)

Student Book **Q2** Read **Source 2**, which is an article from a newspaper.

Source 2

Britain's child soldiers

Denying those under the age of 18 the right to leave the army is outdated, immoral and in breach of UN guidelines

AT 16 YOU ARE not old enough to vote, buy a pint in a pub or ride a motorbike. Yet you can join the armed forces, and commit yourself for four years beyond your 18th birthday. On becoming legally adult you can then be sent to the frontline in Afghanistan. A 16-year-old soldier can train with live ammunition, yet when he goes back to barracks in the evening he isn't old enough to rent an X-rated DVD of *Apocalypse Now*, a film dealing with the horrors of war – because it is too violent.

Notions of childhood change. During the siege of Mafeking in 1900, Robert Baden Powell recruited 12-year-old boys to deliver messages under fire. They wore khaki and their leader was the 13-year-old Warner Goodyear. But today Britain is the only European country to recruit into the regular army at 16. Perversely those young recruits are required to serve two years longer than those recruited at 18. Far from being a curious legal relic, this rule was reintroduced by the Labour government in 2008. After a six-month 'cooling-off' period there is no right to leave. While 'unhappy minors' may leave at the discretion of their commanding officer, the fact that there is no 'discharge as of right' leaves them uniquely open to bullying and that bullying is more serious if it happens because they cannot leave.

The situation of 16-year-old soldiers is sometimes compared to that of apprentices. Yet in what other 21st century apprenticeship can a breach of discipline lead to a court martial and time spent in military prison? In what other apprenticeship do you face such dangers? How many apprentice carpenters, brick layers or plumbers are found dead whether shot in the head or hanging from a beam? Yet that is what happened to four young recruits training at Deepcut barracks. A carpenter's skills are a guarantee of security in an economic downturn. There are more limited openings for trained marksmen. An infantryman returning from Helmand province has no guarantee of a job. David Cameron's call for a 'national change' in attitude towards mental health problems among former soldiers is highly welcome, but could his proposed 24- hour helpline be extended to soldiers who are currently serving or training in barracks?

While the UK no longer has conscription, those joining the army at 16 often come from the poorest and least educated backgrounds. For youngsters without other jobs to go to, a career in the army may be hard to resist. What other choices do they have? It is true that 16- and 17-year-olds are no longer deployed to conflict zones but decisions made as a child have irrevocable consequences as an adult. At the moment a young person making a decision at 16, with his parents' consent, has no right at the age of 18 to review that decision with an informed conscience.

Michael Bartlet, *The Guardian*,
11 March 2011

Worksheet 7.5c: Respond to an English Literature task

The Hero

'Jack fell as he'd have wished,' the Mother said,
And folded up the letter that she'd read.
'The Colonel writes so nicely.' Something broke
In the tired voice that quavered to a choke.
She half looked up. 'We mothers are so proud
Of our dead soldiers.' Then her face was bowed.

Quietly the Brother Officer went out.
He'd told the poor old dear some gallant lies
That she would nourish all her days, no doubt.
For while he coughed and mumbled, her weak eyes
Had shone with gentle triumph, brimmed with joy,
Because he'd been so brave, her glorious boy.

He thought how 'Jack', cold-footed, useless swine,
Had panicked down the trench that night the mine
Went up at Wicked Corner; how he'd tried
To get sent home, and how, at last, he died,
Blown to small bits. And no one seemed to care
Except that lonely woman with white hair.

Siegfried Sassoon

Arms and the Boy

Let the boy try along this bayonet-blade
How cold steel is, and keen with hunger of blood;
Blue with all malice, like a madman's flash;
And thinly drawn with famishing for flesh.

Lend him to stroke these blind, blunt bullet-heads
Which long to nuzzle in the hearts of lads.
Or give him cartridges of fine zinc teeth,
Sharp with the sharpness of grief and death.

For his teeth seem for laughing round an apple.
There lurk no claws behind his fingers supple;
And God will grow no talons at his heels,
Nor antlers through the thickness of his curls.

Wilfred Owen

Worksheet 8.1 Use of imagery

Student Book **Q9** Read the extract from *The Dark Heart of Italy* by Tobias Jones below, and:

- highlight in one colour any **adjectives** or **nouns** (or combinations of them) that describe objects or people (look for the use of the senses)
- highlight in another colour any **verbs of movement**.

> It's a spectacular road that lifts you above the fog of the plain: supported on concrete stilts it struts over valleys, and its long tunnels puncture the mountains. A few hundred metres below the asphalt, picturesque mountain villages huddle around their bell-towers, appearing from above like random piles of matchboxes. Now, in October, the mountain colours are crisp and autumnal: white wood-smoke gusting between dark green pines.
>
> Tobias Jones, from *The Dark Heart of Italy*

Which of these seem to be comparisons of one thing with another? Once you have decided this, fill in the table below.

Imagery	Example	Effect
Metaphors	'struts over valleys'	He personifies the road, making it sound as if it is walking in giant steps, almost boastfully.
Simile		

Worksheet 8.2: Apply the skills: preparing to write

Student Book Q13 Choose **one** of the following three experiences:

- learning to ride a bike or a pony
- helping a relative or family friend out with a job
- going on public transport on your own for the first time.

Use the box below to jot down notes to prepare you for writing.

Who was involved? Write down one or two main people (could be a friend, or someone in authority) and some **basic information** about them (e.g. age, appearance, job):

....

....

....

....

....

What was the **scene**, **setting** or **place** (e.g. your street, a house, a train station?):

....

Now add some **descriptive details**:

....

....

....

....

....

What were your **feelings** about the experience or people involved? (These might be consistent, or they may change over the course of the experience.)

....

....

....

....

....

Worksheet 8.3 — Perform a rehearsed reading

Work in pairs. You are going to perform a 'rehearsed reading' of the text below. Before you do so, you will need to decide between you who is going to read which parts. The point of doing this is to emphasise or draw attention to the repetitions or patterns of language within the text. For example, one of you might read 'smiles down on me' and 'it is not smiling' to draw attention to the repetition of 'smiles/smiling'. Use two highlighters or coloured pens to indicate who will read which sentence or part of the text.

I am sitting on a narrow ledge by the side of the lake. The warm sun makes my skin glow, and the water sparkles and glitters. I am alone, but feel peaceful.

The face of the mountain is calm and smiles down on me.

At first, there is little sign of the storm. There is blue sky and a few fluffy smudges in the distance, but soon these approach the still lake, getting darker all the time. Suddenly, the tiny patch of blue sky has gone.

In a few minutes, rain is spattering my face, and the surface of the sea is a million pinpricks on a black dress. A small boat which was bobbing gently now rocks violently from side to side, the rusted letters of its name blurred and almost invisible. The water swells, and then rises like a dormant beast, waking from its slumber to threaten the path on which I stand.

Now, when I glimpse the mountain it is not smiling.

Worksheet 8.4: Generate ideas for a description

Student Book **Q6** — Your local railway station is running a competition about people's memories of train journeys. Write a description suggested by the picture on page 263 of the Student Book.

Use this sheet to help generate ideas effectively.

Stage 1: Observe carefully: look at the picture for one minute:
- What do you see?
- What can the people see (or feel)?

Stage 2: Choose your method for generating ideas: spider diagram; list; collage; something else? Generate some ideas now using the space below.

Stage 3: Cull and/or connect:
- Cross out any ideas you don't want to use.
- Link any ideas that might be described together.

Stage 4: Add further details and sequence:
- In the same space above, write in some more details about the things you are describing.
- Put them in an order (perhaps add numbers for each paragraph, or re-order them onscreen).

Worksheet 8.5a: Analyse the openings of stories

Student Book **Q3** Read the opening extracts in the table below, and tick the columns that apply to each text. Highlight the particular aspect of each text that tells you this.

Opening	Mood/atmosphere or time	Setting or location	Character or relationship	Key event or action	Direct contact with reader
'They murdered him.'					
'During the whole of a dull, dark, and soundless day in the autumn of the year, when the clouds hung oppressively low in the heavens, I had been passing alone, on horseback, through a singularly dreary tract of country; and at length found myself, as the shades of the evening drew on, within view of the melancholy House of Usher.'					
'The morning had dawned clear and cold with a crispness that hinted at the end of summer. They set forth at daybreak to see a man beheaded, twenty in all, and Bran rode among them, nervous with excitement. This was the first time he had been deemed old enough to go with his lord father and his brothers to see the king's justice done. It was the ninth year of summer, and the seventh of Bran's life.'					
'You must go back with me to the autumn of 1827.'					

Worksheet 8.5b — Plan your story

Student Book Q15 — Plan your own story based on the title 'The Visit' and write the first 2–3 paragraphs of it. Think about how you can engage the reader.

Use this planning grid to plan the stages of the story. Then decide at which point you will actually begin your story. Remember, it doesn't have to be at the 'introduction' stage.

Story element	Details (who, what, where, when, why, etc.)
Introduction	
Complication	
Rising action/ development	
Climax	
Resolution	

© HarperCollins*Publishers* 2015

Writing creatively • 231

Worksheet 8.6: Characterisation and voice

Student Book Q12 Write two opening paragraphs from a story in which your main character arrives in a city from the countryside.

Use the box below to jot down notes to prepare you for writing.

How is your main character travelling as they arrive in the city? (e.g. on foot, bus, bike)

....

What places and sights do they see? Note down two or three, and then think about how you could zoom in on details.

1. ....

2. ....

3. ....

How does what they see (or don't see) reflect their own character or background?

....

....

....

How do they react (if at all)?

....

....

....

Who will your character speak to as they arrive or once they're in the city?

....

....

....

How will this conversation reveal things about them?

....

....

....

Worksheet 8.7 — Plan and write a story opening

Student Book Q6 — Write the opening part of a story that takes place in an abandoned building or setting.

Use this sheet to help plan your ideas. Try to work as quickly and efficiently as you can.

Get ideas:

Who? ....

What? ....

Where? ....

When? ....

Why? ....

Other details:

What's the story/problem? ....

....

Any other characters? ....

....

....

How will you make it original or different? ....

....

....

First paragraph:

....

....

....

....

....

....

Worksheet 8.8a: Plan an assessment task

This task is similar to ones you might encounter in your assessment.

You have been asked to contribute a piece of descriptive writing to an anthology called 'Busy Lives'. Write a descriptive piece suggested by the picture below.

Worksheet 9.1 — Ways of conveying a point of view

Student Book Q7 Positive or negative points of view can be conveyed through using a number of devices. Read the three extracts on pages 281–2 of the Student Book again and complete the table below.

Technique	Negative	Positive	Balanced
Adjective choice			
Verb or verb phrase choice		'I *love* the smell of …'	
Imagery (similes and metaphors)	'Invade our high streets like *alien armies*'		
Types of sentence		Statement: 'I love the smell …'	

Extra challenge: Read this further extract. What is the viewpoint of the writer here? How do you know?

> Despite my own dislike of the way coffee bars are dominating the high street, I thought I should be even-handed and get those who know about such things to explain what the appeal is. Who better than a barista like Sergio Pannetta, who works in our local coffee bar?
>
> 'What's not to like?' he tells me. 'Even people who don't drink coffee like the smell of coffee. Besides, we don't just do coffee – you can get tea, iced drinks, even sandwiches…'. He had a point, but I wasn't convinced. His coffee bar had replaced a bookshop. You can't drink books.

Worksheet 9.2: Select the correct tone and register

Student Book **Q8**

Write the first two paragraphs of each of these texts:
- Write a letter to the headteacher of your school asking them to grant you time off to go to a rock festival.
- Email a friend to persuade them to go with you to a rock festival.

Use the table below to help you.

Letter to headteacher	Email to a friend
Dear Mr/Ms	Hi ....
[para 1] I am writing to you to request...	[para 1] You know that festival that's coming up? Well...
[para 2] I know this may not sound very educational. However...	[para 2] It's gonna be great cos...

Worksheet 9.3 — The language of blogs

Student Book **Q5–6** Read this blog and decide whether the language is suitable for its form – a blog. Then complete the table below. You could write examples of the altered, 'correct' text in the third column.

> It is clear that in the world today, there are a number of jobs that women simply cannot, nor should not do. This is not a matter of equality, nor is it a matter of male pride or domination. No, it is a matter of common sense.
>
> The undeniable evidence is this: in general, women are physically weaker than men. Thus occupations which require muscular strength, such as building work, policing and so on, are simply unsuitable for the female sex.

Blog features	In text?	Changes needed?
Regular reference to 'I', 'me'	Yes/No	
Informal, chatty phrases or vocabulary	Yes/No	
Informal grammar – such as abbreviations, minor sentences, etc.	Yes/No	
Exaggerations to entertain or make a point	Yes/No	
Sense of addressing reader as a friend	Yes/No	

© HarperCollins*Publishers* 2015   Point of view writing • 237

Worksheet 9.4 Select appropriate vocabulary

Student Book **Q3** Read the two student responses and:
- underline adverbs used to strengthen an adjective
- circle adjectives and noun phrases describing clothing or the effect clothes create.

Student 1

I am totally appalled by the influence of branding. I mean, what's the point? Clothes are to be worn... they do a job. They need to be functional, smart (for work) and comfortable. Branding is an unnecessary complication. As long as you don't look a mess, who cares who made them?

Student 2

Brands make a bold statement about who you are. Seeing someone else wearing a brand you like creates an instant, electric connection. They can be incredibly powerful in helping you find like-minded people. Who wants to be an outsider?

Now, complete the table below:

Vocabulary type	Example(s)	Effect
Adverbs used to strengthen an adjective or verb	'totally appalled by...'	How powerfully anti-branding they are. 'Totally' leaves no room for argument.
Adjectives	'functional'	
Nouns or noun phrases	(who wants to be an) 'outsider'	

238 • Point of view writing

Worksheet 9.5: Use a variety of sentences

Student Book **Q10** — Write the opening paragraph to an article in which you write about either the benefits of private reading, or the benefits of sport.

[Writing space]

Now, use this checklist to evaluate your work.

Skill	Yes	No	Not sure
Use simple, short sentences and verbs to state a point of view clearly. (underline these)			
Use longer sentences (such as compounds) to explain your view. (highlight or shade these)			
Use well-chosen verbs to create emotional impact or authority. (circle these)			
Use modal verbs to express levels of certainty. (put a tick over these)			

Worksheet 9.7a: Organise a viewpoint text (1)

Student Book **Q10** Follow this process in order to organise your ideas on the following topic:

> You have been asked to give a talk at your school on your views about whether it is a good idea to take a break when you leave school before you choose a career or go on to further study.

Stage 1: Complete this list of points AGAINST taking a break.

For:	Against
Do something different with my life	I may drift and end up doing nothing
Help me decide what I want to do in the future	
Spend time helping people or volunteering	

Stage 2: Try out Approach 2 – one paragraph FOR, then one paragraph AGAINST. Use this template to help you. (You will need to explain your ideas and develop them in each paragraph as shown here.)

Taking a break might be a good idea as it will enable me to do something different with my life. I will have plenty of time (the rest of my life!) working in a job, having to earn money to support myself, so it will be good to do something that isn't just about money.

Of course, the problem could be that I would end up drifting and doing nothing. I can just see myself ....

....

....

Another good thing about taking a break is ....

....

....

However, you could also argue that ....

....

....

Finally, ...

....

....

Worksheet 9.7b — Organise a viewpoint text (2)

Student Book **Q10** Follow this process in order to organise your ideas on the following topic:

> You have been asked to give a talk at your school on your views about whether it is a good idea to take a break when you leave school before you choose a career or go on to further study.

Stage 1: Note down ideas FOR and AGAINST taking a break.

For:	Against
Do something different with my life	I may drift and end up doing nothing

Stage 2: Organise your ideas into one of the structures you have learned about ('two halves', 'see-saw' or 'point/counterpoint'). Remember that using the last structure is probably the most convincing, as it enables you to 'knock down' counterarguments as you go along.

Stage 3: Before you draft your paragraphs, think about or note down:

- What you are going to include – Statistics? Factual information? A vivid picture to sway the reader?
- What your paragraphs will look like – Short or long for different effects?
- Whether there is a logical order for your arguments – Should one come before the other?
- How you will link your points or ideas – e.g. use of discourse markers?

Stage 4: Draft your three paragraphs.

Extra challenge: Write the whole response, including a suitable introduction and conclusion. Think about effective ways you could begin and end: what length or style of paragraph would work? How will what you put into these paragraphs link to what you are going to say or have just said?

Worksheet 9.8: Discussion record

Student Book **Q10** During your discussion, make notes in the table below based on what you and others say. The task is to explain your viewpoint on the following statement:

The fashion industry is responsible for lots of society's problems.

Pts	Yes, it is responsible …	No, it isn't responsible …
1		
2		
3		
4		
5		
6		

General notes

- Once you have finished, go over your notes and either add further comments or further ideas.
- Decide which argument you find most convincing and begin to plan your blog article around it.

Worksheet 9.9a: Sample point of view task

Read the task, and then write a plan to help you answer the question, using the planning template below.

> *We are wasting unnecessary power by lighting our towns and villages all through the night. All lamplights should be turned off between the hours of 11pm and 7am.*
>
> Write an article for a broadsheet paper in which you explain your point of view on this statement.

My viewpoint

....

....

The key points for my viewpoint

A ....

B ....

C ....

D ....

E ....

Any key points against (which you could acknowledge and then 'knock down')

F ....

G ....

H ....

My structure (the order of my points, e.g. D, E, A, C...)

....

....

....

....

1.1 An introduction to phrases

Assessment objectives

English Language

AO2 Explain, comment on and analyse how writers use language and structure to achieve effects and influence readers, using relevant subject terminology to support their views

AO6 Use a range of vocabulary and sentence structures for clarity, purpose and effect, with accurate spelling and punctuation

English Literature

AO2 Analyse the language, form and structure used by a writer to create meanings and effects, using relevant subject terminology where appropriate

AO4 Use a range of vocabulary and sentence structures for clarity, purpose and effect, with accurate spelling and punctuation

GCSE examinations

- **English Language**
  Paper 1, Question 5
  Paper 2, Question 5
- The same skills and knowledge are also required in
  English Language
  Paper 1, Questions 3, 4
  Paper 2, Question 4
- **English Literature**
  Paper 1, Section A
  Paper 2, Section A

Differentiated learning outcomes

- **All students must** be able to recognise the names of different types of phrases and use some of them in their own writing.
- **Most students should** be able to recognise most different types of phrases, comment on their usage in the reading texts and include a variety of them in their own writing.
- **Some students could** recognise different types of phrases, using them to work out the precise inferences and effects that a writer creates, and also apply them in their own work for effect.

Resources

- **Student Book**: pp. 8–11
- **Worksheets**: 1.1a–b
- **PPT**: 1.1

Getting you thinking

Big question	Recap on the idea that words have different roles to play in a sentence and ask the students to name the parts of speech they remember. Now read the **Big question**: *Isn't a phrase just a cluster of words?* Present the information about phrases in the introductory paragraph in **Getting you thinking** on page 8 of the Student Book. Consolidate this using the definition of 'phrase' in the **Key term** box.

Display **PPT 1.1, slide 1**. Check that the students remember what an adjective is and then read the definition of the noun phrase.

Allow five minutes for the students to work individually to note down their thoughts and ideas about the pairs of noun phrases (**Q1**), before taking feedback and sharing ideas as a class. Consolidate by introducing the **Key term** 'modification'. Ask the students in which other contexts they have heard the words 'modify' and 'modification' (e.g. to 'modify' behaviour; to make 'modifications' to houses). Then discuss **Q2** as a class, bringing out the differences in mood that can arise from changing the adjective.

Explore the skills

Read the information about adjectival phrases in **Explore the skills** on page 8 and introduce the examples and the **Key term** definition of 'adjectival phrase'.
Allow 10 minutes for the students to complete the short creative writing task (**Q3**) independently, pointing out the examples on page 9 of the Student Book to help them make a start.

Give extra support by asking the students to complete the activity in pairs.

Give extra challenge by asking the students to create more complex examples of adjectival phrases.

When the students have finished writing their paragraphs, allow a further two or three minutes for them to consider **Q4**. Then take feedback and share ideas as a class.

Recap on what a preposition is, before asking the students to complete the short revision exercise in **Q5**.

Read aloud the poem 'To His Mistris Going to Bed' by John Donne on page 9 of the Student Book, and discuss **Q6a** and **Q6b** as a class.

Use the paragraph preceding **Q7** at the top of page 10 to consolidate how useful prepositional phrases are in analytical work – for AO2 – when dealing with unseen texts. Then allow approximately 20 minutes for the students to complete **Q7** in pairs or small groups, using the annotations to the poem 'Daffodils' on page 10 and **Worksheet 1.1a**. Take brief feedback as a class. Encourage the students to:

- recognise the surprise element of the daffodils and how they are encountered
- consider how they cover every part of the landscape
- note the continuous nature of the text via the non-finite verbs 'dancing' and 'fluttering', which extend the sentence to the end of the verse – these present a picture of something gentle and elegant, like a corps de ballet or a mass of fairies, seemingly infinite in number and crowding in on the poet as though he is overwhelmed by their scale and beauty.

Develop the skills

Ask the students to recap on what they understand the role of an adverb to be. Then read the introductory paragraph on adverbials and adverbial phrases in **Develop the skills** on page 10. Use the **Key terms** definitions on page 11 to consolidate the students' understanding if necessary.

Then allow 5–10 minutes for the students to complete **Q8** independently.

Display **PPT 1.1, slide 2**, and elicit the difference between the three adverbials. Use the third example to identify the components of an adverbial clause. Recap on the **Key term** 'clause' and ask the students where they have used or heard the term before.

Now read aloud the poem 'Laughing Song' by William Blake on page 11 of the Student Book and elicit some thoughts from the class about the effects of the final two lines.

Allow 15 minutes for the students to explore and discuss the poem in pairs or small groups, using **Worksheet 1.1b** to make notes, annotate and highlight the text (**Q9**). Take brief feedback as a class.

Apply the skills

Read the task in **Q10**. This is a short creative task designed to allow the students to revise the new terminology of phrases and practise their usage.

Allow 30 minutes for the students to complete the main task (**Q10**). Alternatively, this could be used as a creative, follow-up homework task.

Big answer plenary	Once the students have completed the main writing task, ask them to work in pairs to identify and label the phrases their partner has managed to include in their poem. Are they correct? Ask the students to use the definitions in this chapter to check. Then refer back to the **Big question** and ask the students to decide if 'just a cluster of words' is an accurate description of a phrase.
	Ask the students to use the **Check your progress** outcomes on page 11 of the Student Book to evaluate whether they have all achieved Outcome 1. Look back at the responses made in **Q7** and **Q9** to evaluate which students have achieved the higher outcomes.

1.2 Sentence structures and punctuation

Assessment objectives

English Language

AO2 Explain, comment on and analyse how writers use language and structure to achieve effects and influence readers, using relevant subject terminology to support their views

AO6 Use a range of vocabulary and sentence structures for clarity, purpose and effect, with accurate spelling and punctuation

English Literature

AO2 Analyse the language, form and structure used by a writer to create meanings and effects, using relevant subject terminology where appropriate

AO4 Use a range of vocabulary and sentence structures for clarity, purpose and effect, with accurate spelling and punctuation

GCSE examinations

- **English Language**
  Paper 1, Question 5
  Paper 2, Question 5
- The same skills and knowledge are also required in
  English Language
  Paper 1, Questions 3, 4
  Paper 2, Question 4
- **English Literature**
  Paper 1, Section A
  Paper 2, Section A

Differentiated learning outcomes

- **All students must** understand the difference between simple, compound and complex sentences and be able to use all three.
- **Most students should** be able to recognise how each sentence type is constructed and be able to use them in their own work for effect.
- **Some students could** understand how to decode the most complex sentences in order to extract key meanings and be able to use a variety of sentence types in their own work to create precise meaning and effect.

Resources

- **Student Book**: pp. 12–15
- **Worksheets**: 1.2a–b
- **PPT**: 1.2

Getting you thinking

Big question	Refer to the **Big question**: *Some texts use very complex sentences – how do you 'unpack' them?* Introduce the idea that sentences fall into different categories or 'types'.
	Ask the students what they think the difference is between a simple and a compound sentence. Record some of their thoughts on the whiteboard. Use the analogy of adding things together to make a compound in science to help them define what a compound sentence is. You could also use this opportunity to review what compound adjectives are.

Now read the introductory paragraph in **Getting you thinking** on page 12 of the Student Book and link this to their ideas about complex sentences from the start of the lesson.

Display **PPT 1.2, slide 1**, and read aloud the extract from *Harry Potter and the Philosopher's Stone* by J.K. Rowling.

Introduce the names of the four sentence types. Discuss **Q1a–c** as a class, using the extract on the PPT slide, before allowing five minutes for the students to complete **Q1d** independently, using the definitions in the **Key terms** boxes to help them.

Answers to **Q1d**: 1 complex; 2 compound; 3 simple; 4 compound-complex.

Explore the skills

Reinforce the opening statement in **Explore the skills** on page 13, before displaying **PPT 1.2, slide 2**, the first extract from *The Waves* by Virginia Woolf. Allow five minutes for the students to make some initial notes on the extract and to complete **Q2**.

Now display **PPT 1.2**, **slide 3**, the second extract from *The Waves*, and reinforce that in the novel this extract comes before the first one in **Q2**. Discuss **Q3** with the class.

Develop the skills

Reinforce the key ideas in the opening paragraph of **Develop the skills** on page 13. You may wish to allow some time for the students to note down these key points.

Now read the second and third paragraphs, and link the idea of sentence complexity to the nineteenth-century texts the students may be studying in English Literature or may meet in the examination in Paper 2 in an unseen context. Introduce the idea of the 'thought journey' as a useful reading strategy for those complex sentences in nineteenth-century writing. Explain that the punctuation used in complex sentences reflects the natural pauses we should make in helping to unpack the meaning.

Allow ten minutes for the students to complete **Q4** in pairs or small groups, using **Worksheet 1.2a**. They should work out the role of each punctuation mark from the examples given before providing a definition (**Q4a**). Use this activity to re-familiarise the students with the four key punctuation marks they are likely to meet in complex sentences and which they should be using themselves. (Note: this activity works best if you ask the students to complete it with their books closed, as definitions of the punctuation marks are given on page 14.)

Now display **PPT 1.2**, **slide 4**, and feed back as a class. Then allow a further 10 minutes for the students to complete their own examples (**Q4b**).

Refer the students to the table at the bottom of page 14 of the Student Book and introduce the idea of the punctuation 'stage directions'. If time allows, test out the stage directions using the examples given in the table.

Develop this by asking the students to work in pairs, using the stage directions and the extract from *Pride and Prejudice* by Jane Austen on page 15 of the Student Book, to practise their reading of complex sentences (**Q5**).

For **Q6**, allow 20 minutes for the students to complete the 'thought journey' flow chart in pairs or small groups, using **Worksheet 1.2b**. This activity allows the students to unpack the lengthy sentences in the extract idea by idea. Answers to **Q6** can be found on **PPT 1.2, slide 5**.

Apply the skills

Read the task on page 15 of the Student Book. Allow 20–30 minutes for the students to complete **Q7**, using the same format to map out their own 'thought journey' for the additional sentence from *Pride and Prejudice*. If set for homework, this activity could be expanded into a mind-mapping and/or collage task to illustrate the key ideas.

Big answer plenary	Refer back to the **Big question** and the initial ideas the students made about simple, compound and complex sentences on the whiteboard. Ask the students to use the **Check your progress** outcomes to evaluate: • their understanding of the terms • how confident they are using those sentence forms in their own written work.

1.3 Structural effects in sentences

Assessment objectives

English Language

AO2 Explain, comment on and analyse how writers use language and structure to achieve effects and influence readers, using relevant subject terminology to support their views

AO6 Use a range of vocabulary and sentence structures for clarity, purpose and effect, with accurate spelling and punctuation

English Literature

AO2 Analyse the language, form and structure used by a writer to create meanings and effects, using relevant subject terminology where appropriate

GCSE examinations

- **English Language**
  Paper 1, Question 5
  Paper 2, Question 5
- The same skills and knowledge are also required in
  English Language
  Paper 1, Questions 3, 4
  Paper 2, Question 4
- **English Literature**
  Paper 1, Section A
  Paper 2, Section A

Differentiated learning outcomes

- **All students must** be able to understand that using different sentence structures creates different moods or feelings within a text.
- **Most students should** be able to understand that using different sentence structures adds to the meaning and impact of a text for the reader or audience.
- **Some students could** interpret the meanings and effects of a text by deconstructing and commenting on its sentences, phrases and clauses, as well as using those varied structures for effect in their own writing.

Resources

- **Student Book**: pp. 16–19
- **Worksheet**: 1.3
- **PPT**: 1.3

Getting you thinking

| Big question | Read the **Big question**: *Does it make any different what types of sentence you use?* Elicit some initial responses from the class. |

Display **PPT 1.3, slide 1**, and discuss **Q1a–e** with the class. Unpick the key ideas:

- The first sentence is short and dramatic; it forces a stop and acts like a command, as if it is foregrounding some action to come. Link this to the **Key term** 'minor sentence'.

- The second sentence is more descriptive; it has detail and a slow meandering pace, as though we too are walking with the narrator and noticing the details in each clause. Use this opportunity to recap on the terms 'clause', 'subordinate clause' and 'complex sentence'.

Explore the skills

Read the extract from *If Nobody Speaks of Remarkable Things* by Jon McGregor and the accompanying annotations on page 17 of the Student Book. Then allow 15 minutes for the students, working in pairs or small groups, to make notes on the author's use of sentence structure (**Q2**). They can note their ideas on **Worksheet 1.3**.

Take feedback and share ideas as a class. Ensure the students recognise that the listing effects are there to create the sense of the ongoing night and the changing sounds we might expect to hear within it. The word 'sandwiched' reflects the standalone line 'and it stops' as though forming a kind of specific brief moment between the end of night and the beginnings of day. By exploring these kinds of questions, the students are developing an intrinsic understanding of the effects of structure for AO2 work.

Develop the skills

Now read the extract from *Sketches by Boz* by Charles Dickens on page 18. Use this as an opportunity for the students to practise their reading of nineteenth-century texts using the 'stage directions' from Lesson 1.2, which are available on **PPT 1.3, slide 2**. Then allow 20 minutes for the students to complete **Q3** and **Q4**. Before they begin, reiterate that the block of text highlighted in yellow is one sentence, and that the block of text highlighted in blue is also one sentence.

> **Give extra support** by asking one half of the class to work on the yellow sentence and the other half to work on the blue, perhaps in pairs or small groups.
>
> **Give extra challenge** by asking the students to work in pairs, with one student in each pair looking at the yellow sentence, and the other at the blue sentence. They should then discuss their responses to each question **a–d**.

Take feedback as a class. The students should identify ideas such as:

- The old bell is there to alert the shopkeeper not just to customers but also to thieves.
- Beautiful buildings stand alongside more seedy ones, and we get the sense of an area that has become down at heel and is a confused jumble of dirty-looking shops.
- The broker's shops are infested with bugs, and we get a sense of a busy, teeming city life – though it's a life of the poor where all seems squalid, dirty and miserable.

Now ask the students to identify the similarities in the way Dickens and McGregor use sentences for effect (**Q5**). Refer the students to their answers to **Q2–Q4** as a stepping-stone to **Q5**.

Apply the skills

The tasks in this section enable the students to make that vital link between their reading and writing skills; this section will help them to see that all of their skills are interlinked – that the techniques they are able to draw out of texts for AO2 are the ones that they can use for effect as writers in addressing AO5 and AO6.

Allow 45 minutes for the students to complete the written description of a particular aspect of a town or city (**Q6**), working independently. Support this writing by allowing the students to research an image to work from, if the facility is available or if the students are completing this as a homework task.

Alternatively, you could display **PPT 1.3, slide 3**, which contains some interesting images of towns and cities.

Read the task in **Q7**, and highlight the links between writing and reading. This task will allow the students to reflect on their own practice and analyse their own work. Allow 15 minutes for the students to complete the task. This could be set as homework, if the creative writing is done in class.

> **Big answer plenary**
>
> Ask the students to work in pairs and read their partner's creative writing (for **Q6**) and commentary (for **Q7**), and to make two further suggestions for the commentary. Then ask them to use the **Check your progress** outcomes on page 19 of the Student Book to evaluate both the writing and commentary task.
>
> Finally, refer back to the **Big question**. Ask each student to write down one effect that is gained from using different sentence types. Then take feedback and share ideas with the class.

2.1 Explore meanings and interpretations

Assessment objectives

English Language

AO1 Identify and interpret explicit and implicit information and ideas; select and synthesise evidence from different texts

English Literature

AO1 Read, understand and respond to texts, maintaining a critical style and develop an informed personal response; use textual references, including quotations, to support and illustrate interpretations

GCSE examinations

- English Language
  Paper 1, Section A
- English Literature
  Paper 2 Section B

Differentiated learning outcomes

- **All students must** be able to explore and explain possible meanings in texts.
- **Most students should** be able to raise questions about challenging texts, and suggest some of their own answers or interpretations.
- **Some students could** explain how texts can have plurality of meanings and can suggest a range of interpretations supported by evidence.

Resources

- **Student Book**: pp. 22–5
- **Worksheet**: 2.1
- **PPT**: 2.1

Getting you thinking

Big question	Refer to the **Big question**: *What does 'interpreting' a text mean?* Ask the students to discuss the role of an 'interpreter' in politics, sport, etc. Briefly elicit the idea that the interpreter takes the original idea or text and 'translates' it using their own language, for others to understand. In some senses, this is what the students are doing when they interpret a text – finding a new language to describe and make sense of it.

Ask the students to look at the two images on page 22 of the Student Book and to complete **Q1** in pairs. Take brief feedback. They might say:

a Both pictures show a blue starry sky.

b The first picture is photographic and realistic, showing stars as mostly uniform in shape. The second picture is more imaginative, with enlarged, swirly shapes for the stars; it also shows aspects of the landscape other than just sky and trees.

You could follow up by asking: why show these images in a lesson about literature? Take some initial thoughts from the class, but point out that the students will be able to answer this when they have discussed the Venn diagram on page 22.

Explore the skills

Look at and discuss the Venn diagram on page 22 of the Student Book with the class. Establish the idea that an interpretation is a meeting point: it is not a question of them as readers making a wild guess at meaning based on nothing, but is about using ideas that arise *from* the text. Now ask the students to complete **Q2**. This is an extension and development of **Q1**, this time with the students working independently at first. However, once they have made notes, ask them to their share ideas with a partner. As this is an interpretation, there are no definitive answers, but they might mention:

- the different shapes and colours of the stars; the fact they seem to swirl and move; the way in which this swirling is carried through to the tree/plant in the foreground and landscape behind
- the idea that the sky and stars might be seen as active and energetic, rather than as passive, stationary or distant, as in the other image.

Develop the skills

For **Q3** and **Q4**, write the words 'bright' and 'star' on the board (with space between them) and ask the students to write each word on a separate sheet of paper. Then ask them to add the synonyms and connotations for each word. Take feedback as a class, asking, as each word is suggested, what its meaning is, and how it differs from or links with, other interpretations (e.g. 'shining' can mean literally a bright light, but also an impressive achievement).

Now ask the students to complete **Q5**, independently. Take feedback as a class. *Bright Star* is a good title because it is a telling metaphor indicating Keats's brilliance (the original meaning of 'brilliant' is 'shining'); it is also an image used by Keats in one of his own sonnets, which makes it especially apt.

> **Give extra support** by checking that the students are clear about the way connotations can suggest metaphors – the connotations often link to another idea (e.g. the natural world to the human world, and vice versa).
>
> **Give extra challenge** by asking the students what else the idea of a star connotes (if it hasn't come up)? For example, someone who can't be reached? Something that disappears?

In order to develop the students' understanding of interpretation, display **PPT 2.1**, **slides 1–4**, which show some ideas for interpreting William Blake's poem 'The Sick Rose'. As a follow-up/homework task, you could ask the students to copy the poem and go away and puzzle over its possible meanings, without making wild guesses. Alternatively, they could spend five minutes discussing possible interpretations and then report back to the class.

The students should now be in a position to write an informed paragraph about the Van Gogh painting on page 22 (**Q6**). Once they have written their paragraphs, share a few and invite comments on the interpretation given and the reasons suggested for it.

Read 'Virginia' by T.S. Eliot on page 24 aloud to the class. Then ask the students to complete **Q7** and **Q8** in pairs. Take quick feedback, perhaps eliciting the idea that the poem is challenging because it has many repeated words; the beginning and ending of ideas is not always clear (what or who is the subject of the sentence); the combinations seem to be almost 'note-like' missing out articles such as 'the' or 'a' and 'an'. Then run through the recommended process for exploring difficult texts, outlined on page 24.

Now ask the students to complete **Q9** independently, using **Worksheet 2.1**.

Ask the students to read over the two student responses on page 25 and complete **Q10–Q12** independently. Then take feedback as a class. Elicit that the second response is better: it begins with a simple explanation, but then picks up the repetitive phrasing pattern, suggesting the idea of the river's ebb and flow (this is the 'interpretation').

Apply the skills

Read the final task in **Q13**, and ask the students to write the interpretation of 'Virginia' by T.S Eliot, using their annotated worksheets from **Q9** to help them compose their response. Before they begin, refer them to the **Checklist for success** on page 25 and remind them to steer a line between interpretation and guesswork. It is fine to be imaginative and unpick the layers of a text, but the interpretation must be rooted in what is there – and, to some extent, in what is likely.

> **Big answer plenary**
>
> Ask the students to talk with a partner for two minutes about 'interpretation'.
> - What do they understand by the word now?
> - What have they learned about how to interpret texts, especially challenging ones?
>
> Refer back to the **Big question**, and take feedback from the class.

2.2 Explore the conventions of genre

Assessment objectives

English Language

AO1 Identify and interpret explicit and implicit information and ideas; select and synthesise evidence from different texts

English Literature

AO1 Read, understand and respond to texts, maintaining a critical style and develop an informed personal response; use textual references, including quotations, to support and illustrate interpretations

GCSE examinations

- **English Language**
  Paper 1, Section A
- **English Literature**
  Paper 2, Section A

Differentiated learning outcomes

- **All students must** be able to explain clearly how writers use conventions and some of the effects created.
- **Most students should** be able to identify the main conventions of literary genres and make some detailed comments on their use and impact.
- **Some students could** analyse in precise detail how writers use and adapt particular conventions for effect.

Resources

- **Student Book**: pp. 26–9
- **Worksheet**: 2.2
- **PPT**: 2.2

Getting you thinking

Big question

Refer to the **Big question**: *What are conventions and how do writers use them in different ways?* Ask the students to note down, in pairs, ten things they would expect a *Bond* film to include, especially in relation to the story or sequence of events. Then share these ideas (e.g. an initial problematic situation from which Bond eventually escapes) and say that anyone writing a *Bond* film would need to be aware of these conventions. However, you could also point out how the movies sometimes 'play' with these same conventions, even parodying them.

For **Q1**, ask the students to work in groups of three or four. Provide them with sheets of paper and ask them to copy the table on page 26 of the Student Book (note that they need only do so for the two genres: 'sci-fi' and 'teen romance'). Allow five minutes for the students to note down ideas, then take feedback and share ideas from each group with the class. Some of the common conventions might be:

Genre	Location/ settings	Typical characters	Typical plot or themes	Typical language	Other
Sci-fi	spaceship; planet; 'lost world'; futuristic city	explorers; scientists; commanders of spaceships; aliens	threat of invasion; discovery of new species/planet; technology 'biting back'	highly technical; pseudo-scientific; militaristic	gadgets; laser guns; everyday objects with new functions
Teen romance	school; gym; prom/party; cafe/bar	beautiful girl; handsome 'hunk'; best friend; nerd/ geek; teacher; disapproving parents	unrequited love; ugly duckling becomes a swan; facing down bullies; outwitting teachers/adults	teenage slang; authority language from adults	guitar; prom dress; basketball or football; cars or motorbikes; chewing gum

In order to embed the idea of conventions, display **PPT 2.2, slides 1–7**, and play the 'genre game'. Divide the class into small teams, and display each slide for 45 seconds. Each team must note down at least two things for each of the bullet points. At the end, check each team's answers; the team that manages to complete all genres wins.

Explore the skills

Read the extract from *The Castle of Otranto* on page 27 of the Student Book. Use the introductory paragraph of **Explore the skills** to provide the students with some context. One way of ensuring the students get a sense of the atmosphere in the extract is to ask them to work in groups of three to create either a rehearsed reading of the extract (one student as Manfred; one as the narrator; one as Isabella) or a performance.

Remind the students of the main gothic conventions. Then ask them to note down answers to **Q2** and **Q3**. Take feedback as a class. Possible answers to **Q2**:

- Manfred clearly villain; Isabella the beautiful victim
- mystery in the ghostly vision of the helmet; Manfred's desire for Isabella and cruelty towards his wife
- typical objects such as helmet, moon, open window
- location is not obvious, but the setting of a moonlit night seen through a window, matches the mood
- very emotive, emphatic language ('imperiously'; 'seized'; 'shrieked'; use of exclamation marks).

Q3: The atmosphere is one of threat, of fear, of danger to Isabella.

Develop the skills

Ask one or two of the more confident speakers or readers in the class to read the Jane Austen extract on page 28 aloud. Then ask the students to note down answers to **Q4**, in pairs. Take feedback as a class. Answers to **Q4**:

a It sounds unlike a gothic novel for the reasons set out in **b** to **d**.
b Catherine is plain, and seems to prefer sports to 'feminine things', so does not appear weak or in peril.
c No, her parents are well-off and respectable, and she is part of a large family.
d The style is plain and factual, with no action.

Ask the students to complete **Q5a** and **Q5b** independently, and then feed back to the class. These are difficult questions, so elicit what Austen was trying to achieve, which seems slightly tongue-in-cheek, mocking the need for a desperate heroine. To some extent, she 'needs' gothic popularity otherwise she couldn't write her mock account.

> **Give extra support** by pointing out the 'knowing' references to gothic conventions, such as the orphaned child (which Catherine is not!).
>
> **Give extra challenge** by asking in what way Austen's opening does contain or suggest a mystery? (The phrase 'no one ever supposed…' leads us to believe that despite her unlikely circumstances/character, she *is* going to be a gothic heroine.)

Apply the skills

For **Q6**, read aloud the main task and the extract from *Rebecca* on page 29 of the Student Book. Remind the students again of the main gothic conventions they have learned about or are implied in the texts they have read. Then ask them to draft their response to the task, using **Worksheet 2.2** to make notes on first.

Big answer plenary	Ask the students: *How does knowing something about 'conventions' help you engage with or understand a text?* How might they 'practise' conventions in order to see them even more obviously?
	Finish by asking the students to consider the **Check your progress** outcomes on page 29 and identify which outcome they have achieved. Then ask them to note down one thing they need to do, or return to, in order to progress further.

2.3 Explore narrative voices

Assessment objectives

English Language

AO1 Identify and interpret explicit and implicit information and ideas; select and synthesise evidence from different texts

AO5 Communicate clearly, effectively and imaginatively, selecting and adapting tone, style and register for different forms, purposes and audiences. Organise information and ideas, using structural and grammatical features to support coherence and cohesion of texts

English Literature

AO1 Read, understand and respond to texts, maintaining a critical style and develop an informed personal response; use textual references, including quotations, to support and illustrate interpretations

GCSE examinations

- **English Language**
  Paper 1, Section A
- **English Literature**
  Paper 2 Section A

Differentiated learning outcomes

- **All students must** be able to identify some different narrative perspectives, and write an opening which maintains one perspective.
- **Most students should** be able to recognise the differences between narrative voices and perspectives, and try out some of them in their own writing.
- **Some students could** comment on the effects of a range of narrative voices and perspectives, and apply this to convey a particular and convincing tone in their own writing.

Resources

- **Student Book**: pp. 30–3
- **Worksheet**: 2.3
- **PPT**: 2.3

Getting you thinking

Big question	Refer to the **Big question**: *How do writers create interesting narrative voices?* Ask the students to think of a main character in a novel or short story they have read and enjoyed. What made that character distinctive? Was it simply what he or she *did*? Or was it the way in which those events, experiences, etc., were *expressed*?

Read aloud **Text A** on page 30 of the Student Book, and then allow two minutes for the students to discuss **Q1–Q3** in pairs. Take feedback and share answers as a class. Elicit the idea that the narrator interprets particular events in a positive way in terms of the girl's feelings, but from our neutral view as readers – seeing both sides – we can *surmise* that the girl's negative actions are genuine – that she is irritated by the narrator ('ignoring me', 'not responding', 'unfriended').

Explore the skills

Ask the students to complete **Q4** in pairs. Take feedback as a class. Possible responses to the questions are:

a The present tense is mostly used, which gives an immediacy and sense of us living the narrator's life with him.

b 'not responding', 'following', 'watching' all create a slightly obsessive tone, a narrow focus.

c The narrator seems obsessive and locked into his own world, emphasised by his use of words such as 'hidden' and 'secret', which suggest an unhealthy desire.

Read **Text B** on page 31 and ask the students to complete **Q5**, using **Worksheet 2.3** to record their ideas. Again, take feedback as a class. For **Text B**, the main things to draw out are the minor sentences (no verbs); the heightened vocabulary ('golden', 'acolyte' 'believer') that conveys a spiritual, elevated tone; an analogy is drawn with the idea of religious worship and almost transcendental power (in the 'electric' power). There is a final nod towards a Greek mythical figure – Electra – although her story is a violent one as she murders her mother, which may imply that this story will not end well.

Now read **Text C** on page 31 aloud and discuss **Q6** with the class.

For **Q7**, draw the table of comparison up on the board, and allow three or four minutes for the students to make notes before completing the task as a class reading activity. The students should be able to explain that in **Text C**, *negative* verbs such as 'obsessed' and 'creeping' and the use of the name 'Ben' (which is personal rather than the impersonal 'the small, wiry kid… ') make her view of the situation clear. The reference to the 'bus stop' tells us how little the act of 'unfriending' meant – a public, rather than private place.

Then ask the students to complete **Q8** independently.

Develop the skills

Read aloud the extract from 'The Tell-tale Heart' on pages 32–3 of the Student Book.

The students could prepare their own reading of this extract to 'get inside' the voice/character of the text. You could listen to one or two snippets from selected students to see who captures the spirit of the narrator best, and ask them to perform their reading for the class.

Now ask the students to read **Q9** carefully and make some notes for their paragraphs.

Display **PPT 2.3, slides 1–6**, which provide a model of how to begin the analysis required in **Q9**. The PPT presentation shows how much can be distilled from just a few sentences. Talk the students through the model, and then ask them to use their notes to complete their two paragraphs (**Q9**).

Apply the skills

Read the main task in **Q10**. For this final writing task, the students will need to spend some time planning, so if there is not time to complete the written work in class, this could be set as a homework task or finished at the start of the next lesson.

Before the students begin, refer them to the **Checklist for success** on page 33 of the Student Book and ensure that all the students are confident they can meet the criteria.

> **Give extra support** by providing some ready-made ideas. The focus here is not so much on generating ideas, useful though that is, but on getting a sense of voice in the writing. You could suggest that the 'obsession' is for a trophy – perhaps top place in a dance competition or sports event. The protagonist could be the 'obsessed' person, or a friend or rival.
>
> **Give extra challenge** by asking the students to write the whole story. The challenge will be in maintaining the voice, but they may wish to balance this with using dual narrators.

Big answer plenary	Ask the students to note down, on their own, three key ways they can make their narrative distinctive. These are areas of language they should consider each time they produce creative writing. They should be able to say three of the following: • 'narrative viewpoint' (first, second or third person?) • use of sentences and grammar • vocabulary choices to match tone • use of tenses • use of punctuation to match voice and viewpoint • reference 'out' to other stories, ideas (allusion and analogy).

3.1 Understand more challenging texts

Assessment objectives

English Language

AO1 Identify and interpret explicit and implicit information and ideas; select and synthesise evidence from different texts

AO4 Evaluate texts critically and support this with appropriate textual references

English Literature

AO1 Read, understand and respond to texts, maintaining a critical style and develop an informed personal response; use textual references, including quotations, to support and illustrate interpretations

GCSE examinations
- English Language
  Paper 2, Section A

Differentiated learning outcomes
- **All students must** be able to read unfamiliar texts, selecting information and clearly showing their understanding.
- **Most students should** be able to read more challenging texts, selecting information and clearly showing their understanding.
- **Some students could** read and understand more challenging texts, selecting information and showing a perceptive understanding.

Resources
- **Student Book**: pp. 36–9
- **Worksheet**: 3.1
- **PPT**: 3.1

Getting you thinking

Big question	Ask the students to think for a moment about any particularly challenging texts they have encountered – in any subject or situation – and ask them to note down what it was that made them difficult to access. Take some brief feedback as a class. Then refer to the **Big question**: *What techniques can you use to make sense of difficult texts?* Elicit some initial responses.

Begin by pre-teaching or reminding the students what it means 'to infer' when you are reading something. As an example, explain that a writer such as Dickens might describe a shabby, decaying building, and we might infer from this something about the lives of the poor inhabitants, even if we are not told it directly.

Ask the students to discuss **Q1** and **Q2** in pairs, and then take feedback as a class. The students might begin to see that 'shooting' in this context refers to a somewhat different usage than they might expect – that is, 'shooting' as a sporting activity, rather than 'shooting' in an everyday context. The clue might be 'school life', and the somewhat archaic 'passionately fond of...'.

Explore the skills

Read the extract from *The Autobiography of Charles Darwin* on page 37 of the Student Book aloud, pausing at the spaces. This may help the students think about what, grammatically, might fit. Then ask the students to write a paragraph explaining what they learn about Darwin as a boy (**Q3**), which they will refer back to in due course.

Now ask the students to complete the extract using the box of unfamiliar words on page 36 and **Worksheet 3.1** (**Q4**). Once they have completed the task, ask them to compare what they now know with their initial predictions/thoughts (**Q5**). For their interest (although not strictly the point of the task) the missing words, in order, are: *with respect to; much zeal;* named *mineral; some little care; very much; Hempiterous; (Zygaena); Cicindela; White's 'Selborne'; took much pleasure; simplicity; gentleman.*

Emphasise that being faced with unfamiliar words should not prevent the students getting the gist of a text. Then allow two to three minutes for the students to quickly read the next sentence from the extract on page 38 of the Student Book and to add any further information to their paragraph about Darwin as a boy (**Q6**).

Develop the skills

Begin this stage of the lesson by reminding the students of the skills of inference.

For **Q7**, read the task and the longer extract from *The Autobiography of Charles Darwin* on page 38 as a class. Pause to raise the questions in the annotations. There is no need to answer the questions at this point; the focus should be on using questions to interrogate the text, as a way of decoding and unpicking it. Then ask the students to write their paragraphs. Take feedback by asking a small selection of students to read their work for the class, and ask to what extent the questions helped them.

For **Q8**, read the final extract on page 39 aloud and then ask the students to work in pairs to identify the key ideas in each sentence. You could begin by eliciting ideas for the first sentence and modelling it on the board, for example: 'Darwin assists his brother who has set up a laboratory in the garden shed.' You may want to ask the class if this summary captures the idea that Darwin is very much the junior partner at this point; if not, then what could be changed in the summary sentence? ('Darwin assists his brother, who takes the lead in...'?).

Once the students have discussed what they learn from the extract, ask them to work independently to write up their notes. Possible responses for this extract might be:

- Sentence 1: Darwin assists his brother, who takes the lead in setting up a lab in the garden shed.
- Sentence 2: His brother continues the practical work, while Darwin reads about the subject in great depth.
- Sentence 3: Darwin is fascinated by the subject, and both he and his brother work till late.
- Sentence 4: The practical application of the theory taught Darwin more than anything else.
- Sentence 5: His fascination with chemistry gained him a nickname – 'Gas'.
- Sentence 6: The headmaster told him off in front of the other pupils for wasting his energies on such a subject and called him a foreign phrase, which dismayed him as he didn't understand it.

Apply the skills

Before the students begin the main writing task **(Q9)**, remind them to reread all the extracts from Darwin's autobiography. Ask them to go over the notes they have made, and then write a simple plan of about five to six points summing up what they have found out. Point out that they won't be able to include all the points and that they should only include the salient ones – namely, the personal interest/fascination; the link to his brother; the disapproval of the school/headteacher.

> **Give extra support** by providing the key points in bullet form and leaving it to the students to weave them into a fluent piece with evidence.
>
> **Give extra challenge** by asking the students to find the next part of Darwin's autobiography and add a further 75 words about his early life.

As a useful summary of the skills of questioning they have encountered, display **PPT3.1, slides 1–4** as a way of embedding those skills.

| **Big answer plenary** | Ask the students to consider how well prepared they now feel to tackle more challenging texts? Ask them to look at the **Check your progress** outcomes on page 39 of the Student Book and decide which outcomes they have achieved. |

3.2 Use textual support in sophisticated ways

Assessment objectives

English Language

AO1 Identify and interpret explicit and implicit information and ideas; select and synthesise evidence from different texts

AO4 Evaluate texts critically and support this with appropriate textual references

English Literature

AO1 Read, understand and respond to texts, maintaining a critical style and develop an informed personal response; use textual references, including quotations, to support and illustrate interpretations

GCSE examinations

- English Language
  Paper 1, Section A
- English Literature
  Paper 2, Section B

Differentiated learning outcomes

- **All students must** be able to choose quotations carefully to support the points they make.
- **Most students should** be able to select and use relevant quotations and/or close textual references.
- **Some students could** select and use a range of quotations and/or close textual references in a sophisticated way.

Resources

- **Student Book**: pp. 40–43
- **Worksheet**: 3.2
- **PPT**: 3.2

Getting you thinking

Big question	Ask the students to briefly discuss this statement in pairs: *The core skills of analysing and responding to texts can sound very dry and dull, but writing about literature can be as creative as actually writing stories, poems and so on.'* Do they agree? Take feedback, and touch on the challenge of bringing lots of skills together – selecting, analysing, interpreting, making links – and how the way you weave all this together can be quite a creative process.

Read through the poem 'She Walks in Beauty' by Lord Byron on page 40 of the Student Book, together as a class. Allow four to five minutes for the students to discuss any ideas about 'inner' and 'outer' beauty, in pairs. They will be given some ideas to focus on later, but this is useful practice for their own response to texts – they can make use of some of the skills they learned in Lesson 3.1.

Now, in the same pairs, ask the students to complete **Q1**. Take feedback as a class, eliciting these points:

a   The method used is the PEE structure (point-evidence-explanation).

b   The quotation has been used in its entirety and has been introduced by a colon in quite a blunt, factual manner.

Explore the skills

Read the opening paragraph of **Explore the skills** on page 41 of the Student Book. Talk briefly about how the student might have worked in a more sophisticated way, ensuring that the students understand each of the bullet points. Now ask them to copy the table on page 41 and review their own ideas from the discussions earlier in the lesson, adding these to the table, if different from those already given there (**Q2**).

Read the information about embedded quotations and the example on pages 41–2.

Now display **PPT 3.2, slides 1–3**, which provide a further explanation about how to embed quotations. The key thing to draw out is that the embedded quotations must work grammatically while still doing the job of explaining the key point.

Ask the students to select one of the ideas about *inner* beauty from the table in **Q2**, and write an example using an embedded quotation (**Q3**). Remind them that they may need to trim or edit the quotation to make it fit grammatically. Once they have written their examples, ask the students to work in pairs, with each student evaluating the other's example to check that the quotation is both embedded fluently and does the job required.

Develop the skills

Now, look at the quotation on page 42 and discuss the annotations with the class (**Q4**). The key thing to address here is how much can be drawn out of just one or two lines; this opens up the quotation for real exploration and analysis in an interesting way that can shed more light on possible meanings and connections.

For **Q5**, ask the students to select a quotation from the poem on page 40 to annotate. Make sure all the students select a suitable quotation. If they are struggling to identify one, you could suggest:

- 'And on that cheek, and o'er that brow'
- 'So soft, so calm, yet eloquent'
- 'The smiles that win, the tints that glow'.

Read the example response on page 42 aloud; you may wish to dwell on this to point out how the student has 'zoomed in' on key details. Then allow five minutes for the students to make their annotations. Point out that they do not have to use all the ideas in the example response – some may be more suitable or relevant than others. Check the students' annotations before moving onto **Q6**.

Ask the students to complete **Q6**. Once they have converted their annotations into paragraphs, you could display them on the wall anonymously and then ask the class to walk around and select those that they think have most closely fulfilled the task.

Read the paragraph about textual references on page 42 and the example on page 43, and then get the students to quickly identify which lines of the Byron poem are being referenced (**Q7**). (Answer: the first four lines of the second stanza.)

Now read the task in **Q8**, and ask the students to close their books while they write their responses.

Apply the skills

As a precursor to the task in **Q9**, ask the students to work in groups of three or four to read the sonnet and make some initial notes under 'inner' and 'outer' beauty. This should be only an initial 'dip in' to get a sense of the poem.

Now ask the students to complete the main writing task using **Worksheet 3.2** to prepare and make notes (**Q9**). Note that the students will find that there are really no examples given in the poem of inner beauty, but remind them that they still need to comment on this absence.

> **Give extra support** by guiding the students on the first annotation/quotation and the paragraph they write.
>
> **Give extra challenge** by asking the students to compare the treatment of beauty in the sonnet with Byron's poem, rather than a straightforward analysis of one poem.

> **Big answer plenary**
>
> Put the students in pairs and ask them to explain to each other what they have learned about moving on from PEE paragraphs (as discussed in response to **Q1**). Then ask the pairs to report back to the class.
>
> You might also like to ask the students how the techniques they use are more useful for exploring implicit ideas, rather than the more directly obvious ones.

3.3 Synthesise and summarise more challenging texts

Assessment objectives

English Language

AO1 Identify and interpret explicit and implicit information and ideas; select and synthesise evidence from different texts

English Literature

AO1 Read, understand and respond to texts, maintaining a critical style and develop an informed personal response; use textual references, including quotations, to support and illustrate interpretations

GCSE examinations
- English Language Paper 2, Section A

Differentiated learning outcomes

- **All students must** be able to present the ideas from two texts in a clear summary, supported by quotations and accompanied with inferences to show their understanding.
- **Most students should** be able to present ideas from two texts in a fluent and clear way, with relevant quotations and/or close references and inference.
- **Some students could** present ideas from two texts in a detailed way, synthesising evidence from the texts and making perceptive inferences.

Resources
- **Student Book**: pp. 44–7
- **Worksheet**: 3.3
- **PPT**: 3.3

Getting you thinking

Big question	Refer to the **Big question**: *How can you draw together ideas from two related texts in a clear and fluent way?* Discuss as a class: *What are the biggest challenges in reading two texts on similar topics and then writing about how both texts treat similar ideas?* Elicit that the tone and language of each text might be different; that the perspectives might be different too; and that the texts won't necessarily cover exactly the same content or use the same examples.

Read the extract from *The New York Times* on page 44 of the Student Book (**Q1**). Then ask the students to copy and complete the table on page 44 (**Q2**). Possible answers might include:

In Text A, I learn the atmosphere in London is:	Evidence from the text
- especially appealing at night - full of echoes/memories of its literary and cultural history	It has a 'crepuscular kindness'
	'you can see not just how she is, but how she once was, the layers of lives that have been lived here'
	'The dead and the fictional ghosts of Sherlock Holmes and Falstaff, Oliver Twist, Wendy and the Lost Boys'
- made magical at night by the river	'The river runs like dark silk...the bridges dance with light'
- marked of contrasts – there are parts that feel untouched by humans	'There are corners of silence in the revelry of the West End and Soho'
	'in the inky shadows foxes and owls patrol'

Now ask the students to complete **Q3**. It should be relatively straightforward for them, once they have completed the table in **Q2**.

Explore the skills

Read **Text B** on page 45 aloud, and then ask the students to briefly suggest ways in which the two texts are similar and different. This need not be an in-depth task for now, as they will tackle this shortly, but they should, at the very least, recognise that both texts deal with London.

Read the task in **Q4**, and ask the students to suggest how they would need to change the method they used in **Q3** if they were writing about both texts. Draw out the idea that they would need to make links, commenting on both where there are similarities, and where there are key, or more subtle, differences.

For **Q5**, discuss the Venn diagram on page 46 and then ask the students to work in pairs and add further ideas of their own to it. They could use **Worksheet 3.3**, which includes a copy of the Venn diagram for them to add ideas to, as well as some points about each text to give them a head start.

Develop the skills

For **Q6**, ask the students to complete the table on page 47 by finding appropriate quotations from **Text B**. Possible answers are:

Text A	Text B
a 'It's a pretty safe city, and you can walk in most places after sunset.'	'The greatest marvel, after all, is that so few accidents happen in this dim, unnatural light,'
b 'It has a sedate and ghostly beauty.'	'There is something startling in the appearance of a vast city wrapt in a kind of darkness'
c 'The river runs like dark silk through the heart of the city'	'the whole river looks like one huge bed of dense stagnant smoke, through which no human eye can penetrate.'
d 'the bridges dance with light'	'you cannot see the vessel which may at that moment be passing beneath, so heavy is the cloudy curtain which covers the water.'
e 'inky shadows' (at night)	'lighted torches which are carried and waved at the corners and crossings of the streets add greatly to the wild and picturesque effect of the scene, as they flash redly upon the countenances of the passengers'
f 'still illuminated by gaslight'	'a kind of darkness which seems neither to belong to the day nor the night, at the mid-noon hour, while the gas is burning in the windows of long miles of streets.'

Now ask the students to complete **Q7**. Remind them that they need to decide what can be inferred or concluded about the way London is described from the quotations. They could work in small groups, going through the quotations and verbalising the responses.

Ask the students to complete **Q8** independently. Show **PPT 3.3**, **slides 1–5**, which can be used to remind the students how they might express themselves when they want to synthesise ideas.

Apply the skills

Read the task in **Q9**. The students should now be in a position to write their full response to the task. Ask the students to write their summary independently. Remind them to take every opportunity to check the skills they can use by looking at the Student Book and the notes they have made in this lesson.

Big answer plenary	Ask the students to assess, on a scale of 1–10 (high), how confident they now feel about tackling this sort of question in an exam situation. Take feedback and share responses as a class. Identify any remaining problems or issues, which can be targets for improvement.

3.4 Apply your skills to English Language and English Literature tasks

Assessment objectives	GCSE examinations
English Language AO1 Identify and interpret explicit and implicit information and ideas; select and synthesise evidence from different texts **English Literature** AO1 Read, understand and respond to texts, maintaining a critical style and develop an informed personal response; use textual references, including quotations, to support and illustrate interpretations	• English Language Paper 1, Section B

Differentiated learning outcomes	Resources
• **All students must** be able to understand what is required by the questions set and the skills they need to show in their responses. • **Most students should** show their understanding of how to select relevant quotations and references, and, where appropriate, how to synthesise these in their responses. • **Some students could** show that they understand the key elements that distinguish the best responses to texts that require evidence, summary or synthesis of ideas.	• **Student Book**: pp. 48–58 • **Worksheet**: 3.4 • **PPT**: 3.4

Introduction

Explain that AO1, in both English Language and English Literature specifications, refers to the ability to find the most appropriate information in a text or texts. In English Language, the additional requirement in some tasks is to draw on information from two texts and synthesise ideas, referring to differences and similarities between the two texts.

Responding to an English Language task

Read **Your task** on page 51 of the Student Book.

Then read **Q1** on page 48 very carefully and ask the students to work in pairs and think about the implications of the wording:

- What are these extracts about?
- What do we learn about the behaviour of people in authority today and in the past?

What does 'about' mean? (Answer: the main topic or focus). What does 'behaviour' mean? (Answer: the things they do, or have done). Take brief feedback and share ideas with the class.

Now read aloud **Text 1** and **Text 2** on pages 48–50 of the Student Book, reminding the students to bear in mind the preparatory questions. If the students wish, they can make notes of anything relevant as they progress.

Once they have read the texts, ask the students to work quickly, on their own, to note down key ideas under two headings – 'Behaviour in Rio' and 'Behaviour in the Highlands' – using **Worksheet 3.4 (Q2)**. Their notes will help them to assess how well the two responses they will shortly read (pages 52–3 of the Student Book) have picked up on key information.

You may prefer the students to respond to the task before they read the sample responses. If this is the case, then you will need to allow sufficient time for this.

Now read through **Response 1** and the accompanying commentary and annotations on page 52, together as a class. The mark schemes for GCSE English Language could be copied and given to the students. For each response, ask the students to work up the descriptors like a ladder, answering 'yes' or 'no' as to whether they see the skills in place. For **Response 1** they are likely to see Level 3 descriptors in place (**Q3** and **Q4**).

Now read through **Response 2** and the accompanying commentary and annotations on page 53. Ask the students to look at both **Response 1** and **Response 2**, and note down the key differences between the two (**Q5**). In particular, elicit from them:

- the increased use of inference in **Response 2** to dig a little deeper (annotation 3)
- the way the student synthesises ideas (annotation 4).

End by pointing out that, to infer at the highest level, students need to look for subtle differences. In **Response 2**, one of the key ways this is done is when the student picks out a stylistic element in the extract from 'The Crofter Question' – i.e. that everything is reported and the women do not have a 'voice' – whereas in the Rio article, they are at least given names and do speak about their experiences.

Responding to an English Literature task

For **Q1** on page 54 of the Student Book, ask the students to read the extract from 'Odour of Chrysanthemums' by D.H. Lawrence, and then to note down some quick responses to the questions. Take some brief feedback and share answers on the preparatory questions with the class.

If you wish, you could now give the students the task (at the bottom of page 54), and ask them to respond to the first bullet point. They could then measure their own response against the two sample responses on pages 55–6 of the Student Book, or swap responses with a partner and write annotations similar to those on the samples. Using the English Literature criteria, they could then work their way up from the lower responses (Level 3 upwards) to make an evaluation of their own work.

Once the students have written and evaluated their own response, or read the two responses and annotations in the Student Book, ask them to feed back to you what they feel to be the key defining characteristics of the different responses. Are the students now clear on how to write a top-level response?

If you feel they are still struggling to differentiate between the higher levels, use **PPT 3.4** to elicit one key area that demonstrates high attainment.

In order to help the students to understand the subtle difference between the two levels of answer, display **PPT 3.4, slides 1–4**. Show slides 2 and 3 (showing both sentences) and drill down into what is really better about the second than the first (what 'added value' is there in the second example?). Then show slide 4, which explains the first annotation of the **Response 2** more clearly.

Finish by asking the students to look over the **Check your progress** outcomes on page 58, and evaluate which outcome they think they have achieved. Ask them to write down at least two specific targets or objectives for improvement that have come out of the work in this lesson – and in general over the preceding three lessons.

4.1 Analyse and evaluate writers' use of language techniques

Assessment objectives

English Language

AO2 Explain, comment on and analyse how writers use language and structure to achieve effects and influence readers, using relevant subject terminology to support their views

GCSE examinations
- English Language Paper 1, Questions 2, 3
- English Language Paper 2, Question 3

Differentiated learning outcomes
- **All students must** be able to choose clear supporting evidence to explain how one or more language techniques help to communicate the writer's viewpoint.
- **Most students should** be able to select and analyse particular language techniques in detail, linking them precisely to the writer's viewpoint.
- **Some students could** present a succinct overview of the writer's viewpoint, selecting one or more language techniques to analyse thoroughly and in detail.

Resources
- **Student Book**: pp. 60–3
- **Worksheet**: 4.1
- **PPT**: 4.1

Getting you thinking

Big question	Read the **Big question**: *What does 'analyse the effect' mean and how do you do it successfully?* Ask the students to make a note of three or four features that might be termed 'effects'. Take some initial feedback on these ideas for reference during the lesson and then explain that you will be returning to this question at the end of the lesson.

Read the introductory paragraph in **Getting you thinking** on page 60. Draw attention to the idea that writing about language techniques means looking at how a writer has crafted their work in order to communicate ideas to the reader. Reiterate that reference to specific terminology should be seen as a shorthand for analysis rather than an end in itself.

Ask the students to define 'simile', 'alliteration' and 'personification' without referring to the **Key terms** box. Then read the extract from *The Road to Wigan Pier* by George Orwell on page 60 and ask the students to identify these techniques in action. The students can use **Worksheet 4.1** to highlight or annotate the extract if preferred.

Alternatively, display **PPT 4.1, slide 1**, and discuss Orwell's use of simile, alliteration and personification in the extract as a class.

Now allow five minutes for the students to complete **Q1**.

Explore the skills

Display **PPT 4.1, slide 2**, which is a copy of the response on page 61 of the Student Book. Without referring to the annotations in the Student Book, ask the students to identify what they think the response has done well.

Now compare the students' comments with those in the Student Book. Draw attention to or elicit that this response:

- identifies the correct technique and uses the right terminology
- embeds evidence fluently into the student's sentence
- focuses in detail on particular words in the phrase they have chosen
- starts to explore the connotations of particular effects of the simile.

Ask for suggestions of the meaning of the term 'connotation' and then refer to this definition in the **Key term** box.

Display the next extract from *The Road to Wigan Pier* on **PPT 4.1, slide 3**, or read from the Student Book page 61. Then allow five minutes for the students to complete **Q2**.

Read and briefly discuss with the class the connotations of the metaphor 'fiery serpents of iron' using the spider diagram on page 62. Then ask the students to complete **Q3** independently.

Alternatively, ask the students to discuss the spider diagram annotations in pairs, and then complete **Q3** as a paired writing activity.

Develop the skills

Introduce the **Key term** 'semantic field' and ensure the students understand what it means. Allow five minutes for the students to read the complete passage again on pages 60–1 of the Student Book, and then make a list of all the words they feel have connotations of danger (**Q4**).

Now ask the students to read the complete passage again and complete **Q5**. Take feedback as a class:

- For **Q5a**, encourage the students to consider or elicit from them the idea that Orwell is using the semantic field to create a sense of horror and danger associated with working in an industrial setting.
- For **Q5b**, encourage the students to identify the extended metaphor of 'Hell' in the passage. Perhaps draw attention to Orwell's use of colour, images of fire and smoke, sensory imagery such as 'screams', and so on.

Give extra challenge by asking the students to think about what Orwell is comparing these working conditions to and why he might be so shocked by them.

Allow five minutes for the students to discuss **Q6** in pairs. Then take feedback as a class. Possible suggestions might be:

- 'scream' suggests pain/torture
- 'iron' and 'blow' suggests instruments of torture.

For **Q7a** and **Q7b**, the students are being drawn to specifically relate the technique to the writer's viewpoint, which is the point of the lesson. Before they begin, read the paragraph of instructions directly above **Q7** and reiterate that their paragraphs should be no more than 100 words.

Apply the skills

For **Q8**, allow at least 15 minutes for the students to complete the main task. Draw attention to the wording of the task and how it reinforces the writer's viewpoint. Before they begin, refer the students to the **Checklist for success** on page 63 of the Student Book and remind them that they can use any of the ideas and notes they have made during the lesson to support their written work.

Big answer plenary	When the students have completed the written task, ask them to look at the **Check your progress** outcomes on page 63 and to assess which outcome they have achieved.
	Finally, ask the students to write a sentence explaining what they have achieved in this task and how they might improve their skills in order to develop a higher level of attainment.

4.2 Analyse and evaluate writers' use of structure

Assessment objectives

English Language

AO2 Explain, comment on and analyse how writers use language and structure to achieve effects and influence readers, using relevant subject terminology to support their views

GCSE examinations

- **English Language** Paper 1, Questions 2, 3
- **English Language** Paper 2, Question 3

Differentiated learning outcomes

- **All students must** be able to explain clearly how one or more structural features have been used to present the writer's viewpoint.
- **Most students should** be able to consider a range of ways in which the writer has used structural features to present their viewpoint.
- **Some students could** analyse the effects of particular structural features in detail, exploring how they have been used to present the writer's viewpoint.

Resources

- **Student Book**: pp. 64–7
- **Worksheet**: 4.2
- **PPT**: 4.2

Getting you thinking

Big question | Read the **Big question**: *How do structure and organisation make a difference to the ways in which a text is read and understood?* Ask for suggestions about the variety of ways writers might organise and structure a piece of text. The students might suggest: paragraphs, sentence order, sentence length or punctuation for deliberate effect. If the students refer to structural techniques used in poetry, such as stanza length, rhyme scheme or enjambment, explain that while these are all relevant, this lesson will focus only on prose.

Read the scenario in **Getting you thinking** on page 64 of the Student Book, which sets up the parameters of the task and then ask the students to read the example introduction to the article.

Alternatively, display **PPT 4.2, slide 1**, which is a copy of the example, and ask the students to comment on whether they think this is an effective opening.

For **Q1**, ask the students to discuss the example in pairs, making some brief notes on advice they might give to the 'journalist' to make their writing more subtle and compelling. Remind the students to pay particular attention to some of the structural suggestions they have already discussed/offered at the start of the lesson.

Now read the paragraph from *How to Be a Woman* by Caitlin Moran on page 64 of the Student Book (**Q2**).

Allow five minutes for the students to read the extract again and complete **Q3**, using **Worksheet 4.2** to make annotations or notes if needed. Draw particular attention to **Q3b**, which reminds the students of the importance of establishing what the author's viewpoint is rather than merely 'technique-spotting'.

Explore the skills

Ask the students to complete **Q4**, which requires them to identify an example of each of the following structural techniques:

- very short sentence
- rhetorical question
- hyperbolic question
- personal anecdote
- dashes to emphasise a particular idea (or ideas).

Before they begin, refer the students to the **Key terms** 'rhetorical question' and 'hyperbolic question' to ensure they are clear what they mean.

Now display **PPT 4.2, slide 2**, and ask the students to read the example paragraph on the use of dashes. Then allow five minutes for the students to choose another structural technique and complete a similar paragraph (**Q5**).

If time permits, take feedback at this stage; either allow pairs to read each other's work and compare them to the example paragraph, or select two or three students to share their paragraphs with the class. Ensure that they are focused, not only on the effect of the technique, but also on the writer's viewpoint.

Refer the students to the **Key term** 'anecdote' and discuss the effectiveness of using anecdotes with the class. Refer back to **Q3c** and make a connection between the use of personal anecdotes and tone. Elicit how this light-hearted, ironic tone might be working to encourage reader empathy in order to make a more serious point later on in the article.

Display **PPT4.2, slide 3**, and read the next paragraph of the extract from *How to be a Woman*.

Now allow ten minutes for the students to complete **Q6** and **Q7** using **Worksheet 4.2** to highlight or annotate the text.

> **Give extra challenge** Although **Q6** and **Q7** refer to the effects of specific techniques, encourage the students to notice the use of ellipses, or other specific punctuation marks such as the exclamation mark before 'again' and how this helps to create a humorous, self-mocking tone.

Develop the skills

Ask the students to read the final three paragraphs of the article, on page 66 of the Student Book and complete **Q8**, using **Worksheet 4.2** to highlight or annotate the text. Encourage them to consider that the humour is used to draw the reader in, in order to make a serious point overall.

For **Q9**, ask the students to read and discuss the four statements about the article in pairs or small groups. Take feedback as a class: clearly all the points could be said to be true, although the third statement most clearly reflects the overall viewpoint.

Apply the skills

Ask the students to read the annotated quotation from the extract from *How to be Woman* on page 67 (**Q10**).

Then read the task in **Q11** aloud and ask the students to use the model in **Q10** to annotate a similar short section from the extract. If time permits, allow the students to explore and share their ideas in pairs or small groups before proceeding to the main written task.

Alternatively, the extended written task could be undertaken at the start of the next lesson, or as a homework task.

Big answer plenary	Ask the students to return to the **Big question** and make a list of three ways in which Moran uses structure and organisation to create deliberate effects in her writing. These might include whole-text as well as sentence-level features.
	When the students have completed the extended writing task, ask them to highlight one particular technique that they feel they have analysed very effectively, linked to Moran's overall viewpoint. Then ask the students to decide which of the **Check your progress** outcomes on page 67 of the Student Book they think they have achieved.

4.3 Analyse the ways writers create meanings and effects with structure and form

Assessment objectives

English Literature

AO2 Analyse the language, form and structure used by a writer to create meanings and effects, using relevant subject terminology where appropriate

GCSE examinations

- **English Literature**
  Paper 2, Section B
- **English Literature**
  Paper 2, Section C

Differentiated learning outcomes

- **All students must** be able to explain some features of structure or form, making links to the effects being created and making accurate use of technical vocabulary.
- **Most students should** be able to analyse particular features of structure and form in detail, linking them precisely to the overall effect being created and using technical vocabulary to explain effects.
- **Some students could** analyse significant features of form and structure, linking them together to explore how a writer has manipulated them in order to create particular meanings.

Resources

- **Student Book**: pp. 68–71
- **Worksheet**: 4.3
- **PPT**: 4.3

Getting you thinking

Big question	Refer the students to the **Big questions**: *What is the difference between 'structure' and 'form'? Why does the 'form' of a text matter?* Elicit some initial responses from the class. If referring to the previous lesson, some students may suggest aspects of poetic structure and form, which could be a useful reminder at this point. The main point of this lesson is to establish that 'form' relates more to the shape and conventions of a whole text, while structure refers to organisation elements within a particular form.

Ask the students to look at the list of features of a sonnet and complete **Q1**. Remind them that Petrarchan sonnets are in two stanzas of eight and six lines respectively, whereas Shakespearean sonnets are in four stanzas of four, four, four and two lines.

Explore the skills

Ask the students to read 'Sonnet 75' by Edmund Spenser and the notes that explain what type of sonnet it is on page 69 of the Student Book.

Now ask the students to complete **Q2**. For **Q2b**, prompt the students to explore ideas about how poetry can immortalise 'mortal things' such as a person or an emotion. For **Q2c**, encourage ideas about how love can conquer time and the forces of nature.

Develop the skills

Read the information about Petrarchan sonnets on page 70 of the Student Book and ask the students to list the structural differences between Petrarchan and Shakespearean sonnets.

Refer to the **Key term** 'volta' and ask the students to make a note of the definition.

Now read aloud 'How to Leave the World That Worships *Should*' by Ros Barber on page 70 of the Student Book and ask the students to complete **Q3**, using **Worksheet 4.3** to make notes and annotations.

Then take feedback as a class. Responses might include:

a This poem is a sonnet, but it is not about romantic love; it is more about the love of life and the love for our environment.

b The volta marks a shift in focus from the mundane ordinariness of our working lives with the word 'above'. This shifts the focus to looking around us at the world we live in, rather than being focused on the small details and aggravations of daily life. The poem is about encouraging us to appreciate the world around us.

Ask the students to read the **Key terms** 'enjambment' and 'caesura' and make a note of their definitions. Then refer back to the difference between 'structure' and 'form' and draw out that the 'form' is that of a sonnet but these key terms are structural features within that form.

> **Give extra challenge** by asking the students to look at the notes on 'caesura' and 'enjambment' on the copy of the poem on page 70 of the Student Book and to select one and analyse the effect it creates.

Apply the skills

Read the task in **Q4**, which is the main task for this lesson. Before the students begin the task, refer them to the prompts, possibly collating responses on the board for reference as the task is completed.

- Prompt 1: refers to the extension of one line by one syllable; possibly this is to extend the idea that taking time to appreciate the simplest of life forces is fundamental and is therefore being given extra significance. Also, this line needs more breath when read out loud, so the message about filling the lungs with air is reinforced by the physical act of breathing.

- Prompt 2: the final word is isolated structurally; perhaps because it is the main point of the poem, intensified as a command.

- Prompt 3: the students can use their notes on caesura and enjambment for this.

- Prompt 4: the 'love' in the poem is not romantic but more about love for ourselves, each other and the beauty of the natural world.

Big answer plenary	Refer back to the **Big question** and ask the students to work in pairs and write a definition of 'structure' and of 'form' on sticky notes. Display these on the whiteboard for the students to read and ask them to make a note of the ones they think are the best in their books.
	Then ask the students to swap their final piece of written work with a partner and use the **Check your progress** outcomes on page 71 of the Student Book to assess which outcome their partner has achieved.

4.4 Apply your skills to English Language and English Literature tasks

Assessment objectives

English Language

AO2 Explain, comment on and analyse how writers use language and structure to achieve effects and influence readers, using relevant subject terminology to support their views

English Literature

AO2 Analyse the language, form and structure used by a writer to create meanings and effects, using relevant subject terminology where appropriate

GCSE examinations

- English Language Paper 1, Questions 2, 3
- English Language Paper 2, Question 3
- English Literature Paper 1
- English Literature Paper 2

Differentiated learning outcomes

- **All students must** be able to explain some features of language, structure or form, making links to the effects being created and making accurate use of technical vocabulary.
- **Most students should** be able to analyse particular features of language, structure and form in detail, linking them precisely to the overall effect being created and using technical vocabulary to explain effects.
- **Some students could** analyse significant features of language, form and structure, linking them together to explore how a writer has manipulated them in order to create particular meanings.

Resources

- **Student Book**: pp. 72–82
- **Worksheets**: 4.4a–b
- **PPT**: 4.4

Responding to an English Language task: Language

This topic in the Student Book may take about three lessons if the tasks themselves are completed in class.

Display **PPT 4.4, slide 1**, and ask the students to write a sentence in their own words explaining what skills they have to demonstrate for AO2.

Explain that AO2 refers to anything that the writer has done deliberately in order to make meaning; anything that shows understanding that the writer is 'the maker of the text' and, as such, is making conscious decisions about particular words, particular techniques, particular structural features and the order in which they are used.

Now read aloud the extract from *Lord of the Flies* by William Golding on pages 72–3 of the Student Book. Then ask the students to complete **Q1**, using **Worksheet 4.4a** to highlight or annotate the text.

Read the main task in **Q2**, which is to look at a section from the extract in more detail and analyse the writer's use of language.

Display **PPT4.4, slide 2**, which shows this section of the extract, and annotate it as the students give some initial ideas (**Q2**). The students can then use the annotations for reference as they complete the written task.

Now display **PPT4.4, slide 3**, and discuss the **Checklist for success** with the class, so that they have a clear idea of the success criteria for this task.

Allow no more than 15 minutes for the students to complete the written task.

Now ask the students to read **Response 1** (**Q3**) and the accompanying **Comments** on page 75 of the Student Book, and discuss **Q4** as a class.

Then ask the students to read **Response 2** and the accompanying **Comments** on page 76 of the Student Book, and discuss **Q5** as a class.

The mark schemes for GCSE English Language could be copied and given to the students. For each response ask them to work up the descriptors like a ladder, answering 'yes' or 'no' as to whether they see the skills in place.

If preferred, the students could complete **Q4** and **Q5** on page 75 by taking one section from **Response 1** and rewriting it, using the comments on **Response 2** to improve it.

Alternatively, ask the students to discuss the two responses in pairs and identify three ways in which **Response 1** could be improved.

Responding to an English Language task: Structure

Display **PPT 4.7, slide 4**, which is a copy of the task and the **Checklist for success** on page 76 of the Student Book. This time, ask the students to work independently to respond to this question on whole-text structure. Before they begin, refer the students to the **Checklist for success** and explain that this can be used to scaffold and organise their response.

When the students have finished the task, read the two sample responses and their accompanying comments on pages 77–8 of the Student Book. Then complete **Q1–Q4** as a class, which can be used to identify:

- one element of their work that they are particularly pleased with
- one element of their work that needs to be improved.

Responding to an English Literature task

Read aloud the poem 'The Swan' by Mary Oliver on page 79 of the Student Book. Point out that, even though the poem is referring to a very different genre of text, the skills required for reading are exactly the same.

Now allow five minutes for the students to reread the poem and to complete **Q1** independently, using **Worksheet 4.4b** to highlight or annotate any features that they notice. This is a useful message as it reinforces the transferability of reading skills, and reminds the students that the approach is the same regardless of form, genre or examination question.

Display **PPT 4.4, slide 5**, and read through the final task, which is an independent response to the poem 'The Swan' (**Q2**).

Before the students undertake their own response to this task, read **Responses 1** and **2**, and the **Comments** on the two responses, on pages 80 and 81 of the Student Book. Discuss **Q3–5** as a class and then ask the students to select one element of good practice that they could aim to incorporate into their own response. The GCSE English Literature mark scheme for Paper 2, Section B could be given to the students to place the responses into the appropriate Level (Level 6 for **Response 1**, Level 8 for **Response 2**).

Allow approximately 20 minutes for the students to complete their own response. Alternatively they could complete the task as homework.

As a final task, ask the students to use the **Check your progress** outcomes on page 82 to identify a target for future work.

5.1 Explore how writers use different settings to develop characters

Assessment objectives

English Literature

AO1 Read, understand and respond to texts, maintaining a critical style and develop an informed personal response; use textual references, including quotations, to support and illustrate interpretations

AO2 Analyse the language, form and structure used by a writer to create meanings and effects, using relevant subject terminology where appropriate

AO3 Show understanding of the relationships between texts and the contexts in which they were written

GCSE examinations
- English Literature Paper 2, Section A

Differentiated learning outcomes
- **All students must** be able to use context to help them explain ideas and comment in detail on the language and structure of a text.
- **Most students should** be able to use context to help them explore ideas thoroughly and analyse the effects of language and structure.
- **Some students could** include ideas about context in a clear overview that focuses sharply on the question in order to analyse and evaluate ideas about language and structure.

Resources
- **Student Book**: pp. 84–9
- **Worksheet**: 5.1
- **PPT**: 5.1

Getting you thinking

| Big question | Refer the students to the **Big question**: *How can ideas about a place help you to understand a character?* Elicit some initial responses. |

Display **PPT 5.1, slide 1**, and ask the students to note down initial responses to **Q1**.

Take feedback as a class and elicit what similarities and differences there are between the two images, both of which portray an old woman in a rural setting. The students could be pushed to explore the idea that the point of view of the observer, with their own ideas and stereotypes, can make as much difference as the content of the images.

Explore the skills

Read the extract from 'The Darkness Out There' by Penelope Lively on page 85 of the Student Book and ask the students to complete **Q2–Q5** in pairs or small groups. Take feedback as a class. The students might notice:

Q2: Exaggerated fairy tale references like 'witches, wolves and tigers' as well as the archetypal setting of the dark wood, with its scary branches looking like 'faces and clawed hands'.

Q3: The references to 'skittering' and 'giggling and shrieking' make it sound as if being scared was more of a game than about real fear. We enjoy being frightened sometimes but in a safe, controlled way. Why are horror films so popular, for example?

Q4: Lack of details as to who the girl was, who the attackers were, etc. Maybe it was a story made up by adults to keep children away from the woods – a modern fairy tale, perhaps?

Q5: Sandra still seems to believe the 'people at school' and thinks that evil is easy to spot like the very clear-cut villains of fairy tales.

Develop the skills

Display **PPT 5.1, slide 2**, and read the second extract from 'The Darkness Out There' on page 86 of the Student Book and ask the students to gather material to help them answer **Q6–Q8**, using **Worksheet 5.1**, to make notes on or annotate the text.

Collate the students' ideas on the board, before asking the students to write responses to **Q6–Q8**. Take feedback as a class. Responses might include:

Q6: 'cottage-loaf'; 'composed of circles'; 'creamy smiling pool of a face'

Q7: The details about Mrs Rutter tend to be soft, circular and stereotypical of Sandra and Kerry's view that Mrs Rutter is an 'old dear'. This is also backed up by the description of the objects in the room. You could compare this to Steinbeck's portrayal of Crooks in Chapter 4 of *Of Mice and Men*, if the students are familiar with it.

Q8: The phrases 'her eyes snapped and darted' and 'Her eyes investigated, quick as mice' do not fit with the rest of the description and could suggest the personality behind the appearance.

Now read the third extract from 'The Darkness Out There' on page 87 of the Student Book and ask the students to complete written responses to **Q9–Q11**. Possible student response might be:

Q9: Lively focuses on the youth of the airman, calling for 'mutter' suggesting a stereotypical view of women as carers, he is desperate for the comfort and love of his family.

> **Give extra support** by explaining to the students that 'Mutter' is the German word for mother.

Q10: Mrs Rutter uses unexpectedly harsh language, e.g. 'bastard', 'tit-for-tat', in her otherwise matter-of-fact and almost heartless description of the events (as in her use of weather as an excuse for not helping the airman and the fact that she went back to have another look at the dying man). She seems to feel no remorse – only indifference.

Q11: Sandra is paralysed by shock and unable to act. Kerry reacts more physically, dropping his spoon, which 'clattered to the floor' and is more assertive – 'shoved his chair back from the table', 'I'm going'.

Read the final extract from the story on page 88 of the Student Book and ask the students to complete written responses to **Q12**. Take feedback as a class. The students might notice:

- Sandra's changed opinion of Kerry
- her realisation that appearances are deceptive and the world is 'unreliable'.

Some students might notice the tone of narrative voice in 'but everything is not as it appears, oh no.' – a hint of fairy-tale narrator.

Apply the skills

Display **PPT 5.1, slide 3**, and read through the task and **Checklist for success**. Then discuss the qualities of a successful response to the task as a class.

Read the student response on page 89 of the Student Book and discuss the annotations. Ask the students to set themselves one or two targets to focus on while they respond to the main task (**Q13** and **Q14**).

Big answer plenary	Ask the students to peer-assess their responses to the main task with partners and to highlight references to places and settings in their responses. The students could then write a WWW/EBI comment for their partners.

5.2 Explore how writers use different time periods to develop themes and ideas

Assessment objectives

English Literature

AO1 Read, understand and respond to texts, maintaining a critical style and develop an informed personal response; use textual references, including quotations, to support and illustrate interpretations

AO2 Analyse the language, form and structure used by a writer to create meanings and effects, using relevant subject terminology where appropriate

AO3 Show understanding of the relationships between texts and the contexts in which they were written

GCSE examinations
- English Literature Paper 2, Section B

Differentiated learning outcomes

- **All students must** be able to use context to help them explain ideas and comment in detail on the language and structure of a poem.
- **Most students should** be able to use context to help explore ideas thoroughly and analyse the effects of language and structure in a poem.
- **Some students could** include ideas about context in a clear overview that focuses sharply on the question and analyse and evaluate ideas about the language and structure of a poem.

Resources
- Student Book: pp. 90–3
- Worksheet: 5.2
- PPT: 5.2

Other Student Book pages
- Lesson 3.2, pp. 41–2

Getting you thinking

Big question	Refer students to the **Big question**: *How can understanding a text's historical setting help you to understand its themes and ideas?* Elicit some initial responses. Ask the students if they can think of any examples of things they have read with historical settings that affect the way the text is received. What were the main themes of the text? How did the author use the historical setting to highlight those themes?

Read the extract about 'The Great Famine' on page 90 of the Student Book and ask the students to complete **Q1**. Take feedback and reach agreement as a class as to what the three most important points are.

Explore the skills

Read aloud the first part of the poem 'At a Potato Digging' by Seamus Heaney on pages 90-1 of the Student Book. Discuss the annotations with the class and ask for any further suggestions.

Then ask the students to complete **Q2** working individually. Before they begin, encourage the students to embed quotations in their responses and refer back to the guidance on how to do this given in Lesson 3.2 (Student Book pages 41–2).

Develop the skills

Read sections II and III of the poem on page 91 of the Student Book. Then ask the students to copy and complete the table in **Q3**.

Give extra support by discussing the examples already in the table.

Give extra challenge by asking the students to think about how Heaney shows the flashback.

Now ask the students complete **Q4** and **Q5** working in pairs. Take feedback as a class. The students might comment on:

Q4: The repetition is shocking and emphasises the horrific effects of famine because the same words are used to describe the inanimate and the living person. It emphasises the influence of the past on the present, and also creates a dramatic shift in time.

Q5: The faster rhythm hints at the desperation of the famine victims. The insistence of rhythm could represent the gnawing hunger of famine itself.

Ask the students to complete **Q6**, working in the same pairs and using the table in **Worksheet 5.2**.

Give extra support by reading through the example response in the table and discussing it with the students, before asking them to complete the rest of the table in a similar style.

Apply the skills

Read section IV of the poem on page 92 of the Student Book and ask the students to complete **Q7** and **Q8**.

Give extra support by putting the students into pairs or small groups in order to discuss the questions.

Take feedback as a class. Possible responses may be:

Q7: The phrases 'dead-beat' and 'flop' are dysphemistic (i.e. shockingly direct – the opposite of 'euphemistic') when referring to the modern workers, but they echo the real effects of the famine in 1845, when a million people did actually die.

Q8: The imagery suggests a primeval, pre-Christian relationship between humans and the land. Fear of famine is still present and engenders superstition.

Display **PPT 5.2, slide 1**, which is a copy of the task in **Q9** and the **Checklist for success** on page 93 of the Student Book. Check that the students are clear about the task and the success criteria.

Read the sample response on page 93 of the Student Book and discuss the annotations with the class.

Before the students begin the task, ask them to identify two things the sample response does particularly well, and to use them as targets for their own written response (**Q10**). You could also ask them to set themselves a skills target, using wording from the **Checklist for success** on page 93 of the Student Book, or on **PPT 5.2, slide 1**.

Now ask the students to complete their written response to the task in **Q9**.

Big answer plenary	Discuss the following questions as a class: • Has the poem altered your view of Ireland and its relationship with the UK? • How does our understanding of the past influence our views of the present? Then refer back to the **Big question**; elicit further responses and discuss with the class.

5.3 Explore how ideas about literary context can inform your reading of a text

Assessment objectives

English Literature

AO1 Read, understand and respond to texts, maintaining a critical style and develop an informed personal response; use textual references, including quotations, to support and illustrate interpretations

AO2 Analyse the language, form and structure used by a writer to create meanings and effects, using relevant subject terminology where appropriate

AO3 Show understanding of the relationships between texts and the contexts in which they were written

GCSE examinations

- English Literature Paper 1, Section B

Differentiated learning outcomes

- **All students must** be able to show a clear understanding of the ways a text fits into a particular genre, using evidence from the text to support points.
- **Most students should** present a thoughtful, detailed explanation of the ways a text fits into a particular genre, using detailed references to the text to support points.
- **Some students could** explore and analyse the ways in which the text fits the genre with precise supporting details.

Resources

- **Student Book**: pp. 94–7
- **Worksheet**: 5.3
- **PPT**: 5.3

Getting you thinking

Big question	Refer to the **Big question**: *How do writers create authentic childhood narrative voices?* Ask the students for their initial thoughts on why a writer might want to include a childhood voice in a narrative. There are many possible reasons (e.g. to provide an 'innocent' perspective on events), but some students may say that this will enable the writer to show how a character develops into maturity.

Ask the students to complete **Q1** and **Q2** in pairs, using **Worksheet 5.3**. Then take feedback as a class. Ask the students to justify the reasons for their selections. Is there any agreement about which characteristics are typical of older or younger people?

Explore the skills

Read the three introductory paragraphs of **Explore the skills** on page 95 of the Student Book. Ensure the students are clear about the definition of *bildungsroman*.

Now read aloud the extract from *Great Expectations* on page 95 and ask the students to complete **Q3** and **Q4** independently. Take feedback as a class. Possible answers:

Q3: 'Powerless', 'innocent', 'naive' and 'imaginative' are all words that might apply to the young Pip.

Q4: The students may notice that the narrative voice is retrospective: older Pip is narrating the experience of younger Pip.

Read the extract from *David Copperfield* on page 95 and ask the students to complete **Q5**. Take feedback and share ideas as a class. Students might comment on:

- the retrospective narrative voice
- both are orphans
- references to gravestones
- use of first-person narrator
- descriptions of earliest memories
- feelings of loneliness/isolation.

Develop the skills

Ask the students to read the information about *bildungsroman* in the introductory paragraph of **Develop the skills** on page 96, which takes the explanation of the term further.

Now read the second extract from *David Copperfield* on page 96 of the Student Book and ask the students to complete **Q6**. The students might notice:

- that the extract highlights the powerlessness of the young David, but he is portrayed as someone who will fight against injustice
- the fact that he is more concerned about his own 'crime' (biting Mr Murdstone's hand) than the humiliation and cruelty he has suffered, suggesting that he is already reflective and concerned with improving his own character.

Now read the extract from *Jane Eyre* by Charlotte Brontë on page 97 of the Student Book and ask the students to complete **Q7**, discussing the questions in pairs.

Take feedback and share ideas as a class. The students might suggest:

- Both are treated unfairly because of the cruelty of adults around them.
- Both hold inferior positions of power in their respective households.
- David appears wiser than Jane at this point in his development.
- The younger Jane seems less reflective and more focused on the injustice of the situation.
- The older Jane recognises that her younger self is headstrong.
- Dickens uses questions and exclamations to highlight David's vulnerability.
- Brontë uses emotive vocabulary to highlight Jane's agitation.

Apply the skills

Display **PPT 5.3, slide 1**, which is a copy of the task in **Q8** and the **Checklist for success** on page 97 of the Student Book. Check that the students are clear about the task and the success criteria.

Before the students begin the task, ask them to look back at the list of words in **Q1** and then to reread the four extracts carefully. Tell the students to refer to their copy of the Venn diagram on **Worksheet 5.3** so they can match to the words from this list with the characters in the extracts. Then ask the students to complete the written task, using their notes and ideas from the lesson.

This task could be undertaken during a subsequent lesson, as it would be useful to allow the students an extended period of time to complete a detailed analysis.

> **Give extra support** by allowing the students to focus on two, rather than three, of the characters.
>
> **Give extra challenge** by focusing in detail on the language Dickens and Brontë use to describe the emotional state of their characters – in particular David and Jane – and what this suggests about their respective characters at that point in their development.

Big answer plenary	Refer back to the **Big question** and ask the students to reflect on the three 'voices' they have studied. Which do they feel is the most 'authentic' and why? Which most accurately reflects the words they selected from the Venn diagram as applying best to childhood?
	Ask the students to use the **Check your progress** outcomes on page 97 of the Student Book to self- or peer-assess their completed written task and to set targets for the assessment task at the end of the chapter.

5.4 Apply your skills to an English Literature task

Assessment objectives

English Literature

AO1 Read, understand and respond to texts, maintaining a critical style and develop an informed personal response; use textual references, including quotations, to support and illustrate interpretations

AO2 Analyse the language, form and structure used by a writer to create meanings and effects, using relevant subject terminology where appropriate

AO3 Show understanding of the relationships between texts and the contexts in which they were written

GCSE examinations
- English Literature Paper 2, Section A

Differentiated learning outcomes
- **All students must** be able to use context to help explain ideas and comment in detail on the language and structure of a text.
- **Most students should** be able to use context to help explore ideas thoroughly and analyse ideas about the language and structure of a text.
- **Some students could** include ideas about context in a clear overview that focuses sharply on the question, and could analyse and evaluate ideas about language and structure.

Resources
- **Student Book**: pp. 98–102
- **Worksheet**: 5.4
- **PPT**: 5.4

Using context to broaden your interpretation of a literary text

Display **PPT 5.4, slide 1**, and read the summary of the play *Hamlet* by William Shakespeare aloud to the class. Ensure the students understand where the scene from *Hamlet* used in this lesson fits in to the play as a whole.

Now display **PPT 5.4, slide 2**, which contains information the students need to think about in order to understand how different audiences might understand the ghost in *Hamlet*. Ensure the students understand all the terminology.

Read the extract from Act 1 Scene 5 of *Hamlet* by William Shakespeare on page 98 of Student Book.

Then move on to discuss the possible reasons why Shakespeare included the ghost as an important character. Emphasise that different audiences might view the inclusion of a ghost in different ways (as outlined on page 99 of the Student Book):

- a convention of Revenge Tragedy – Revenge Tragedies were extremely popular in Shakespeare's time and usually featured a ghost who gives the central character a motive for revenge against a powerful and dangerous opponent

- a 'real' event – more people in Shakespeare's time believed in the supernatural than in modern times and therefore, this could be seen as a realistic representation of a possible event

- an insight into Hamlet's unconscious mind – the ghost could be seen by a modern audience to represent thoughts and feelings of which Hamlet is not aware, following the ideas of psychoanalysis which became popular in the twentieth century.

Ask the students to collect evidence from the extract to support these three interpretations of the ghost. Put the students into groups of three. Ask each student in each group to collect evidence on *one* of the three interpretations. The students then debate the three interpretations within the group.

Then take feedback as a class, with each group justifying which interpretation they think is the best.

Display **PPT 5.4, slide 3**, and read the information about psychoanalytic criticism. Ensure the students understand how this approach can be applied to *Hamlet*.

Responding to an English Literature task

Display **PPT 5.4, slide 4,** which shows the main written task in **Q1** and the **Checklist for success** on page 99 of the Student Book. Read through the task with the class. Ensure the students understand the task and the success criteria.

Read **Response 1** and the accompanying **Comments** on page 100 of the Student Book and elicit any advice the students might give to improve it (**Q2** and **Q3**). Advice they might give the student includes:

- linking ideas about context more closely to evidence from the extract
- commenting on the effects of language, structure and form in more detail.

Then read **Response 2**, the annotations and the accompanying comments on page 101. Using the annotations, briefly discuss as a class the ways in which this response is successful.

Ask the students to complete **Q4** using **Worksheet 5.4** to make notes on or annotate the text. Refer the students again to the **Comments on Response 2** to help them.

If preferred, the students could complete **Q3** and **Q4** by taking one section from **Response 1** and rewriting it, using the comments on **Response 2** to improve it.

Now ask the students to complete their written response to the main task (**Q1**).

As a final task, ask the students to use the **Check your progress** outcomes on page 102 to identify a target for future work.

6.1 Understand critical reading

Assessment objectives

English Language
AO4 Evaluate texts critically and support this with appropriate textual references

English Literature
AO1 Read, understand and respond to texts, maintaining a critical style and developing an informed personal response; use textual references, including quotations, to support and illustrate interpretations

GCSE examinations
- English Language Paper 1, Question 4
- English Language Paper 2, Question 4
- English Literature key skill across all components

Differentiated learning outcomes
- **All students must** be able to understand that there is more than one way to read and interpret a text – that there is no one correct answer.
- **Most students should** be able to understand that by asking particular types of questions you can form an interpretation of a text.
- **Some students could** demonstrate that they can ask precise questions about a text and thereby build an individual and original interpretation of it.

Resources
- **Student Book**: pp.104–7
- **Worksheet**: 6.1
- **PPT**: 6.1

Getting you thinking

| Big question | Explore with the students the connotations of the word 'critical' and what it usually means to them. Steer them into defining what a critic is and what they do for a job. Then refer to the **Big question**: *How is reading critically different from the usual comprehension work?* Elicit some initial responses. |

Display **PPT 6.1, slide 1**, which shows the two extracts from the film reviews on page 104 of the **Student Book**, and ask the students to read them (**Q1**).

Discuss and 'unpack' both reviews with the class (**Q2**). Elicit that the first review seems to suggest the film defies convention, while the second one confirms it is still a 'costume drama', but one that has a difference. Both reviews suggest something 'alien' or apocalyptic about the film.

Explore the skills

Explore the concept that making a viewpoint on a text is also an academic discipline. Use this opportunity to explain the nature of academic studies of literature and introduce the concept of critical theory and the critical essay.

Use the information in the introductory paragraphs of **Explore the skills** on page 105 of the Student Book to support the discussion.

When introducing the ideas of feminist theory, display **PPT 6.1, slide 2**, and read through it with the class. Then ask the students to think of any texts they might have read at home, or as part of their English Literature studies, that would lend themselves to feminist study – for example, novels such as *Wuthering Heights* or *Jane Eyre*, Shakespeare's plays such as *Much Ado about Nothing*, *Twelfth Night* or *A Midsummer Night's Dream*, or poetry such as Browning's monologues.

Read the extract from *Romeo and Juliet* by Shakespeare on page 105 of the Student Book, either using two volunteer readers to perform it for the class, or with the students working in pairs. Before they begin, read the introductory paragraph to give the extract context and set the scene. Then ask the students to complete **Q3** and **Q4**.

Give extra support by asking the students to work in pairs or small groups to consider the questions.

Take feedback and share ideas as a class. The students should be able to pick up on:

a   Capulet's presentation of a dominant self through the pronoun usage

b   his reference to 'wife' as a common noun rather than using her name

c   the use of imperatives and the definite tone of the modal verbs.

Allow the students some time to explore what this suggests about the role of women in Shakespeare's time – can they draw any modern parallels?

You could extend this task by presenting this text alongside a contemporary news article on the topic of arranged marriages between young people to add to the Paper 2 skills set. This could also be used to stretch and challenge the idea that this practice is something only to be found in Shakespeare's time and therefore only relevant to women in past centuries.

Develop the skills

Display **PPT 6.1**, **slide 3**, and introduce the concerns of Marxist theory. Again ask the students to reflect on their previous reading to suggest works that might have resonance with the ideas in Marxist theory: perhaps *Wuthering Heights*, work by Dickens or Priestley, or the more radical Romantic poets, for example.

Read aloud the extract from *Love on the Dole* by Walter Greenwood and the accompanying annotations on pages 106–7 of the Student Book. Then put the students into pairs or small groups and ask them to explore the text and complete **Q5** and **Q6**. The students should pick up on:

- the way the narrator separates himself and is almost hiding his shame – he behaves and feels guilty or like a criminal
- the deliberate use of a colloquial working-class voice, showing where he is placed in society – at the mercy of the wealthy business owner for his living; even other working men are disparaging and lacking sympathy
- the idea that as industry grows and becomes more mechanised, there is less room for people to have jobs
- the way the ending seems like a war poem, using ghostly imagery – as though these men do not exist in society's eyes.

Apply the skills

Read the task in **Q7** and ask the students to choose one of the 'mini' essay titles. Then allow the students 20–25 minutes to write their two to three paragraphs using the notes they have compiled in the lesson on *Romeo and Juliet* and *Love on the Dole*.

Big answer plenary	Ask student to work in pairs, read each other's responses and, using the questionnaire on **Worksheet 6.1**, evaluate their partner's progress.
	Refer back to the **Big question** and ask the students to comment on how the type of work they have done in this lesson is different from basic comprehension work.

6.2 Construct a convincing response to literary texts

Assessment objectives

English Language
AO4 Evaluate texts critically and support this with appropriate textual references

English Literature
AO1 Read, understand and respond to texts, maintaining a critical style and developing an informed personal response; use textual references, including quotations, to support and illustrate interpretations

GCSE examinations
- English Language Paper 1, Question 4
- English Language Paper 2, Question 4
- English Literature key skill across all components

Differentiated learning outcomes
- **All students must** be able to write a response containing a clear interpretation of the poem.
- **Most students should** be able to present a convincing interpretation of the poem.
- **Some students could** demonstrate their ability to present a convincing, compelling and imaginative interpretation of the poem.

Resources
- **Student Book**: pp. 108–11
- **Worksheet**: 6.2
- **PPT**: 6.2

Other Student Book pages
- Lessons 3.1–3.4, pp. 36–58
- Lessons 4.1–4.4, pp. 59–82

Getting you thinking

Big question	Discuss the meanings of the word 'interpretation' and ask the students to comment on what this might mean in terms of their English Literature studies. What method or skill have they learned already, where they need to draw on clues or read between the lines of a text and 'unravel' it? Refer back to Chapter 3 to ensure the students realise that their skills in *making inferences* are vital in addressing this Assessment Objective. Referring back to Chapter 4, if required, ask the students to recap on the method they should use to comment on *language and structure*. Note: the skills for AO4 are essentially a synoptic combination of AO1 and AO2. Now refer to the **Big question**: *You have gathered ideas about a text – how do you put it all together?* Explain that in this lesson the students are going to consolidate their skills of inferential and critical reading in order to build secure responses.

For **Q1**, display **PPT 6.2, slide 1**, which is a copy of the main task, and ask the students to pick out the key words. They should focus on: 'critical evaluation'; 'exploring'; 'presents'; 'power'; and 'man versus nature'.

Now display **PPT 6.2, slide 2**, and work through the key words unpacking what each one actually means and asking the students for synonyms to check their understanding. You could record ideas on the whiteboard in a mind-map/spider diagram format and then link this to the bullet-pointed list of skills on page 108 of the Student Book. Elicit which ideas/synonyms link to comprehension skill; which ideas/synonyms link to language; and which ideas/synonyms link to structure.

Explore the skills

Display **PPT 6.2, slide 3**, and explain that in writing something evaluative that is based on critical reading, the students should always use a combination of the skills mentioned in **Q1**. They should aim to show something of all their skills – critical evaluation demands a synopticity – in the same way that a well-made cake has a perfect combination of ingredients to produce something wholly delicious.

Read the opening three stanzas of Blake's poem 'The Tyger' and the accompanying notes on page 109 of the Student Book, and explain the colour coding of the text.

Allow ten minutes for the students, perhaps working in pairs, to add to and comment on the notes, using **Worksheet 6.2**. Can they shed any light on some of the areas the student is questioning? Do the student's notes trigger any additional thoughts for the class? If time allows, take brief feedback.

Now read the entire poem from the beginning, this time including the annotations to the final three stanzas on page 109. Allow 15–20 minutes for the students to complete **Q2** in pairs or small groups, using **Worksheet 6.2** to make notes or add annotations. Encourage the students to uncover ideas that lead to discussion of:

- the images of industry and production/the links to the industrial revolution (you could recap here some of the key ideas of Marxist theory discussed in Lesson 6.1)
- the image of the stars crying, as though nature watching down on us is mourning what is happening as the nation becomes more industrialised
- how the religious reference relates to God and his work in the Creation – comparing the Lamb (potentially the Lamb of God, i.e. Jesus and his sacrifice) with the Tyger (potentially the industrial magnate: the desire for wealth and power/capitalism/the dissipation of all that is spiritual).

For **Q3**, allow 5–10 minutes for the students to look back at the whole poem and compile more detailed notes in preparation for the main writing task.

Develop the skills

Use the information in the introductory paragraph of **Develop the skills** on page 110 to introduce the idea of the *defining statement*. Explain how this gives a useful and definite focus to students' work, particularly when writing a response under examination conditions.

Display the example of a defining statement on **PPT 6.2, slide 4**, before giving the students five minutes to write their own (**Q4**). Take feedback and share some student examples with the class to show the range of possible ideas and interpretations. Then allow a further 5–10 minutes for individual reflection on the selection of material (**Q5**).

Display the exemplar opening paragraph on **PPT 6.2, slide 5**, and discuss **Q6a** and **Q6b** as a class. Explain how it can be useful to blend ideas that link together well from different areas of their notes – just as you would blend the eggs, sugar and flour to make the cake. Show how the example uses the notes made by the student in **Q2** and blends the ideas on language, usefully with the ideas on mood. Then allow five minutes for the students to complete **Q6c** independently.

Display the exemplar concluding paragraph on **PPT 6.2, slide 6** and again use **Q7a** and **7b** to generate whole class discussion.

Apply the skills

Read the task in **Q8**, which leads the students into creating a whole essay-style response. Allow up to 45 minutes for the students to complete the task. If time is short, you could ask them to write the opening paragraph in class, and set the middle section and conclusion as an extended homework task. Refer students to the **Checklist for success** on page 111 of the Student Book as a means of recapping on the method. Explain that they have completed the first three bullet points in their classwork so far.

> **Give extra support** by allowing students to use the exemplar paragraphs as a writing frame.
>
> **Give extra challenge** by allowing students free rein to complete their own critical evaluation, using the examples only as style guides.

Big answer plenary	Refer back to the **Big question**, and ask students to draw a flow chart of the method or process they need to use when writing critical responses to literary texts.

6.3 Construct a convincing response to non-fiction texts

Assessment objectives

English Language
AO4 Evaluate texts critically and support this with appropriate textual references

English Literature
AO1 Read, understand and respond to texts, maintaining a critical style and developing an informed personal response; use textual references, including quotations, to support and illustrate interpretations

GCSE examinations
- English Language Paper 1, Question 4
- English Language Paper 2, Question 4

Differentiated learning outcomes
- **All students must** be able to plan, write and support a response to a non-fiction text which shows their own convincing interpretation.
- **Most students should** be able to gather and organise their ideas to present a convincing interpretation of the text.
- **Some students could** gather and organise perceptive ideas to present a convincing and compelling argument for their original interpretation.

Resources
- **Student Book**: pp. 112–15
- **Worksheets**: 6.3a–b
- **PPT**: 6.3

Other Student Book pages
- Lesson 6.2, pp. 108–11

Getting you thinking

Big question	Refer to the **Big question** and reinforce the key opening information in **Getting you thinking** on page 112 of the Student Book: that writing an evaluative essay for non-fiction uses exactly the same skills as writing one for literature. Reassure the students that the key to success is using a clear methodology – the one that they have already acquired the skills for through study of Core Chapter 6 and/or Advanced Chapters 3, 4 and 6.

Read through and recap on the three key skills listed in the introductory information on page 112, informally testing the students on their knowledge of the key terms, if necessary. For example, can they remember what is meant by, or can they define, 'language', 'structure', 'tone', 'attitude' and 'interpretation'?

Display **PPT 6.3**, **slide 1** and read the task aloud. Allow the students two to three minutes, possibly in pairs, to think about how they would tackle this task (**Q1**), and then discuss **Q2a** and **Q2b** to elicit ideas from the whole class.

Explore the skills

Look through the extract from *Strands* by Jean Sprackland on page 113 of the Student Book and explain that there are questions to work on linked to the four key areas of investigation: language; structure; tone; and key messages.

Read the extract aloud and ask the students to complete **Q3a–d**, using **Worksheet 6.3a**. This activity would work well as a small-group investigation, with different groups working on each area, followed by a plenary feedback session. You could ask the students to collate their ideas onto A3 paper with markers, which could then be pinned up at the front during feedback. The students may pick up on the following:

a **Language**: references to 'plague' – how the ladybirds helped to stop the plague of greenfly but became a plague themselves; the verbs ('fill', 'blunder', 'drip') create the sense of the swarm and how overwhelming it is – the scale of the 'plague'; the reference to 'ticklish' a reminder of their past innocence and link to childhood; the swift change in tone of the description – how can they be both enchanting and a curse – the volume of them changes our perception of them.

    b **Structure**: the innocent and lovely memory of the opening contrasts with the implied 'fear' of the ladybirds being something to run from; the ladybirds become objectified and the repetition of the structure suggests the volume and number of ways they become a plague together with the simple, tense, curt structures; sense of anxiety and worry through the questioning; the broken dialogue of the friend suggests how thick the air is with them; the strong judgement of the dog walker is paradoxical compared to the introduction.

    c **Tone**: swift change in the perception of the creature; this conjures the memory of other swarms and the stuff of horror films, e.g. Hitchcock's *Birds*; the humour of the end makes us laugh at the man's response and we find it odd and funny that this tiny creature could instil panic, fear and contempt.

    d **Key messages**: we move from the innocent and helpful garden creature to a menacing pest; suggests there is a wider concern here as to why this may have happened – an environmental phenomenon; suggests that things in small numbers are good and positive but when anything grows and multiplies, it becomes a threat – maybe a wider message about the relationship between people, the planet, overconsumption and exploitation of resources.

Develop the skills

After taking feedback for **Q3**, recap on the concept of a 'defining statement' from Lesson 6.2.

Display **PPT 6.3, slide 2**, which shows the defining statements in **Q4**. Discuss the possibilities of each one as a whole class before allowing five minutes for individuals to choose one to work with, or to write their own (**Q4**).

Now allow 20 minutes for the students to gather and select evidence individually, using **Worksheet 6.3b** (**Q5**).

Remind the students of the main writing task in **Q1** and display **PPT 6.3, slide 3**, which shows a possible model introduction.

Allow 5–10 minutes for the students to write their introductory paragraph (**Q6**). Then, if time allows, take feedback and share one or two good efforts you have noted when moving around the class.

> **Give extra support** by suggesting the students use the model as a style guide to get their own introduction underway.

Apply the skills

Allow 30 minutes for the students to write up their work from the planning table in **Worksheet 6.3b** (**Q7**).

Before they begin, refer the students to the **Checklist for success** on page 115 of the Student Book and remind them of the skills they learned in Lesson 6.2.

Alternatively, you could ask the students to complete this section of their response as a homework task if necessary.

> **Big answer plenary**
>
> In plenary, display the extract from a model conclusion on **PPT 6.3, slide 4**, which shows how a student returns to their defining statement in their conclusion. Explain how this method will give their interpretation of a text structure and cohesion.
>
> Ask the students to work in pairs and read each other's responses. Then allow the students time to work together to draft cohesive conclusions to both of their pieces using the model paragraph for guidance and support.
>
> Then ask the students to use the **Check your progress** outcomes on page 115 of the Student Book to assess which outcome they think their partner has achieved, explaining the reasons for their decision.

6.4 Apply your skills to English Language and English Literature tasks

Assessment objectives

English Language
AO4 Evaluate texts critically and support this with appropriate textual references

English Literature
AO1 Read, understand and respond to texts, maintaining a critical style and developing an informed personal response; use textual references, including quotations, to support and illustrate interpretations

GCSE examinations
- **English Language** Paper 1, Question 4
- **English Language** Paper 2, Question 4
- **English Literature** key skill across all components

Differentiated learning outcomes
- **All students must** be able to present relevant and detailed interpretations of texts, using evidence to support them and including sensible analysis of methods.
- **Most students should** be able to present convincing and effectively supported responses, showing increasingly sophisticated analysis.
- **Some students could** present a compelling interpretation with perceptive and original aspects of analysis, with seamlessly integrated references and support.

Resources
- **Student Book**: pp. 116–24
- **Worksheets**: 6.4a–b
- **PPT**: 6.4

Other Student Book pages
- Lesson 6.3, pp. 112–15

The final lesson of this chapter provides good practice of the skills learned in the chapter. These can be done under examination conditions, as individual assessments if required.

Responding to an English Language task

Before the students read the extract from *The Kite Runner* by Khaled Hosseini, read the introductory paragraph on page 116 of the Student Book to provide them with some context.

Now display **PPT 6.4, slide 1**, which shows the key questions student should think about while reading the extract. Allow 15 minutes for the students to read the extract and complete **Q1**, using **Worksheet 6.4a** to annotate or make notes on the text.

> **Give extra support** by reading the extract aloud for the students and allowing them five minutes thinking and annotating time.

For **Q2**, display **PPT 6.4, slide 2**, which is a copy of the main task. Elicit the focus of the task, and the key skills needed to tackle it. Consolidate the students' understanding of the method needed by displaying **PPT 6.3, slide 3**, which shows the **Checklist for success** from Lesson 6.3.

Before the students begin, refer them also to the **Checklist for success** on page 117 of the Student Book.

Then allow 45–50 minutes for the students to plan and write their response to the task. Allow five minutes for the students to carefully check their own work.

Now read aloud **Response 1** on page 118 of the Student Book. Point out the skills that have been shown using the annotations.

Ask the students to annotate their own work in a different colour to show where they have used any of the four skills shown in the example.

Read aloud the **Comments on Response 1** on page 118.

Allow five minutes for the students to discuss in pairs how **Response 1** could be improved (**Q3**). Ask each pair to write down one piece of advice they could give to this student (**Q4**). Take feedback and share ideas as a class.

Read aloud **Response 2** on page 119. Again, point out the skills that have been shown in the annotations and ask the students to annotate any of those skills that are evident in their own work.

Read aloud the **Comments on Response 2** on page 119, and ask the students to complete **Q5** independently. Ask each student to write down one key tip they could take from this example response. Take feedback and share ideas with the class.

Responding to an English Literature task

Ask the students to read the poem 'The Convergence of the Twain' by Thomas Hardy on page 120 of the Student Book. Before they read, display **PPT 6.4, slide 4**, which shows the key questions students should think about while reading the poem; then allow 15–20 minutes for the students to read the poem and complete **Q1**, using **Worksheet 6.4b** to annotate or make notes on the text.

> **Give extra support** by reading the poem aloud for the students and allowing 10 minutes thinking and annotation time.

For **Q2**, display **PPT 6.4, slide 5**, which is a copy of the main task from page 121 of the Student Book. Elicit the focus of the task, and the key skills needed to tackle it. Then display **PPT 6.4, slide 6**, and talk through the **Checklist for success** (from page 121 of the Student Book) to consolidate their ideas.

Allow 45 minutes for the students to plan and then write their response to the task (**Q2**).

Allow five minutes for the students to carefully check their own work.

Now read aloud **Response 1** on page 122 of the Student Book. Point out the skills that have been shown using the annotations.

Ask the students to annotate their own work in a different colour to show where they have used any of the four skills shown in the example.

Read aloud the **Comments on Response 1** on page 122.

Allow five minutes for the students to discuss in pairs how **Response 1** could be improved (**Q3**). Ask each pair to write down one piece of advice they could give to this student (**Q4**). Take feedback and share ideas as a class.

Read aloud **Response 2** on page 123. Again, point out the skills that have been shown in the annotations and ask the students to annotate any of those skills that are evident in their own work.

Read aloud the **Comments on Response 2** on page 123, and ask student to complete **Q5** independently. Ask each student to write down one key tip they could take from this example response. Take feedback and share ideas with the class.

> **Give extra challenge** by allowing the students to work collaboratively in small groups to work on the two responses. Groups could spend 20–25 minutes:
> - reading the samples in turn
> - working through the annotations
> - writing a series of advice tips for the class
> - using the responses to peer-evaluate each other's responses and add advice
> - matching the responses – both the exemplars and their own – against the Level criteria in accredited mark scheme grids.

7.1 Compare how writers use tone to convey viewpoints and perspectives

Assessment objectives

English Language

AO3 Compare writers' ideas and perspectives, as well as how these are conveyed, across two or more texts

GCSE examinations
- English Language
  Paper 2, Question 4

Differentiated learning outcomes

- **All students must** be able to make clear comparisons of viewpoint based on inferences from the text.
- **Most students should** be able to present a detailed comparison between the viewpoints expressed in two texts, inferring meaning from a range of evidence.
- **Some students could** form an analytical comparison of the viewpoints and the ways in which they are presented in two texts, analysing a range of evidence to support their comparison.

Resources
- **Student Book**: pp. 126–9
- **Worksheet**: 7.1
- **PPT**: 7.1

Getting you thinking

Big question	Read the **Big question**: *What is irony and how do writers use it for humorous effect?* It may be useful to discuss the term and ask the students what they think it means. Explain that 'irony' is a concept often misunderstood and that the purpose of this lesson is to gain a clear understanding of what irony is and how it is used by writers to present viewpoints.

Read the definition of irony in the introductory paragraph of **Getting you thinking** and the first example of irony on page 126 of the Student Book. Elicit an explanation from the class as to why it is ironic.

Read the second example of irony and discuss **Q1** as a class. Elicit that the statement is ironic because the 'gap' is created by Mrs Bennet's apparent ignorance of the fact that she has just complained.

Allow five minutes for the students to think of their own examples of irony in real life, using the examples as prompts. Then take feedback as a class.

Explore the skills

Ask the students to imagine that they are visiting a new city for the first time and have the chance to ask three questions about the place they are visiting. Allow five minutes for the students to discuss this in pairs, before taking feedback and sharing ideas as a class.

Read the first extract from 'Six to Eight Black Men' by David Sedaris on page 126 of the Student Book. For **Q2**, ask the students to compare the questions Sedaris asks his cabdriver with the ones they suggested. Do his questions appear to be more trivial, perhaps? Why would he need to know this kind of information?

Before looking at the annotated version on page 127 of the Student Book, read the second extract from 'Six to Eight Black Men' using **PPT 7.1, slide 1**. Ask for the students' initial reactions. Use the following prompts if necessary:

- What is your reaction to the first sentence of this paragraph?
- Is there a particular point in this paragraph that makes you laugh?
- What do you think of the tone of this essay so far?

Now read the second extract and the annotations at the top of page 127. At this stage, focus the students on the ironic 'gap' – ask them what is ironic about the questions Sedaris asks and how they differ from the kinds of questions you might expect someone to ask about a new place (**Q2**).

Read the third extract from 'Six to Eight Black Men' on page 127. Again, ask the students to suggest one particular part of this third paragraph that they find amusing.

Now ask the students to read the sample response to the final sentence of this paragraph, on page 128. Draw attention to how the student is unpicking the ironic 'gap' between the author's attitudes and more traditional attitudes to Christmas.

For **Q3**, allow five minutes for the students to select one of the annotated sections of the second extract and write a paragraph of their own about the way Sedaris uses irony to create humour.

Allow a further ten minutes for the students to look at all three extracts and complete **Q4**. Then take feedback and share responses as a class, possibly comparing them with the sample student paragraph or using the **Check your progress** outcomes on page 129 of the Student Book.

Develop the skills

Read the extract from *Travels in West Africa* by Mary Kingsley on page 128 of the Student Book. **Q5–Q9** focus on the extract and the ways Kingsley uses irony to create humour. This part of the lesson should be used to develop the students' ability to look for ironic 'gaps' and understand how they create humour.

Allow 10 minutes for the students to complete **Q5–Q9** independently, using **Worksheet 7.1** to annotate the text. Note that extended written responses are not necessary at this stage as students will be doing an extended piece of writing in **Q10**.

> **Give extra support** by encouraging the students to recognise that Kingsley appears surrounded by information and advice that is strongly discouraging a visit to West Africa.
>
> **Give extra challenge** by encouraging the students to focus on how the ironic 'gap' has been created through the preoccupation with warnings and potential dangers rather than the expected encouragement and excited anticipation.

Apply the skills

Display **PPT 7.1, slide 2**, which shows a simple comparative question. Ask the students to suggest ways to tackle the question. Do not refer to the suggestions on page 129 of the Student Book yet. Collate the students' suggestions on the whiteboard. Then ask the students to compare these with those on page 129 of the Student Book.

Now read the task in **Q10**. Refer the students to the prompts on the whiteboard and the **Checklist for success** on page 129. Remind them that these can be used to structure their piece of extended comparative writing. Allow at least 20 minutes for the students to complete this extended writing task. If preferred, this could be used as a homework task or as an extended writing activity for the next lesson.

Big answer plenary	When the students have completed the extended comparison, ask them to use the **Check your progress** outcomes on page 129 of the Student Book to assess which outcome they have achieved.
	Return to the **Big question** and ask the students to complete the sentence: *Irony is ...*
	Then, ask them to write one or two sentences explaining how either Sedaris or Kingsley has used irony in their writing.

7.2 Compare the influence of poetic voices over time

Assessment objectives

English Language
AO3 Compare writers' ideas and perspectives, as well as how these are conveyed, across two or more texts

English Literature
AO2 Analyse the language, form and structure used by a writer to create meanings and effects, using relevant subject terminology where appropriate

GCSE examinations
- English Literature Paper 2, Section B

Differentiated learning outcomes
- **All students must** be able to compare the ways ideas about the sublime are presented in two poems, using relevant evidence to support their ideas.
- **Most students should** analyse the similarities and differences between the ways ideas about the sublime are presented in two poems, looking closely at the effects of a range of ways the writers have presented their ideas.
- **Some students could** present a comparative evaluation of the ways in which ideas about the sublime are communicated, making a judgment about which one is the more successful.

Resources
- **Student Book**: pp. 130–3
- **Worksheet**: 7.2
- **PPT**: 7.2

Getting you thinking

Big question	Ask the students to look at the background photographs across pages 130–3 and elicit their impressions of these two different settings. Collate their responses on the board. Then read the **Big question**: *How can two writers see such different things in the same setting?* Elicit some initial responses from the class.

Read the introductory paragraphs about Romanticism and the sublime on page 130 of the Student Book. Explain that, for the Romantics, the relationship between human beings and the natural world was a key concern.

If time permits, ask the students to undertake some independent research into the Romantic movement. They could be asked to find out:

- the names of some of the most significant Romantic poets: Blake, Wordsworth, Coleridge, Byron, Shelley and Keats, for example
- features and concerns of the movement – for example, emotion over reason; the power of the natural world; the power of ordinary lives; using emotions to create art.

Remind the students of the **Key term** 'personification' and that it is a form of metaphor. Then read the poem 'Spellbound' by Emily Brontë, on page 130 of the Student Book and ask the students to identify any aspects of personification in the poem (**Q1a**). The main reference here is 'a tyrant spell has bound me', which refers to the storm.

Now ask the students to complete **Q1b–d**, which should draw them to infer that the storm is seen as dangerous and overwhelmingly powerful by Brontë.

Explore the skills

Read the poem 'Below the Green Corrie' by Norman MacCaig on page 131 of the Student Book and ask the students to complete **Q2**. Take feedback as a class. The students might suggest:

- 'The mountains gathered round me like bandits'
- 'Their leader swaggered up close'
- 'it was they who stood and delivered'
- 'They gave me their money and their lives'
- 'that swashbuckling mountain'
- 'wearing a bandolier of light'.

Refer the students to the extracts from both poems placed side by side at the bottom of page 131. Ask them to write down one comment they could make about these two extracts, beginning with the word 'both'. Take feedback and share ideas as a class.

For **Q3**, allow ten minutes for the students to find evidence for each of the statements in the table, using **Worksheet 7.2**. This could be done in pairs.

Q4 gives the students the opportunity to use the information in the table as prompts for a short comparative paragraph about these two poems. There is flexibility in this task depending upon the time available: either the students could select one point for development and exemplification with evidence, or you could ask them to write a longer piece that uses more of the information in the table.

Develop the skills

Read the poem 'Night on the Mountain' by George Sterling on page 132 of the Student Book. Allow five minutes for **Q5**, as the students are simply identifying and making a quick list of ideas here.

For **Q6** and **Q7**, the students are starting to gather evidence to use in a comparison between 'Below the Green Corrie' and 'Night on the Mountain'. Again, allow five minutes for making a quick list of ideas.

Apply the skills

Refer the students to the **Key term** 'evaluate' and explain that it is a very useful term for comparing poems.

Ask the students to complete **Q8**. The task here is to evaluate the two poems in terms of their ideas and attitudes about mountains (or the power of the natural world).

Refer again to the information about the sublime on page 130. Then ask the students to complete **Q9**, which is the prompt for an evaluative statement.

Read the main task in **Q10**, which is a comparative analysis of the ways in which the two poets, Sterling and MacCaig, reflect ideas about the sublime.

Before they begin, refer the students to the **Checklist for success** on page 133 of the Student Book, and remind them that their notes and ideas from this lesson can be used to plan their responses.

As this is a developed task, it may be useful to use this lesson as preparation and the following lesson for completion of the extended written outcome.

Big answer plenary	Refer back to the **Big question** and ask the students to write one sentence explaining the key difference in perspective between the two poets' views of the natural world.
	Alternatively, give the students a sticky note and ask half of the class to write one word describing the dominant feeling in 'Below the Green Corrie' and the other half to complete the same task for 'Night on the Mountain'. Then stick the notes on the board for the students to refer to when writing their answer to the main task.
	Ask the students to self- or peer-assess their responses to the main task using the **Check your progress** outcomes on page 133 of the Student Book, and to assess which outcome they have achieved.

7.3 Compare and evaluate how writers explore similar ideas in poetry

Assessment objectives

English Literature

AO2 Analyse the language, form and structure used by a writer to create meanings and effects, using relevant subject terminology where appropriate

GCSE examinations
- English Literature
  Paper 2, Section C

Differentiated learning outcomes
- **All students must** be able to compare the ways ideas about childhood innocence are presented in two poems, using relevant evidence to support their ideas.
- **Most students should** be able to analyse the similarities and differences between the ways ideas about childhood innocence are presented in two poems, looking closely at the effects of a range of ways the writers have presented their ideas.
- **Some students could** present a comparative evaluation of the ways in which ideas about childhood innocence are communicated, making a judgement about which one is the more successful.

Resources
- **Student Book**: pp. 134–7
- **Worksheet**: 7.3
- **PPT**: 7.3

Other Student Book pages
- Lesson 6.1, pp. 104–7

Getting you thinking

Big question	Ask the students to look up the definition of 'evaluate' and then share some ideas about the meaning of the word. Refer the students back to Lesson 6.1 to remind them, if necessary.
	Then read the **Big question**: *What is an evaluative comparison and how do you do it?* Discuss this question with the class.

Read the explanation of 'evaluating' in the introductory paragraph of **Getting you thinking** on page 134 of the Student Book. Then allow five minutes for the students to discuss **Q1** in pairs or small groups. Take feedback as a class and share ideas on how they reached their conclusions. Elicit that in order to evaluate something, you have to know exactly what your criteria are.

Explore the skills

Display **PPT 7.3, slide 1**, and read the poem 'Children in Wartime' by Isobel Thrilling. As they read, ask the students to think about what they learn about the experience of being a child in a war-torn area (**Q2**). (The poem is also available on **Worksheet 7.3**.)

Now display **PPT 7.3, slide 2**, and ask the students to focus on this small section of the poem in more detail. Allow five minutes for the students to look at these two lines in close detail with reference to the thinking prompt in **Q2**; what are they learning about the experience of being a child in a war-torn area?

Take feedback and share ideas as a class. Then read the annotations on these two lines on page 135 and briefly compare students' ideas with the ones given there.

Before moving on to **Q3**, refer the students back to the explanation of 'evaluation' on page 134. Explain to the students that they have just been:
- looking carefully and analytically at a text
- weighing the ideas and details against an idea, or a concept, or against a different text
- reaching a conclusion.

In other words, the students have already begun the process of 'evaluating'.

Now allow 5–10 minutes for the students to select two more small details from the poem and focus on how these details enable the reader to learn something about this child's experience of being in a war-torn area (**Q3**).

For **Q4**, refer the students to the **Key term** 'synthesise' and read the definition on page 135. Then allow ten minutes for them to complete their paragraphs.

If preferred, ask the students to work in pairs or small groups, reading each other's responses to **Q3** and then synthesising their ideas across a wider selection of points.

Display **PPT 7.3, slide 3**, and read the poem 'Incendiary' by Vernon Scannell. (This poem is also available on **Worksheet 7.3**.) Explain to the students that they are going to apply their learning to a new poem. Their evaluative focus this time is to establish the poet's attitude towards the child. During the reading, the students should also think about what this poem has in common with 'Children in Wartime' (**Q5**).

Display **PPT 7.3, slide 4**, and look at the first two lines of the poem in detail and the accompanying notes on page 136 of the Student Book.

Q6 applies the learning from **Q3** to a new task. Again, ask the students to focus in detail on two small sections from the poem, keeping their focus on what they are learning about the poet's attitude towards the child.

Develop the skills

The students are now going to start comparing the two poems more systematically.

For **Q7** and **Q8**, read the three statements about both poems and allow 5–10 minutes for the students to write a summary of the similarities between them. Introduce the idea that comparison refers to differences as well as similarities.

> **Give extra support** by allowing the students to use the opening sentence below **Q8** on page 136 of the Student Book.

Display **PPT 7.3, slide 5**, which is a copy of the example student response on page 137 of the Student Book. Read the extract aloud.

Then ask the students to discuss the ideas in **Q9** in pairs or small groups, and then to use their ideas and the sample paragraph to complete **Q10** independently.

Q11 could be completed prior to writing the paragraph in **Q10** in order to give the students more material to include. Alternatively, discuss the ideas in **Q11** – the use of perspective – as a class as part of the preparation for the extended writing task in **Q12**.

Apply the skills

Read the main task in **Q12**. In this task the students are drawing together all of their notes and ideas into an extended response. Before they begin, refer the students to the **Checklist for success** on page 137 of the Student Book, which the students could use as the basis for a plan.

If you prefer, this task could be completed as a homework exercise or during the following lesson.

Big answer plenary	Refer back to the **Big question** and ask the students to write a sentence explaining the two terms: 'evaluate' and 'synthesise'.
	Then ask the students to look at their piece of extended writing and identify one sentence of their own where they feel they have made an effective evaluation. Share these with the class, either in class feedback or via sticky notes.
	Finally, ask the students to use the **Check your progress** outcomes to self- or peer-assess their piece of extended writing.

7.4 Apply your skills to English Language and English Literature tasks

Assessment objectives	GCSE examinations
English Language AO3 Compare writers' ideas and perspectives, as well as how these are conveyed, across two or more texts **English Literature** AO2 Analyse the language, form and structure used by a writer to create meanings and effects, using relevant subject terminology where appropriate	• English Language Paper 2, Question 4 • English Literature Paper 2, Section B • English Literature Paper 2, Section C

Differentiated learning outcomes	Resources
• **All students must** be able to compare the ways ideas are presented in two poems, using relevant evidence to support their ideas. • **Most students should** analyse the similarities and differences between the ways ideas are presented in two texts, looking closely at the effects of a range of ways the writers have presented their ideas. • **Some students could** present a comparative evaluation of the ways in which ideas are communicated, making a judgement about which one is the more successful.	• **Student Book**: pp. 138–46 • **Worksheets**: 7.4a–c • **PPT**: 7.4

Introduction

Recap on the learning from this chapter by asking the students to write a couple of sentences explaining the most useful ways of approaching and constructing a comparative task. They should aim to include:

- looking for the key 'hooks' or connections between the texts
- using *'both ... however ... whereas'* to structure their response.

Responding to an English Language task

Read **Source 1**, on page 138 of the Student Book and ask the students to complete **Q1**, using **Worksheet 7.4a**. At this stage they are gaining an overview of the passage. Encourage them to highlight, annotate or underline anything they notice. Remind the students of the learning from previous lessons, in particular the ways in which synthesis and evaluation are attained by gaining a comparative overview of writers' viewpoints and perspectives, and by focusing in on particular details. Therefore, it is important to gain a clear idea of the writer's viewpoint and to select three or four details to use to exemplify this.

Alternatively, the students could work in pairs or small groups, annotating the extract together.

Now ask the students to read **Source 2** on page 139 of the Student Book and to complete **Q2** using **Worksheet 7.4b**.

Read the task in **Q3** and refer the students to the **Checklist for success** on page 139. Allow 10 minutes for the students to read both texts again and make a short set of notes on the similarities and differences between them. It may be useful for the students to use the worksheets so that they can have the two sources side by side as they read. These ideas may include:

- Both are about boxing.
- Both are about particular attitudes towards boxing.

- **Source 1** is more general than **Source 2**.
- **Source 2** is more descriptive than **Source 1**.
- The two texts share a topic but have different purposes and viewpoints.

If the task is being used for examination practice, display **PPT 7.4**, **slide 1**, which is a copy of the task and the **Checklist for success** on page 139 of the Student Book. Allow at least 15 minutes for the students to complete their written responses to the task.

Alternatively, refer the students to the **Comments on Response 1**, on page 140 of the Student Book. If preferred, read **Response 1** (**Q4**) prior to completion of the independent task (**Q3**) in order for the students to see what is effective and for you to identify where further scaffolding may be needed. Display **PPT 7.4**, **slide 2**, and point out the strengths of this response. Ask the students to use these points to set a target for their own completion of **Q3**.

Q5 asks the students to consider the strengths of **Response 1**. This could be completed by considering their own response alongside **Response 1** and reflecting on which they think is stronger.

Once the students have completed the task, read **Response 2** on page 141 of the Student Book and ask the students to note down any advice needed to improve it (**Q6**). Then ask them to look again at their own response. This activity can be used to identify:

- one aspect of their work that they are particularly pleased with
- one aspect of their work that needs further improvement.

Responding to an English Literature task

Display **PPT 7.4**, **slide 3**, and read the poem 'The Piano' by D.H. Lawrence. Then ask the students to complete **Q1** on page 142. Draw attention to the fact that, although this text appears on a different examination paper and is in a different genre, the reading skills needed to analyse it are exactly the same.

Now display **PPT 7.4**, **slide 4**, and read the poem 'Background Material' by Tony Harrison. Then ask the students to complete **Q2**.

Allow 5–10 minutes for the students to quickly read both poems again, and summarise the similarities and differences between them. Similarities might include:

- Both are about the speaker's attitudes towards parents.
- Both are in first person.
- Both are about memories and the past.

Now, using **Worksheet 7.4c**, ask the students to highlight or underline:

- one particular line, phrase or couplet from each poem that they feel presents one of these strong connections
- three words from each poem that particularly stand out for them.

The final task in **Q3** is a comparative response to 'The Piano' and 'Background Material'.

Display **PPT 7.4**, **slide 5** which is a copy of the task and the **Checklist for success** on page 143. Read the task and refer the students to the success criteria. Then ask them to complete their written responses.

If preferred, complete **Q4–Q6** prior to completion of the task in **Q3** by reading **Response 1** and **Response 2** first. Then ask the students to select one element of good practice and aim to incorporate it into their own response.

Big question	The **Check your progress** outcomes on page 146 of the Student Book provide an opportunity for the students to reflect on their learning and progress. They can be applied either to both tasks in this section or just to the final task.

8.1 Engage the reader through original forms of narration

Assessment objectives

English Language

AO5 Communicate clearly, effectively and imaginatively, selecting and adapting tone, style and register for different forms, purposes and audiences. Organise information and ideas, using structural and grammatical features to support coherence and cohesion of texts

AO6 Use a range of vocabulary and sentence structures for clarity, purpose and effect, with accurate spelling and punctuation

GCSE examinations
- English Language Paper 1, Section B

Differentiated learning outcomes
- **All students must** be able to create different narrative voices and perspectives.
- **Most students should** be able to create some engaging and convincing narrative voices and perspectives.
- **Some students could** create a range of convincing, original and compelling narrative voices and perspectives that engage the reader from the first sentence of the story.

Resources
- **Student Book**: pp. 148–51
- **Worksheet**: 8.1
- **PPT**: 8.1

Getting you thinking

Big question

Refer to the **Big question** and ask the students to discuss the following statement in pairs (and then with another pair) for three to four minutes in total: *The most important decision you make as a writer is who your narrator is.*

You do not need to take any feedback for now – you will revisit this at a later stage.

Read aloud the extract from 'Wreckage' on page 148 of the Student Book and ask the students to complete **Q1–Q3** in pairs. Then take feedback as a class. Answers:

- **Q1**: the wrecked car
- **Q2**: The car had a relationship with Suki, the driver, which is now 'finished'.
- **Q3**: The impact of the narrator announcing their own death and yet speaking is surprising and makes us curious.

Explore the skills

Read through the list of possible narrators. Then ask the students to complete **Q4** and **Q5** independently.

Give extra support by providing specific examples for each of the bulleted points in the list of types of narrator. For example, if the students are unclear what 'inanimate' means you might refer them back to the first text about the car, or suggest a love story in which a mirror in a room tells the story.

Give extra challenge by asking the students to think of other unusual narrative voices not covered by the list (e.g. multiple narrators, the 'author', or someone purporting to be the author).

Take feedback as a class. In **Q4** the narrators are: **a** not human (a dog); **b** unusual position/situation; **c** observer; **d** 'older self' – a form of phantom/double.

Answers to **Q5**: **a** dog and owner; **b** patient and father/relatives; **c** stall-owner and couple; **d** younger/older self and best friend.

Use the internet to find a copy of Edward Hopper's famous painting 'Night-hawks' and display for the students. Ask them to suggest who might narrate it if this was the opening scene from a story. Which would make the most unusual narrator?

Develop the skills

Now ask the students to read the extract from *High Fidelity* by Nick Hornby aloud to each other in pairs (each student has a go at reading it). This should help them to get a sense of the voice and tone.

Allow six to seven minutes for the students to complete **Q6–Q8** independently. Then put them in groups of three or four to discuss their responses. Take feedback and share ideas as a class. Possible answers:

Q6: He is addressing Laura, but also, of course, us as readers.

Q7: There seems to be an element of contradiction here – Laura is the focus of the passage, so the fact that she doesn't make 'the top five' makes us wonder why she's worth talking about.

Q8: The style of list partly dehumanises the girls, almost as if they were just bits of music, but also suggests an inability to deal with relationships normally. This is linked to the novel's title because music can be in 'hi-fi' – meaning both a music system (CD player, speakers, etc.) and a type of high-quality sound (faithful to the original), while fidelity links to 'faithfulness' in terms of relationships.

Allow 10 minutes for the students to complete **Q9** independently, using **Worksheet 8.1**. Then put the students back in their groups again to discuss and agree on the answer to **Q10**. Take feedback and discuss **Q10** as a class - it's a difficult question – perhaps you could say 'slightly bitter', 'reflective', 'unreliable' or 'subtly humorous'?

Now ask the students to complete **Q11** independently. Then take feedback. There are no definitive responses for this, but all the examples here have an observant, contemplative, and occasionally sad or quiet tone with varying degrees of passivity. In the example given, the mention of the 'cold tide' has a cold, ominous tone, too.

Q12 could be completed in class, with the students writing just one further paragraph, or the extracts could be developed and used as a springboard for a longer piece (suitable as a homework task). If completed in class, share some of the students' work; compliment those who have managed to sustain the tone and narrative perspective.

Apply the skills

Read the task in **Q13**. Then ask the students to work in pairs to come up with ideas around the photo and / or the title. The students should use the opportunity to use speaking skills to develop and build ideas – e.g. by encouraging, asking questions, summing up. 'So, what else could 'division' refer to? A body splitting in two? Perhaps someone feeling split in two – like in love with two people…what do you think?'

Once the initial discussion is over, allow five minutes for the students to gather their ideas, add any further possibilities and then begin writing their first three paragraphs. Make sure you have checked with each student, before they begin, that they have a clear, planned idea about the narrative voice, tone and perspective.

If time permits, share some of the openings and ask for comments from the class about the style of narrator and what effect particular techniques have. Encourage the students to avoid simply saying what they like or dislike – ask them to give responses that methodically 'reflect' what they get from reading / hearing the openings (e.g. 'The way you've written it, the narrator sounds very distant…is that what you wanted?')

Big answer plenary	Refer back to the **Big question** – what are the students' views now? Ask them to make their own evaluation of where they are in terms of the **Check your progress** outcomes on page 151 – was there anything they particularly struggled with? If so, could this be tackled here and now?

8.2 Use imagery and symbolism to enhance narrative and descriptive power

Assessment objectives

English Language

AO5 Communicate clearly, effectively and imaginatively, selecting and adapting tone, style and register for different forms, purposes and audiences. Organise information and ideas, using structural and grammatical features to support coherence and cohesion of texts

AO6 Use a range of vocabulary and sentence structures for clarity, purpose and effect, with accurate spelling and punctuation

GCSE examinations
- English Language Paper 1, Section B

Differentiated learning outcomes
- **All students must** use some imagery to make their writing more vivid.
- **Most students should** be able to use appropriate imagery and symbolism in their writing to create vivid narratives.
- **Some students could** sustain a powerful range of ideas through their selection of imagery and symbols.

Resources
- **Student Book**: pp. 152–5
- **Worksheet**: 8.2
- **PPT**: 8.2

Getting you thinking

Big question	Refer to the **Big question** and explain that the objective for the lesson is to find out how to make writing 'distinctive' using particular techniques. Write the word 'distinctive' on the board and ask the class to suggest words that link to it, or are synonyms of it. They might suggest: 'easy to see', 'vivid', 'with a clear shape or appearance', 'standing out', 'original', 'individual', 'separate' (link to 'distinct'), etc.

Read aloud 'The Warning' by Adelaide Crapsey on page 152 of the Student Book. Ask the students how easy they found it to visualise this poem. How 'distinctive' was it? Then allow two to three minutes for the students to discuss **Q1a** and **Q1b** in pairs. Take brief feedback as a class: the answers are not definitive but the 'white moth' could be linked to death or age – moths tend to appear at night, and eat or destroy clothing, fabric or carpets. The skill is to suggest ideas without making them totally explicit, so we are left with a distinctive image or feeling, but an indistinct meaning.

Explore the skills

Introduce the idea of the 'pathetic fallacy': the idea that nature reflects the emotions or narrative being shown (such as thunderstorms for passionate or dramatic moments; rain running down a window to suggest a character's unhappiness or loneliness). Explain that this idea is very strong in literature and in other media, such as film.

Now ask the students to complete **Q2** independently.

> **Give extra support** by doing the first example with the class, before the students work on b) and c) independently. If they are struggling for suggestions, you could prompt them to produce something along these lines:
>
> *Here lies*
> *The fallen tree:* – What could this represent? Someone who has died?, something fruitful that has ended, like a relationship?
> *Splintered branches dying,* – What distinctive image would work?
> *An ice cold wind drifting over* – Can I bring in another sense to link to another idea?
> *Grey stones.* – Can I suggest war graves – the fallen?

Now read aloud the extract from 'The Rain Horse' by Ted Hughes on page 153 of the Student Book, and ask the students to complete **Q3** and **Q4** independently. Take feedback as a class. Possible answers:

Q3: a He seems to have got slightly lost – even though it is a place he once knew
   b it has started to rain and is getting heavier.
   c The phrase 'he had come too far' might suggest all is not well. Also, why is he returning – and so unsuitably dressed?

Q4: It suggests the place he remembered with fondness ('dreamily') is not quite as wonderful as he'd hoped – perhaps he shouldn't have come back?

Read the second extract on page 153 and ask the students to complete **Q5** and **Q6**. For **Q6**, consider the idea of the 'him' not recognising the land and vice versa, to make sure the students understand the symbiotic relationship between these two things – this is more than just a ruined walk, but is tied up with identity and emotion.

Complete **Q7** as a class discussion, taking suggestions, such as: 'back'; 'body' or 'face'; 'gaped wide/opened its jaws'.

For **Q8**, display **PPT 8.2, slides 1–2**, to model a response to the first set of features, so that the students can visualise how to convey the unwelcoming response of the land. Share some examples with the class and peer-assess by ticking off the techniques.

Develop the skills

Read aloud the third extract from 'The Rain Horse' on page 154.

For **Q9**, put the students in groups of three or four to discuss and make notes. The ideas here are quite challenging, so you may need to identify a separate group for guided work. Ask groups to reread the text for themselves, and then look at it in detail, line by line, before making their own individual notes. Points to bring out:

- The way the horse blocks out the light (associated with joy, insight, etc.) and is then 'inside his head' suggests it has crossed over from the physical to the metaphorical.
- He is no longer thinking about his ruined suit, just about how to survive.
- He has become primitive and animalistic himself – 'like a madman'; the fact that his business suit – which might represent human progress, the world of work – is ruined implies there are deeper forces that govern us, but also that we have become detached from the 'real' world – that of nature.

Apply the skills

Read the task in **Q10** and ask the students to make notes using **Worksheet 8.2** to plan and set out their key ideas before completing their written responses.

Give extra support by providing a version of **Worksheet 8.2** with some ideas already completed so that the students need only add a few of their own.

Give extra challenge by asking the students to write the full-length story or description. Or, building on the work done in Lesson 8.1, ask them to write it from an unlikely perspective (e.g. from the perspective of the horse).

Big answer plenary

Once the students have completed their paragraphs (or whole story), ask them to write the key success criteria onto several sticky notes: 'relationship verbs', 'relationship nouns', 'personification', 'imagery: similes or metaphors'. Then ask them to work in pairs and to stick the appropriate criteria to each other's work. Finally, ask them to assess which outcome their partner has achieved from the **Check your progress** on page 155.

8.3 Use structures to create memorable texts

Assessment objectives

English Language

AO5 Communicate clearly, effectively and imaginatively, selecting and adapting tone, style and register for different forms, purposes and audiences. Organise information and ideas, using structural and grammatical features to support coherence and cohesion of texts

AO6 Use a range of vocabulary and sentence structures for clarity, purpose and effect, with accurate spelling and punctuation

GCSE examinations

- English Language Paper 1, Section B

Differentiated learning outcomes

- **All students must** be able to link ideas effectively using some structural devices.
- **Most students** should use structural devices to make writing coherent and engaging.
- **Some students** could use structural devices fluently and inventively to create a range of ideas and effects.

Resources

- **Student Book**: pp. 156–9
- **Worksheet**: 8.3
- **PPT**: 8.3

Getting you thinking

Big question	Ask the students to think about this question: *Is it possible to have a story without the events or actions in some sort of order or sequence?*
	Spend two to three minutes opening the floor to the students to explore this idea. You could elicit from them the fact that the very act of reading – we go from left to right and down the page – means that even if stories don't mention time, as readers we experience them in time sequence (unless we read the ending before the beginning!). You might also touch on the idea that as readers we try to organise events, so even if we are not told things logically, we turn them *into* a story as a way of understanding them.

Read the sentence from 'Miss Brill' by Katherine Mansfield on page 156 of the Student Book and ask allow two to three minutes for the students to consider **Q1–Q4**. Take feedback as a class:

Q1: Miss Brill

Q2: nothing directly, but we assume Miss Brill is visiting the *Jardins Publiques*.

Q3: It could have started, 'Miss Brill was glad...fur.'

Q4: She wanted to draw attention to the weather and the setting before mentioning Miss Brill.

Explore the skills

Read aloud the bullet list explaining the functions of an opening. Refer to the complete opening paragraph from 'Miss Brill' on page 157. The key thing to reinforce is the explanation of the clause order of the first sentence – the foregrounding of the cautious 'Although ...'.

Now read aloud the complete opening paragraph from 'Miss Brill' and reiterate the importance of time and order of events. Point out that by beginning in the 'heart of the story' (Miss Brill in the gardens), the actual focus of events here is not on what happened earlier, important though it is.

Allow five minutes for the students to complete **Q5-Q8** in pairs. Then take feedback as a class. Answers are:

Q5: We are told about Miss Brill taking the fox fur out of its box and putting it on.
Q6: She uses the past perfect 'had taken'.
Q7: She likes having the fur and wants to treat it like a naughty, but lovable child.
Q8: 'biting'.

Ask the students to complete **Q9** independently. They can add further details to the first sentence if they wish.

> **Give extra support** by suggesting situations for the second sentence in **Q9** – for example, getting ready to go out; eating in a cafe; leaving their house or flat; meeting each other.
>
> **Give extra challenge** by asking if the first sentence (when completed) could be swapped around so it begins with an adverbial, e.g. 'Scattering the pigeons...'.

Develop the skills

Now ask the class as a whole to suggest responses to **Q10** and **Q11**.

For **Q10**, Mansfield uses 'but' after 'The air was motionless,' and then in the sentence, 'But the nose...' to tell us it needs repair.

Q11 is more challenging – the students need to search for subtle descriptions – there is the 'chill' in the air, even the 'leaf drifting' suggesting summer is over. Later, the fox though dead seems to 'snap' and of course its nose had 'taken a knock' – rather a sad sight. Finally, the 'tingling' and the 'something gentle' in her chest might hint at illness, however subtly.

Now ask the students to complete **Q12** independently: accept any response that uses conjunctions.

You could display **PPT 8.3** as a model.

For **Q13**, ask the students to read the end of the story to themselves, and then go back to the opening and read that again, to get a good sense of the structural links. Then ask them to complete the two questions independently, before sharing responses with a partner. Take feedback as class:

- The references to 'stupid old thing' and 'silly old mug at home', the question 'who wants her?' and the fact she has her weekly treats for herself, all suggest her solitude, as does her 'little dark room' (no mention of anyone else).

- The replacing of the fox fur – which she had seemed to be proud of and which offered her a sort of companionship – links back to her taking it out. Also, as before the 'red eiderdown' is mentioned, and the 'crying' of the fox connects with its imagined voice at the start ('What's been happening to me?'). This could be seen to reflect Miss Brill's own experience and feelings.

Apply the skills

Read the task in **Q14** and ask the students to make notes for their story, using **Worksheet 8.3**. The advantage of the model in the worksheet is that it doesn't have to be the order the story is told in – this shows a different line altogether, which can jump backwards and forwards.

Big answer plenary	Ask the students to note down the three most important things they have learned about structuring narrative from this lesson. Then, ask them to evaluate their progress against the **Check your progress** outcomes on page 159 of the Student Book.

8.4 Apply your skills to an English Language task

Assessment objectives

English Language

AO5 Communicate clearly, effectively and imaginatively, selecting and adapting tone, style and register for different forms, purposes and audiences. Organise information and ideas, using structural and grammatical features to support coherence and cohesion of texts

AO6 Use a range of vocabulary and sentence structures for clarity, purpose and effect, with accurate spelling and punctuation

GCSE examinations
- English Language Paper 1, Section B

Differentiated learning outcomes
- **All students must** be able to write creatively, drawing on voice, imagery and effective structural ideas to create impact.
- **Most students should** be able to make their creative writing engaging and coherent through their use of effective narrative voice, careful choice of vivid imagery and use of structural devices.
- **Some students could** create convincing and original texts through their use of compelling narrative voices, powerful imagery and inventive structures.

Resources
- **Student Book**: pp. 160–4
- **Worksheet**: 8.4
- **PPT**: 8.4

Introduction

Explain that AO5 and AO6 refer to the ways in which the students are able to craft and compose their own descriptive and narrative writing in order to make an impact on the reader. They deal with the conscious manipulation of words, sentences and the overall text for effect, and, in the case of descriptive/imaginative writing, at the highest level they describe the ability to create original and compelling writing that sustains interest from the first to the last word.

Responding to an English Language task

Read out the set task in **Q1** and ask the students to look at the photo on page 160 of the Student Book. Allow five minutes for the students to note down ideas related to the photo independently. Remind them that they might wish to consider unusual or original perspectives. Remind them, also, that they should think about what is suggested or implied by the photo as much as what is actually visibly present.

Refer the students to the **Checklist for success** on page 160 and ask them to explain what each of the bullets refers to:

- What is a 'convincing, original' voice or perspective?
- What does 'vivid' mean?
- What sort of possible structures are there that they could consider?

The students could, at this point, plan a response and draft a first paragraph, or, if you wish to remain focused on the evaluation and assessment of skills, you could move straight on to **Q2** and **Response 1**.

Read through **Response 1** and the accompanying annotations and commentary on pages 161–2 together as a class.

The mark schemes for GCSE English Language could be copied and given to the students. For each response ask them to work up the descriptors like a ladder, answering 'yes' or 'no' as to whether they see the skills in place. For **Response 1** they are likely to see Level 6 descriptors in place.

For **Q3**, display **PPT 8.4, slides 1–4**, which model one way to improve **Response 1**. The particular idea here is that the reader is both left to work out more (they are told less), and at the same time they are *shown* more (there is more detail). Finally, the structure changes, with the focus on the character shifted to the end of the first paragraph.

The **Comments on Response 1** on page 162 also recommend a more inventive overall structure. Make the point that creativity also comes in the way patterns can be used in descriptive writing – treating the text more like a poem and less like a narrative.

Next read aloud **Response 2** on pages 162–3 in order to accentuate the sound patterns and structural devices that are a particular feature of the text. Then ask the students to read the accompanying annotations and **Comments**.

Ask them to look at both **Response 1** and **Response 2**, and note down the key differences that they observe between the two (**Q4**). In particular, elicit from them:

- the inventive imagery, which is developed into expanded metaphor around the idea of an 'orchestra' (but also how the mere idea of a 'dead orchestra' allows a set of creative ideas to flow out)
- the sound and word patterns that chime with the subject matter (it is important to point out that such patterns have to be appropriate, if possible, not just introduced for the sake of it)
- the way the voice of the text seems to speak, beyond the grave, to the reader.

The students could then complete their own full response to a similar task using **Worksheet 8.4.** This shows a photo of a bookshop and asks them to write a description based on it. Decide whether the students should do a full practice response without any assistance, or whether they should be provided with some initial guidance – for example, discussing the picture as was done with the one of the wreck at the start of the unit. Completing this full response may take more than the time immediately available, in which case the task could be completed for homework.

Once the students have completed the task, they should look again at the two sample responses and their own, and make a judgement as to which response they think they are closer to (in level). Then, ask them to select and note down:

- one aspect or feature they are particularly pleased with in their own work
- one aspect of feature they could improve.

Alternatively, they could exchange their work with a partner and, using the English Language mark scheme, work their way up from the bottom and decide which of the levels they feel the response fits best. Following this, they could rewrite their response in the light of the comments proposed.

9.1 Convey convincing and original voices in your writing

Assessment objectives

English Language

AO5 Communicate clearly, effectively and imaginatively, selecting and adapting tone, style and register for different forms, purposes and audiences. Organise information and ideas, using structural and grammatical features to support coherence and cohesion of texts

AO6 Use a range of vocabulary and sentence structures for clarity, purpose and effect, with accurate spelling and punctuation

GCSE examinations
- English Language Paper 2, Section B

Differentiated learning outcomes

- **All students must** be able to write a convincing article that has a clear style and a sense of voice.
- **Most students should** be able to recognise different styles of voice in texts and choose from some of the techniques writers use to create their own text.
- **Some students could** select from a range of distinctive voices and language techniques to create a convincing, original voice of their own.

Resources
- **Student Book**: pp. 166–9
- **Worksheet**: 9.1
- **PPT**: 9.1

Getting you thinking

Big question	Authors often talk about 'finding their voice'. Ask the students what they think this means. Take brief feedback: it might mean settling on subjects and ways of writing about those subjects that are unique to the writer. It could also mean adopting a style that readers recognise as theirs. The students may be able to mention favourite writers who have this uniqueness.

Read the extract from Tim Dowling's article 'Hounded out' on page 166 of the Student Book, and ask the students to discuss **Q1–Q3** in pairs. Then take feedback as a class. Responses might include:

Q1: He doesn't like them, and hates one of them.

Q2: She is persuasive and despite his moaning, he does as she suggests.

Q3: The title is a pun (dog/hound) and the text has some slightly humorous comments, so it is light-hearted.

Explore the skills

Look over the table on page 167 of the Student Book with the class and read it aloud. From this, the students should be able to see that what appears to be fairly 'throwaway' text is actually quite carefully constructed for effect.

For **Q4**, display **PPT 9.1, slides 1–5**, to develop a modelled response with the class. Each slide shows the different stages put together, so reveal one at a time, explaining the reasoning as you do so. You could give the students the first two slides to look at, and then create a shared response, with them suggesting how the text might develop. When the students have completed their own paragraphs, share some of them with the class as a whole. Were they able to emulate Tim Dowling's style?

Develop the skills

Now read aloud the extract from '*The Amazing Spider-Man 2* review' by Xan Brooks on page 167 of the Student Book, and ask the students for an initial response to the tone/voice. Is it the same as Tim Dowling's? If different, how?

For **Q5-Q8**, allow five minutes for the students to discuss the questions in pairs and then join up with another pair to compare responses. Take feedback from each group of four, and share ideas with the class. Possible answers:

Q5: The extended metaphor is that of a romantic relationship.

Q6: 'outgrow us'; 'moved on'; 'embraced'

Q7: The metaphor suggests that this was an important and powerful part of his younger life, so much so that he is still 'in love', even as a grown man.

Q8: a Here, the metaphor is related to 'thread' – the idea that the relationship is 'sewn together'.

  b It is particularly relevant because of the idea of a spider's web and the thread a spider uses to capture its prey.

  c The final pun is on the word 'yarn', which can mean fabric that is woven together and is also an old-fashioned word for 'story'.

Now ask the students complete **Q9** independently.

> **Give extra support** by placing less confident students in the class into a guided writing group so they can work together to compose a paragraph or the start of it. You could begin by getting them to think of vocabulary or phrases around disease or addiction, such as 'next fix', 'sweaty palms', 'shaking limbs', 'cold turkey'.
>
> **Give extra challenge** by asking the students to review a film they hate, using a different sort of metaphor – perhaps a plague, a nightmare or a dreadful voyage.

Read the extract from the article 'Good friends are hard to find – and even harder to keep' by Tim Lott on page 169. Before the students attempt to answer **Q10**, get them engaged with the tone of the text by using the grid in **Worksheet 9.1** to 'unpick' the text through its language.

Take feedback, drawing out the generally simple nature of the statements, the use of the present tense, and the simile ('like a good marriage') and metaphor ('battle-scarred veterans') mentioned on page 169 of the Student Book.

Now ask the students to complete **Q10**. Take feedback as a class.

a The students should be able to find examples such as: 'Simply this – an absence of pride.' (and any of the sentences that follow in the final paragraph.)

b Lott recognises that friendship is about accepting your own failings – and those of your friends – rather than looking for perfection.

Apply the skills

Read out the task in **Q11** and check all students are clear about what the statement is saying. Ask them to restate the viewpoint in the question in their own words, something which can then be used in their first paragraph, for example: *'The idea that our friendships change over time and we can be guilty of giving too much importance to hanging on to them, is one I can understand, but fundamentally disagree with...'*

Then, using the **Checklist for success** on page 169 of the Student Book, ask the students to plan their three paragraphs, deciding what they are going to include in each. They should then spend 20 minutes drafting their three paragraphs, bearing in mind the overall objective to develop a distinctive tone of voice. Their voice doesn't have to be identical to those of Tim Lott, Xan Brooks or Tim Dowling – but each of these provides an idea of differing tones they can emulate.

> **Big answer plenary**
>
> Once they have completed their draft, ask the students to exchange texts with a partner and, using the **Checklist for success** and **Check your progress** outcomes on page 169 of the Student Book, to make an assessment of their partner's work before redrafting where necessary. Then, ask them to make an assessment of their own work using the three outcomes.

9.2 Manipulate structure to create effects in point of view writing

Assessment objectives

English Language

AO5 Communicate clearly, effectively and imaginatively, selecting and adapting tone, style and register for different forms, purposes and audiences. Organise information and ideas, using structural and grammatical features to support coherence and cohesion of texts

AO6 Use a range of vocabulary and sentence structures for clarity, purpose and effect, with accurate spelling and punctuation

GCSE examinations

- English Language Paper 2, Section B

Differentiated learning outcomes

- **All students must** be able to write in a structured manner using clear paragraphs to build a persuasive argument.
- **Most students should** consider some different structures and choose one that makes their point of view clear and coherent.
- **Some students could** select from a range of structures and use them in inventive and engaging ways in point of view writing.

Resources

- **Student Book**: pp. 170–3
- **Worksheet**: 9.2
- **PPT**: 9.2

Getting you thinking

Big question — Refer to the Big question: *How can you structure points in an opinion piece to create impact in an original, yet clear way?* Then ask students what the structure of a front page news report tends to be – in terms of what comes in the first paragraph or two, and so on. Then ask them if this is the same for feature articles or opinion pieces within the paper – why not? Because the main purpose of these types of articles is not primarily to report the general news, but to comment on an issue of specific concern to the writer as a person.

Give extra support by pre-teaching some of the terms before reading the extract from George Monbiot's article aloud – 'pesticides', 'eco-systems', 'neurotoxins', 'correlation', 'causation' and 'precipitous'.

Ask the students to discuss **Q1–Q3** briefly in pairs. Possible responses:

Q1: He believes production of a particular type (neonicotinoids) should be stopped while trials take place.

Q2: There is more impact in the first paragraph – it puts the choice to the 'world' and the reader first, thus foregrounding his worries.

Q3: The use of technical language related to the topic gives his article – and his argument/opinions – credibility and authority.

Explore the skills

Read the opening paragraph in **Explore the skills** on page 171 together with the class, and point out the three sentences in the box. You could display **PPT 9.2** to show how the text operates, highlighting the different parts on **slides 2** and **3**.

Then, ask the class to look at **Q4** and feed back responses ('We are just beginning to understand what we've walked into' and 'At this rate, it doesn't take long to engineer a world without song.'). In both cases, these are the final sentences of the paragraph.

Then ask the students to identify the technical language Monibot uses to support his argument (**Q5**).

For **Q6**, display **PPT 9.2**, **slide 4**. Once the students have identified the 'emotional trigger' ('Nature is a monochrome canvas, empty of life.'), ask them to look at the different options for where to place the sentence, before copying out their preferred option. You can then display **PPT 9.2**, **slides 5–8**, which show the sentence in the different positions. The best one is probably as it is in Monbiot's text – i.e. with the sentence placed at the end of the paragraph, but point out that it doesn't have to be.

Read the sentence in **Q7** aloud, and then allow four to five minutes for the students, working in pairs, to compose and add a trigger sentence to the front or end of the paragraph. They will need to be clear what the viewpoint expressed in the paragraph is. Once they have completed the task, take some suggestions and write them up on the board to share with the class – which ones do the students feel do the job of tugging at the reader's conscience most successfully?

Develop the skills

Read the task in **Q8** aloud and check that the students are clear what the viewpoint expressed is. Allow three or four minutes for the students to make notes on how they might approach the task. If the students can think of any other arguments against access to global produce (**Q9**), list them on the board for everyone in the class to see.

For **Q10**, allow five minutes for the students to list arguments on the other side (in favour of global produce), working in small groups. These points might include:

a   It provides an income to poorer countries that they might otherwise not have.
b   Global demand will eventually drive up wages.
c   It gives the consumer more choice.
d   It enables consumers to understand more about different cultures through the types of food that are available.
e   It encourages consumers to be more adventurous in their eating – possibly more healthy.
f   It drives down cost of food.

Then, give the students five minutes to debate the issue, using the arguments they have listed, plus the ones from the Student Book. Is there a consensus at the end?

Now, go through the structure table on page 173 of the Student Book carefully, making sure the students are clear what the different structures indicate. Once this has been done, ask the students to complete **Q11**.

Apply the skills

Read the task in **Q12** and refer the students to the **Checklist for Success** on page 173. Encourage them to go back over the topic if they need to be clearer about the skills needed to complete the task. Then ask them to draft their three paragraphs, using **Worksheet 9.2** to help them decide how they are going to marshal their arguments. Stress that *how* they introduce each point is up to them. For example, is there a 'killer' point they want to make? If so, is it best up front, or to build up to it? There are no right or wrong answers in this respect, but it's important that students understand they need to navigate the reader around the arguments, in the direction they want.

> **Give extra support** by choosing a structure for less confident students – perhaps the simple 'essay of two halves'.
>
> **Give extra challenge** by asking the students to write the full article. They could do their own research and add in relevant factual data, technical terms, etc.

Big answer plenary	Ask the students to write down three things they have learned about structure from the lesson. Take feedback from the class and, if time permits, read some opening paragraphs from the final task. Ask if the students can identify a clear structure that has been used.

9.3 Match style and tone to purpose and audience

Assessment objectives

English Language

AO5 Communicate clearly, effectively and imaginatively, selecting and adapting tone, style and register for different forms, purposes and audiences. Organise information and ideas, using structural and grammatical features to support coherence and cohesion of texts

AO6 Use a range of vocabulary and sentence structures for clarity, purpose and effect, with accurate spelling and punctuation

GCSE examinations

- English Language
  Paper 2, Section B

Differentiated learning outcomes

- **All students must** be able to write in a tone that matches audience and purpose to create a clear point of view article.
- **Most students should** be able to use a range of suitable rhetorical effects and patterns to make an argument clear and convincing.
- **Some students could** create a compelling and convincing argument through careful selection of language and linguistic patterns to match tone, audience and purpose.

Resources

- **Student Book**: pp. 174-7
- **Worksheet**: 9.3
- **PPT**: 9.3

Getting you thinking

Big question	Refer to the **Big question**: *How can you pitch your style perfectly to match the task.* Explain to the students that any topic can be approached using the style they select (serious subjects are often dealt with in a light-hearted manner by comedians on television panel shows, for example), but they should be aware that if they don't match the style to the audience – or equally importantly, the style to the outcome they want – then the text won't work.

Read aloud the first sentence of the extract from the article 'This surveillance bill puts our hard-won freedom in peril' by Harry Leslie Smith on page 174 of the Student Book. Ask the students what they notice about the style (length of sentence, use of vocabulary, etc.). They might mention how long the sentence is and how complicated the structure is – it needs to be read a couple of times, because the whole of the section preceding the verb 'is' is the subject of the sentence (which you could sum up as 'the government's inaction on data').

Now read the rest of the article before asking the students to complete **Q1** in pairs. Take brief feedback.

a This will have been made clear by looking at the first paragraph: Smith's general viewpoint is that government should be doing more to stop companies holding private data about us, but the specific argument relates to the bill and his opposition to it.

b His purpose is to persuade parliament to at least discuss the bill, as well as to enlist readers' support/sympathy.

c The tone is serious and cautionary (warning the reader).

d The audience consists of readers of the paper/people who care about such matters.

Explore the skills

Read through the guidance on the powerful usages and the rhetorical flourishes in the table on page 175. Then allow five to six minutes for the students to complete **Q2** and **Q3** in the same pairs. Take feedback as a class.

Q2: 'Since the dark ages, human society has fought to remove the yoke of state...'
'It is incumbent upon our parliament to debate this bill...'

Q3: 'Since the dark ages human society has fought.../all people must fight...'
'...is more than an affront to/it is an affront to...' (note the balancing effect of the semi-colon here)

For **Q4**, display **PPT 9.3** to help model the first few words of the text that need strengthening. You could focus on the verb phrases, adverbs and adjectives, as shown in the slides. The suggested change from 'you' to 'we' fits with the style of an article that sounds like a speech, drawing everyone in.

Ask the students to complete **Q4**, using **Worksheet 9.3** to underline or highlight the words or phrases they think need to change, before rewriting the text in the table provided.

Develop the skills

Now ask the students to complete **Q5** and **Q6** in pairs. Take feedback as a class. Possible responses:

Q5: These references give the text 'weight' – this is a writer who can draw on references to history and war, which add to the impression of an important point being made that is not just relevant today but has longer-term impact.

Q6: The further metaphor is *'put a leash on the human spirit...'*, the idea of our liberty being controlled like a dog on a lead.

Ask the students to complete the task in **Q7** using the second half of **Worksheet 9.3**.

> **Give extra support** by prompting the students to think of appropriate ideas. For example, for the first gap, point out that if we are 'shining a light into the ... of terrorism', then that place must be dark. What comparison could be made? What other dark places are there (e.g. dark pit, cave, forest, night)?
>
> **Give extra challenge** by asking the students to write a further paragraph of their own in favour of the legislation, using some or all of the skills they have learned.

Apply the skills

Read the task in **Q8** and allow 10 minutes for the students to list ideas for and against the statement. Once they have done this, they can decide which view they would take on the issue. As you go around the class, make sure that everyone has a sufficient number of points to write their three paragraphs.

Before the students begin their response, ask them, as a class, to identify the key things they have learned, referencing some of the texts they have looked at. They will be expected here to take a fairly serious tone, so it should not be too far away from the tone Harry Leslie Smith uses.

> **Big answer plenary**
>
> Once the students have completed their three paragraphs, ask them to exchange with a partner and, using their partners' other points, see if they could quickly write a further paragraph. Once they have done this, listen to some samples from the students and ask the others to comment on the extent to which they have fulfilled the task brief.

9.4 Apply your skills to an English Language task

Assessment objectives

English Language

AO5 Communicate clearly, effectively and imaginatively, selecting and adapting tone, style and register for different forms, purposes and audiences. Organise information and ideas, using structural and grammatical features to support coherence and cohesion of texts

AO6 Use a range of vocabulary and sentence structures for clarity, purpose and effect, with accurate spelling and punctuation

GCSE examinations
- English Language Paper 2, Section B

Differentiated learning outcomes

- **All students must** be able to express their viewpoint clearly using a simple two-part essay structure, with topic sentences and simple adjectives and verbs.
- **Most students should** be able to write paragraphs with a clear focus, use negative and positive vocabulary and appropriate formal or informal language.
- **Some students could** adapt tone and register, use punctuation for effect, and select from a range of styles, structures and language techniques to express their views.

Resources
- **Student Book**: pp. 178–82
- **Worksheet**: 9.4
- **PPT**: 9.4

Other Student Book pages
- Lessons 9.1–9.3, pp. 166–77

Introduction

Explain that the relevance of AO5 and AO6 to this assessment is that they refer to the ways in which they, as the students, structure and craft their own point of view writing in order to express their viewpoint clearly and persuasively. These Assessment Objectives refer to the students' use of thoughtful organisation and deployment of language, matched to particular audiences and conventions, to create influential and well-argued texts.

Responding to an English Language task

Read the sample task about solitude/loneliness on page 178 of the Student Book. Then allow two to three minutes for the students think about the subject and decide what their own view is. Then ask them to join with two or three others to share and discuss these views.

Now ask the students to work in the same small group to list key techniques or ways they could go about arguing their point of view in a convincing and compelling way (**Q1**). The students have considered this in the earlier lessons, but revisit what they understand those terms to mean:

- 'convincing' here, means that their text must read as if they really do believe the case they're making
- 'compelling' means that, whatever their viewpoint is, they can argue it in a way that makes it impossible for readers not to agree.

These should naturally draw on what they have done in Lessons 9.1 to 9.3.

Display **PPT 9.4, slides 1–5**, to help explain the key areas that the students should consider in order to be 'convincing' and 'compelling'.

Now read **Response 1** and the accompanying annotations and comments on pages 178-9 of the Student Book and ask the students a series of questions to ensure they have followed and understood the annotations (**Q2**). For example:

[1] *How does the opening paragraph not address issue immediately?* (It expresses the writer's wish to 'become a hermit', which does not tell us at this point what the issue is.)

[2] *How is humour used to create sense of voice/exaggerated persona of writer?* (It gives a perhaps exaggerated view of his relationship with his anxious mother.)

[3] *How does the dialogue build the 'angle' being pursued?* (He is using it as an example of the 'hassle' he gets from others; it also gives us a distinctive sense of his voice – it's unlikely the writer would tell his teacher he's becoming a hermit.)

[4] *How does the long paragraph develop the idea by painting a picture of writer's own room?* (The repeated sequence – closing curtains, cat off bed, etc. – emphasises idea of difficulty finding solitude in the family house.)

[5] *How does the metaphor take the argument in a new direction?* (It does this by describing the mind as a creative machine that needs space to operate.)

[6] *What are the repeated rhetorical patterns?* (The 'if' clauses set up questions that have causal responses related to solitude – 'you're a weirdo'.)

[7] *How does the short final paragraph links back to beginning of article?* (It does this by mentioning hermits.)

At this point the mark schemes for GCSE English Language could be copied and given to the students. For **Response 1** ask the students to work up the descriptors like a ladder, answering 'yes' or 'no' as to whether they see the skills in place (**Q3**). For **Response 1** they are likely to see Level 3 descriptors in place.

Now read **Response 2** and the accompanying annotations comments on pages 180–1 of the Student Book. Ask the students to look at both **Response 1** and **Response 2**, and note down the key differences that they observe between the two. Has **Response 2** met the descriptors at Level 4 in the GCSE English Language mark scheme? As before, ask them to work up the descriptors like a ladder, answering 'yes' or 'no' as to whether they see the skills in place (**Q4**).

The students could complete their own full response to a similar task using **Worksheet 9.4**. This gives them a task and also provides a planning template to help them get started.

Decide whether the students should do a full, practice response without any assistance, or whether they should be provided with some initial guidance – for example, discussing the title and generating ideas around the viewpoint. Completing this full response may take more than the time immediately available, in which case the task could be completed for homework.

Once the students have completed the task, they should look again at the two sample responses and their own, and make a judgement as to which they think they are closer to (in level). Then, ask them to select and note down:

- one aspect or feature they are particularly pleased with in their own work
- one aspect of feature they could improve.

Alternatively, they could exchange their work with a partner and, using the English Language mark scheme, work their way up from the bottom and decide which of the levels they feel the response fits best.

Following this, they could rewrite their response in the light of the comments proposed.

Worksheet 1.1a — William Wordsworth's 'Daffodils'

Student Book **Q7** Look at the following extract from the poem 'Daffodils' by William Wordsworth. Answer the questions in the annotations on page 10 of the Student Book, by focusing on the information in the prepositional phrases, which have been highlighted for you.

> I wandered lonely as a cloud
> That floats on high o'er vales and hills, [1]
> When all at once I saw a crowd, [2]
> A host, of golden daffodils;
> Beside the lake, beneath the trees, [3]
> Fluttering and dancing in the breeze. [4]
>
> Continuous as the stars that shine [5]
> And twinkle on the Milky Way, [6]
> They stretched in never-ending line [7]
> Along the margin of a bay:
> Ten thousand saw I at a glance, [8]
> Tossing their heads in sprightly dance. [9]
>
> William Wordsworth, from 'Daffodils'

1 What type of cloud does Wordsworth want you to picture?	
2 How does this prepositional phrase connected to time show the impact the daffodils make on Wordsworth?	
3 How do these prepositional phrases help you to imagine the quantity of daffodils in the landscape?	
4 How is a sense of movement created and what sort of movement do you imagine?	
5 How does this help us picture the number of flowers?	
6 How does this add to the beauty of the image?	
7 What sense is created here?	
8 What speed is conveyed here? How does this help us see Wordsworth's message about natural beauty?	
9 How does he capture the innocence and beauty of the flowers here?	

Worksheet 1.1b — William Blake's 'Laughing Song'

Student Book Q9 Read the following poem by William Blake, which is made up entirely of adverbial clauses, except for the final two lines. Think about the effect this creates before answering the questions below.

Laughing Song

When the green woods laugh with the voice of joy,
And the dimpling stream runs laughing by;
When the air does laugh with our merry wit,
And the green hill laughs with the noise of it;

When the meadows laugh with lively green,
And the grasshopper laughs in the merry scene,
When Mary and Susan and Emily
With their sweet round mouths sing 'Ha, ha, he!'

When the painted birds laugh in the shade,
Where our table with cherries and nuts is spread,
Come live, and be merry, and join with me,
To sing the sweet chorus of 'Ha, ha, he!'

William Blake

---

a What image of the natural world does Blake create through the adverbial clauses?

....

....

....

b What kind of a 'time' is created though the adverbial clauses? How would you describe it?

....

....

....

c When Blake invites his love to 'Come live, and be merry, and join with me', how is this made more innocent than in the Donne poem in Activity 6, because of the adverbial clauses in the rest of the poem?

....

....

Worksheet 1.2a: Punctuation in complex sentences

Student Book **Q4** The main punctuation marks we find in complex sentences are listed in the chart below. Examples are given of them in both creative writing and analytical writing.

   a Work out what the punctuation marks are doing in each case before writing your own definition of their role.

   b Then, practise using the punctuation marks by completing the chart.

	In analysis	In creative writing	Definition
Comma	As well as being a dramatist, Shakespeare wrote many sonnets, many of which were about love.		
Semicolon		The train grudgingly pulled out of the station; we were going to war.	
Pairs of commas, pairs of dashes (parenthesis)	Blake wrote many poems about religion – though he was against organised religion himself – and the theme of spirituality can be seen in…		
Colon		Peterson checked out the room, mentally recording all he could see: burnt CDs, recording equipment, laptop and fresh milk on the counter. Someone had been here recently	

314 • Key technical skills

Worksheet 1.2b: Thought journey

Student Book **Q6a** Complete the map of the thought journey through the extract, which is all one sentence.

Main clause

The news about Lydia has made Elizabeth forget her own problems.

Quotation = 'Lydia – the humiliation, the misery, she was bringing on them all – soon swallowed up every private care;'

Separated by: a semicolon

Additional ideas:

1 Lydia has brought a lot of shame to the family.

Quotation = ...

Separated by: pair of dashes

2 ....

Quotation = 'and covering her face with her handkerchief, Elizabeth was soon lost to everything else;'

Separated by: ....

3 After a few minutes Darcy's voice brings her back to reality.

Quotation = ...

Separated by: ....

4 ....

Quotation = 'who, in a manner, which though it spoke compassion, spoke likewise restraint, said,'

Separated by: ....

Worksheet 1.3: Unusual sentence structures

Student Book **Q2** Read the following extract from by Jon McGregor where he describes a city at night. Explore how the writer has used unusual sentence structures for effect by answering the questions in the annotations.

So listen.

Listen, and there is more to hear.

The rattle of a dustbin lid knocked to the floor. [1]

The scrawl and scratch of two hackle-raised cats. [1]

The sudden thundercrash of bottles emptied into crates. [1] The slam-slam of car doors, the changing of gears, the hobbled clip-clop of a slow walk home. [2] The rippled roll of shutters pulled down on late-night cafes, a cracked voice crying street names for taxis, a loud scream that lingers and cracks into laughter, a bang that might just be an old car backfiring, a callbox calling out for an answer, a treeful of birds tricked into morning, a whistle and a shout and a broken glass, a blare of soft music and a blam of hard beats, a barking and yelling and singing and crying and it all swells up all the rumbles and crashes and bangings and slams, all the noise and the rush and the non-stop wonder of the song of the city you can hear if you listen the song [3]

and it stops [4]

in some rare and sacred dead time, sandwiched [5] between the late sleepers and the early risers, there is a miracle of silence. [6]

Everything has stopped. [7]

Jon McGregor, from *If Nobody Speaks of Remarkable Things*

---

1 What is unusual about each of these three sentences? Do they have a subject?	
2 Is this a sentence? What do notice about the listing?	
3 Is this a sentence? What effect is the writer trying to create through the use of syndetic listing?	
4 Has the sentence finished yet? How does the structure here bring you up short? Does this change the pace?	
5 What do you think is the importance of this word in relation to the structure of the sentence?	
6 Look back at the whole sentence. Is it understandable in this context? How is additional impact created when the sentence stops? How does the sentence reflect the night itself?	
7 What is the impact of the spacing and the simple sentence at the end? Why does this sentence become unusual in relation to the previous ones?	

Worksheet 2.1: Interpret T.S. Eliot's 'Virginia'

Student Book Q9 Use the copy of the poem to begin to 'unpick' and explore it. Use this sequence of questions to help you annotate the poem and add notes.

> **Start** with the simple things: what is obvious? What is happening in the poem?
>
> **Move on** to a deeper exploration:
> - What stands out or is noticeable in the poem?
> - Do any particular words, phrases or lines seem particularly powerful?
> - What questions are raised by these words or phrases?
> - Can you think of possible answers?
> - What connotations or ideas come to mind from particular words or phrases?

Virginia

Red river, red river,
Slow flow heat is silence
No will is still as a river
Still. Will heat move
Only through the mocking-bird
Heard once? Still hills
Wait. Gates wait. Purple trees,
White trees, wait, wait,
Delay, decay. Living, living,
Never moving. Ever moving
Iron thoughts came with me
And go with me:
Red river river river.

T.S. Eliot

Worksheet 2.2: Understand the gothic genre

Student Book **Q6** Use this worksheet to make notes based on the extract from the novel *Rebecca* by Daphne du Maurier.

A sense of mystery	An atmospheric location
A character who seems alone or vulnerable	**References to the supernatural**
Heightened, highly descriptive and exaggerated language	**A sense of violence or threat**

Worksheet 2.3: Compare tone and style in two texts

Student Book **Q5** Use this grid to help you explore the differences in tone and style between Text A and Text B on pages 30–1 of the Student Book.

Feature	Text A	Text B
Type of sentences and use of grammar	Standard, conventional sentences for the most part with no minor sentences or one-word sentences. Use of a rhetorical question directed at the reader.	
Vocabulary and how information is conveyed	Some informality – slightly everyday usages such as 'clincher'. Particular actions and events are described in a straightforward manner.	
Analogies or allusions		
Anything else you notice		

© HarperCollins*Publishers* 2015   Key concepts • 319

Worksheet 3.1 Understand more challenging texts

Student Book **Q4** Can you place these words and phrases into the text by Charles Darwin below the box?

with respect to	much zeal	*named* mineral
some little care	very much	Hemipterous
(Zygaena)	Cicindela	White's 'Selborne'
took much pleasure	simplicity	gentleman

……………………………… science, I continued collecting minerals with ……………………………… , but quite unscientifically — all that I cared about was a new ……………………………… , and I hardly attempted to classify them. I must have observed insects with ……………………………… , for when ten years old (1819) I went for three weeks to Plas Edwards on the sea-coast in Wales, I was ……………………………… interested and surprised at seeing a large black and scarlet ……………………………… insect, many moths ………………………………, and a ……………………………… which are not found in Shropshire. I almost made up my mind to begin collecting all the insects which I could find dead, for on consulting my sister I concluded that it was not right to kill insects for the sake of making a collection. From reading ………………………………, I ……………………………… in watching the habits of birds, and even made notes on the subject. In my ……………………………… I remember wondering why every ……………………………… did not become an ornithologist.

Adapted from Charles Darwin, *The Autobiography of Charles Darwin*

320 • Reading, understanding and responding to texts © HarperCollins*Publishers* 2015

Worksheet 3.2: Ideas about beauty in Sonnet 130

Student Book **Q9** Begin your work by selecting ideas about inner and outer beauty and add them to the table below.

Outer beauty	Inner beauty
Her lips are red in colour, but they are not as bright as coral, which is 'more red'.	She is not like a goddess – she is 'on the ground', nothing spiritual or heavenly in that sense…

Choose some quotations and annotate them here:

Quotation 1

Quotation 2

Quotation 3

Worksheet 3.3 — Summarise ideas in a Venn diagram

Student Book **Q5** Use the Venn diagram below to record your points about the two texts. Some possible points have been placed in the diagram for you, and some others are included under the diagram for you to add in the correct places.

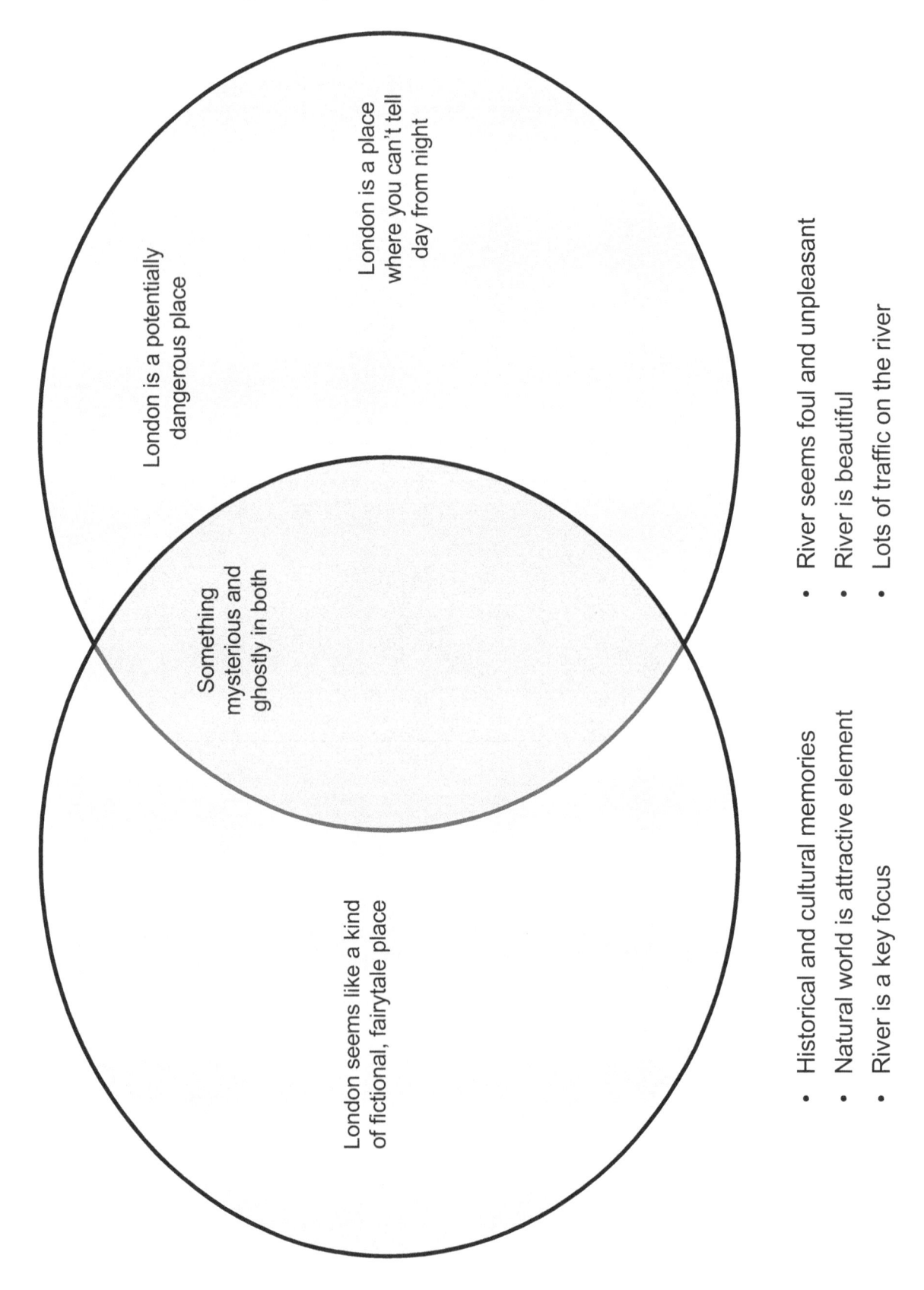

Top circle:
- London is a potentially dangerous place
- London is a place where you can't tell day from night

Overlap:
- Something mysterious and ghostly in both

Bottom circle:
- London seems like a kind of fictional, fairytale place

Points to add:
- River seems foul and unpleasant
- River is beautiful
- Lots of traffic on the river
- Historical and cultural memories
- Natural world is attractive element
- River is a key focus

Worksheet 3.4: Summarise and synthesise information

Student Book Q2 Using details from both sources, write a summary of the behaviour of the authorities towards the poor in Rio compared to in the Highlands in the past.

To enable you either to write your own response or to evaluate responses written by others, use this table to summarise the key ideas and add evidence. You could then use a highlighter or arrows to link any points of similarity, or where the same sort of idea/area is being addressed or commented on.

(In the exam, you may not have time to write all the ideas down and then make links, so to 'work smart' you could try to find similar or related ideas and place them alongside each other immediately, using the designated rows.)

Behaviour of Rio authorities	Behaviour of Highlands authorities
Areas of Rio being demolished in preparation for the World Cup. ('buildings...have been levelled')	People in Greenyard being removed or evicted. ('evicting schemes')

Worksheet 4.1: Language techniques in Orwell's *The Road to Wigan Pier*

In this section of *The Road to Wigan Pier*, George Orwell uses a range of language techniques in order to express a particular viewpoint.

A slag-heap is at best a hideous thing, because it is so planless and functionless. It is something just dumped on the earth, <u>like the emptying of a giant's dust-bin.</u> [1] On the outskirts of the mining towns there are frightful landscapes where your horizon is ringed completely round by jagged grey mountains, and underfoot is mud and ashes and over-head the steel cables where tubs of dirt travel slowly across miles of country. Often the slag-heaps are on fire, and at night you can see the <u>red rivulets</u> [2] of fire winding this way and that, and also the slow-moving blue flames of sulphur, which always seem on the point of expiring and always spring out again. Even when a slag-heap sinks, as it does ultimately, only an <u>evil brown grass</u> [3] grows on it, and it retains its hummocky surface. One in the slums of Wigan, used as a playground, looks <u>like a choppy sea suddenly frozen</u> [4]; 'the flock mattress', it is called locally. Even centuries hence when the plough drives over the places where coal was once mined, the sites of ancient slag-heaps will still be distinguishable from an aeroplane.

At night, when you cannot see the hideous shapes of the houses and the blackness of everything, a town like Sheffield assumes a kind of sinister magnificence. Sometimes the drifts of smoke are rosy with sulphur, and serrated flames, like circular saws, squeeze themselves out from beneath the cowls of the foundry chimneys. Through the open doors of foundries you see fiery serpents of iron being hauled to and fro by redlit boys, and you hear the whizz and thump of steam hammers and the scream of the iron under the blow.

George Orwell, from *The Road to Wigan Pier*

Worksheet 4.2 — Analyse a writer's use of structure

Student Book Q3 What is your response to this opening paragraph?

> Why did I get fat? Why was I eating until I hurt and regarding my own body as something as distant and unsympathetic as, say, the state of the housing market in Buenos Aires? Obviously, it's not wholly advisable to swell up so large that, on one very bad day, you get stuck in a bucket seat at a local fair and have to be rescued by your old schoolmaster, but why is being fat treated as a cross between terrible shame and utter tragedy? Something that – for a woman – is seen as falling somewhere between sustaining a sizable facial scar and sleeping with the Nazis?

Student Book Q6 Read the next paragraph of Moran's article. As you read, notice how she uses parentheses (brackets).

> Why will women happily boast-moan about spending too much ('…and then my bank manager took my credit card and cut it in half with a sword!'), about drinking too much ('…and then I took my shoe off and threw it over the bus stop!'), and about working too hard ('…so tired I fell asleep on the control panel, and when I woke up, I realized I'd pressed the nuclear launch button! Again!') but never, ever about eating too much? Why is unhappy eating the most pointlessly secret of miseries? It's not like you can hide a six-Kit-Kats-a-day habit for very long.

Student Book Q8 What is the difference between the tone at the start and at the end of the article? Which is more serious? Why do you think Moran has structured her text in this way?

> I sometimes wonder if the only way we'll ever get around to properly considering overeating is if it does come to take on the same perverse, rock 'n' roll cool of other addictions. Perhaps it's time for women to finally stop being secretive about their vices and instead start treating them like all other addicts treat their habits. Coming into the office looking frazzled, sighing, 'Man, I was on the pot roast last night like you wouldn't believe. I had, like, MASH in my EYEBROWS by 10 p.m.'
>
> Then people would be able to address your dysfunction as openly as they do all the others. They could reply, 'Whoa, maybe you should calm it down for a bit, my friend. I am the same. I did a three-hour session on the microwave lasagna last night. Perhaps we should go out to the country for a bit. Clean up our acts.'
>
> Because at the moment, I can't help but notice that in a society obsessed with fat – so eager in the appellation, so vocal in its disapproval – the only people who aren't talking about it are the only people whose business it really is.
>
> Caitlin Moran, from *How to be a Woman*

Worksheet 4.3 Analyse form and structure in a sonnet

Student Book **Q3** As you read, make notes in response to the following questions.

  a What do you think this poem is about? Is it about love or something else?

  b What changes between the octet and the sestet? What is different about the meaning between the two stanzas?

How to Leave the World that Worships *Should*

Let faxes butter-curl on dusty shelves.

Let junkmail build its castles in the hush

of other people's halls. Let deadlines burst

and flash like glorious fireworks somewhere else.

As hours go softly by, let others curse

the roads where distant drivers queue like sheep.

Let e-mails fly like panicked, tiny birds.

Let phones, unanswered, ring themselves to sleep.

Above, the sky unrolls its telegram,

immense and wordless, simply understood:

you've made your mark like birdtracks in the sand –

now make the air in your lungs your livelihood.

See how each wave arrives at last to heave

itself upon the beach and vanish. Breathe.

Ros Barber

Worksheet 4.4a: Respond to an English Language task

Student Book Q1 This extract is from the first chapter of the novel *Lord of the Flies*. As you read it, think about and make some immediate notes on the questions in the Student Book.

The Sound of the Shell

The boy with fair hair lowered himself down the last few feet of rock and began to pick his way toward the lagoon. Though he had taken off his school sweater and trailed it now from one hand, his grey shirt stuck to him and his hair was plastered to his forehead. All round him the long scar smashed into the jungle was a bath of heat. He was clambering heavily among the creepers and broken trunks when a bird, a vision of red and yellow, flashed upwards with a witch-like cry; and this cry was echoed by another.

'Hi!' it said. 'Wait a minute!'

The undergrowth at the side of the scar was shaken and a multitude of raindrops fell pattering.

'Wait a minute,' the voice said. 'I got caught up.'

The fair boy stopped and jerked his stockings with an automatic gesture that made the jungle seem for a moment like the Home Counties.

The voice spoke again.

'I can't hardly move with all these creeper things.'

The owner of the voice came backing out of the undergrowth so that twigs scratched on a greasy wind-breaker. The naked crooks of his knees were plump, caught and scratched by thorns. He bent down, removed the thorns carefully, and turned around. He was shorter than the fair boy and very fat. He came forward, searching out safe lodgments for his feet, and then looked up through thick spectacles.

'Where's the man with the megaphone?'

The fair boy shook his head.

'This is an island. At least I think it's an island. That's a reef out in the sea. Perhaps there aren't any grownups anywhere.'

The fat boy looked startled.

'There was that pilot. But he wasn't in the passenger cabin, he was up in front.'

The fair boy was peering at the reef through screwed-up eyes.

'All them other kids,' the fat boy went on. 'Some of them must have got out. They must have, mustn't they?'

The fair boy began to pick his way as casually as possible toward the water. He tried to be offhand and not too obviously uninterested, but the fat boy hurried after him.

'Aren't there any grownups at all?'

'I don't think so.'

William Golding, Lord of the Flies

Worksheet 4.4b: Respond to an English Literature task

Student Book **Q1** Read the following poem, 'The Swan' by Mary Oliver. As you read, think about the questions in the Student Book (page 78).

The Swan

Did you too see it, drifting, all night, on the black river?

Did you see it in the morning, rising into the silvery air –

An armful of white blossoms,

A perfect commotion of silk and linen as it leaned

into the bondage of its wings; a snowbank, a bank of lilies,

Biting the air with its black beak?

Did you hear it, fluting and whistling

A shrill dark music – like the rain pelting the trees – like a waterfall

Knifing down the black ledges?

And did you see it, finally, just under the clouds –

A white cross streaming across the sky, its feet

Like black leaves, its wings

Like the stretching light of the river?

And did you feel it, in your heart, how it pertained to everything?

And have you too finally figured out what beauty is for?

And have you changed your life?

Mary Oliver

Worksheet 5.1: Development of character in 'The Darkness Out There'

Student Book **Q6–Q8** In this extract, Sandra is inside Mrs Rutter's cottage.

6. Find words and phrases which suggest Mrs Rutter looks like a typical 'old dear'.
7. How does Lively's description of Mrs Rutter's house reinforce this impression of her?
8. Is there anything in the description which suggests Mrs Rutter might not be as harmless as Sandra thinks?

She seemed composed of circles, a cottage-loaf of a woman, with a face below which chins collapsed one into another, a creamy smiling pool of a face in which her eyes snapped and darted.

'Tea, my duck?' she said. 'Tea for the both of you? I'll put us a kettle on.'

The room was stuffy. It had a gaudy lino floor with the pattern rubbed away in front of the sink and round the table; the walls were cluttered with old calendars and pictures torn from magazines; there was a smell of cabbage. The alcove by the fireplace was filled with china ornaments: big-eyed flop-eared rabbits and beribboned kittens and flowery milkmaids and a pair of naked chubby children wearing daisy chains.

The woman hauled herself from a sagging armchair. She glittered at them from the stove, manoeuvring cups, propping herself against the draining-board. 'What's your names, then? Sandra and Kerry. Well, you're a pretty girl, Sandra, aren't you. Pretty as they come. There was – let me see, who was it? – Susie, last week. That's right, Susie.' Her eyes investigated, quick as mice. 'Put your jacket on the back of the door, dear, you won't want to get that messy. Still at school, are you?'

Penelope Lively, from 'The Darkness Out There'

Worksheet 5.2: Analyse Heaney's use of language

Student Book **Q6** Complete the following table.

Animal/plant image	Effect
'wolfed the blighted root'	
'faces chilled to a plucked bird'	
'beaks of famine snipped at guts'	
'grubbing, like plants, in the bitch earth'	A strange image: 'grubbing' suggests the starving people are now less than human, focusing on finding food like insects would. Perhaps comparing people to 'plants' suggests how connected people were to the natural world; the image adds to the dehumanising effect of the famine. The 'black mother' who brought the good harvest is now the 'bitch earth' showing that nature can deny as well as provide. The word 'bitch' suggests spite and is linked closely to the word 'earth'; both are one syllable with short vowels and harsh 'th' consonant sounds adding to the idea of something spiteful and deliberate.
'hope rotted like a marrow'	

Worksheet 5.3: Characteristics of narrative voices

Student Book **Q1** Look at the words in boxes below and think about how you might group them.

Q2a Which words do you think carry positive connotations? Which carry negative connotations? Which might be a mixture of both? Use the Venn diagram to place the words where you think they should go.

Q2b Which of these words would you associate with a young person, and which would be more likely to describe an older, wiser person?

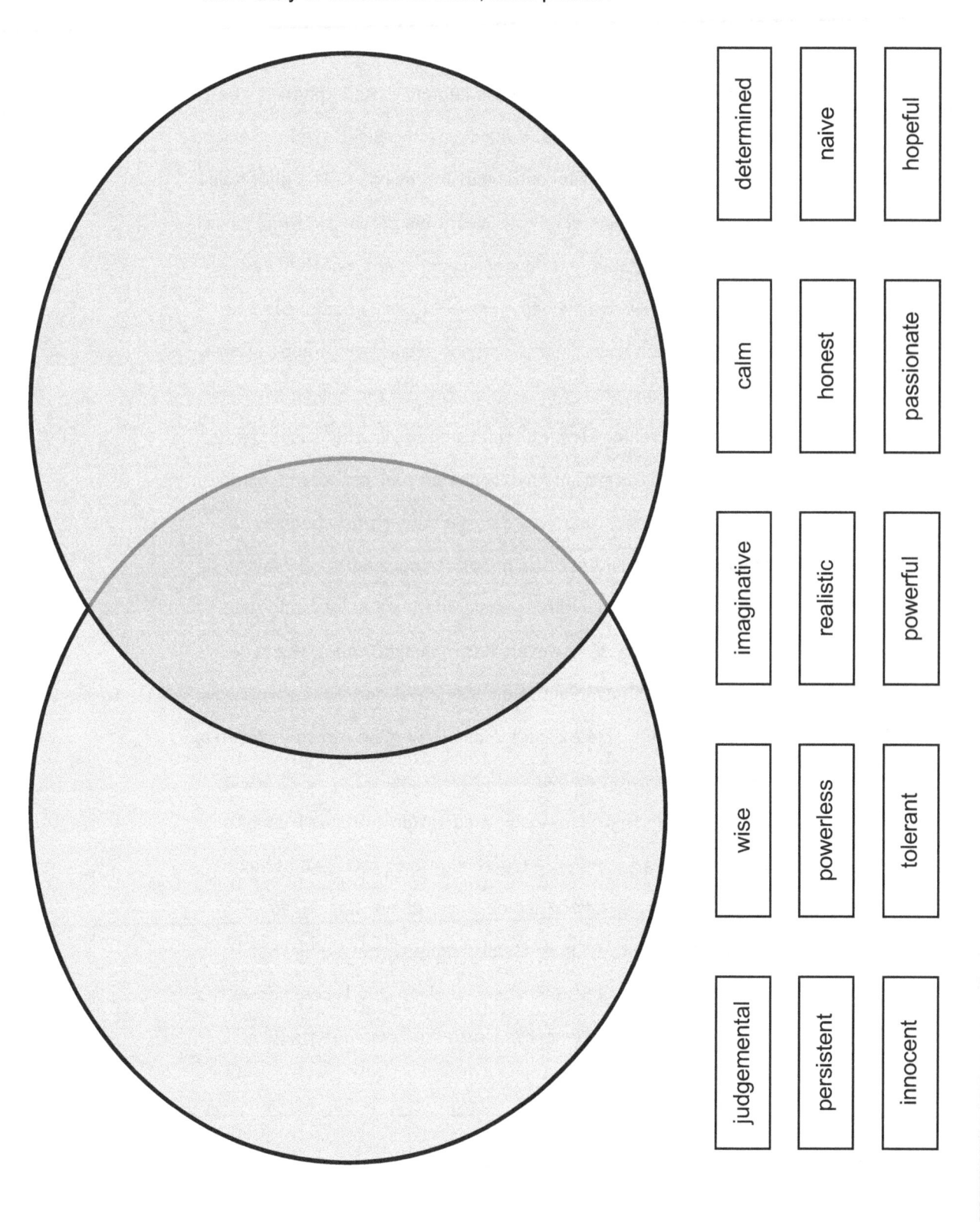

- determined
- naive
- hopeful
- calm
- honest
- passionate
- imaginative
- realistic
- powerful
- wise
- powerless
- tolerant
- judgemental
- persistent
- innocent

Worksheet 5.4: Assess a student's response to an English Literature task

Student Book **Q4** As you read Response 2 below, think about what the student has done well.

Response 2

The appearance of a ghost in Act 1 of a revenge tragedy would be expected by a Shakespearean audience. As expected, the ghost provides the central dilemma of the play with his demand to 'revenge his most foul and unnatural murder'. The ghost also reveals that his murderer now 'wears his crown' setting Hamlet against a formidable and dangerous opponent, another key feature of a revenge tragedy. However, many audiences see Hamlet as much more than a revenge tragedy; it can be viewed as a powerful psychological exploration of the human condition. The ghost is telling Hamlet something he already suspected as revealed by his comment 'my prophetic soul' and seems to be giving him a perfect motive to act; a modern psychoanalytic interpretation could see the ghost as representing Hamlet's unconscious desire to kill his uncle or what Freud would have called the id. The id, however, has a balance called the superego, which is similar to a conscience, and you can already see it working in this extract. Hamlet says he will take revenge with 'wings as swift as meditation or thoughts of love', which sounds fast at first. However, 'meditation' hints at Hamlet's flaw: he thinks too much. Also 'thoughts of love' is a strange simile to use in this situation as love and murder are so different. Perhaps Hamlet is unconsciously revealing that he is happier thinking about love than murder. This foreshadows the inner conflict which torments Hamlet throughout the play.

Worksheet 6.1: Evaluation questionnaire

1. Does the work look at the text from a clear viewpoint? Yes ☐ No ☐
2. Does it begin to interpret the text from that viewpoint? Yes ☐ No ☐
3. Does it back up the ideas using textual support/quotation? Yes ☐ No ☐

Your colleague has reached Outcome 1. Give them two ideas they could have added to the work to improve it.

....

....

4. Does it use the questions on the text to dig deeper into two or three key ideas? Yes ☐ No ☐
5. Does it support those ideas with examples from the text? Yes ☐ No ☐
6. Does the work include some inference to help build an interpretation based on feminist or Marxist ideas? Yes ☐ No ☐

Your colleague has reached Outcome 2. Give them one additional suggestion that would have made this work even better.

....

....

7. Does the response use some original ideas in addition to the ones in the questions? Yes ☐ No ☐
8. Are those ideas supported with interesting and/or unusual details from the text? Yes ☐ No ☐
9. Does the interpretation take a convincing feminist or Marxist viewpoint whilst also showing some original thought? Yes ☐ No ☐

Your colleague has reached Outcome 3. Tell them which part of their work you liked the best.

....

....

Worksheet 6.2 Blake's 'The Tyger'

Student Book **Q2** Read the whole of William Blake's poem 'The Tyger' adding your own annotations.

The Tyger

Tyger Tyger, burning bright,
In the forests of the night;
What immortal hand or eye,
Could frame thy fearful symmetry?

In what distant deeps or skies.
Burnt the fire of thine eyes?
On what wings dare he aspire?
What the hand, dare seize the fire?

And what shoulder, & what art,
Could twist the sinews of thy heart?
And when thy heart began to beat,
What dread hand? & what dread feet?

What the hammer? what the chain,
In what furnace was thy brain?
What the anvil? what dread grasp,
Dare its deadly terrors clasp!

When the stars threw down their spears
And water'd heaven with their tears:
Did he smile his work to see?
Did he who made the Lamb make thee?

Tyger Tyger burning bright,
In the forests of the night:
What immortal hand or eye,
Dare frame thy fearful symmetry?

William Blake

Worksheet 6.3a: Jean Sprackland's *Strands*

Student Book Q3 Read the following extract from the book *Strands* by Jean Sprackland. She describes walking on her local beach and encountering an unusual event.

When I was a child, it was said to be lucky to have a ladybird land on your sleeve.[2] My dad certainly liked it when they visited the garden, because they ate the greenfly that plagued [1] his raspberry canes. There was an air of [3] mild enchantment [4] carried by the single ladybird – the one that chose you and rested on you,[3] perhaps just for a minute or two, before unfolding itself and flying away home. [...]

One muggy August day [2], there is a phenomenal swarm [3] of seven-spot ladybirds on this coast. Millions of them divert onshore, interrupting their journey from who-knows-where. (...) They're [2] bizarrely out of place [4] on the beach. They [2] fill the air, and seagulls make slow predatory circles overhead. They [2] blunder [1] drunkenly on the ground, turning the sand red. They [2] drip [1] from fence posts and pool underneath.

We walk on the beach with our faces covered in scarves, though it's midsummer. Still they land on our eyelids and in our hair and tumble ticklishly [1] down inside our clothes. As we walk, they crunch [1] underfoot; they're everywhere. Families abandon their picnics and flee. People lock themselves inside their cars.[2] [...]

These childhood gifts, these small enchantments [1], are suddenly so extravagantly numerous that their currency has collapsed. They've become worthless, and worse than worthless. Now they look like tiny curses.[4]

[...]

What is it about swarms that raises the hair on the back of our necks?[3] Ladybirds are not harmful: they don't sting like wasps, and they don't devastate crops like locusts. But it seems we can have too much of a good thing.[4] A sudden onslaught on this scale feels threatening; it feels like a plague [1]. Things are out of kilter.[4] What does it mean? What will come next? [2] Is it an omen of some kind; a judgement on us? [...]

'Ladybird Books,' laughs my friend.[2] 'Remember their slogan? *Everybody loves a ....*' He stops abruptly and spits one out.[3] The beach is almost deserted by now, and this is starting to feel apocalyptic.[4]

A dog walker coming the other way calls out: 'Aren't they horrible little bastards [1]?' And he breaks into a run. [3]

Jean Sprackland, from *Strands*

Key:
[1] language
[2] structure
[3] tone
[4] key messages

Worksheet 6.3b — Select and gather evidence

Student Book **Q5** Now *select and gather* the evidence you would like to use in your response to the task in the grid below. Remember to select the points that will most usefully support the *defining statement* of your argument.

d Key messages	
c Points about tone	
b Structure points	
a Language points	

- Forming a critical response

Worksheet 6.4a — Khaled Hosseini's *The Kite Runner*

Sitting cross-legged, sunlight and shadows of pomegranate leaves dancing on his face, Hassan absently plucked blades of grass from the ground as I read him stories he couldn't read for himself. That Hassan would grow up illiterate […] had been decided the minute he had been born, perhaps even the moment he had been conceived […] – after all, what use did a servant have for the written word? But despite his illiteracy, or maybe because of it, Hassan was drawn to the mystery of words, seduced by a secret world forbidden to him. I read him poems and stories, sometimes riddles – though I stopped reading him those when I saw he was far better at solving them than I was.

[…]

One day I played a little trick on Hassan. I was reading to him, and suddenly I strayed from the written story. I pretended I was reading from the book, flipping pages regularly, but I had abandoned the text altogether, taken over the story, and made up my own. Hassan, of course, was oblivious to this. To him, the words on the page were a scramble of codes, indecipherable, mysterious. Words were secret doorways and I held all the keys. After, I started to ask him if he liked the story, a giggle rising in my throat, when Hassan began to clap.

'What are you doing?' I said.

'That was the best story you've read me in a long time,' he said, still clapping.

I laughed. 'Really?'

'Really.'

'That's fascinating.' I muttered. I meant it too. This was … wholly unexpected. 'Are you sure, Hassan?'

He was still clapping. 'It was great, Amir. Will you read me more of it tomorrow?'

[…]

I gave him a friendly shove. Smiled. 'You're a prince, Hassan. You're a prince and I love you.'

That same night, I wrote my first short story. It took me thirty minutes. It was a dark little tale about a man who found a magic cup and learned that if he wept into the cup, his tears were turned into pearls. But even though he had always been poor, he was a happy man and rarely shed a tear. So he found ways to make himself sad so that his tears could make him rich. As the pearls piled up, so did his greed grow. The story ended with the man sitting on a mountain of pearls, knife in hand, weeping helplessly into the cup with his beloved wife's slain body in his arms.

That evening, I climbed the stairs and walked into Baba's smoking room, in my hands the two sheets of paper on which I had scribbled the story. (…)

'What is it, Amir?' Baba said reclining on the sofa and lacing his hands behind his head. Blue smoke swirled around his face. His glare made my throat feel dry. I cleared it and told him I'd written a story.

Baba nodded and gave a thin smile that conveyed little more than feigned interest. 'Well, that's very good, isn't it? He said. Then nothing more. He just looked at me through the cloud of smoke.

I probably stood there for under a minute, but, to this day, it was one of the longest moments of my life. Seconds plodded by, each separated from the next by an eternity. Air grew heavy, damp, almost solid. I was breathing bricks. Baba went on staring me down, and didn't offer to read.

Khaled Hosseini, from *The Kite Runner*

Worksheet 6.4b: Thomas Hardy's 'The Convergence of the Twain'

The Convergence of the Twain

In a solitude of the sea
Deep from human vanity,
And the Pride of Life that planned her, stilly couches she.

Steel chambers, late the pyres
Of her salamandrine fires,
Cold currents third and turn to rhythmic tidal lyres.

Over the mirrors meant
To glass the opulent
The sea-worm crawls – grotesque, slimed, dumb, indifferent.

Jewels in joy designed
To ravish the sensuous mind
Lie lightless, all their sparkles bleared and black and blind.

Dim moon-eyed fishes near
Gaze at the gilded gear
And query: 'What does this vaingloriousness down here?' …

Well: while was fashioning
This creature of cleaving wing,
The Imminent Will that stirs and urges everything

Prepared a sinister mate
For her - so gaily great –
A Shape of Ice, for the time far and dissociate

And as the smart ship grew
In stature, grace and hue,
In shadowy silent distance grew the iceberg too.

Alien they seemed to be:
No mortal eye could see
The intimate welding of their later history,

Or sign that they were bent
By paths coincident
On being anon twin halves of one august event,

Till the Spinner of the Years
Said 'Now!' And each one hears,
And consummation comes, and jars two hemispheres.

Thomas Hardy

Worksheet 7.1: Mary Kingsley, *Travels in West Africa*

Student Book Q6–10 In her travelogue *Travels In West Africa*, published in 1897, Mary Kingsley writes about her reactions to advice on a planned trip to West Africa

> I think many seemed to translate my request for practical hints and advice into an advertisement that 'Rubbish may be shot here.' This same information is in a state of great confusion still, although I have made heroic efforts to codify it. I find, however, that it can almost all be got in under the following different headings, namely and to wit:
>
> - The dangers of West Africa
> - The disagreeables of West Africa
> - The diseases of West Africa
> - The things you must take to West Africa
> - The things you find most handy in West Africa
> - The worst possible things you can do in West Africa.
>
> […]
>
> It was the beginning of August '93 when I first left England for 'the Coast.' Preparations of quinine with postage partially paid arrived up to the last moment, and a friend hastily sent two newspaper clippings, one entitled 'A Week in a Palm-oil Tub,' which was supposed to describe the sort of accommodation, companions, and fauna likely to be met with on a steamer going to West Africa, and on which I was to spend seven to The Graphic contributor's one; the other from The Daily Telegraph, reviewing a French book of 'Phrases in common use' in Dahomey. The opening sentence in the latter was, 'Help, I am drowning.' Then came the inquiry, 'If a man is not a thief?' and then another cry, 'The boat is upset.' 'Get up, you lazy scamps,' is the next exclamation, followed almost immediately by the question, 'Why has not this man been buried?
>
> Mary Kingsley, from *Travels in West Africa*

Worksheet 7.2 Find evidence and connections

Student Book **Q3** Look at the ideas collected in the following table. Find the evidence to support each detail. See how many more connections you can find between these two extracts from the poems.

Detail	Quotation	Effect
Both use repetition.		Both poets suggesting the overwhelming presence of the natural world.
Both use an image of darkness.		Both seem to be suggesting that there is a dark, ominous presence about the natural world.
Both personify the natural world.		Both suggest that the natural world has a life-force which is dangerous and threatening.
Both suggest the idea of attack.		Both suggest the idea that nature is a threat to humans.

Worksheet 7.3: Compare two poems about childhood

Student Book Q12 Compare the ways two poets present ideas about childhood innocence in 'Children in Wartime' and 'Incendiary'.

Children in Wartime

Sirens ripped open
the warm silk of sleep;
we ricocheted to the shelter
moated by streets
that ran with darkness.
People said it was a storm,
but flak
had not the right sound
for rain;
thunder left such huge craters
of silence,
we knew this was no giant
playing bowls.
And later,
when I saw the jaw of glass,
where once had hung
my window spun with stars;
it seemed the sky
lay broken on my floor.

Isobel Thrilling

Incendiary

That one small boy with a face like pallid cheese
And burnt-out little eyes could make a blaze
As brazen, fierce and huge, as red and gold
And zany yellow as the one that spoiled
Three thousand **guineas** worth of property
And crops at Godwin's Farm on Saturday
Is frightening – as fact and metaphor:
An ordinary match intended for
The lighting of a pipe or kitchen fire
Misused may set a whole menagerie
Of flame-fanged tigers roaring hungrily.
And frightening, too, that one small boy should set
The sky on fire and choke the stars to heat
Such skinny limbs and such a little heart
Which would have been content with one warm kiss
Had there been anyone to offer this.

Vernon Scannell

Worksheet 7.4a — Attitudes towards boxing (1)

Student Book **Q1** Read Source 1, which is an editorial article from *The Guardian* about boxing, published in 2000. As you read it, make some notes on what you are learning about the writer's viewpoint on boxing

Source 1

Few would doubt Muhammad Ali's place as one of the great figures of the last century. He achieved global fame as an athlete, became a powerful spokesman for his people and a principled advocate for social justice – even forfeiting his champion's title rather than serve in Vietnam. But perhaps his greatest achievement is not yet complete. The eloquent testimony of his own deterioration into disability may yet prove his lasting legacy. For Muhammad Ali, once boxing's shining exponent, is now a living warning of the dangers of the ring. He has been reduced to virtual immobility, his once-fast tongue slowed and slurred – all because he took punches for three decades.

We mention him now because of the fate of a less-starred fellow boxer. On Saturday night Paul Ingle sustained serious brain injuries after losing to South Africa's Mbulelo Botile in Sheffield. He spent yesterday in hospital, in a 'critical but stable' condition after surgeons laboured for two and half hours to remove a blood clot from his brain. Predictably, the British Boxing Board of Control has put on its concerned face, promising 'to launch an inquiry' and look for 'lessons to be learned'.

But these cliches are no longer good enough. Boxing cannot sincerely 'inquire' into the circumstances of Saturday's fight or look for lessons, as if what happened to Paul Ingle was a freak accident – like a plane collision or a rail crash. When a disaster of that kind strikes, it is because something wholly unexpected has happened. But for a man to suffer brain damage after his brain has been pummelled – deliberately and with precision – is wholly to be expected. It is no surprise at all. Ask Michael Watson, still confined to a wheelchair after his fight against Chris Eubank in 1991. Ask Gerald McClellan, beaten into a coma in 1995 and now in need of 24-hour-a-day care. Ask the family of Bradley Stone, killed by his 1994 bantamweight bout. Or take one last look at Muhammad Ali.

No liberal calls for a ban on any activity lightly. But we repeat our long-held belief that boxing has no place in a civilised society. To those who say a ban would only drive the sport underground, we point to bear-baiting and cock-fighting: they were banned and have all but vanished from British life. We wish the same fate for the sport which has laid waste to too many young men, including the greatest among them.

Leader, 'Ban this barbaric sport',
from *The Guardian*, 18 December 2000

Worksheet 7.4b — Attitudes towards boxing (2)

Student Book **Q2** Now read Source 2, which is an essay on boxing by William Hazlitt written in 1822. Again, as you read, think about what you are learning about this writer's viewpoint on boxing.

Source 2

> In the first round every one thought it was all over. After making play a short time, the Gas-man flew at his adversary like a tiger, struck five blows in as many seconds, three first, and then following him as he staggered back, two more, right and left, and down he fell, a mighty ruin. There was a shout, and I said, 'There is no standing this.' Neate seemed like a lifeless lump of flesh and bone, round which the Gas-man's blows played with the rapidity of electricity or lighting, and you imagined he would only be lifted up to be knocked down again. […]
>
> If there had been a minute or more allowed between each round, it would have been intelligible how they should by degrees recover strength and resolution; but to see two men smashed to the ground, smeared with gore, stunned, senseless, the breath beaten out of their bodies; and then, before you recover from the shock, to see them rise up with new strength and courage, stand steady to inflict or receive mortal offence, and rush upon each other, 'like two clouds over the Caspian' – this is the most astonishing thing of all: – this is the high and heroic state of man! […] Ye who despise the FANCY, do something to show as much pluck, or as much self-possession as this, before you assume a superiority which you have never given a single proof of by any one action in the whole course of your lives! – When the Gas-man came to himself, the first words he uttered were, 'Where am I? What is the matter!' 'Nothing is the matter, Tom – you have lost the battle, but you are the bravest man alive.'
>
> William Hazlitt, from 'The Fight'

Worksheet 7.4c: Compare two poems

Student Book **Q3** Compare the ways poets present attitudes towards the past in 'Piano' and 'Background Material'.

Piano

Softly, in the dusk, a woman is singing to me;
Taking me back down the vista of years, till I see
A child sitting under the piano, in the boom of the tingling strings
And pressing the small, poised feet of a mother who smiles as she sings.

In spite of myself, the insidious mastery of song
Betrays me back, till the heart of me weeps to belong
To the old Sunday evenings at home, with winter outside
And hymns in the cosy parlour, the tinkling piano our guide.

So now it is vain for the singer to burst into clamour
With the great black piano appassionato. The glamour
Of childish days is upon me, my manhood is cast
Down in the flood of remembrance, I weep like a child for the past.

D H Lawrence

Background Material

My writing desk. Two photos, mam and dad.
A birthday, him. Their ruby wedding, her.
Neither one a couple and both bad.
I make out what's behind them from the blur.

Dad's in our favourite pub, now gone for good.
My father and his background are both gone,
but hers has my Welsh cottage and a wood
that still shows those same greens eight summers on,
though only the greenness of it's stayed the same.

Though one of them's in colour and one's not,
the two are joined, apart from their shared frame,
by what, for photographers, would mar each shot:

in his, if you look close, the gleam, the light,
me in his blind right eye, but minute size –

in hers, as though just cast from where I write,
a shadow holding something to its eyes.

Tony Harrison

Worksheet 8.1: Features of a distinctive voice

Student Book **Q9** What language features can we see here that contribute to the distinctive voice and style? See if you can find examples of any elements in the table below. Not all the features are present.

Feature	Examples
Informal, chatty vocabulary and turns of phrase.	'that lot'
Vivid, descriptive setting	
Directly addressing another character	
First-person narrator	
Reflective thoughts on emotions	
Semicolons used to add a clarification to the previous statement	
Third-person narrator	
Past tense references to past events	'These were the ones that really hurt.'
Present tense references to current situations	
Exclamation marks for shock or anger	

Are there any other features of narration that aren't mentioned in the table? If so, list them here with examples:

Feature	Examples

Worksheet 8.2 — Plan your story

Student Book **Q10** Use this planning template to help you plan your story.

Key planning questions	My notes and plans
Who is lost? (Think about age, gender, job or role – if relevant.)	
Will there be *anyone else or anything else* in the story? (Like the horse, or perhaps an object or machine?)	
Where are they lost? (Consider exterior and interior settings – could be good to think of a local place you know or have seen.)	
Where have they *come from*? (You don't need to mention this explicitly – it could be implied.)	
How did it happen? (How did they come to be lost? Did they do something stupid? Or was it someone else's fault? Will there be consequences?)	
What is the 'relationship' between the new environment and the main character? (Is it unwelcoming, as in 'The Rain Horse, or a haven or escape?)	

Worksheet 8.3 — Plan events using a time line

Student Book **Q14** Use this model to help plan your story called 'The Anniversary'.

You could begin by creating a **time line** of events for your story, so for example:

A Morning: wife goes to work	**B** Mid-morning: stay at home	**C** Husband goes out and buys flowers	**D** Early evening: cooks meal, gets flowers out, etc	**E** Wife phones, says she's gone for drinks – back late

But, this doesn't have to be the order things are told in. For example:

Start of story as written:

- **D** Husband is cooking meal, and putting out flowers. It is close to the time when she/wife gets back. He's in a hurry – eager to please her on this special day – their 10th anniversary.
- **A** He recalls her going off to work.
- **B** We find out he's a stay at home husband, takes kids to school
- **E** The phone rings (that's all reader is told)
- **C** Recalls buying flowers and posh food
- **E** The rest of the phone call – she's staying out. Story ends with him sitting alone at table, drinking the champagne.

Try it for yourself:

Time-line and events: (doesn't have to be over one day)

Sequence as revealed in story

....

....

....

....

....

© HarperCollinsPublishers 2015 Writing creatively • 347

Worksheet 8.4 Apply your skills to an English Language task

Student Book Q1 You are going to enter a creative writing competition. In the competition you have to write a description suggested by this photo.

Make sure you:
- generate ideas and plan your task
- consider the success criteria for the higher levels of attainment.

Worksheet 9.1: Tim Lott's use of language

As you read Tim Lott's text about friendship, use the table below to record your findings about the language and language features he uses.

Feature	Explanation	Example/s
Narrative voice (first, second or third person)		
Main tense or tenses used		
Length of sentences		
Variety of sentences (i.e. simple, complex, statements, questions)		
Dialogue or speech		
Imagery or metaphor		
Distinctive punctuation		
Vocabulary (technical, everyday, etc.)		
Verbs		

© HarperCollins*Publishers* 2015

Point of view writing • 349

Worksheet 9.2 — Organise your argument

Student Book **Q11** Here are some of the key ways of arguing for/against stores only stocking local and seasonal produce.

For	Against
• Point about the negative impact of global trade on local producers.	• Provides an income to poorer countries they might otherwise not have.
• A personal anecdote about a recent visit to a local supermarket.	• An anecdote regarding not being able to get what you need at a local store and high prices.
• A description of someone on the other side of the world working on a farm.	• Global demand will eventually drive up wages.
• Point about the way having so much food choice has changed people's expectations and wants.	• Gives the consumer more choice.
• Point about how eating seasonal produce links us more closely to weather, times of year and our local community.	• Enables consumers to understand more about different cultures through what is available.
	• Encourages consumers to be more adventurous in their eating – possibly more healthy.
	• Drives down cost of food.

My essay structure

Now think about how you might use some of these in your essay.

Paragraph 1

....

....

Paragraph 2

....

....

Paragraph 3

....

....

Further paragraphs

....

....

....

....

....

Worksheet 9.3 — Strengthen your text

Student Book **Q4** This text is from **Q4** in the Student Book.

- Highlight or circle any words or phrases that don't seem sufficiently powerful or assertive (e.g. get rid of or replace weak adverbs, adjectives or nouns and consider using 'will' or 'must')
- Underline any sentences that could be combined into a more fluent, flowing single sentence, with repeated verb patterns as in Smith's.

It's really important that you can find out about what villains are up to or get info on terrorists who have ideas up their sleeve for attacking the UK. The country's safety is the issue, I reckon, and it would be a bit silly to ignore this. In fact, my and your safety is also an issue. This bill could make life a bit safer for all of us. Better for you and safer for your family. Also, people at work or those who run the country.

Rewrite the text here:

....

....

....

....

....

....

....

....

....

Student Book **Q7** This text goes with **Q7** in your book. Add appropriate metaphors to the gaps.

We need this Bill so we can shine a light into the .... of terrorism.

Without it, criminals will be able to unlock the .... of government.

Britain needs to remain a ....

out of the reach of those who wish to do us harm or destroy our liberties.

Worksheet 9.4: Apply your skills to an English Language task

Read this task and then plan and answer it.

> 'We are wasting unnecessary power by lighting our towns and villages all through the night. All lamplights should be turned off between the hours of 11pm and 7am.'
>
> Write an article for a broadsheet paper in which you explain your point of view on this statement.

You can use the planning template below to help you answer the question:

The key points for/against my viewpoint

For	Against

Now, on a separate sheet of paper, decide how you will order your points and paragraphs.